The DEFINING MOMENTS IN BENGAL

The DEFINING MOMENTS IN BENGAL

1920–1947

SABYASACHI BHATTACHARYA

OXFORD
UNIVERSITY PRESS

OXFORD
UNIVERSITY PRESS

Oxford University Press is a department of the University of Oxford. It furthers the University's objective of excellence in research, scholarship, and education by publishing worldwide. Oxford is a registered trademark of Oxford University Press in the UK and in certain other countries

Published in India by
Oxford University Press
YMCA Library Building, 1 Jai Singh Road, New Delhi 110 001, India

First Edition published in 2014

ISBN-13: 978-0-19-809894-2
ISBN-10: 0-19-809894-4

Typeset in Berling LT Std 9.5/13
by Alphæta Solutions, Puducherry, India 605 009

CONTENTS

PREFACE

It may be useful, by way of a prefatory statement, to tell the reader how this work is structured. This is an attempt to explore some constitutive elements of the life and mind of Bengal in the twentieth century. From that point of view Bengal, as we know it today, emerged in the years between the 1920s and Independence and Partition. It is one of the arguments in this book that in the 1920s there began a redefinition of Bengal's identity. That trend distinguishes twentieth-century Bengal from the past, the era of the 'Renaissance' and its climactic moment, the movement against the Partition of Bengal. The rise of a new Muslim middle class with the spread of education was also distinctly a new feature of the early decades of the twentieth century. In the 1920s, the vernacularization of the language of politics, increasing focus on Bengali language and culture in the academic world, a regional patriotism nurtured by public spokesmen like Chitta Ranjan Das or Prafulla Chandra Ray or A. K. Fazlul Huq, and persistent negotiations between regional loyalties and Indian nationalism of a wider ambit and significance—these were some of the signs of a new 'Bengali Patriotism' of the *bhadralok* elite. At the same time, there emerged a new *bhadra mahila*, with the commencement of a critique of conventional notions like chastity, as well as the entry of women into politics and the public sphere. The history of women's entry into political activities from the Non-Cooperation Movement onwards has often been criticized in recent days on the ground that male hegemony in the public sphere remained intact. While that generalization is by and large sustainable, in this work it has been argued that entry into the public sphere had many liberating potentials for women even though those might have been unintended consequences. On the whole, when we look at these trends the impression one gathers is that we are looking at a Bengal distinctly different from nineteenth-century 'Renaissance' Bengal. That is what the first two chapters are about.

In the third chapter, we turn to what some contemporary observers called 'the Hindu social order' and the place it assigned to those who were not Hindu *bhadralok*. Those beyond the pale in that scheme of things were substantial in number, in fact the majority of the population of Bengal. In respect of these communities the old social order was not uniformly exclusive—they were placed at different points along a continuum of exclusionary practices. Similarly, the development of community identity did not occur uniformly among these communities. Among the backward and untouchable castes this consciousness began to develop in the early decades of the twentieth century but in only a few instances did it head towards a confrontational position. Muslim identity consciousness developed at a much faster rate and it is one of the arguments in this work that it will be incorrect to simplify and reduce that complex history into the catchphrase, 'spread of communalism'. While on the one hand there were tendencies towards syncretism across the Hindu–Muslim community boundaries, in both communities there were contradictory impulses towards contestation. Further, while on the one hand the so-called Hindu social order accommodated the lower castes, on the other hand there was a rigid hierarchy and abominable inequality. The general picture is one of trends towards integration, counter-acted by those that were tantamount to subordination or social exclusion in respect of the lower castes, or of the non-Hindu communities.

How these social fault lines, generally taken for granted earlier on, acquired a centrality in the years from the 1920s is the theme of the fourth chapter. To get away from stereotypes about communalism we have looked at the domain of culture and unusual sources of information like the childhood experiences recorded in some Muslim memoirs, or debates about importing Arabic and Persian words into the Bengali language and the Hindu reaction to 'Muslim Bangla', or the communal issues in history textbooks as sites of contestation. Given the trend from 1905 onwards the spread of higher education and the growth of a new

Muslim middle class in Bengal—one can understand the emergence of Muslim identity consciousness in Bengali Muslim newspapers and magazines; but we must also listen to the contrary voices, rare as they are, critical of the communal anti-Hindu stance. This chapter aims to show that the roots of communalism are in cultural and social practices, in daily social transactions, and not so much in the activities of political parties that monopolize most historians' attention. Communal political parties only helped bring out into the public domain what was latent in quotidian life.

The chapters that follow focus on political and economic history, as distinct from the focus in the first four chapters on the deep structure of society and culture. Chapter Five considers Gandhian politics in the era of the Non-cooperation and Civil Disobedience Movements, 1920–35. It is argued in this work that Bengal differed from most other regions in India in consistently exploring some alternatives to the Gandhian path. Hence, parallel to the politics of the Gandhian Congress, important roles were played by the Swaraj Party, the *biplabi* or revolutionary nationalist movement and, finally, the Socialist and Communist alternative to Gandhism. In the first section of this chapter, we examine the impact of Gandhian politics and the efforts of C. R. Das to devise in the freedom movement an alternative strategy such as that of the Swaraj Party. The second section of this chapter studies *biplabi* activities, which began long before Gandhism came on the scene and continued till the late 1930s. The revolutionary nationalists' differences with Gandhi's non-violence was obvious. However, in the course of the 1920s and 1930s many *biplabi*s began to eschew violence and some joined the Congress and the others, the Left. The third section of this chapter is about Communism or variants of Socialism that began to be influential in Bengal after the Russian Revolution, particularly in the industrial labour movement. However, the Left was quite marginal at this time, and the movement is of interest chiefly because of its importance in future history.

Politics took a new turn in Bengal, as they did in almost all parts of India, from after the formation of elected provincial governments under the Government of India Act of 1935. The salient trend in the politics of Bengal in the decade 1936 to 1946, discussed in Chapter Six, was the exclusion of Congress from political power and the increasing strength of the Muslim League during the League ministries. Despite some contrary tendencies such as a brief revival of the Congress in 1942, or the efforts of the nationalist Muslims in Bengal to keep Muslims in the Congress fold, this was the general pattern of politics. The policy adopted by the central Congress leadership prevented the Bengal Congress from entering into any alliance—although A. K. Fazlul Huq of the Krishak Praja Party was keen on such an alliance to form a ministry. The agrarian economy was in crisis due to the World Depression and its aftermath. As the struggle intensified between the rent-paying *praja* and the rent-collector *zamindar*, the Congress failed to respond to the situation and the Hindu political elite in the Congress became known as pro-*zamindar* or anti-peasant. Internally, the Bengal Congress was splintered into several factions such as those led by J. M. Sengupta and Subhas Chandra Bose. In contrast, M. A. Jinnah managed to suppress factionalism in the League and to emerge as the sole spokesman of the Muslim community; while the Bengal Congress watched impotently, the Muslim League ministries expanded their support base by using the power they enjoyed for a decade. One man who might have taken the Bengal Congress out of the morass it was in was Subhas Chandra Bose. But he was expelled from its ranks by the Congress and incarcerated in his home by the British Indian government. Later, when he appeared on the eastern war front with the Azad Hind Fauj, contrary to his expectations, there was no uprising in India, even when his troops set foot on Indian soil in Manipur. (Special wartime laws throttled the media, news of the heroic exploits of the Azad Hind Fauj was suppressed in the newspapers, and the radio broadcasts by Bose were accessible to only a minuscule part of the population that owned radio sets and had the courage to tune in to banned broadcasts. The impact of Subhas Bose was felt only on the eve of Independence when some Azad Hind officers were put on trial.) While the Bengal Congress was in a state of unprecedented decline, the Hindu Mahasabha failed to effectively challenge the Congress among their Hindu constituents. The best evidence was the fact that in the General Election of 1946 thirty out of thirty-one Mahasabha candidates were defeated, Syama Prasad Mookerjee being the only one to get elected. The Hindu segment of the electorate did not abandon the Congress, though it was faction-ridden, out of power, out of contact with the Muslim masses, and without a single national-level leader to speak for Bengal since the expulsion of Subhas Bose.

The crisis in the Bengal Congress was only one of a multitude of crises in the 1940s (Chapter Seven). The Second World War not only caused scarcity of food and clothing and fuel in the urban centres but also deprivations of various kinds in the rural areas subject to the government's 'Denial Policy', that is, policy of anticipating the entry of enemy forces and denying them supply of food, provisions, boats, and so on. by removing or destroying them. The outbreak of the Second World War brought in its wake a massive price inflation that adversely affected the fixed-income-earning salaried class. The industrial workers and some residents in the city were partly protected by dearness allowance and rationing; that was part of the government's policy, since Calcutta was a vital supply base for the southeast Asian theatre of war. Few of the *bhadralok* were entitled to such protection against inflation. Wartime inflation brought into the Bengali lexicon the word 'black market' and into Bengali society a new class of nouveau riche who profited from trading in scarce commodities on the black market, providing supplies to British and Allied Forces personnel, and hoarding food or cloth or kerosene. In the meanwhile, the scarcity of cement and iron brought construction to a halt in Calcutta, except for army barracks and military facilities; and thus urban congestion increased and slums for new immigrants began to proliferate. Statistical indices like the number of persons per municipal premises, or quantity of water available per head, indicate a degradation of the quality of urban life in Calcutta. These problems remained unresolved not only due to the wartime short-run factors, but also some long-run trends such as the decline in the efficiency of the Municipal Corporation, a failure of social leadership, and the low level of indigenous capital participation in developing industry in that colonial metropolis. In 1943, the Great Bengal Famine, a consequence of procurement of rice for military consumption, hoarding by traders, and denial of shipping for rice import, killed more civilians in Bengal than the total number of British and American soldiers during the entire World War. Thousands of famine-stricken farmers came to Calcutta to beg in vain and die of starvation on the streets, an experience that deeply scarred the city's morale and the self-regard of the *bhadralok* who witnessed it. The famine was in part also one of the many instances of the rise in the level of corruption in public life; what started the famine was a monopoly irregularly awarded to a favoured business house by a minister, a monopoly to procure for the government rice from the market. Corruption in public life, ranging from bribery to secure votes in the Legislative Assembly, to underhand dealings in the Calcutta Municipal Corporation or the rationing system, became for the first time the subject of comment by many observers in the 1940s. Finally, in 1946, the communal riot in Calcutta on the day declared by the Muslim League and Chief Minister H. S. Suhrawardy as Direct Action Day to attain the goal of creating Pakistan, was a holocaust that signalized an irreparable rupture between the Hindu and Muslim communities. Calcutta was never the same again. To sum it up, the series of crises in the 1940s overwhelmed Bengal and the proud city of Calcutta we saw in the first chapter of this book. These years brought to Bengal the warning signals of an all-encompassing crisis that would engulf Bengal and cast a shadow over many decades in the future beyond 1947.

The last two chapters of this book aim to describe the political processes leading to Independence and Partition. Viceroy Mountbatten, given to making dramatic statements, wrote to the Secretary of State for India: 'We are sitting on the edge of a volcano' and Bengal was a crater where an explosion might occur any time. The private and official papers of Mountbatten reveal that initially he had a plan known to his inner circle as 'Plan Balkan' that would have allowed independent decision-making to units and territories comprising British India and the Princely States in respect of accession to India or Pakistan. In particular, he wanted to recognize the Princes' sovereign rights upon the termination of British Paramountcy. Private and adverse advice to Mountbatten from Jawaharlal Nehru averted that disaster. Another plan that Mountbatten had to give up was to keep Calcutta separate from West Bengal, to allow East Bengal access to the port city. Similarly, the leaders of the Bengal Congress found it impossible to give effect to their agenda, creation of a separate 'United Bengal'—the last flicker of the 'Bengali patriotism' we met with in the first chapter of this book. The efforts of Sarat Chandra Bose and others to persuade the central leadership failed and it was too late to obtain the concurrence of their Muslim counterparts. In the meanwhile, turbulence in Bengal reached a climax in a number of communal incidents including the infamous Noakhali riots that brought Gandhi to Bengal. The recurrence of flare-ups and the memories of the 1946 Calcutta riot compelled Congress leaders, including Gandhi, to accept Partition as an inevitability.

Opinion hardened on both sides of the communal divide in favour of Partition. In accordance with the modalities devised by the three chief negotiators at the top, Mountbatten, Nehru and Jinnah, the Bengal legislators dutifully voted in favour of the Partition scheme. The Radcliffe Commission swiftly decided in a few weeks the territorial division, just in time for the ceremonious Declaration of Independence and the second partition of Bengal. That was the outcome of the decades-long negotiations, recorded in this work through the eyes of contemporaries, swinging between 'Bengali patriotism' and an overarching Indian nationalism. The Partition was not easy to accept. Perhaps it was an agonizing moment, particularly for Gandhi who fought communalist separatism all his life. But his mind was compelled to accept what his heart rejected. He wrote a sad letter to Sarat Chandra Bose on 8 June 1947 to say that he accepted 'a frank partition, it being a recognition of the established division of hearts'.

ABBREVIATIONS

ABP	*Ananda Bazar Patrika* (newspaper), National Library, Calcutta
AICC Papers	All-India Congress Committee files in Nehru Memorial Museum & Library, New Delhi
AITUC	All-India Trade Union Congress files, Nehru Memorial Museum & Library, New Delhi
BCR	Dr Bidhan Chandra Roy's private papers, Nehru Memorial Museum & Library,, New Delhi
BPCC	Bengal Provincial Congress Committee
BPML	Bengal Provincial Muslim League
BS	Bangla San/Sal, or the Bengal Era
CE	Common/Christian Era
CWMG	*Collected Works of Mahatma Gandhi*
FIC	Famine Inquiry Commission, papers and *Report*, National Archives
Home (Pol.)	Home Department, Political Branch, Government of India
IESHR	*Indian Economic and Social History Review*, New Delhi
MAS	*Modern Asian Studies*, Cambridge, UK
NAI	National Archives of India, New Delhi
NMML	Nehru Memorial Museum & Library (Private Papers section), New Delhi

QA	*Qaid-i-Azam Jinnah Correspondence*, ed. S. Pirzada, Karachi, 1977
RPC	*Rajendra Prasad Correspondence*, ed. Valmiki Choudhary, New Delhi
RR	*Rabindra Rachanavalee* (collected works of Rabindranath Tagore)
SI	*Star of India* (Muslim League newspaper), National Library, Calcutta
SPM	Syama Prasad Mookerjee's Private Papers, Nehru Memorial Museum & Library, New Delhi
SPJJ	*Samayik patre jiban o janamat, 1901–30*, ed. Nurul Islam, Dhaka, 1977
TF	*Towards Freedom*, document series, General Editors, S. Gopal and Sabyasachi Bhattacharya, Indian Council of Historical Research
TOP	*Transfer of Power*, document series, ed. N. Mansergh, P. Moon, HMSO, London
WBSA	West Bengal State Archives (Calcutta)

I

REINVENTING BENGAL
The 1920s

It is one of the arguments of this book that in the 1920s there began a redefinition of Bengal's identity. To this process can be traced the major themes that dominated Bengal's history through the twentieth century. It involved, first, rethinking on Indian nationalism and the growth of a new 'Bengali patriotism'. Political leaders articulated a regional identity—not necessarily incompatible with loyalty to the Indian nation—while intellectuals gave a certain 'body' to it in their construal of Bengal's history, language, and cultural traditions. Bengal's political marginalization in the all-India arena, or a perception of that sort, added strength to this regional identity consciousness. Second, the 1920s also witnessed a trend that may be called the vernacularization of politics. This meant not merely the increasing use of the Bengali language to address the newly enfranchised part of the electorate unfamiliar with the English language. It also meant an indigenization of the idiom and style of expression and action in the entire public sphere.[1] In a general way, we might also say that the digits of discourse begin to change in the 1920s.

A diminution of the hegemony of Calcutta, hitherto the fountain of 'English knowledge', occurred along with the vernacularization of politics. The rate of growth of Calcutta was lower than that of Dhaka and small towns in the districts; and the new educated urban public in the smaller towns began to matter. A part of this process was the growth of the Muslim middle class, till now limited to a few *ashraf* (of high lineage) families and fewer educated professionals in that community.

Moreover, Calcutta itself changed in the early decades of the century. By the end of the 1920s a large proportion of the Calcutta intelligentsia consisted of first-generation migrants from the districts, essentially outsiders and, not infrequently, *Bangal*, that is, from East Bengal. These newcomers were closer to village Bengal than the old Calcuttans had ever been. A recurring theme infuses creative writings from the 1920s: a rural–urban dialogue, reflecting a nostalgia for the village that was left behind and, on the other hand, an ambivalent surrender to the attraction of the life and mind of the city.

Again, in the 1920s a new wave in literature, usually identified with the *Kallol* group of authors, opened up new horizons, thematically and ideationally. Whether or not these new writers—mostly from villages and small district towns—were able to overcome the overwhelming presence of Tagore, they certainly brought innovations into creative writing. For one thing, the proletariat and the sub-proletariat and various kinds of marginal men and women appear as protagonists in fiction for the first time. The new literary radicalism also meant the exploration of themes from which the *bhadralok* litterateur averted his eyes till the *Kallol* era (1923–9).

The 1920s also saw the culmination of an effort to redefine the gender question. No doubt the patriarchal values persisted but, at the same time, efforts were made to negotiate a new relationship between men and women, beyond the patriarchal prescriptions and proscriptions. The stereotype of unqualified and unquestionable patriarchal domination of women appears to be analytically inadequate, at least for the 1920s; on the other hand, the radical and reformist intellectual critique and agenda did not constitute the life experience of Bengalis. There were attempts to negotiate a transition as a result of a conflict between those who stood for change and their opponents.

This leads us to a more general point. There seemed to be a great distance between two parallel discourses coexisting in Bengal at this time, a great distance between the world of high culture and the world that is revealed in the commonplace writings in chapbooks printed in run-down printing presses using woodblocks and obsolete typefaces, the ephemeral tracts by obscure authors, manuals produced for housewives and householders, pamphlet literature promoting various causes ranging from caste mobility to protection of women's 'chastity' and, above all, the quotidian social interactions recorded in personal narratives.

This vast 'sub-literature' and particularly the Bengali newspaper—once you got down to the small print beyond the headlines—are as instructive as the best of writings of the best of minds. To the extent we are able to access those unconsidered trifles and ephemera below the level of high culture, the nuanced quality of the conversation between the two worlds of culture in Bengal's society can be regained. We shall also argue in the following pages the importance of individual experience and practice in the private space, as distinct from the well-researched public sphere; hence our emphasis on face-to-face interactions in daily life, or the patterns of association between so-called high and impure castes and the Muslim community, or the changing conjugal relationship.

In this chapter, and in the next three, we address themes that stem from the deep structure of Bengal's life and culture, while in the subsequent chapters we look at the constitutive elements shaping Bengal's economy and politics. To begin with, let us look at the interplay between the old concept of nationalism and a new 'Bengali patriotism', the old Anglicist style and the new vernacular culture of politics, the inescapable city and the village of nostalgic imagination, the traditional Calcutta elite and the 'outsiders' from the *mofussil*, the literary establishment and the new wave from 1923, anticipating the post-Tagorean era (Chapter 1). Then we will proceed to look at the old *antahpurika*, women of the secluded inner quarters, and the new *bhadra mahila* emerging in the public sphere (Chapter 2). This will be followed by an attempt to situate, in the social and sacral order of Hinduism, castes and communities that were engaged in contestation of that order (Chapter 3). And we turn, finally, to the interplay between the concept of one Bengal and that of two Bengals, inherent in the ascendancy of a new Muslim identity consciousness (Chapter 4).

A New 'Bengali Patriotism'

There occurred a redefinition of Bengal's identity in the 1920s in a way distinct in several ways from the earlier thinking. First, the context had changed substantially. Unlike the period of the Swadeshi movement in reaction to the partition of Bengal in 1905, there was now a fairly widespread nationalist consciousness in many other parts of India—a consciousness that was qualified by the simultaneous process of regional identity formation. Not only in Bengal but also elsewhere in the ranks of politically advanced people, there now developed a perceptible dichotomy, though not necessarily a conflict, between 'nationalist' and 'regional' loyalties. Bengali political consciousness up to the 1910s was characterized by a confident assertion of being 'advanced' compared to the rest of India. It was as if Bengal was the custodian of national consciousness. It was no longer so in the 1920s when Marathi, Gujarati, Tamilian and north Indian participation in the nationalist movement was more pronounced and thus Bengali pre-eminence in politics became a thing of the past. More on that later. Secondly, another difference, notably in Bengal, between the 1920s and earlier decades was that the idiom and style of politics was increasingly vernacularized. A good deal of the nationalist speeches and writings of the late 19th century appeared to be an echo of noises off-stage, the source being Europe. 'For a long time', Rabindranath Tagore wrote in 1921, 'our political leaders did not cast their eyes to anyone except the English-educated section, for theirs was a country which belonged to the books of English history. Theirs was a country which was made of gaseous effusions in the English language, and ghostly shades of Burke and Gladstone and Garibaldi used to float around'.[2] The emergence of a specifically Bengali discourse—not only in language, but in the cultural idiom and political style—from the 1920s has not been noticed by historians because of the nature of the sources they are accustomed to use. The increasing volume of writings on public matters in Bengali pamphlets and tracts and newspapers, and the use of the Bengali language as the medium in public meetings, in place of the flood of Victorian English, were marked features of the 1920s. In the *mofussil*, the new crop of middle-level leaders felt more comfortable in the Bengali medium. As we shall see later, the quality of the political rhetoric was also markedly different.

Around 1920, one notices an assertion of a new 'Bengali Patriotism'. A long essay in Bengali under that title (the English word 'patriotism' was used in the title '*Bangaali* Patriotism') was written by Pramathanath Chaudhury (1868–1946), the famous author and the editor of the literary journal *Sabuj Patra*.

> National consciousness was something that everyone talked about in the Swadeshi era [that is, 1906–7]. In those days our people understood

> this only in its political sense. In those days, what we meant by consciousness of ourselves was an awareness of our deplorable lack of independence. Needless to say, in that narrow sense the identity consciousness as an Indian and as a Bengali is one and the same thing.[3]

Chaudhury went on to say that there was more to national identity consciousness than that; or else, independent countries would have no national consciousness. He said that if he were charged with 'Bengali patriotism', he would plead guilty, and that he had no faith in the 'memorised words, mimicry of thoughts' typical of political conferences, 'Congress patriotism', and of 'a mind fed on foreign textbooks'. These books taught a sort of nationalism that all educated Indians shared, but at another level there was a cultural identity that varied from region to region. The future growth of civilization would be sustained by that deeper cultural level. These cultures of the regions had a need for 'self-realization' and, therefore, the patriotism that grew out of those roots should not be brushed aside as provincialism.

Having offered this cultural and political rationale for 'Bengali patriotism', Chaudhury made two other points. 'Some politicians gasp in horror at the mention of regional patriotism, because in their view that attitude of mind indicates narrow-minded nationalism of a selfish sort'. But actually, he argued, there was no contradiction between Indian nationalism and regional patriotism such as that of Bengal; the 'patriotism of the provinces' of British India was a consciousness of individuality that should not be suppressed for it formed the basis of the consciousness of Indian unity. 'To unite the many is a good thing, but to assimilate all would be a form of suppression', almost tantamount to a '*Swadeshi* imperialism'. The trend towards 'self-determination of small nations'—it will be recalled that the post-World War I settlement in Europe was taking place when he wrote—offered a lesson to India. Bengal, like other regions in India, might legitimately maintain her cultural identity and be a part of the Indian nation at the same time.

Thirdly, Chaudhury made an extremely interesting point about the future. The struggle for Swaraj was bringing about unity, but what of the future after attainment of Swaraj? The 'friendship of convicts in a jail' is not the same as the friendship of free individuals. Freedom would bring a different form of unity that would allow the development of different cultural personalities, the *swadharma* of each constituent of the Indian nation. However, he warned, there may develop conflict; but his concept of Bengali patriotism, he argued, belonged to the realm of culture, and such conflicts had to do with the realm of material interests. The currency of the realm of culture are ideas and creations which enrich everyone by exchange; these are not material assets that one would keep to oneself. Thus he was optimistic in that he expected regional cultures to be the bases of integration, although there may be conflicts in terms of material interests.

This trend of thinking in Pramatha Chaudhury reflects a general tendency among opinion makers in Bengal in the 1920s. The site of contestation around the question of 'Bengali patriotism' was the realm of culture. But it was also the trend among the political spokesmen of Bengal. One such was Chitta Ranjan Das (1870–1925), the man Mahatma Gandhi called the 'uncrowned King of Bengal'. This theme appears in the important political statements he made in the last decade of his life: at the Bengal Provincial Literary Conference in 1916 (Bankipore), at the Bengal Provincial Conference of the Congress in 1917 (Calcutta), and again at the last conference of that body he attended in 1925 (Faridpore). In the first of these statements, his Presidential Address, Das made 'Bengali consciousness' his theme: in fact in the first paragraph, remarkable for its rhetorical flourishes, the word 'Bengali' occurs twenty times in about one hundred and fifty words.[4] He spoke of the uniqueness of the culture of Bengal, tracing its roots to the *Sahajiya* lyrics of late medieval times, the Vaishnava lyrics of Chandidas and Vidyapati, the poetry of Ramprasad Sen, the *kabiwallahs* (folk-ballad singers) of the 18th and 19th centuries, and so on. Das was the author of a few works of fiction and poetic anthologies, but he was evidently asked to preside over a literary conference because of his pre-eminence in public life and a political message of 'Bengali consciousness' underlay his entire speech. The next year, at the Congress Provincial Conference, which for decades had been an important political platform in Bengal, Das spoke of 'our national culture and civilization'. He argued that 'the nationality of the Bengali existed even before the advent of the British people, only the shock of an alien civilization was needed to make us conscious of this spirit', that is, the spirit of *jatir jatitwa*, the nationhood of the people.[5] This speech in April 1917 was also remarkable because, for the first time, such an address was delivered in the Bengali language, not in English. The speech entitled 'Banglar Katha' (Of Bengal) began with an invocation of the great cultural figures of Bengal, Chandidas and the Vaishnava poets, Ramprasad Sen, Bankimchandra Chatterjee, Vivekananda, and others, representing 'the spirit of Bengal'. 'Our political movement is a spiritless, abstract, illusory thing. If you want to make it real you have to comprehend the totality of Bengal' and not isolate the political discourse from that totality.[6]

This approach leads to Das's second major theme: Having founded his conception of *desh* in Bengal's cultural identity, Das launches into a critique of the 'mimic Anglicism' of the Nationalist leaders of the generation of Sir Surendra Nath Banerjea (1848–1925). Das devotes several pages to the characterization of that European-style politics as a 'huge failure'. In thus distancing himself from the previous generation of political leaders, Das lost their support—Surendra Nath was an implacable critic in the remaining part of his political life—but Das gained a position in contemporary Bengali perception as its spokesman. Here was a man who not only broke with the earlier tradition of speaking in English—not easily accessible to the class of people who now thronged the political meetings and had gained a voice with the expansion of the franchise since the Government of India Act of 1919—but also gave Bengaliness a centrality in his scheme of things. Das's heady rhetoric must have impressed his political audience: 'The Bengali cannot forget that he is a Bengali first and last … he has a distinct character.… Alas, the force of another civilization has made us powerless and feeble…', and so on.[7]

The third theme developed by Das was that a Bengali cultural identity would keep the different religious communities together. The Hindus and Muslims of Bengal had imbibed each other's culture for generations and 'influenced by the same culture, the two together form the real Bengali nation'.[8] In the face of the widening rift between the two religious communities, Das claimed that 'much of it was a myth. Before the Swadeshi movement it never existed at all'. Since the Swadeshi days the Muslims showed a new political consciousness; Das was confident that cultural unity would prevail over religious disunity. These were sentiments expressed by many others but what was new in C. R. Das's stance was that he did not decry Muslim political consciousness. Instead, he hoped to co-opt that into a common struggle for Indian independence. And to give a concrete basis for such co-option he proposed the Bengal Pact which met, halfway, Muslim aspirations to a share of electoral seats and government jobs. Later on, we shall look into the details of the Bengal Pact and the reasons why it failed.

C. R. Das's approach was also characterized by an attention to rural Bengal, a blind spot of the urban elite in pre-Gandhi Congress politics. In his Presidential Address at the Provincial Conference in 1917, he focused attention on the question: What ailed rural Bengal which had been 'the centre of the cultivation of our culture?' Das pointed to the destruction of rural industries, the concentration of resources in the city, the lack of agricultural capital and rural credit, the enfeeblement of the village community, the poor state of health due to lack of potable water, prevalence of malaria, and so on. Rabindranath Tagore, among others, had spoken of these problems over and again, especially in his celebrated essay 'Swadeshi Samaj' which later became the ideational basis of his Sriniketan experiment from 1921. But C. R. Das put this on the agenda from a high political forum in 1917 for the first time. The increasing presence of the rural voter, after the enactment of the Government of India Acts of 1919 and 1935, soon revealed to political leaders the relevance of this rural agenda.

C. R. Das's Bengal-centric stance left one question unanswered. How would such a regional patriotism relate to the pan-national political movement led by the Congress? Das was to unavoidably confront this question later in his life, because he attained a national stature when he was in the Congress or in the Swaraj Party. The clearest statement he made on this was in his last political testament, his speech at the Bengal Provincial Conference on 2 May 1925, a few weeks before his death. He put forward the view that there was no clash between local patriotism and Indian nationalism for

> nationalism is merely a process of self-realization, self-development, and self-fulfilment. It is not an end in itself.... It seeks a Federation of the States of India; each free to follow, as it must follow, the culture and the tradition of its own people; each bound to each in the common service of all; a great federation within a greater federation, the federation of free nations....[9]

As we shall see later, this federal idea became a key concept in many Bengal political leaders' thinking from the 1920s.

The idea of a sovereign united Bengal that found expression (ineffectually and without much public support in Bengal) in an abortive scheme in 1947 was a variant of an old notion of a Bengal that could preserve its autonomy in some sort of loose federation. Two great spokesmen of Bengal formulated such an idea, although neither organized any popular movement centred on such a federalist notion. One was C. R. Das who said in the last political statement he made that he desired Bengal to be part of a federation of states. The other Bengal leader was A. K. Fazlul Huq (1873–1962); who moved the well-known resolution on Pakistan in the Lahore Session of the Muslim League in 1940: Huq had proposed Pakistan as a federation of states.

If C. R. Das was the most important political spokesman of what Pramatha Chaudhury had called 'Bengali patriotism', Sir Prafulla Chandra Ray (1861–1944) articulated most effectively its economic agenda. A renowned professor of chemistry, he himself was an entrepreneur, being the founder of the Bengal Chemical and Pharmaceutical Works (1901) and the promoter of some other Bengali enterprises. In the 1920s he was influential not only as an intellectual but also because he had carved for himself a niche in the public arena: he was a prominent supporter of Gandhi, was a leader of many social service initiatives sponsored by the Congress and, above all, was a tireless missionary propagating a message to the Bengali people.

This message is conveyed in many pamphlets and tracts he wrote in the 1910s and 1920s: 'The Bengali Intellect and its Abuse' (1910, reprinted in 1920 and 1927), 'The Future Livelihood of the Bengalee Youth', 'The Economic Problem: What Is the Position of the Bengalee People?' (1910), 'The Internal and External Obstacles to Nation-building' (1921), 'The Problem of Livelihood' (1928). The central message of these tracts, written in Bengali and in a style close to the colloquial language, was as follows: For many centuries before the beginning of British rule in Bengal, Brahmanic hegemony had stultified the people's mind, particularly since the decline of Buddhism: much subtlety and pedantry was used in arguments on trivialities, while the constraint of traditionalism hampered rational and free enquiry. Despite the opening of new intellectual horizons from the days of Rammohun Roy, the Bengali middle classes had become oriented to a kind of 'English' education that made them fit for only clerical services. The space that was left by British capitalists for indigenous enterprise in Bengal was occupied by north Indian business communities. Instead of emulating such businessmen, the *bhadralok* looked down upon them. The villages were ruined by the destruction of handicrafts, the migration of the rural elite to the cities, and also by epidemics and endemic diseases. The upbringing and education of the middle-class youth made them ideal office employees but they acquired consumption habits unequal to their incomes. The poorer classes of Bengal were unable to compete with the labouring poor of Bihar, Orissa, and north India who migrated to Calcutta and proved to be better at hard manual labour. Finally, P. C. Ray was sceptical of the beneficial effect of 'higher education' in national life for it was unrelated to the realities of life in Bengal. When 95 per cent of the people were illiterate and illiteracy was even greater among women, how could the consciousness of the people be engaged in the nation-building endeavour?

Like all people with missionary zeal P. C. Ray's was a somewhat reductionist approach to complex problems, but in most matters he hit the mark. He was, as must be evident from the views sketched above, a stern critic of his own people. And yet, in the formation of a sort of Bengali patriotism his was an important contribution in adding to it an economic dimension and in addressing the problem of the impoverished *bhadralok*. While this engendered an awareness of the need to develop an entrepreneurial and technological base for economic development in Bengal (of which the application of the professor's knowledge of chemistry to the pharmaceutical industry was a fine example), this attempt to take up the unfulfilled agenda of the Swadeshi days of 1906–10 produced little impact on his Bengali audience. His exhortation to them to emulate the Marwari or Gujarati or Parsi business communities fell on deaf ears; indeed, it generated, on the contrary, a resentment of the 'sons of the soil' against non-Bengali entreprenuers. As we shall see later, P. C. Ray's critique of other aspects of Bengali society, for example, the caste system, caste hierarchy, and the stupid pretensions of the upper caste, scarcely left a mark on the Bengali mind. This man of science who combined a radicalism in thought with pragmatism in action remained an ineffectual prophet. He was revered but not followed. Ironically, he was to be remembered in later times chiefly as a spokesman of the grievances of the 'sons of the soil' against the rest of the world.

The concern for delineating the Bengali identity that we have seen in the litterateur Pramatha Chaudhury, the political leader Chitta Ranjan

Das, and in the 'economic missionary' Prafulla Chandra Ray, was also reflected in the academic and intellectual work of that period. In 1921, a Bengali student of linguistics had his doctoral thesis on 'the origin and development of the Bengali language' accepted at the University of London. The author of the thesis, to be published in 1926, was Suniti Kumar Chatterji (1890–1977). He writes that 'the idea of systematically investigating the history of my mother tongue' struck him when he was a student and the result was, ten years later, eleven hundred pages of a linguistic history that included a study of the 'racial, historical and cultural background' of Bengal in the first two hundred and fifty pages. Chatterji traced 'the evolution of a common nationality and of one type of culture and literature among the people of heterogeneous origins in West Bengal, in East Bengal, in North Bengal'—*Rarha, Vanga,* and *Varendra.*[10] One of his major conclusions was that 'by the middle of the 10th century (A. D.) to which period the earliest extant specimens of Bengali can be referred, the Bengali language may be said to have become distinctive, as the expression of the life and religious aspirations of the people of Bengal, with the nucleus of a literature uniting the various dialectal areas'.[11] In elucidating for the first time the origin and growth of the language community that became the Bengali people, Chatterji traced the origins of the unity of Bengal to the Pala dynasty which gave a political form to a cultural identity. He pointed out that by extension of the term *Vanga,* the deltaic region, the appellation of *Bangalah* was given to what was known as '*bhasha* or current speech, as opposed to Sanskrit or Persian'; the Portuguese spoke of 'idioma Bangalla' and the early Indo-Persian texts mention 'Zaban-i-Bangalah' in this manner. However, the term *Gauda bhasha* was also in use, at least from the 16th century; its use till the 19th century is evident in the title of Rammohun Roy's book of Bengali grammar *Gaudiya vyakarana* (1833). Curiously enough, it seems that even as the speech of the *Gauda* country, that is, western and north-central Bengal, became the standard form of Bengali, the appellation *Gaudiya bhasha* was replaced by the term *Bangla bhasha* and the English used no other name for the language. In showing the historical basis of the linguistic and cultural identity of the 'Bengali people', Chatterji contributed more than just another scientific treatise.

The other aspect of Suniti Kumar Chatterji's work that merits attention is that it served to underline Bengal's linguistic identity in relation to the classical Sanskrit matrix from the days of 'old Bengali' (950 to 1200 CE) and 'transitional middle Bengali' (1200 to 1300 CE), and also acknowledged Bengali's indebtedness to Persian from the 18th century, particularly in regard to vocabulary. We shall see later that the communal divide in Bengal in the decades preceding the Partition of 1947 brought into existence a tremendous cultural turbulence on the question of 'Muslim Bengali'; the effort of a small section of Hindu *bhadraloks* to de-Persianise the Bengali language went against the grain of the catholicity of that language in accepting and absorbing, for centuries, vocabulary from not only Persian but also Portuguese, English, and other languages.

Another issue germane to Bengal's cultural history in the twentieth century is the relationship between the dialects of West and East Bengal. Chatterji pointed out that while there were strong pan-Bengali characteristics, the dialect peculiarities distinguished the *Rarha, Varendra, Kamarupa* (parts of north Bengal), and *Vanga* groups from each other. He also pointed to 'communal peculiarities' (for example, of the Brahmans, on the one hand, and Kaivartas, on the other) side by side with an ongoing process of 'communal inter-dialectal influencing'.[12] But these individualities, it seems, were increasingly overtaken by a hegemonic influence:

> Calcutta became the intellectual centre of the Bengali people, and through literature and actual contact in life, the Calcutta form of Bengali spread and infected the dialects.... The actual spoken language (of Calcutta) gradually came to its own in a mass of unconventional literature, and in ephemeral poetry: and it attained to dignity in the early writings of Rabindranath Tagore.... The colloquial of Calcutta has become the speech of educated classes everywhere in Bengal....[13]

A metropolitan hegemonic Calcutta looking askance at the provincial *Bangal* east of the river Padma, the representations of that relationship in literature, the stereotypes regarding 'provincialism' as perceived by the cultural centre in Calcutta, the change in language individualities under the influence of a Bengali upper-caste and urban-based mandarinate—these are important elements of a cultural history of Bengal's personality. So far as dialect forms are concerned, Chatterji's work was a landmark.

The importance of Suniti Kumar Chatterji's work on the Bengali language is revealed now in retrospect. Though it might have been admired as a piece of scholarship—did not Amit Ray in Tagore's *Shesher Kavita* hold it in his hands?—it is doubtful how widely it was read. The more widely read authors were those who laid the basis of a history of the Bengali people. As usual, in the construction of a collective identity historiography played a vital role. Ramaprasad Chanda's (1873–1942) work on the dynasties of pre-Muslim Bengal, *Gauda-raj-mala* (1912), Akshay Kumar Maitreya's (1861–1930) epigraphic research in *Gauda-lekha-mala* (1912), Rakhaldas Bannerji's (1885–1930) history of Bengal (volumes I and II in 1915 and 1917 respectively), and the Marathi author who wrote in the Bengali language, Sakharam Ganesh Deushkar (d. 1916) laid the basis on which historiography in the Bengali language developed from the 1920s. Among others, Haraprasad Sastri (1853–1931) who discovered in Nepal the earliest Bengali manuscripts called the *Charyapadas* (1912), Dinesh Chandra Sen (1866-1939), Jogesh Chandra Ray (1859–1956), S. Wajed Ali (1890–1951) and Muhammad Shahidullah (1885–1969), played important roles in locating the language and culture of Bengal in historical tradition to give a certain 'body' to regional identity consciousness.

Institutional efforts in the same direction are also notable. Akshay Kumar Maitreya took a lead in founding the Varendra Research Society (1910) along with Chanda, R. G. Basak, Ghulam Yazdani and many younger scholars who published their research in the 1920s. The Bangiya Sahitya Parishad played a part in collecting and publishing old manuscripts and folk ballads. The annual Bangiya Sahitya Sammelan in the 1920s had a separate section on history—a forum for the presentation of essays by Bengal historians. In the University of Calcutta, Ramprasad Chanda taught, from 1919, Ancient History and Anthropology. His colleague in that university was Dinesh Chandra Sen who published between 1923 and 1932 old Bengali ballads in eight volumes. The 'recognition' of Bengali by the University of Calcutta during the vice-chancellorship (1906–14) of Sir Asutosh Mookerjee (1864–1924) was itself a landmark. In 1921, Mookerjee took the initiative to change the rules of 'matriculation' (that is, the final school examination and commencement of undergraduate education) to allow the option of the mother tongue in place of English as a medium of instruction and examination; in 1932 this effort finally succeeded.[14] In the meanwhile the 'Department of Indian Vernaculars' from 1925 created a space for Bengali in postgraduate studies. The foundation of the University of

Dhaka in 1921 provided a second nucleus of advanced studies: as for Bengal studies, the lead was given by Muhammad Shahidullah. These are some of the institutional developments that fed the stream of historical and cultural studies of Bengal around the 1920s.

In the late nineteenth century, Bankimchandra Chatterjee had said that the Bengali people were unaware of their past, that they lacked a sense of the historical and neglected to write their own history. Akshay Kumar Maitreya in his Preface to Ramaprasad Chanda's work on the dynastic history of Bengal quoted Bankim and wrote that what Englishmen had written about the history of Bengal did not exhaust the possibilities of further research, their work had shown the need for further research. And such research was the responsibility of Bengalis. 'Those who have from misty antiquity, generation after generation made this their homeland, those who have arrived at their present state through many twists and turns of history, those are the people who can relate to the history of this country most intimately'.[15] At the same time, Maitreya was careful to avoid the sort of parochialism that characterized the writings of some of his contemporaries. He profusely acknowledged the path-breaking work of A. Cunningham, W. W. Hunter, H. Blochmann, and others, and he spoke of the need to locate Bengal's history in a larger perspective.

> That Bengal has been the meeting place of many cultures and traditions, the focus of synthesis of many apparently contrary outlooks, a region which has seen fascinating endeavours towards assertion of its identity—is known to us in many ways.... The history of the Bengali people cannot be comprehended if one limits oneself to the chronicle of what happened within the boundaries of Bengal in an isolated manner. What has been the history of Bengal is also an aspect of the history of mankind.[16]

These are noble sentiments, but departure from such norms was not unknown, particularly in respect of 'Muslim rule' in Bengal. However, Akshay Maitreya's injunction echoes a trend of thinking to which we now turn.

While we have argued that a kind of 'Bengal patriotism' was ascendant in the second and third decades of this century, two qualifications need to be made. The first is easily disposed of. The iconization of Mother Bengal had taken place much earlier—in fact, Bankimchandra's

'Vande Mataram' was addressed to her and to no other entity—and the Swadeshi era witnessed its worship on a scale unknown in India till then; moreover, in the popular theatre dramatists hailed her and poets and *kabiwallahs* (folk balladeers) sang her praise. What was new in the second and third decade of this century was a political case being made for Bengali patriotism, along with an intellectual effort to give a 'body' to it with cultural, historical, and linguistic arguments to establish the Bengali identity. Moreover, there is a self-evident difference between the earlier era when Mother Bengal was accepted as a representation of the *desh* as conceived in Bengal, and the new era when resurgent Indian nationalism in the subcontinent as a whole posited a dichotomy between regional patriotism and a supraregional nationalism. Therefore, it can be argued that this 'Bengali patriotism' of the 1920s was something that was *new.* Ironically, to validate its claim, Indian nationalism had to postulate its prior existence in the form of a qualitatively different regional patriotism of the earlier era and claim that as its own. As a historian noted many years ago,

> the concept of patriotism was at the centre of traditional Indian notions of *watan, qaum, pitribhumi, Aryavarta, Hindostan,* and so on. Nationalism, a construct of European origin, comes later but it does not displace the older concept of patriotism. That concept of patriotism was a part of the mental world of the common people who were unaware of Mazzini and Garibaldi or the history of the European nation states.[17]

The subsumption of this older notion of patriotism, usually rooted in regional culture, was on the agenda of the nationalist leadership; and when that was attempted in Bengal, or for that matter elsewhere in India, the notion of 'patriotism' underwent a mutation. This was necessary for the legitimation of the new Bengali patriotism in the 1920s, a part of the project of reinventing Bengal.

Our depiction of the rise of Bengali patriotism around the 1920s calls for an important qualification. Among the opinion-makers and leaders of thought in Bengal there were some dissenters. Not that they rejected Bengali patriotism, but they underlined the fact that it would be wrong to mistake the part for the whole, and that the heady brew of local patriotism might befuddle people into forgetting the fundamental unity that integrates Bengal and all other parts into the civilization called India. Rabindranath Tagore seemed to have thought on these lines.

At the turn of the century, Tagore wrote a celebrated essay, 'The History of *Bharatvarsha*'. He argued that '*Bharatvarsha* has always endeavoured to merge diversities into unity, to direct different paths towards one end, to inwardly comprehend the many as one—to capture the inner unity without destroying the distinguishing particularities which can be perceived externally'.[18] In 1921, he wrote another essay, 'The Course of Indian History', again emphasizing 'the genius of India to mould the disparate many into one'.[19] This was a recurrent theme in Tagore's writings till the end, often in a language and rhetoric reminiscent of his interpretation of Upanishadic monotheism. (Could the *Vaishnava* in Chitta Ranjan Das or the *Shakta* in Pramatha Chaudhury share it?) As far as the individuality of Bengal's culture was concerned, Tagore was willing to recognize it, and in fact he was one of its makers. But his overwhelming emphasis was on the unity of India as a civilization. This view was echoed in the writings of some intellectuals, most notably in an influential book written by Radhakumud Mookherji (1884–1963), *The Fundamental Unity of India, from Hindu Sources* published in 1914.

Since the days of Edward Thompson and Sachin Sen, commentators contemporaneous with Tagore, the fact that the latter was critical of nationalism is well known. This has been reiterated by later commentators periodically. Therefore, it is pointless to devote much space to it. What is worthy of note is that even such a Bengali icon as Tagore was attacked on this ground by many in Bengal, including the great Chitta Ranjan Das himself. Das, in his Presidential Address to the Bengal Provincial Congress in 1917, singled out Rabindranath Tagore for criticism on the ground that Tagore was a recent convert to 'internationalism'.[20] What was this 'internationalism' in Tagore that C. R. Das found unacceptable? As early as 1901, Tagore writes that patriotism is one of those stereotypes 'to which man does not apply his mind' and 'blind nationalism is a deep-rooted disease' and 'coercion, bullying, injustice and deceit' were practices inherent in the nationalism of the European model.[21] About this time, he wrote profusely on political questions in a journal he edited. Basically, his view was that nationalism was a European phenomenon and Indian society and civilization had inherent values that were not consistent with the European type of nationalism.[22] Prominent in the agitation against the partition of Bengal of 1905, Tagore became a critic of nationalism from around 1917, as a consequence of the impact of World War I on his mind. For example, he writes in 1921 that European nationalism had, in the form of imperialism, devastated Asian victims and then nationalism devoured its own progenitors in Europe itself during the World War.[23] And again, in 1925, during his debate with Mahatma Gandhi, he goes out of his way in an essay on the *charkha* to launch a critique of nationalism and a paean of praise for the recently founded League of Nations.[24] That sort of thing did not endear him to people like C. R. Das, nor to the *Ananda Bazar Patrika* which once wrote editorially:

> Those who are familiar with the Swadeshi era know how much the new nationalism or patriotism of Bengal or of India owes to Rabindranath Tagore. Today, after only a few years, the same Rabindranath is putting all his force against nationalism! Perhaps the terrible destructiveness of the last World War of Europe and the ugly visage of nations at loggerheads, have hurt the poet's soul. But, however much the poet's soft and idealistic soul may be hurt ... there is no denying that nationalism is a necessity for the oppressed countries like India.... In the present world, binding the strong and the weak by the bond of love may be nice to imagine, but it is hopeless as a practical proposition.[25]

To sum it up, by the 1920s Tagore's universalistic ideas about the innate unity of mankind had no room for nationalism, not to speak of regional sub-nationalism. And this was far from being a popular approach to the politics of the day in Bengal at that time; the views of the *Patrika* or C. R. Das cited above are typical of numerous contemporary critics of Tagore. A new Bengali patriotism ruled the public mind.

If we may anticipate a later development, in the late 1930s Tagore's attitude underwent another change. The marginalization of Bengal in national politics, the sorry state of the Congress riven with dissensions in Bengal, the series of events leading to the virtual removal of Subhas Chandra Bose from Congress presidentship in 1939, and so on. appear to have influenced Tagore. In 1939, he wrote an essay on the Congress in which he observed: 'The complaint that Bengalis were slighted in the last meeting of the Congress has been heard all over Bengal. To give credence to such a grievance is a sign of weakness'. At the same time, he said, 'Fatal symptoms of lack of feeling of unity between one province and another have become unfortunately evident, although the Congress was founded to serve as the point of confluence for this country'. He was unwilling to accept complaints against the Congress, but he says nevertheless: 'In these times of turmoil my mind clutches to itself Bengal. If Bengal grows greater in our hands, India will be the gainer…'.[26] There is another piece of writing in 1939 reflecting the same sentiments; it was meant to be an address in honour of Subhas Chandra Bose, but it remained undelivered and unpublished till Tagore's death. Subhas was under attack in the All-India Congress Committee and Tagore appeals to Bengal to stand by him. What is more important, Tagore reflects upon Bengal in relation to the rest of India:

> Let no one mistake me that I want, out of a sense of provincial arrogance, to detach Bengal from India … so that Bengal may not be emasculated and fail to be in the forefront, so that Bengal's union with India be complete, that is why I make this appeal. In the great national union today, each province must give its best to the sacrificial fire.[27]

In one of his last public speeches, in 1939 in Calcutta, Tagore reverted to this theme. Bengal, he said, had led India in the days of Rammohun Roy to usher in a new age, but 'the firmament in Bengal today is dark'. The need for the hour was that 'Bengal's strength should strengthen India, Bengal's voice should truly utter India's message, Bengalis should never waste themselves in an impasse of self-alienation, away from the struggle to liberate India'. Above all, Tagore reiterated what he had said so often before, Bengal's endeavour for 'self-realisation' was inseparable from India's endeavour.[28] One can see in these and other writings of Tagore, his deep anxiety about the future of the Bengali people, his unwillingness to surrender to the prevailing spirit of regional patriotism although he partly shares the concern of its proponents in respect of Bengal, and his deep distrust of murky party politics, and yet an abiding faith in the 'unifying genius' of Indian civilization. Tagore reflects, admittedly at a rarefied level, the rich discourse of Bengali patriotism *and* its interrogation; he reflects the highly nuanced quality of that patriotism.

We shall see later that the 'Bengali patriotism' we have noted in the 1920s intensified in the next two decades. C. R. Das had said at the Coconada session of the Indian National Congress: 'You cannot delete Bengal' from the history of the Congress. This was when the Hindu–Muslim Pact designed by C. R. Das was rejected at the AICC meeting and he was shouted at: 'Delete the Bengal Pact'.[29] Das had never faced such heckling and he rose to say, furiously: 'You can delete the Bengal Pact, but you cannot delete Bengal from the history of the Indian National Congress'. It was the pride of Bengal that it was the head and front of the Congress at one time. From the 1920s, Bengal was gradually marginalized in national politics, as we shall see later. It remained an important element in the body politic; in numbers, the Bengali-speaking population was the second-highest in India according to the Census of 1931: speakers of Hindi and its variants and Urdu all put together numbered 79.3 million, Bengali speakers 53.4 million, Telugu 26.4 million, Tamil 20.4 million, Marathi 20.9 million, and Punjabi 15.8 million. It was, however, not so much a question of their numerical strength but their place in the leadership of the national movement. That leadership in the early history of modern India was a matter of pride to the Bengali people. From what was conceived by them to be a glorious past, was Bengal destined to slip down a slope of historical inevitability? We shall return to that question in a later chapter.

The Vernacularization of Politics

Along with the growth of a new 'Bengali patriotism' there began a process that may be called the vernacularization of politics. Into the making of it went various elements, not just the increasing volume of a political discourse in the Bengali language: the diminution of what used to be a monopolistic hold of the metropolis of Calcutta in the public sphere not only in politics but beyond; intergenerational change in leadership style and the obsolescence of the style of the generation of Sir Surendra Nath Banerjea; the rise of a *mofussil* leadership in prosperous small towns with their 'bar libraries' and colleges and proto-political voluntary associations; the expansion of the franchise and the increasing presence of a new type of voter, distinct from the 'English-educated' intelligentsia who had dominated Congress and the Legislature; a new language and rhetoric of politics, using the idioms and symbols and imagery familiar to the Bengali-speaking audience. All this made for the vernacularization of politics and in this process the cultural ambience created by a new young set of literary personalities, often from the *mofussil*, played a role; the literary movement usually called the *Kallol* (1923–9) era brought into the cultural discourse themes and concerns closer to the life of the village and the small town and the vast 'hinterland' of Calcutta, themes untouched by the hitherto dominant Calcutta elite.

We have seen already that Chitta Ranjan Das was as much critical of 'the mimic Anglicism' of the previous generation of political leaders as was Tagore who made fun of the ghostly presence of Gladstone or Garibaldi in the English speeches of those Bengali leaders. The archetype of that old-style leader was Sir Surendra Nath Banerjea and his chief critic—and successor to leadership in Bengal politics—was C. R. Das. An event in 1918 marked their final break and Banerjea's marginalization. In his deposition before the Montagu-Chelmsford Committee, Banerjea took a very moderate position and this provoked a manifesto, a counter-statement, from C. R. Das, Fazlul Huq, and other younger leaders. Banerjea wrote bitterly in his newspaper *The Bengalee*, 'Old people have no voice, we are wiser than our fathers'.[30] In his speech at Chittagong, Das replied in words that signalized the final break with the old leadership:

> We have been told that the leaders of yesterday are the only people who can lead us.... I want them to lead us. But if a man comes and says, look here you will have to do this, it does not matter what the people of Bengal want, I am the leader of Bengal ... then my answer is 'Thou Imposter'.[31]

At this time, Das was thirty-eight years of age, Fazlul Huq thirty-five, and Sir Surendra Nath sixty. Waiting in the wings were two leaders who served as Das's lieutenants and later fought for the mantle of succession. These were Jatindra Mohan Sengupta (1885–1933) and Subhas Chandra Bose (1897–1945) aged thirty-three and twenty-one respectively in 1918 when the 'old guard' was challenged by Das.

C. R. Das showed great perspicacity in comprehending and responding to the need to transit from the late-19th-century style of thinking and articulating politics. In C. R. Das's brief career as a political leader—eight years from 1917 when he was elected President of the Bengal Provincial Conference of the Congress, till his death in 1925—Subhas Bose was very close to him for the last four; Bose made some insightful observations on his *guru* on the occasion of the publication of the biography of Das in 1926. '*Deshbandhu* (C. R. Das) used to say quite often—if we want to extend any Indian movement to Bengal we must put the stamp of Bengal on it'.[32] Subhas sought this Bengali stamp in the ideational affiliation of C. R. Das's thoughts and writings. He pointed to Das's deep-rooted link with Bengal's tradition in three ways. First, Bengal's Vaishnavism gave Das not only a personal faith but also, in public life, an openness to other points of view and freedom from restrictive dogmatism. In particular, according to Subhas, Das's belief in the *dvaita–advaita* doctrine enabled him to reconcile contradictions. 'Deshbandhu was a *dvaita–advaitabadi*. Cultures are many, but culture is also one.... If each nation develops its culture, then the culture of mankind is enriched. If you eschew your national culture you cannot help the advancement of mankind'. Secondly, according to Subhas, Das's conception of the motherland was, as in the case of Bankimchandra, D. L. Roy and Tagore (Subhas is wrong about Tagore), formed by the Bengal tradition of *shakti* worship and Tantra. Thirdly, the cultivation of *nyaya* or logic in Bengal, says Subhas, has encouraged the Bengali mind to excel in debate and this characteristic, as a lawyer and public man, Das shared with his people. It is not necessary for the present to go into the question whether Subhas Bose was right in postulating these continuities affiliating Das to the tradition of Vaishnavism, *Shakti* worship and *nyaya*; what is significant is that among his followers Das was perceived in this light and thus accepted as truly a Bengali. And we have seen that right from his first major political statement as President of the Bengal Provincial Conference in 1917—a speech not in English but in the Bengali language for the first time in the history of the Provincial Conference—Das tried to cultivate that image of being a 'Bengali first and last' as he put it. In place of Edmund Burke and Gladstone and John Stuart Mill, he invoked the names of Bengal's poets and religious teachers and the like. And his regard for the cultural identity of Bengal and of other parts of India was such that he talked of 'federation of cultures' (as Subhas Bose put it), the counterpart of the 'federation of states' he recommended as the appropriate form of unifying India.[33] Das was reaching for a Bengali idiom in politics to address a constituency beyond the limits of Calcutta.

We may now turn to the phenomenon of the growth of *mofussil* towns, that is, the towns in the districts outside of the periphery of the three cities of Calcutta, Howrah, and Dacca in the first decades of the 20th century. This is not only of demographic interest but it affected the politics of Bengal in that metropolitan dominance was reduced, the political participation of the *mofussil* town inhabitants became more significant, and a new leadership—particularly the Muslim leadership—based itself in these peripheral towns. A quick look at the statistics in the Census Report (1931) of A. E. Porter will be helpful. Bengal had three cities with over 100,000 population in 1931: Calcutta, with suburbs, had a population of 12.59 lakh, Howrah 2.25 lakh, and Dhaka 1.39 lakh; together they accounted for about 42 per cent of Bengal's urban population.[34] But the smaller towns were growing much faster. In the decade 1921–31, in the three cities (that is, above 1 lakh population) the growth rate was 11.2 per cent whereas class II towns (50,000 to 1 lakh) grew by 15.3 per cent, and class III towns (20 thousand to 50 thousand) by 19.2 per cent. The same applied to the two previous decades. Population growth in the three class I cities of Calcutta, Howrah, and Dhaka, was 3.3 per cent in 1911–21 and 8.1 per cent in 1901–11; the growth rate was much higher in class II towns—22.5 per cent in 1911–21 and 78.4 per cent in 1901–11; in class III towns also the growth rate was high, 6.3 per cent in 1911–21 and 17.4 per cent in 1901–11.

To sum it up, the Census figures establish that medium- and small-sized towns out in the districts were doing much better than the three big cities, among which, again, the decadal growth rate of population was greater in Dhaka—21, 10, and 16 per cent in the three decades 1901 to 1931; in Howrah, it was 18.6, 9.1 and 15.2 per cent over the same period. The corresponding rates for Calcutta (9.9, 3.3, and 11.1 per cent) compare unfavourably. It was evident that Calcutta was losing the race, growing at a much slower rate than the other cities, and medium and small towns.[35]

This in itself does not mean that the Calcutta urban agglomeration was losing its premier position; nor did the shifting of the capital of British India from Calcutta to New Delhi mean that. Calcutta remained in advance of the rest in terms of municipal services, filtered water supply (only 40 towns had it, and all on smaller scale), density of population (over 36 thousand per square mile compared to about 22 thousand in Howrah and 25 thousand in Dhaka in 1931), and cosmopolitan character (33.2 per cent of Calcutta's population in 1931 was from outside Bengal); and it still had all the advantages of being a provincial capital, a port city, and the centre of an industrial conurbation.

Nevertheless, the fact was that Calcutta was not growing as much and as fast as the small and medium towns 'out in the districts' or in the *mofussil*.

The term *mofussil*, which has found its way into the *Oxford English Dictionary*, was part of the colonial English argot. It was adopted from Hindustani to indicate rural localities as opposed to the administrative centre in the city. The towns in the *mofussil* were subordinate administrative bases, business centres, and the focus of such higher level educational and intellectual activities as there were in the districts. The stereotype that these were sleepy little nooks was the creation of sahibs, white and brown, in whose scheme of things Calcutta had a centrality. The officers in civil and judicial administration, the inevitable *babus* who assisted them, the small-town lawyers, the college and school teachers, traders and merchants serving these town inhabitants—these were the people who constituted the administrative *mofussil* town at the turn of the century. The composition was more variegated if the town happened to be a *gunge* or a mart or the centre of an artisanal industry or a mode of transport service like the railways or steamboats. By the 1920s, these towns had undergone considerable politicization. Since the 1880s, the working of local governments and municipalities with representatives elected by taxpayers had created a political consciousness at the level of electoral politics, as distinct from ephemeral agitational politics. The increase of litigation leading to the growth of a numerous lawyer class in the lower courts, the habit of *zamindars* of the district to maintain a 'town house', and the increase in the number of educational institutions serving the needs of male members of rich peasant families and the professionals—all these added to the numbers of the semi-urban middle class in the district headquarters. They were semi-urban, first, because many of them, as in the case of many residents of Calcutta, had a house or accommodation (*basha*) in the town and their home (*bari*) was in the village they belonged to; secondly, the small towns did not have all the urban characteristics by way of civic amenities and living conditions.[36] Many of these *mofussil* towns, the Census Report of 1931 stated, 'differ but little in their conditions from large villages, except in the provision by the municipality of an infrequent lamp-post'.[37] In these semi-urban communities there developed a public sphere; its sites were the elected district boards, municipalities and local bodies, the bar library of the pleaders and other law-related professionals, the governing bodies of educational institutions, the voluntary associations devoted to social work or cultural activities and, finally, in the big towns, local branches of political parties and caste associations, and so on, which had lateral and vertical links spreading beyond the towns. Unlike urban politics of the metropolitan cities, the dynamics of public life in *mofussil* towns remain unexplored.[38]

Of the many political leaders who arose out of this background we may take Abul Hashim (1905–74), the general secretary of the Bengal Muslim League 1943–7, as typical—a contrast to the type represented by the man he replaced as general secretary, H. S. Suhrawardy.[39] Abul Hashim's career reads as follows: born in 1905, brought up in the town of Burdwan; studied in Burdwan Raj College after having spent a few disagreeable months in Presidency College, Calcutta; after his B. A. in 1928, admitted to Aligarh Muslim University but left it within a few weeks for Burdwan; organized the Burdwan Muslim Youths' Association in 1928; enrolled as lawyer in Burdwan in 1931; elected from Burdwan district to the Bengal Legislative Assembly in 1937 and retired from legal profession; elected president of the Burdwan District Muslim League in 1938; general secretary of Bengal Muslim League in 1943. Similar were the political career trajectories of many *mofussil* men, though few attained to the high position he did. In 1943–7, Hashim executed his programme of establishing a fully working branch and office of the Muslim League in every district town; from small towns and villages over five lakh members were recruited in 1944. Thus, from being a Calcutta-based party with nominal presence in the district towns, Hashim and his colleagues from towns like Burdwan, Murshidabad, Jessore, Comilla, Khulna, Rangpur, and so on, converted the Muslim League into a party with active links with Muslim middle-class townsmen and, less effectively, with village-level political activities. Thus, organizationally he did for the League what the Congress had done in the early 1920s under C. R. Das.

> Except for the Legislative Assembly, my political activities were limited to the Burdwan district. I had been to no district outside of Burdwan, nor did I hold any public meeting outside the district. The Burdwan District Muslim League was being thoroughly organised.... However limited the field, if a man can prove his competence within that limited field, he will prove himself in a larger arena beyond those limits.[40]

These words of Abul Hashim in his autobiography—reflecting on his early political career—could have been said equally appropriately by many political leaders who rose from the *mofussil* towns in the 1920s and 1930s in Bengal. It is also to be noted that many of these men, like Hashim, belonged to a network of familial and traditional connections with roles in the public sphere. Abul Hashim's father, who graduated from Presidency College in Calcutta, was an active supporter of Sir Surendra Nath Banerjea and served both in the provincial and central legislatures under the Montagu-Chelmsford dispensation of 1919. Hashim's maternal grandfather, Nawab Abdul Jabbar, after serving the Bengal Government as a deputy magistrate and the Bhopal State as prime minister, retired to his ancestral village in Burdwan. Hashim's paternal great-grandfather was a subordinate judge in the service of the East India Company.[41] Families such as these were what English officers posted in the districts would have called 'local notables' in villages or towns; the role of these notables was multifarious in Bengal's society. Transition from serving the state, to being spokesmen of 'public interest', to political leadership came naturally to the notables at the top of that social order.

While the new entrants into politics from the *mofussil* towns effected an end to the monopolistic hold of the Calcutta elite, there took place another parallel development: the expansion of franchise. A large number of people began to exercise their power to vote and elect representatives to the legislatures in each province of British India. This was the consequence of the Government of India Act of 1919, following the Montagu-Chelmsford scheme (and later Government of India Act of 1935). In Bengal in 1921, the lowering of the property qualifications and the consequent enlargement of franchise meant an addition of about 100,000 voters from the urban middle classes and the well-to-do peasantry. The Report of the Indian Central Committee headed by Sir Sankaran Nair in 1929, reviewing elections to form governments in 1921, pointed out that despite Congress agitations hostile to registration of voters about 5.3 million were registered all over India, and in 1926 the registration increased to 6.4 million. 'The growth of population, increase of wealth bringing more citizens above the qualifications level, improved methods of registration, and the extension of female suffrage have contributed to the increase' along with 'the policy of council entry and the consequent quickening of public interest in politics'.[42]

The outcome of extension of franchise, however limited it might have been (said to be below 3 per cent of the population, according to the Nair Committee), meant that there were now many voters who qualified by property qualification, the criterion under the Act of 1919. They included a large number who were not literate in the English language; hence a need to bring out newspapers in Bengali and to address meetings in Bengali. An additional factor was a strong pre-existing trend in Bengal among the nationalistically inclined to use Bengali whenever possible. How far this trend was pushed is recorded humorously by Abul Mansur Ahmed (1898–79)—raised in a village in Mymensingh and later a lawyer in Mymensingh town and eventually a distinguished editor and political activist in the Krishak Praja Party. Eschewing English, the entire vocabulary of the game of foot-ball was Sanskritised by him and his friends.[43] The ideal of oratory, an art much overrated in Bengal, was no longer the Gladstonian language of Sir Surendra Nath Banerjea, but the chaste Sanskritic Bengali of C. R. Das, or the Bengali closer to the people's language used by A. K. Fazlul Huq (1873–1962). Curiously enough, the language used in the legislature continued to be English but, more often than not, the electoral battles, the public meetings, and political conferences were conducted in the medium of the mother tongue.

An interesting consequence of this development occurred in the Muslim community. There began a debate whether Bengali or Urdu was the appropriate language for the community in the public arena. There were a very few families who spoke Urdu at home, for example, families related to the former royal houses at Dhaka or Murshidabad, or recent immigrants like the families of Abul Kalam Azad (1888–1958) or Abu Sayeed Ayub (1906–82). But this minuscule section apart, Bengali was the language of the Muslims; nevertheless for public speeches and published writings, should Urdu be the language? It would have been ironical had the shift from English brought about a switch to Urdu. In the 1910s and 1920s there were indeed some proponents of Urdu as the right medium for Muslims. 'A few non-Bengali Mosalmans who have settled in Calcutta' were, writes Muzaffar Ahmed (1889–1973) in 1917, 'trying to force on Bengalee Mosalmans Urdu in place of Bengali'; they forget that Bengal is bigger than Calcutta.[44] T. Ahmed writes in 1926: '*Sharif* or well-born Muslim status can be claimed only if the mother tongue is changed', as if one's mother tongue is a matter of shame to this section of Muslims; they are trying to impose

Urdu on rural Bengal which is Bengali-speaking. Abdul Majid in 1930 writes: 'Even in this twentieth century there are "great" people who are proud of their aristocracy and look upon Bengali as damaging to their *sharafat*'.[45] Thus there appears to be a sub-text behind the Bengali versus Urdu debate: the identification of Urdu as the language of a small number of city dwellers and *ashraf*, as distinct from the village dwellers and the common people, the *atraf*. On the whole, in the contemporary journals the opinion was overwhelmingly in favour of Bengali, the mother tongue.

While there was this general opinion against Urdu replacing Bengali, another question that came up was the question of the 'national language' to link Bengal with the all-India Muslim community. Mohammad Wajed Ali (1896–1954) of Khulna district writes in 1918 that Arabic should be the national language, although Bengali is the mother-tongue of Bengali Muslims, because 'you cannot give life to nationhood among Bengali Muslims if you eliminate Arabic and Urdu'.[46] Maulana Akram Khan (1868–1968), the leading Muslim League intellectual, said in his Presidential Address at the Bengal Muslim Literary Conference in 1918: 'In our party the radicals have now begun to say that Bengali is not only our mother-tongue but also our national language. In my humble judgement this is totally illogical.... Muslim nationalism is totally on the basis of religion.... It will be disastrous if we forget that the national language of Muslims is Arabic'.[47] The editor of the journal published by the same Literary Conference writes at the same time: Arabic is the universal language of Muslims in the world, but 'we shall never accept Arabic as our national language.... A nation is not the same as a particular religious community. In that perspective, Bengali is the national language of all inhabitants of Bengal'.[48] Thus, Muslim opinion on Bengali and even the concept of nationhood was by no means univocal.

Another aspect of the vernacularization of the language of politics, at least agitational and electoral politics, in Bengal in the 1910s and 1920s was the expansion of the vocabulary of the Bengali language used in the public sphere. Satyendranath Majumdar (1891–1954), who worked in *Ananda Bazar Patrika* from 1922, and was editor from 1926, reflected on this:

> Classical ornamental language [Bengali] in newspapers is difficult for the readers with limited education, so news began to be written in a

> language common readers could follow.... English is the language of the government. The administration uses only the English language.... The Bengal newsmen have to translate all that. Constitutional changes have brought in an astonishing number of new words.... Bengali news media have, on the one hand, introduced neologisms to enrich the language and, on the other, have taken the responsibility of education in the mother tongue in the field of political science.[49]

At one time in Bengal, Rabindranath Tagore writes in 1923, 'It was a matter of pride to write in the English language, to deliver speeches in English. Today it is the opposite in Bengal. Today some people say regretfully, "They speak better English in Madras". This adverse certificate we should wear like a medal'.[50] In this essay and a crop of similar essays and speeches in the 1920s, Tagore responded to the new trends in that decade with his usual imaginative insight. He was, of course, happy that the position he had adopted decades ago was at last vindicated. 'To keep out Bengali and to adopt any other language, whatever it may be, will emasculate the independence of our mind'.[51] He recalls that Latin was at one time the common language of the learned all over Europe: when the modern languages emerged and began to be the medium of creative and scholarly writing, Europe's civilization was advanced rather than retarded. Likewise, English served as a lingua franca but true unity of mind could not be achieved by artificial means. The self-expression of people in their mother-tongue would create diversity in cultures, but that was a natural organic development, and it was preferable to a mechanical unity created by imposing English.[52]

In these writings of Tagore in the 1920s there is more than just a plea to replace English with Bengali. Wrestling with the problem of how language and literature relate to the nation-formation process, he asked the question in 1923, were Bengalis a nation? His answer was that politically they were far from forming a nation state, socially they were divided infinitesimally by the caste system, in terms of religion there was a divide between Hindu and Muslim communities, and as regards racial origins the baffling mixture of races precluded any claim to common origin. What then constitutes Bengaliness? 'It is not being born in Bengal which makes one Bengali, it is access to the human mind through a particular language which makes one Bengali'.[53] He argued that the self-realization of each culture through its own language alone could be the basis of relating with other cultures; thus the formation of

Indian nationhood would, far from being impeded, be advanced by the development of each language and its literature.

'The political enthusiasm in the country today, however much we may value it, is only an external phenomenon. The internal consciousness of the self is greater than the calculation of gains and losses [in politics], and it finds free expression in Bengal's language and literature…'.[54] It is not easy to translate Tagore's highly nuanced language, but the above summary may serve our purpose. The nationalist movement was a battle for the mind of the people. And Tagore argued that only the languages of the peoples of India could reach into their minds, only their own language and no other. Bengal's self-expression through her own language and literature would bring about the unity of her mind with that of India. Inevitably, Tagore played an important role in promoting the literary conference of non-resident Bengalis or the Prabasi Banga Sahitya Sammelan at which his speeches as founder-president have been cited above. Tagore believed that such conferences, meeting in different parts of India outside Bengal, would enhance mutual understanding between different linguistic groups and diminish Bengal's cultural parochialism. On the latter point: 'The chief vice of the Bengalee people is vanity; therefore, they are not satisfied unless they hear their own praise endlessly. They are insatiably thirsty for the wine of praise, if that is in short supply they are unhappy. This vanity, greed for flattery, is baseless and creates a miasma of self-deception…', and so on. Tagore hoped that Bengalis outside Bengal would be free of this self-deceiving vanity, and help interpret Bengal to India.

The politicization of the language question had one more interesting aspect: the controversy over 'Musalmani Bangla' in the 1920s and 1930s. Bengali infused with Urdu or Persian words was called Musalmani Bangla by the votaries of Sanskritized Bengali; some Muslim literary journals also accepted that appellation, judging by their use of the term 'Musalmani Bangala' in the 1910s. We shall return to this issue later.

Hegemonic Calcutta and Village Bengal

The relationship between Calcutta and village Bengal has always been complex and it was never more so than when Calcutta's hegemony began to be challenged in the 1920s. We have seen that challenge in the rise of the *mofussil* towns; in the growth of a Muslim professional middle class that did not claim Calcutta culture as its patrimony; in the expansion of the franchise and party machinery in rural Bengal affecting the foundations of political parties hitherto parochially Calcutta-centred; in the disparagement occasioned outside West Bengal by the presumptuous use of the Calcutta dialect as Bengal's literary language; and, above all, in the entire complex of processes we have called vernacularization of politics. All of that meant a diminution of Calcutta's advantage over the rest of Bengal as the heterogenetic city offering 'English' knowledge and culture.

And yet Calcutta continued to matter. Gopal Haldar (born 1902), raised in Noakhali town and a very self-conscious *mofussilite* who migrated to Calcutta, says that every Bengali has two homes: one is the place where he was born and the other is Calcutta.[55] This puts very aptly Calcutta's position as the cultural capital of Bengal. For many residents of Calcutta this statement would have had another significance in the 1920s or 1930s: many Bengali residents in Calcutta looked upon their accommodation in Calcutta—from the clerk's hovel to the *zamindar*'s palace—as their *basha*, just a house, while the home or *bari* was in the village they belonged to. This was, of course, more true of the large numbers who came to work in Calcutta from the east and north Bengal districts. Thus a good number of Calcutta citizens were, so to speak, commuters between the village and the urban world. The village continued to occupy a good deal of their mental space. Visits to the village, especially during the Durga Puja, were important moments in their lives. A 1929 editorial entitled 'Puja Holiday' in the *Ananda Bazar Patrika*, quite perfectly mirrors the middle-class Bengali mind:

> For the home-loving Bengali the Puja Holiday is a prized opportunity. The Bengali is going home.... Again in those infinitely wide expanses, those green and cool uncrowded village homes with all the world's love and a multitude of memories, await the footsteps of the sons who shall return.... This love for his home of the Bengali abroad, fills his mind with nostalgia when the Puja holidays arrive.... But year after year, the village he sees in his imagination is not the village that he sees in reality....There is the altar but not the goddess there was, there is the village but gone are its beauty, its abundance, its joyousness....[56]

This reflects very well the early twentieth century predicament of the urban mind: there is a village of one's imagination to which one would like to return and one cannot return to it. From the early decades of the twentieth century to Satyajit Ray's Apu trilogy in the mid-twentieth century, a recurring theme in Bengali creative works has been the loss of the village, the nostalgia of the prisoners of the city for a rural past that cannot be regained.

In the complex relationship between Calcutta and village Bengal, the challenge of Calcutta's hegemony that we have spoken of opens a window. Alongside the processes we have touched upon there was, in the 1920s and 1930s, an immense impact in the literary world made by a host of people who came from outside Calcutta, from villages and small towns remote from the metropolis. A lot of their literary themes were also derived from that background. It is interesting to find out where the formative years, childhood, and early youth, were spent in the lives of creative writers who entered the field of Bengali literature during this era: Tarasankar Banerji (1898–1971) in the district of Birbhum and a chronicler of life in that district; Bibhuti Bhushan Mukhopadhyay (1896–1987) in Darbhanga district in Bihar; Balai Chand Mukherji, known by his pen-name 'Banaphul' (1899–1979) in Jessore in a village later included in the 24 Parganas; Sailajananda Mukherji (1901–76) in Burdwan town and in the collieries districts of Bengal and Bihar where he spent most of his life; Dinesh Das (1888–1941) in Chittagong and Dhaka; Buddhadeva Bose (1908–74) and Ajit Datta (1908–74) in Dhaka; Jibanananda Das (1899–1954) in Barisal, where he taught for the major part of his life; Saradindu Bannerji (1899–1970) in Munger and Patna in early life and out of Calcutta for the most part; Rajshekhar Bose (1880–1960) in Darbhanga and Patna; Pramatha Nath Bishi (1901–85) in Santiniketan in Birbhum district; Amiya Chakrabarty (1901–86) in Hazaribagh in Bihar, Annada Sankar Ray (b. 1904) in Orissa and Bihar; the list seems endless of authors whose formative periods were spent out of Calcutta, in its vast hinterland. There were also others who spent relatively shorter periods there and moved into Calcutta earlier in their life than those mentioned. Such was the pattern with Kazi Nazrul Islam (1899–1976) from Burdwan district; Premendra Mitra (1904–88) from Banaras and Mirzapore; Humayun Kabir (1894–1968) from Faridpur; Manish Ghatak (1902–79) from Baharampur; Sajani Kanta Das (1902–62) from Dinajpur and Bankura; Manik Bandyopadhyay (1908–56) from Bihar and Bengal district towns where his father was posted; Naresh

Chandra Sengupta (1883–1964) from Munger in Bihar. Some of these authors spent most or all of their working lives out of Calcutta, for example, Tarashankar, 'Banaphul', Jibanananda Das, Jagadish Chandra Gupta (1886–1957, place of work Birbhum), Mohitlal Majumdar (1888–1952, in Dhaka from 1928 to 1944), Achintya Kumar Sengupta (1903–76, who mostly held district postings in government service), Amiya Chakrabarty, and others. Who then were the literary men who spent their formative years in Calcutta in childhood and youth? The list is relatively small: Premankur Atarthi (1890–1964), Manindra Lal Bose (1897–1986), Gokul Nag (1895–1925), Prabodh Kumar Sanyal (1905–83), Bishnu De (1909–82), and Samar Sen (1916–87) are some names that readily come to mind.[57] Some of them were actually of families originally from East Bengal; Samar Sen in his memoirs says that although he was a boy of Baghbazar, Calcutta, his grandfather, the great scholar Dinesh Chandra Sen, spoke the East Bengal dialect; but young Samar's parents forbade him from using it—an interesting point about the *Bangals*' acculturation in Calcutta.

It is not that these facts have much significance from the literary and aesthetic point of view. But from the social aspect to search for such data is perhaps worthwhile. The impregnable fort of Calcutta was assailed in the 1920s and 1930s by rank 'outsiders', many of them *Bangals*, and East Bengalis at that. The earlier generation, say those born before the 1890s, included among the literary men a few who were likewise outsiders, for example, Prabhat Kumar Mukhopadhyay (1873–1932) or Ramananda Chatterjee (1865–1943) of Allahabad until he moved to Calcutta in 1908, or Atul Prasad Sen (1871–1934) who made Lucknow his home. But there had been an overwhelming presence of Calcuttawallahs, including naturally those connected by descent or marriage or socialization with the Tagore family and a few old families of Calcutta and places in the immediate neighbourhood. The new generation of literary men were from a different background, with greater familiarity with the truly rural or with terrains which were exotic to the true Calcuttan. Themes beyond the ken of the Calcuttans were addressed by this new generation of creative writers who invaded Calcutta.

In the process of co-optation of these newly arrived, *adda* played a role. To give Calcutta its due, it was an open city. A young man who joined Presidency College in 1914 with medals from Faridpur District

School and Anushilan Samiti booklets in his baggage, Nirmal Chandra Bhattacharya (1897–1984), has described the co-optation process in his memoirs of those times.[58] The premier educational institutions located in Calcutta attracted the best from all over eastern India; the hostels, such as Hindu Hostel in Presidency College schooled the newcomers. For the poorer students, poorly paid clerks, and the like, the 'mess', often organized and segregated district-wise, was a school for the new citizens of Calcutta. But, above all, there was the institution celebrated in Bengal, the *adda* where conversation flowed and minds flowered, a glasshouse nursery for young minds thirsty for a culture beyond the range of *mofussil* society. The *adda-dhari* might graduate to higher levels of *adda* nucleating around eminent authors, a literary journal, a scientist, a publishing house, or even a tea shop with interesting habitués. Sudhir Chandra Sarkar (1892–1968), a well-known publisher and host of a famous *adda* for decades, writes that these literary gatherings also had a dress code. 'At that time [the 1920s] the young writers developed a special fashion of dressing. Most poets and literary men would wear a bushy hair style, French-cut beard, silk *dhoti*, and ochre-coloured *kamiz* (shirt).... These days [that is, in 1968] however, it is difficult to make out who is a literary man and who is not, from the way he dresses'.[59] However, it was not all external appearance and a pose. Even Nirad C. Chaudhuri, who belonged to one literary group assembled around a journal—before he 'came to the conclusion that Bengali literature itself had no future'[60]—recognized a certain intellectual solidity in the literary men in the 1920s: 'At that time there was no inclination in Bengali literary circles to banish learning or even the pose of learning to academic zoos, instead of accepting it as a normal feature of civilized life in its literary expression'.[61]

The point I have made about the invasion of 'outsiders' beyond the pale into Calcutta's intellectual world and, on the other hand, their co-optation into that world, was reflected in the sensibilities displayed in the literary works of the 1920s and 1930s. The new citizens of Calcutta brought with them an awareness of rural Bengal—and in a broader sense an awareness of Nature, enriching the rural–urban dialogue that infuses Bengali writings of those times.

Two representative works of this kind of the period under study are *Pather panchali* (The song of the road) and *Putul nacher itikatha* (A tale of the puppets), published in 1929 and 1936 respectively.

The first, written by Bibhuti Bhushan Bandyopadhyay (1894–1950), is partly autobiographical; in fact the author signed the copy he gifted to Sajani Kanta Das as 'Apu'—the name of the boy at the centre of the narrative. Later, the author wrote, in a letter to his wife, that when he was compelled to work for a living in Bhagalpur, away from his village home, he remembered his own childhood and wrote this book.[62] Unfortunately, the book is often read merely as a nostalgia trip into 'the lap of nature'. That undoubtedly is true of the novel. There is also, in an equally large measure, nostalgia for the village home left behind, and Satyajit Ray captured that beautifully. This is the recurrent theme of the last section of the novel, the third one entitled 'Akrur Sambad' (this part has remained untranslated in the English, French, German, and Russian versions). Of many similar passages, one may recall the last pages when Apu, in the middle of an alien city, watches the dusk descending and remembers their abandoned home in the village:

> This is when the shadows are beginning to gather in the yard of their home in the woods ... those sweet, silent, calm afternoons ... surely that yellow bird comes to perch on the bamboo near the wall.... A few more moments, and their home will be covered by the dark, and no one to light the evening lamp, ... in that house without a single soul, crickets will sing in the bush, owls will hoot in the thickly wooded part behind their house.... No man will tread those pathways, no one would ever know of the lime tree mother had planted, no one to see the flowers that will bloom, no one to take the fruits that will ripen, and only the yellow bird will cry and whirl about. For all times to come those beautiful magical afternoons will waste in the woods.[63]

There is another aspect to it. The village locates people in a history that Calcutta scarcely possesses. Apu's family is not one of great status and wealth, but even such a family traces itself back to a past many generations before British rule. This is what the first section of the novel is about. And the author reflects: numberless generations of men have been in the *bhita* (the homestead or the seat of the family); the British *sahibs* came and went 'like the flotsam and the foam of the river' which is likened to 'the flow of boundless time'. Not only is there a sense of wide expanse of space in the novel, but also a sense of almost limitless time. The village and its people possess a past that is recovered by them, and by Apu, in family lores, legends of the village; and the people also locate themselves in relation to a tradition in *Puranic* tales they read or listen to or see dramatized in folk theatre. The village accesses the Great Tradition, or at least the learned among them do, like Apu's father, the brahmin in a priestly vocation. A failure in life, his only legacy to his son was a sensibility alert to a tradition: 'The father whom they today put on the funeral pyre ... a man defeated in the life-struggle, he is but a shadow, not known to Apu ... but there was another whom Apu had known ... his father who sang: *Kale varshatu parjjanyam prithivee shashyashalinee lokah santu niramayah...*'.[64]

The city, particularly a colonial heterogenetic city like Calcutta did not have the organic link the village had with the traditions that made Indian civilization. This is what Apu gained, and lost, along with the bounties of Nature. On the other hand, did not the city represent 'modernity', freedom from the dead weight of tradition translated into constraints of a narrow conception of life, and escape from what Marx called 'rural idiocy?' The tension between the culture of the city and of village Bengal is a major theme in a famous novel of the 1930s.

The Tale of the Puppets by Manik Bandyopadhyay (1908–56) has its main protagonist, Shashi, coming back to his village after completing his studies at the Medical College in Calcutta. When he had gone to Calcutta

> his mind was narrow, his mental faculties were blunt, his tastes were unrefined. The narrow path of a village householder's life was all that he could see in the future. In Calcutta his sensibilities were refined by the books he read and by his friends.... Then, when he came back to the village as a doctor he, at first, felt claustrophobic.... Is the rest of his life to be spent in the midst of these uneducated men and women, these tanks and ponds, these bushes and jungles and fields. Ye Gods, there is not even a library here! But slowly Shashi's mind settled into acquiescence.... Things he had learned from books, things to aspire and hope for, he now learned to regard as things that belong to books.[65]

That is how we first get to know Shashi and at the end of the book: 'Where would Shashi go, leaving his village? What is there beyond the village limits that Shashi would want? An enormous lifeless world, innumerable unknown people. What is there for Shashi?' He accepts, though with a heavy heart, the inevitability of staying where he belongs. In these and other inner dialogues in Shashi's mind, the thread that keeps the narrative of a rather eventless kind is the dithering between the life and mind of the city and the village. Likewise, he dithers in relation to the only woman in his life, Kusum, entirely a village person. The unfulfilled hankering for 'something beyond', the contempt for the rural idiocy and at the same time the sense of belonging that ties Shashi to the village—in short, the ambivalences of a mind caught in the tension between two cultures and ways of life of the city and the village have been dissected by Manik Bandyopadhyay with a surgeon's scalpel.

Manik Bandyopadhyay accurately reflects the ambivalence of the Bengali intellectual with regard to the city of Calcutta in those days. It was put so well by Premendra Mitra in 'Mahanagar' (The Big City) in 1933:

> Come with me to the Big City that spreads itself to the sky like a wound of the Earth, the Big City that soars in *minar*s and spires and high-rises to the stars like the prayers of the human soul.
>
> Come with me to the streets of the Big City, streets that are labyrinthine like the course of weak men's lives, streets that are wide and luminous like the irresistible ardour of the human mind.[66]

Among those who scarcely perceived the city as a luminous focus was the quintessentially urban poet, Samar Sen (1916–87). His poem 'Nagarik' (Citizen):

> The pale day comes to the big city, and then the tar-dark night.
> And then again the day
> Filled with the sound of roller machines
> The distant flash of the red *golmohur*, far away
> The breeze carries the smell of molten tar....
> How much more of scarlet *saris* and soft breasts, and smooth men with finely parted hair
> How much more of Gold Flake cigarette smoke wafted in the breeze
> Oh, Big City! ....
> Cholera and the factory's siren, and gonorrhoea and the pox....[67]

There is something sharp and yet brittle about the sensibilities of the poets who could not draw upon life experience beyond the city. Nirad C. Chaudhuri left his home in East Bengal in 1927 and was never to see the region again.

> My ancestry and early life have made me incapable of being a contented city-dweller, although I have had to live in big cities ever afterwards. Thus I have remained a countryman, unchanged and unchangeable in my habits and outlook. Moreover, it is by drawing on the memories of

> boyhood in East Bengal that I have been able to resist that atrophy of sensibilities which city life brings about inexorably. But not only atrophy, something worse—fossilization, has come over the mind of Hindu Bengalis on account of the separation of their life from its natural environment....[68]

Chaudhuri claims, with his usual modesty, that he was personally exempt from this diminution of sensibilities, particularly because he did not live in Calcutta after the Partition of 1947. His observation, based on his very intimate knowledge of the Calcutta intellectuals, appears to be near the mark when one 'Namierizes' the leading literary figures of the 1920s and 1930s in terms of their background and formative periods in their life.

The New Wave in Literature

In so far as Bengali literature was at all able to overcome the overwhelming presence of Rabindranath Tagore, the 1920s marked a beginning. Conventional history of literature has it that a new era commenced with the famous Calcutta literary magazine *Kallol* (1923–9).[69] As with all conventions, this is a description useful for chapterizing textbooks and doctoral theses. The roots in the immediate past of the magazine lay earlier in the decade in a group that called itself the Four Arts Club and in the activities of the students of Dhaka University.[70] It also seems that even earlier there were anticipations of what *Kallol* stood for: for example, in the writings of Naresh Chandra Sengupta's psychosexual fictional writings or in attempts at social 'realism' a la western exemplars in Charu Chandra Bandyopadhyay, before *Kallol* came out.[71] Nor did Rabindranath Tagore go unchallenged earlier, though the perpetrators of that crime were quite second-rate literary figures, with the possible exception of D. L. Roy. Nor is it true that all the authors in that group found their voices for the first time in *Kallol*; some of them had already been published in standard journals before that, for example, Achintya Sengupta, Premendra Mitra, and Shailajananda Mukherjee.[72] And yet, despite these continuities and anticipations, when *Kallol* arrived on the scene it did mark a disjuncture. We cannot talk of the 1920s without taking notice of it.

Since this book is not a history of literature, our concern with the literary movement beginning in 1923 is limited: to explore what it tells us about the historical conjuncture Bengal found herself in. The impact of World War I, the increasing numbers of the industrial working class in and around Calcutta, the sub-proletariat in the city's unorganized sector merging into the 'criminal classes' in an underworld that had always been there, the misery of the educated unemployed in the lower middle classes, the new inner world opened up in the Freudian discourse on psychosexuality, the emergence of 'realism' as perceived by Bengali readers of translations of the literature of continental Europe, the resistance of the literary establishment in Calcutta to new endeavours of the younger generation—all these constituted the scene that saw the birth of this literary movement. But there was, perhaps, more to it than that. It was not merely these circumstances, but a new spirit that invaded the mind of a new generation of creative writers, says Achintya Kumar Sengupta (1903–88), a participant—chronicler of the movement.

> Youth inspired by idealism and frustrated by the reality—this was the anguish of that age. He batters on doors that remain closed, there is no room for him anywhere, the place he is given in the scheme of things is too little for his inner being—he lacks a sense of fulfilment and this rends him to pieces.... There is a mismatch between his dreams and the reality. Thus there is restless defiance, on the one hand, and an enervating sense of defeat, on the other. What is called the 'malady of the age' or the anguish of the era is inscribed in deeply etched lines on the face of *Kallol*.[73]

Some of this *angst* was of the generic kind, true of many young men and women at any time, at any place. Premendra Mitra (1904–88), a fellow-member of the *Kallol* group, writes in a letter to Sengupta at that time:

> If the primitive tribe of Bushmen in Africa get a 20th-century aircraft, their predicament would be like ours with our life. We do not know what this life is, and what it is for. We do not know its inner logic, its purpose, its significance. Maybe now and then we manage to turn this knob or the other and turn the propellers and we think it is like a cooling fan for our comfort, or when the machine injures someone we think it is an instrument of torture. This analogy is not actually very good because the aircraft will be simplicity itself to the Bushman, compared to the meaningless puzzle life presents us....[74]

But there were purposes more specific to Bengal's predicament in the 1920s in the Kallol movement, not merely the 'frustration'—undoubtedly a key word, even till the mid-twentieth century in Calcutta—of youthful idealism. Some of the most fiery spokesmen of militant nationalism were close to *Kallol*. One of them was Kazi Nazrul Islam (1898–1976) who battled not only foreign rule but also oppression in all forms: of labour under capitalism, of women under patriarchal domination, and of freedom of the mind as opposed to religious fanaticism. His writings in his journal, *Dhumketu* put him in jail for a year on the charge of sedition; that is when he wrote his first poem for *Kallol* at the beginning of its life.[75] Many members of this group also found common cause with a journal for the working classes called *Sanghati*; it was patronized by the veteran nationalist Bipin Chandra Pal (1858–1932) and among the authors it attracted was a leading *Kallol* contributor Sailajananda Mukhopadhyay (1901–76) who wrote about the life of coal miners.[76] Among the nationalist leaders, Chitta Ranjan Das was supported by *Kallol* editorially, particularly after his death. Among the tributes to Das, an interesting observation was made, in reaction to the historian Sir Jadunath Sarkar's disparaging comment. 'Pundits may not recognise Chittaranjan, but the people of the country did. That is why they called him *Desh-bandhu*. That name suggests what his hold was over people's mind. Pundits may not see that, because there is a kind of punditry which fails to see anything significant in contemporary history, because books do not tell him about it'.[77]

However, the literary movement was not memorable for its stance on political questions. Its significance lay in its new, purportedly Post-Tagorean trend, in literature. To underline its newness they challenged Tagore's authority on occasions. Achintya Kumar Sengupta wrote a poem, still worthy of recall, declaring: 'Even though Rabindra Thakur might block the way forward', progress in literature will be made, for Achintya Kumar represents the future.[78] Themes never touched upon in the classical Tagorean era were the favourite ones for many *Kallol* authors. One of them was Manish Ghatak (1902–79) who, Sengupta notes, 'began to write about things that have always been there; though the guardians of morality in Bengal had always averted their eyes from them. This was another world of the failures and the unsung … beggars, goons, burglars, pick-pockets … these were brought into the pages of literature'.[79] There was not always a social or political purpose in this endeavour. Dinesh Ranjan Das (1888–1941), the founder–editor, educated up to college level in Chittagong and Dhaka, was far from thinking of a political agenda; 'his aim was to struggle, at the cost of self-deprivation, for an ideal in society' and this was 'the ideal of truth in literature'.[80]

The Kallol group undertook similar literary enterprises in the 1920s, such as the magazines *Pragati* (Progress, 1927) and *Kali Kalam* (Pen and Ink, 1926–7). The new generation of authors liked to band together, a togetherness closer in adversity than that brought about by the genteel *adda* of the writers of the olden days. Jibanananda Das writes in a letter from Barisal to Achintya Sengupta during the Kallol days: 'We are besieged by people without sympathy. A few of us are like-minded, and we should try to bind ourselves together. We have no money, nor creature comforts, but let us enjoy the pleasures of wayfaring together, however arduous the journey...'.[81] This strong 'we–they' consciousness was reciprocated by the establishmentarian factions in literary circles. Nirad C. Chaudhuri (1897–1999) played a role, perhaps a role unworthy of him, in lampooning the new generation. But he realized that his 'literary campaign' produced the opposite of the result desired: 'As things turned out our campaign was a total failure. Instead of checking the new trends, we established them by the publicity we gave them'.[82]

There were indeed some people in the new literary movement, as in any similar group, who could be accused of being poseurs, poorly educated greenhorns, and imitators of the European masters. Mean and savage lampooning of opponents was an old tradition in Bengal. And the controversy whipped up at this time fell into the pattern of *dala-dali* or faction-fight reminiscent of the days of Rammohun Roy and Radha Kanta Deb, not in terms of the quality of the discourse but the intensity of partisanship. In the manner of the old days, the issues fought over were placed before a *samajpati* (that is, leader of society, sometimes a caste group). Tagore was that arbiter. What happened at the court of arbitration need not detain us. Basically, Tagore seemed to show his sympathy for the 'new literature' and at the same time held on to the view, expounded by him earlier as well, that the decisive question was not *what* was the theme or subject matter of literary works, but *how* it was written; that is to say, the supremacy of the aesthetic criterion. Two points he made suggest that his sympathy for the new literature was qualified (his antipathy towards its critics, including the journal Nirad Chaudhuri was associated with, was quite evident). He said he was willing to concede that he could not comprehend the mentality of the poorer classes; but to make a fetish of crying one's eyes out 'for the poor' might be merely a pose, and it did not necessarily ensure great literature. Secondly, he conceded that to offer a critique of society and its principles and rules was part of the freedom of the realm of literature; however, to make that a creed for a group or faction to be deliberately formed for that purpose went against the grain of creative writing, for creative writing was the job of an individual mind.[83] These discussions and controversies in 1927–8 ensured for the new literary movement recognition of sorts. Those groups soon perished, *Kallol* in 1929 and the others even earlier, and the authors went their separate ways. The rebels became establishment icons. But, for a while in the 1920s, that burst of energy and a push for new horizons left a mark on that decade.

Notes

1. The term 'nationalism' was usually translated into Bengali as *jatiyatabad*, and 'patriotism' as *desha-prem*—the distinction being rather fuzzy in the early twentieth century.
2. Rabindranath Tagore, 'Satyer ahvan', *Prabasee* (Kartik, 1328 BS); reprinted in *Kalantar* (Calcutta, 1376 BS), p. 201.
3. Pramatha Chaudhury, 'Bangaali patriotism', *Sabuj Patra* (Agrahayan, 1327 BS) (my translation).
4. The text of the speech is reprinted in Appendix, N. C. Ghosh, *Chittajayee Chittaranjan* (Calcutta, 1378 BS), p. 557.
5. The text of the speech is reprinted in Chitta Ranjan Das, *Deshbandhu Chitta Ranjan: Brief Survey of Life and Work, Provincial Conference Speeches, etc.* (Calcutta, 1926), pp. 1–83.
6. Das, *Deshbandhu Chitta Ranjan*, pp. 60–1.
7. Das, *Deshbandhu Chittaranjan*, p. 6; Ghosh, *Chittajayee Chittaranjan*, pp. 5–10, text of speech by C. R. Das.
8. C. R. Das, *India for Indians: Speeches, October 1917–February 1921* (Madras, 1921).
9. C. R. Das, Speech at Provincial Conference, Faridpur, 2 May, 1925, as quoted in Ghosh, *Chittajayee Chittaranjan*, p. 336.
10. Suniti Kumar Chatterji, *The Origin and Development of the Bengali Language* (Calcutta, 1st edn 1926; reprint 1985), vol. I, pp. i, xiv, 147.
11. Chatterji, *Bengali Language*, vol. I, p. 81.

12. Chatterji, *Bengali Language*, vol. I, pp. 138–41.
13. Chatterji, *Bengali Language*, vol. I, p. 135.
14. Calcutta University, *Hundred Years of the University of Calcutta* (Calcutta, 1957), chs 6–7. For a list of historical publications, see Prabodh Chandra Sen, *Bengal: A Historiographical Quest* (Calcutta 1995; Bengali edn 1953). There is no standard work on Bengal historiography.
15. Akshay K. Maitreya, preface to R. P. Chanda, *Gauda-raja mala* (Calcutta, 1st edn 1912, reprint 1973), p. 19.
16. Maitreya, preface to *Gauda-raja mala*, p. 37.
17. Sabyasachi Bhattacharya, *Oupanibeshik bharater arthaniti* (The Economy of Colonial India) (Calcutta, 1989), p. 19.
18. Rabindranath Tagore, 'Bhartvarsher itihas' was published 1309 BS, *Bangadarshan* (new series) and in the volume entitled *Bharatvarsha* (Calcutta, 1905); reprinted in *Rabindra Rachanavalee* (Calcutta, 1989) [hereafter cited as *RR*], vol. II, p. 705 (my translation).
19. Tagore, 'Bharatvarsher itihaser dhara' published in *Pravasee*, 1319 BS, and reprinted in *RR*, vol. IX, p. 591.
20. C. R. Das, Speech at Bengal Provincial Conference, 1917, in *Deshbandhu Chitta Ranjan*, pp. 18–19.
21. Tagore, 'Birodhmulak adarsha', published in *Bangadarshan*, 1308 BS, reprinted *RR*, vol. V, p. 759.
22. See Tagore's essays 'Nation ki?' ('What is a nation?', a discussion of Renan's views) and 'Bharatiya samaj' (Indian society), published in 1901 and reprinted in *RR*, vol. II, pp. 619–25.
23. Tagore, 'Shikshar milan' (Unity through education), published in 1930 in *Pravasee* and reprinted in *Kalantar* (Calcutta, 1969), p. 186.
24. Tagore, 'Charka', published in 1925 in *Sabujpatra* (1332 BS, 1925 CE), and reprinted in *Kalantar* (Calcutta, 1969), p. 260.
25. *Ananda Bazar Patrika* [hereafter cited as *ABP*], 5 June 1923; see Sabyasachi Bhattacharya (ed.), *The Mahatma and the Poet: 1915–1944* (Delhi, 1997), 'Introduction'.
26. Tagore, 'Congress', in *Modern Review*, July 1939; this English translation is mine—the last passage quoted above was deleted in the English translation (probably by Amiya Chakrabarty) published in 1939; the Bengali original I have used is from *Kalantar* (Calcutta, 1953), pp. 371–82.
27. Tagore, 'Deshanayaka', *Kalantar*, p. 387; written in 1939, it remained unpublished till Tagore's death (my translation).
28. Tagore, 'Maha jati sadan', published in *Pravasee* (1346 BS); reprinted in *Kalantar*, pp. 389–91 (my translation).
29. Ghosh, *Chittajayee Chittaranjan*, p. 248.
30. *The Bengalee*, 6 June 1918.

31. C. R. Das's speech at Chittagong, 18 June 1918, in Ghosh, *Chittajayee Chittaranjan*, p. 88.
32. Subhas Chandra Bose (Mandalay Jail) to Hemendra Prasad Dasgupta, biographer of C. R. Das, 20 February 1926, in Bose, *Taruner swapna* (Calcutta, 1928, reprint 1967), p. 97.
33. Bose to Dasgupta, 20 February 1926, in Bose, *Taruner swapna*, p. 116.
34. A. E. Porter, ICS, *Census of Bengal 1931*, Subsidiary Table III, p. 85; paras 97–100 on distribution and variation of urban population, pp. 74–9.
35. Porter, *Census of Bengal 1931*, Subsidiary Table IV, p. 85.
36. S. Ahmad, 'Urbanization and Urban Classes' in *History of Bangladesh*, ed. S. Islam, (Dhaka, 1992), vol. III, p. 229. Sirajul Islam, 'Life in the Mofassal Towns of 19th century Bengal', in *The City in South Asia*, eds K. Ballhatchet and J. B. Harrison (London, 1980) is insightful on an earlier period.
37. Porter, *Census of Bengal 1931*, pp. 78–9.
38. On Calcutta and Howrah, Rajat K. Ray, *Urban Roots of Indian Nationalism: Pressure Groups and Conflict of Interests in Calcutta City Politics, 1875–1939* (New Delhi, 1979); Amal Das, *Urban Politics in an Industrial Area: Aspects of Municipal and Labour Politics in Howrah, 1850–1928* (Calcutta, 1994).
39. Abul Hashim, *Amar jiban o bibhag-purva bangladesher rajniti* (1st edn 1978, Dhaka; reprint 1988, Calcutta; I was unable to obtain the English version, *In Retrospection*; quotations are translations by me from the 1988 edition), pp. 1–35.
40. Hashim, *Amar jiban*, p. 33.
41. Hashim, *Amar jiban*, pp. 1–5.
42. Government of India, *Report of Central Committee* (Sir Sankaran Nair, Chairman), Calcutta, 1929, p. 35.
43. Abul Mansur Ahmad, *Amar dekha rajnitir panchas bacchar* (Dhaka, 1995), ch. 1.
44. Muzaffar Ahmed, 'Urdu Bhasha o Bangiya Musalman', *Al Islam*, III, no. 4 (1324 BS), in M. N. Islam, *Samayik patre jiban a janamat 1901–1930* (Bangla Akademi, Dhaka, 1977), p. 318; this is a collection of extracts reprinted from newspapers and journals which I found invaluable; hereafter it is cited as *SPJJ*.
45. Tasaddak Ahmad's speech in *Shikha*, I (1933 BS), *SPJJ*, p. 323; Abdul Majid, 'Bangla Bhasha o Mussalman', *Muazzin*, II, nos 9–10 (1337 BS), *SPJJ*, p. 332.
46. M. Wajed Ali in *Bangiya Musalman Sahitya Patrika*, I, no. 4 (1325 BS), *SPJJ*, p. 325.
47. M. Akram Khan, Presidential Address, 3rd Bengal Muslim Literary Conference, *Bangiya Musalman Sahitya Patrika*, I, no. 4 (1325 BS), *SPJJ*, p. 326.

48. Khan, Presidential Address, p. 326.
49. S. Majumdar, *Nirbachita rachana sangraha* (Calcutta, 1984), speech at Bengal Literary Conference, 1938, pp. 109–112.
50. Tagore, Presidential Address, Pravasee Banga Sahitya Sammelan, Banaras, 3 March 1923, reprinted in *RR*, vol. XII, Appendix to *Sahityer pathe*, pp. 495–501.
51. Tagore, 'Sahitya sammelan', speech at Calcutta in 1926, reprinted in *RR*, vol. XII, Appendix to *Sahityer pathe*, p. 545.
52. Tagore, Speech at Banaras, Majumdar, *Nirbachita rachana sangraha*, 4 March 1923, reprinted in reprinted in *RR*, vol. XII, Appendix to *Sahityer pathe*, pp. 501–4.
53. Tagore, *RR*, vol. XII, Appendix to *Sahityer pathe*, p. 496.
54. Tagore, *RR*, vol. XII, Appendix to *Sahityer pathe*, p. 500.
55. Gopal Haldar, *Rupnaraner kule* (Calcutta, 1st edn 1969; reprint 1992), vol. I, p. 32.
56. *ABP*, editorial 'Pujar chhuti', 8 October 1929.
57. In order to identify authors commonly considered as significant contributors to literature—from out of the vast numbers who wrote and were published—I have used an arbitrary criterion, that is, I have focused attention on those mentioned in a standard history of Bengali literature, Sukumar Sen's *Bangla sahityer itihas* in four volumes and *History of Bengali Literature* (Delhi, 1979). For biographical details I have used S. C. Sengupta (ed.), *Sansad bangla charitabhidhan* (Calcutta, 1994). My reference to the speech habit cultivated by Samar Sen is based on his *Babu brittanta* (De's Publishing, Calcutta, 1978, pp. 13–14), a classic among Bengali memoirs. It seems that being thus acculturated came easily to immigrants from East Bengal, for example, Mrinal Sen's account of his love affair with the city of Calcutta, from the age of seventeen. Mrinal Sen, *Always Being Born: Memoirs* (Stellar, Calcutta, 2005), ch. 1.
58. Nirmal Chandra Bhattacharya, *Bismrita bangla* (Calcutta, 2007), ch. 4.
59. S. C. Sarkar, *Amar desh, amar kal* (Calcutta, 1994), pp. 108–9.
60. Nirad C. Chaudhuri, *Thy Hand, Great Anarch! India 1921–1952* (London, 1987), p. 234.
61. Chaudhuri, *Thy Hand, Great Anarch!* p. 226.
62. Bibhuti Bhushan Bandyopadhyay to wife, Roma, 10 October 1940, cited in J. Chakraborti, 'Introduction' to *Pather panchali* (Calcutta, 1985), p. 8.
63. Bibhuti Bhushan Bandyopadhyay, *Pather panchali* (Calcutta, 1985), ch. 35 (my translation).
64. B. B. Bandyopadhyay, *Pather panchali*, p. 186.
65. Manik Bandyopadhyay, *Putul nacher itikatha* (Calcutta, 1987, 19th edn), pp. 12–13.

66. Premendra Mitra, 'Mahangar', *Desh*, I, nos 1–8 (24 November 1933) (my translation).
67. Samar Sen, 'Nagarik'.
68. Chaudhuri, *Thy Hand, Great Anarch!* p. 203.
69. *Kallol* means the 'sound of waves'; it was the title of founder–editor Dinesh Das's poem in the first number of the journal *Kallol* in 1923.
70. The standard historical works on the *Kallol* era are Jeebendra Sinha Roy, *Kalloler kal* and Debkumar Bose, *Kallol juger katha sahitya*; I have also used extensively the memoirs of a leading member of the literary group, Achintya Kumar Sengupta, *Kallol yug* (Calcutta, 1950), which contains some letters of that period.
71. Sukumar Sen, *Bangla sahityer itihas*, vol. IV, p. 250.
72. A staid old journal, *Pravasee*, had published Sengupta, Mitra, and Mukherjee before *Kallol*'s appearance.
73. A. K. Sengupta, *Kallol yug*, p. 61.
74. Premendra Mitra's letter to Sengupta, n. d., circa 1925, in A. K. Sengupta, *Kallol yug*, p. 65.
75. A. K. Sengupta, *Kallol yug*, pp. 26–7, 32.
76. A. K. Sengupta, *Kallol yug*, p. 18.
77. Atul Chandra Gupta, 'Deshbandhu', *Kallol* (1925), cited in A. K. Sengupta, *Kallol yug*, p. 86.
78. A. K. Sengupta, *Kallol yug*, p. 84.
79. A. K. Sengupta, *Kallol yug*, p. 55.
80. A. K. Sengupta, *Kallol yug*, p. 36.
81. A. K. Sengupta, *Kallol yug*, p. 99.
82. Chaudhuri, *Thy Hand, Great Anarch!* p. 234.
83. Reports of this celebrated encounter between the establishment and the new wave authors are, from varying points of view, available in Chaudhuri, *Thy Hand, Great Anarch!* ch. 4; A. K. Sengupta, *Kallol yug*, pp. 186–8; in *Pravasee* (Baishakh 1335 BS) or Tagore, *Sahityer pathe*, *RR*, vol. XIV, pp. 511–23; and, in a satirical vein, in *Shaniharer chithi* (Baisakh, 1335 BS).

2

THE GENDER QUESTION AND THE NEW *BHADRA MAHILA*

In some works in the area of gender history today there is perhaps an interpretative tendency presenting a rather monotonic picture of the nineteenth and early twentieth century discourse on the 'woman question'; while there can be no doubt that the picture is accurate in focusing on the dominant patriarchal values, the facts of the 1920s and 1930s being characterized by active contestation and, at another level, ambivalences on the part of those in adversarial roles debating the woman question, need to be taken into account. These ambivalences, the sensibilities brought into play by the gender issue, and the nuances of the debate cannot be easily reduced to essentialist formulae. No doubt, the nineteenth-century patriarchal system survives well into the twentieth century, but it is not a Skinner Box labelled 'Patriarchy' that produces a predictable set of reactions to a given set of stimuli.

If a Martian were to read the literary journals we have been looking at in the previous chapter, he would have thought that Bengal had attained a high level of consciousness on the gender question. He would have read Rabindranath Tagore's 'Letter from the Wife' (1914), or Sarat Chandra Chatterjee's 'The Worth of Women' (1924), or critiques of traditional patriarchy written by women (here the Martian would have to be careful, for many men, including the great Sarat Chandra himself, wrote under a feminine pen-name), or he would have read declarations of 'free love' from the more radical members of the new literary movement of the 1920s.[1] But our hypothetical Martian's judgement would be wrong. There were two parallel discourses in Bengal at the time, and one realizes this when one looks at the commonplace writings and utterances belonging to a vast 'sub-literature' of newspapers and tracts, the chapbooks produced in crude printing presses using obsolete type fonts and woodblock pictures, the textbooks and 'manuals for housewives', the quotidian social transactions, and the unconsidered trifles in the web of Bengali culture taking us into a conceptual world altogether different from that of the denizens of high culture. That the latter constituted the life experience of Bengalis in the 1920s is something only a Martian could have believed.

It will be useful to identify certain key concepts to provide entry into the mindset we are trying to get at, as well as its interrogation, increasingly obstreperous, by proponents of change. These are the concepts commonly used in the kind of written texts we have mentioned earlier; *sateetwa* (chastity of women), *garhyastha dharma* (household regimen or duties), *vaidhavya dharma* (duties of widowhood), *naree shiksha* (women's education), *adhikar* (right or realm, according to the context), and *prem* (love). We may look at texts written around the 1920s and 1930s and note that they focus on the *bhadra mahila*, women of the educated *bhadralok*'s family; the silence of these texts on the non-*bhadralok* women is, needless to say, itself of obvious significance. In respect of the *bhadra mahila* there are a fair number of wide-ranging studies by historians; the question we will focus upon is whether the nineteenth-century discourse changed substantially in the early decades of the twentieth century.[2] Arguably, there was a change by the 1920s in some ways. That is what we shall try to explore.

Notion of Chastity Defended and Contested

The old digits of discourse of nineteenth-century vintage continued to be in use. One of these was *sateetwa* or women's chastity, a vital means of controlling women's sexuality. This old war horse, *sateetwa*, was drafted into battle by one set of opinion-makers and, of course, it was too tempting a target for the radicals. To give a flavour of the debate, here is an essay presented by one Ashrumati Devi at the Conference of Youths in Jessore,[3] chaired by Jyotirmoyee Ganguly (1889-1945), daughter of the Brahmo Samaj leader Dwarkanath, and herself a prominent Congress activist. Writing in1929, she says: 'The heavy weight of *sateetwa* has been sitting on the chest of our society ... this old rotten corpse of a custom must be forthwith put on the funeral pyre.... *Sateetwa* is inherent in a woman who is noble and strong in spirit. From this viewpoint, to have a husband or none or many is not the essence of it'.[4] The author pointed out that Ahalya, Draupadi, and Kunti would not have qualified as *satee* if one were to apply the criterion that a *satee* was a woman who belonged exclusively to one man. Man has created 'constraints on sex relations.... Nature allows freedom.... By the construction of *sateetwa* man has violated the law of Nature'. And there are reflections on conjugal love: 'There can be no love within constraints. No doubt there can be play-acting by husband and wife within an enforced give-and-take relationship; there can be no love. The *Vaishnava* poets had said so explicitly'. Finally, Ashrumati says that 'the garbage of *sateetwa*' did not bring into the world Veda-Vyasa, Karna, Arjuna, or Yudhishthira. What is particularly interesting is that the argument is not cast in terms of an appeal to modernity or exemplars from the West; *shastra* as an authority is not invoked but figures of the classical Indian past are recalled to demolish the twentieth-century caricature of *sateetwa*. A foaming-at-the-mouth editorial in a popular newspaper was quite unable to cope with that, but European inspiration was attributed: 'consumers of tidbits from the table of European sexologists', 'free sex and lax morals', 'brainless, enervated perversions', and so on, were some of the milder words used in an editorial. It was said that not only were some such perverse men 'taking advantage of the women's liberation movement' (*naree swadhinta*), but also 'regretfully we note, some women ... excessively educated'; that the youth organizations were also being 'contaminated' was proven by the fact that the essay quoted was presented at the conference of a reputed youth organization. 'What next!' seemed to be the tone of the editorial, the title of which was 'Freedom and Licentiousness'. At the same time, the editorial view seems to be that there are forces behind this 'unfortunate' piece of writing by an educated *bhadra mahila*, forces that must be negotiated with. It was conceded, while contesting the attack on *sateetwa*, that 'it is our responsibility to bring to an end the state of women in seclusion in a position tantamount to that of slaves, in a state of stupor due to superstitiousness and lack of knowledge, in a condition no different from lifeless matter...'. Noticeably absent is any appeal to *shastric* authority or the tradition of the past. The object is posited as 'freedom of this country and the betterment of this society'.

In fact, this freedom from dependence on *shastric* authority seems to be a characteristic of many of the writings in this decade. *Ananda Bazar Patrika* in 1929 says of the Sarda Bill which raised age of consent for women: 'The problems of society of the twentieth century will be solved by the leading minds of the twentieth century; it is foolish to resort to some dead or obsolete *smriti shastra* citations'.[5] 'Men do not observe the injunctions of Manu, but the unmanly men are always ready to subject women to those injunctions'. Even the most traditional household manuals for housewives, for example, *Garhasthya-dharma* (1904) by Nagendra Bala Mustafi, *Griha-dharma* (1934) by Priyanath Bose, *Swamee-stree* (1933) by Nandlal Mukherji, and so on, rarely depend on the authority of the *shastras*. Though the object might be to defend a traditional institution or practice, the presentation is in terms of 'social needs in modern times'. It is often no more than a garb for a highly conservative message. For example, a series of lessons for the housewife in the form of conversation between husband and wife by Prafulla Kumar Dhar (1925) run as follows: 'In our country a section of our educated persons are eager to bring about the liberation of women (*stree swadhinata*). But how far this will be good for this country lacking independence—that is to be considered. Having been encaged like birds, century after century, ... our women cannot freely fly when you free them from the cage...'.[6] While in Iswar Chandra Vidyasagar's times the case for widow remarriage rested mainly on reinterpretation of the *shastras*, in the late 1920s discussions on the Sarda Bill against child marriage tended to appeal to such an authority only incidentally.

Manuals for Housewives

However, the trends mentioned above did not by any means suggest that enlightenment had dawned on the votaries of tradition. Those manuals for housewives contain gems of archaic sentiment and rhetoric. Mrs Mustafi writes in 1904 in such a manual (recommended by the Bengal Textbook Committee as a book to be purchased for school libraries and as suitable for giving away as prize at schools):

> It is true that now steps are being taken to educate women, but that education is unsuitable for preparing women for household duties (*garhasthya dharma*).... A little learning does not bring wisdom, but it imparts a false sense of independence, women's nature becomes

> undisciplined, and thus education causes unrest in society. Nowadays a little learning imparted to women has disturbed our society in many ways.... True education would prevent such problems.[7]

Prafulla Kumar Dhar in 1925 attributes to an ideal young wife these words: 'Although I am a mere girl, I am a Hindu woman. I know that your advice is like the words of the *Vedas* to me. Bless me that I may give you happiness and die at your feet' (literally, with my head touching your feet), says the wife. The husband responds: 'I pray to God that your wish be fulfilled'.[8] Priyanath Bose in a householders' manual (1934) has this to say in a chapter on 'The Awakening of Women':

> Today we hear on all sides things about the Awakening of Women. Many men shudder to hear of it. Many women wonder what it is....In conversation, behaviour, and interactions, a sort of inversion (*ulta-britti*) has taken place. Men and women have lost their capacity to play their ordained roles (*dharma*); that is perhaps the reason why such a problem has arisen.[9]

Another similar work (1934), which had more than one imprint, was Mukherjee's, written in the form of conversations between husband and wife; this form of didactic writing was common in the *Puranas* and was followed even in the *Panjika* or Hindu calendar which began invariably with a conversation between the divine beings Shiva and Parvati. '*Sateetwa* contains within itself the virtues of the Woman, the Mother, and the Goddess. That is why it is the essence of a woman's life. The woman who can protect her chastity is in need of nothing ... a sacred luminosity shines around her ...', and so on.[10] Needless to say, across the communal border, the *purdah* was defended in the same manner as *sateetwa*. Mohammad Abdussalam's *Purdah tattwa* (Theory of the Purdah, 1926) is an interesting specimen.[11] Variations on the theme of chastity are to be found in the writings on *vaidhavya dharma*, a specially dangerous area of controlling feminine sexuality. One Nakul Chatterjee writes a typical book of this kind, *Bidhaba bandhab* (Friend of Widows, Dhaka, 1923). Incidentally, voluntary desertion of their homes by widows, described as abduction, was not uncommon; Muslims were often accused in the Hindu-controlled media of the crime of abduction and thus communal passions were engaged in defence of chastity.

There is a great deal of this kind of writing and it is easy to put it together to expose 'tradition' ruling the mind. But there was simultaneously an effort to negotiate with the challenge to tradition. This effort seems to emerge not so much as a concern with "modernity' or the 'Enlightenment Project' and what have you, as a concern for the immediate pragmatic context. After all, why do manuals for housewives proliferate and who were they meant for? In the traditional joint-family, vertically or horizontally extended, the elders among the women of the family would mould the young bride and fashion her personality to suit the wifely role. A substitute for that was needed when families began to nucleate with migration to the small towns and the three cities of Calcutta, Howrah, and Dhaka. In the city of Calcutta there were large numbers of single male migrants—but this was more true of upcountry labourers and Bengali labourers than of middle-class *bhadraloks* settled in an employment. This also applied, to a lesser degree, to a few smaller 'industrial towns' where jute mills, coal mines and railway centres were located. Compared to industrial towns, the vast majority of the towns that were administrative headquarters or trade centres attracted more female migrants, that is, families (or part of the family, some members remaining in the home village). In 99 such non-industrial towns (less than 1 lakh population), the number of females per 1000 males was 787 in 1931, a higher figure than the number of females per thousand in large industrial cities.[12] These were towns like Burdwan, Bankura, Krishnanagar, Baharampur, Jessore, Khulna, Rajshahi, Jalpaiguri, Faridpur, Agartala, Pabna, Rangpur, and so on. The smaller towns attracted more migrants with families than did the bigger ones. In fact, the census figures show that as the towns grew bigger, the female population as a ratio of the total tended to decline in the early twentieth century. At any rate, what emerges is the migration of more women to small towns, a trend in the 1911–31 censuses, which suggests that some part of the old joint-family was left behind in the village home. Hence housewives, part of a smaller family in the small towns, were target readership (the literate housewives, of course) for the 'housewife's manuals' and similar 'educational' writings. This kind of publications imparted the sort of 'traditional knowledge' that used to be passed on from the elders to young women. Typical manuals would include chapters on herbal medicines for common diseases, child care, handling of contagious disease, diet for pregnant women and related matters, treatment for burns, what to do to resuscitate a person rescued from drowning, or one who had ingested a poisonous substance—all manner of things. It was not just moral lessons on *chastity* of women. Nor were they philosophical essays of the genre of Bhudeb Mukhopadhyay's *Paribarik prabandha* (1882).

In so far as these works by quite obscure but widely read authors addressed broader social questions, we have seen that the hold of tradition was strong, but at the same time one notices efforts to enter into a dialogue with new ideas, to negotiate a transition. Priyanath Bose, a diehard conservative in his attitude to women's education, not only deplores ill-treatment of the wife by the mother-in-law, but also acceptance of dowry; and he says that 'the husband's relationship with the wife is based on love, not on domination, coercion or chastisement'.[13] Mrs Mustafi, also critical of the formal education women were into, writes (1904) that 'women should not be confined' to the limited job of taking care of the family and the household chores; there are women's duties but 'women's life has higher aims as well ... the cultivation of self (*atma*)'; she means that in the spiritual sense and commends women who 'ascend to the higher sphere of *jnana*'.[14] Whatever one may make of her spiritual prescription, this perhaps expresses, in the idiom of those times, a dissatisfaction with the view that for the woman the be-all and end-all was the household. Mohammad Abdul Rauf's tract (1923), in the form of a conversation between husband and wife, is a rare example of reflections on conjugal relationships in the Muslim social context. The wife, talking about her place in her husband's family, says: as a person the wife has special rights in her husband's family and those rights must not be trampled upon by others, for that would be detrimental to her self-respect and 'there is nothing in the world greater than self-respect'.[15] The husband declares at the end of the conversation: 'You are not a plaything, but my companion in life...'. This is, of course, an unusually advanced sort of sentiment for 1923, but this too was a part of the effort to negotiate with a transition.

Women's Education

We have tried to see how the concepts of *sateetwa* and *garhasthya dharma* were handled, concepts derived from the past. *Naree-shiksha* (women's education) was a more recent introduction into the discourse, originating in the late-nineteenth-century Bengali *bhadralok* endeavour to reconstruct femininity by bringing into the *antahpur* (the inner quarters of the women) education of the kind that would produce the *bhadra mahila*. In the nineteenth century, proponents and participants in women's education appear to be doing something daringly novel, if not subversive. Ras Sundari Devi (1809–99) writes in the 1860s: 'Let alone voicing my innermost feelings, my heart used to quiver at the thought of anyone guessing how I felt: so much so that if I saw a sheet of paper which had been written on, I used to look away. This was in case anyone accused me of wanting to study'. Jnanada Nandini Devi (1851–1941) reminisces:

> One night I suddenly woke up and raising my head I saw my mother writing or reading something. Seeing me she quickly hid all those, fearing that as I was a child, I might tell someone. One of our elderly neighbours knew how to read and write but, for fear of being ostracized, engaged in these activities behind closed doors. Nevertheless, people got to know, and she was publicly denigrated by residents of the locality.

Sarala Devi Chaudhurani (1872–1945) recalls:

> I would have studied botany at Bethune [College]—for which no really complicated apparatus was required. But I was firmly resolved to learn physics, just like the boys of the household.... In my mind, a tremendous restlessness set in. I wanted to leave home, which was like a cage, and rush out on some purposeless and random journey. Like my brothers, I wanted to earn an independent livelihood.[16]

These writings from about the 1820s, 1850s and the 1880s suggest that women's education was a novel enterprise. By the 1920s it was no, longer a question whether education should be offered to women; in fact, even to the conservative-minded, the only question was how much. Education can be—and this is a point that we often miss when we take it for granted or look at intentions and not the outcomes—subversive of the established order of things. We have heard Nagendra Bala Mustafi railing against the 'little learning' imparted to women by way of formal education as 'disturbing to our society'. Likewise, another author complains in 1926 of 'alien education and non-Hindu education which does not allow women, when they get married, to relate with our tradition'; this education also made young persons 'intolerant'.[17]

The same author concedes, however, that education is necessary to allow 'a meeting of minds' between wife and husband.[18] A more forthright adversary of education says:

> Your [that is, women's] education does not mean that you will take the air like a *memsahib* roaming the streets hand-in-hand with your husband or just sit like a queen devouring novels, or speechify.... Women must be taught to read and write and be independent, on the one hand and, on the other, they must observe rules of wifely behaviour—cook, raise children.....[19]

We find an echo in the words of the Vice-Chancellor of Calcutta University, the historian Sir Jadunath Sarkar (1870–1958) speaking at Bethune College for Women in 1927: 'In our country, the woman's place is in the home and the family; the nature of girls is also different from that of boys. In these circumstances, education for women should be appropriate to the household, family, society and nature of women in our country'.[20] The *Ananda Bazar Patrika* editorially supported this view, with its own gloss that a 'national pattern' specific to India must evolve.[21] As late as 1934, Priya Nath Bose writes that the Bengali family needs a healthy, compliant, and dutiful daughter-in-law rather than 'an educated girl who is poor in health, dolled up with soap and pomade (*pomatom*), quarrelsome, and sickly pale'.[22] What kind of education was desirable for women? In 1929, a Conference on Women's Education in Calcutta, chaired by Mrs P.K. Ray, suggested a curriculum: religious education, domestic work and management, treatment and nursing of patients, child rearing, arts and crafts, music, and physical fitness exercises.[23] Quaint and indeed reactionary as it was in delimiting women to certain 'womanly' roles, this kind of attitude coexisted with fairly advanced ideas. For instance, the same body of people at the parallel session of the All-India Women's Conference, led by Lady Abala Bose (1864–1951), wife Sir J.C. Bose the scientist, Maharani Sucharu Devi of Mayurbhanj, and Kamala Devi Chattopadhyay, passed strong resolutions in support of the pending Sarda Bill against child marriage.[24]

A Quantitative Index

Leaving aside these issues pertaining to the content of formal education, how many women in Bengal had any basic education at all? As an index of women's status, the proportion attaining literacy is very important. In less developed countries it is a standard measure of women's status and quality of life. While development economists use this measure whenever the data base allows it, historians have not shown an awareness of this aspect although very sophisticated approaches to the gender question have been developed.

In Bengal in the 1920s, the literacy level—even after decades of exposure to Macaulay's machine for the dispersal of Enlightenment—was abominably low in general, and particularly that of the female population. The position at the end of that decade is reflected in the ratios worked out in Table 2.1 on the basis of A.E. Porter's report on the Census of Bengal in 1931.

The total in the table includes some other religious communities (2 per cent of the total), each with small populations, such as Jains, Parsis, Buddhists, Christians, Animists, and Confucians. Literacy was defined in the census as 'ability to read and write a letter from and to a friend'.

In terms of absolute numbers, in the total female population of 2.45 crore in Bengal there were only 99,000 literate in English, and 6.6 lakh literate in the vernacular. As is well known, the rate of literacy was lower in the Muslim community than in the Hindu community at that time. To their credit, the Muslim elite tried to push forward an agenda for female education: the Purdahnashin Madrasa opened by Suhrawardiya Begum in Calcutta in 1913, the Muslim Educational Conference, Rokeya Sakhawat Hossain's (1880–1932) school founded in 1911, Shamsun Nahar Mahmud's (1909–1964) collaboration with Rokeya in the Anjuman-i-Khawateen-e-Islam to promote social welfare among backward Muslim women, the admission of larger numbers of Muslim women in Dhaka University founded in 1921 and, finally,

Table 2.1 Percentage of Population, Male and Female, Literate in the Vernacular and in English in 1931

Religious Community	In the Vernacular		In English	
	Male	Female	Male	Female
Hindu	22.43	4.18	5.88	0.55
Muslim	9.71	1.41	1.71	0.14
Total	15.36	2.71	3.64	0.41

Source: A.E. Porter, ICS, *Report in the Census of Bengal in 1931* (Calcutta, 1932).

the Lady Brabourne College started in 1939 under the patronage of Chief Minister Fazlul Huq—these were some landmarks in the Muslim women's education movement.[25]

When we consider that only a small section of the literate population had received formal education—this number was not recorded in the census—one realizes what a minuscule population constituted the catchment area for recruitment to the educated *bhadra mahila* category. But a significant fact was the concentration of the literate female population in some caste brackets. The figures for these so-called upper castes in Table 2.2 indicate this concentration.

These figures, worked out from the census tables of 1931, show how a 'community of the educated' could develop among the upper-caste women, although the literate and educated women were spread very thinly over the total population. Most noteworthy is the Vaidya caste (numbering about 110,000—both male and female) which attained a high rate of female literacy. Vaidya women registered 38.34 per cent literacy in Bengali, more than double the male literacy level in the vernacular in Bengal's total population; again, literacy in English among Vaidya women, 11.29 per cent, was three times the percentage of male literacy in English in the total population of Bengal. The Brahmins (much more numerous, about 14.5 lakh) and the Kayasthas (about 15.6 lakh) also showed levels of female literacy much higher than the average female literacy level, though they were nowhere near the Vaidya caste. In these so-called 'high' castes, men's access to education, employment, the professions, urban life and institutions, and so on. constituted a resource that women could partly share—although that share was exceedingly small—and the associative activities among these *bhadraloks* appear to have created among the higher castes norms different from that of the rest in respect of women's education.

Table 2.2 Percentage of Female Population Literate in the Vernacular and in English in 1931 in the Upper Castes

Caste	In the Vernacular	In English
Brahmin	17.53	2.69
Vaidya	38.34	11.29
Kayastha	16.96	2.87

Source: A.E. Porter, ICS, *Report in the Census of Bengal in 1931* (Calcutta, 1932).

Among the other castes, there are some who do better than the average and some worse. Table 2.3 looks at the more numerous of these castes.

The castes involved in trade and artisanal industry, some upward mobile peasant castes, and some groups with a specific cultural tradition (for example, the Vaishnavas) appear to do better than the average. The level of literacy in English is not included here because it was insignificantly low.

There are many shortcomings in these statistics, including those of categorization. However, the overall picture is clear: a low level of female literacy in general, and concentration of a higher proportion of literate women in the so-called upper-caste brackets, the site of the emergence of the Bengali *bhadra mahila*. Apart from the caste factors, one suspects that there were also spatial variations tending towards regional concentration. In East Bengal, Hindu women seemed to have greater access to education than in West Bengal, though there is no quantitative evidence for this. Perhaps, relatively recent migration to East Bengal loosened the ties of tradition in 'high-caste' families. The spread of Brahmoism was, of course, a very important factor, creating a new model of Bengali womanhood; thus the sections affected by Brahmoism, directly or by demonstration effect, adopted the Brahmo agenda for women's education. Unfortunately, the census classification does not allow us to separate Brahmos from the Hindus. Christians, through their missionary activities, led the others in female literacy in

Table 2.3 Percentage of Female Population Literate in the Vernacular in Selected Castes, 1931

Saha	6.93
Barujeebee	5.65
Mahishya	3.24
Vaishnav	3.16
Bengal Average	*2.71*
Napit	2.54
Goala	2.43
Charmakar	1.55
Dom	0.65
Vyagra-Kshatriya	0.45

Source: A.E. Porter, ICS, *Report on the Census of Bengal in 1931* (Calcutta, 1932).

the 19th century: in 1931, 32.16 per cent of Christian women were literate in Bengali and 24.86 per cent in English. Thus, socially and spatially, there were concentrations of literate women. Hence the possibility of the formation of what we may call the critical minimum needed to form a communication community. Ironically, this was the consequence of caste and status inequality affecting access to education. Such a communication community was a prerequisite for associative activities, including a women's movement.

In passing, we may note that the educated *bhadra mahila* became role models for many, so much so that they set the fashion in apparel. As a sociologist has pointed out, there is no Bengali word for 'fashion' and 'style' and the English words are used as the need arises.[26] However, the Bengali *bhadra mahila* set the trends in fashion for several decades beginning in the late nineteenth century, not only for small-town womenfolk but also for the advanced urban middle classes in many parts of India. Their style of wearing the sari with pleats in front and the braid on the left shoulder is now almost universal, except amongst the truly rural who retain the traditional styles local to different parts of India, or amongst the super-sophisticated in their occasional 'ethnic' moments.[27] This style was created in Calcutta by Jnanadanandini Devi, Rabindranath Tagore's sister-in-law and wife of Satyendranath Tagore, who fused the Bengali and Parsi styles; having spent many years in Bombay Presidency where her husband served in the Indian Civil Service (ICS), she was familiar with the Parsi mode.[28] It is a fact that this new style originating in Calcutta was widely accepted in urban society in almost all parts of India but it is difficult to explain the phenomenon. Perhaps the Bengali *bhadra mahila* was perceived widely as a role model for urban educated women in other parts of India. Or perhaps the influence of film-makers of the generation of Pramathesh Barua (1903–51) and Bimal Roy (1909–66) in Calcutta or in Bombay had something to do with it. Likewise, there was an influential cultural example, Tagore's Santiniketan. Be that as it may, from the early twentieth century, the new style of wearing the sari and certain additional apparel and accessories to go with it, marked out the educated townswoman from her sisters in less privileged circumstances. It was as a mark of privilege, access to education and 'modernity', that the sari worn in the new style was considered worthy of imitation.

Women's Rights

The 1920s or 1930s did not see anything like a women's movement. But there were straws in the wind. The term *nareer adhikar* (women's rights) was heard now and then. 'Bengali society', said an editorial in a Bengali daily in 1923, 'shows great anxiety to point to women's duties, and an equally great disregard for women's rights'.[29] Women's voting rights were recognized in 1922 in municipalities and corporations, subject to property qualifications applying to men as well. On women's voting rights in elections to the legislature, the *Ananda Bazar Patrika* editorialized: 'In our country many people accept women's equal rights as a principle; when it comes to action they raise objections and excuses. They say that education has not spread among women in this country ... and that seclusion of women and social customs are inimical to conferment of rights on women'.[30] This sums up the substance of the debate on women's political rights occasioned by the proposal being considered in 1925 in the Bengal legislature to extend the franchise to women. By the last half of the 1920s most provinces, including Bengal, had thus extended the franchise to women on the same terms as men. But it was a bit of a hoax. The Government of India in their despatch to the Secretary of State for India in 1930 observed, quite correctly, that the extension of franchise to women was 'a gesture of high significance' but it was 'only a gesture, because few women in India own property in their own right' and property qualification was the basis of voting rights.[31] An important Bengali tract of those times was *Women's Rights* (1925) by Nanilal Bhattacharya. The history of the suffrage movement in England is traced and the origins of a modern point of view traced to Mary Wollstonecraft's tract of 1792. From Indian history, the author cites examples of women who were great rulers, scholars, sages, and so on, to refute the view that Indian women were unfit for citizenship or franchise.[32] The Indian National Congress eventually approved in 1931 a resolution demanding universal adult franchise.[33]

Other issues in the 1920s were civil rights, age of consent, and right of succession. A Bill on Hindu Succession was moved in the Indian Legislative Assembly, but most Hindu members opposed it, including Madan Mohan Malaviya who contended that non-Hindus had no right to support or oppose the Bill since it concerned only the Hindu community. A last-ditch attempt by a member from Bengal, S.P. Sinha, to keep the matter open to public debate or a referendum, was rejected by a massive majority of 48 against 14.[34] This question continued to be a subject of contention through the 1940s: women's rights of succession were looked upon as an imposition in addition to the dowry, and it was even claimed, amazingly, that women's succession rights would destroy Hinduism since they would bring in matriarchy![35]

The question of raising the age of consent to eliminate child marriage came to a head in 1929 when Harbilas Sarda proposed in the Indian Legislature his celebrated Bill. This was one issue on which there was a concerted agitation by women's organizations against conservative opinion. Typical of the latter was the Hindu Provincial Conference (later to merge with the Mahasabha). Meeting at Dhaka in August 1929, the Hindu Provincial Conference of Bengal resolved against the Sarda Bill.[36] Some journals, most prominently the *Basumati*, strongly opposed the Bill. The conservative argument was that to wait till the girls attained the age of sixteen would encourage premarital sex; there was also a section of conservatives opposed to child marriage, but also to legislation because that would allow the state to intervene in matters that ought to be left to Hindu society to take care of. The refutation of these absurdities was easily achieved by the supporters of the Sarda Bill; what is interesting in this conflict was the forthright denunciation of *shastric* authority. For example: 'Opposition to the effort to stop child marriage is medieval barbarism. Jeemutavahana in the fourteenth century, Raghunandana in the sixteenth, prescribed the appropriation of women's social and economic rights ... for the last few centuries unspeakable torture of womanhood has taken place'; 'irrational *shlokas* from the *smriti-shastra* (law books)' were irrelevant in the twentieth century; the 'dominance of a dead *smriti shastra* combined with absence of rationality' characterized the conservative outpourings, but what would you expect in this 'reactionary, superstition-ridden, society devoid of commonsense'; it was also said that Muslims did not share the reverence for *shastras*, but their social practices and those of the Hindus coincided on one objective, the subordination of women.[37]

It is true that on this issue, as on others, the prominent spokesmen on both sides treated in their writings women as objects rather than subjects, and women's participation in the debates was very limited. However, on the Sarda Bill there was an unusually organized agitation initiated by women. A memorable event of 1929 was a meeting of Bengali women at Albert Hall on College Street in Calcutta. Among those who addressed the meeting were Sneha Sheela Chaudhary (1886–1955) a prominent Congress activist in Jessore since 1921, and Sucharu Devi (1874–1961) the wife of the Maharaja of Mayurbhanj and more generally known as daughter of Keshab Chandra Sen. Resolutions were passed by the assembled Bengali women in support of the Sarda Bill and against the institution of child marriage. Perhaps equally significant and more remarkable is the statement made by Sneha Sheela Chaudhuri: 'Love [*prem*] is not born in the mind of a girl at the age of twelve or thirteen.... Do the makers of laws [*shastras*] look upon women as manufacturing machines?'[38] What the reactions were went unreported, but it was a momentous statement from a woman, demanding 'love' in conjugal relationship.

The All-India Women's Conference met in Calcutta in January 1929. Lady Abala Bose (1864–1951) was the secretary and Maharani Sucharu Devi was chairman of the Reception Committee. Abala Bose, having been denied admission to Calcutta Medical College, was trained in the Madras Medical College in 1882–6; she founded in 1919 the Naree Shiksha Samiti in Calcutta and about two hundred girls' schools in rural areas, and was one of the initiators in the intervention made by the All-India Women's Conference (AIWC) in support of the Sarda Bill. It is interesting to note that in those days Muslim and Christian women also attended the AIWC sessions, although on most other public platforms the communal divide had appeared.

The organized efforts to push the 'women's cause' into the public sphere, particularly in respect of legislation and franchise, was accompanied by the nationalist political leadership's attempts to appropriate that cause, provided it could be moulded to its own purposes. There was a routine cant about nation building and the new role of women: 'If the nation's womenfolk are not a strong force, the nation will be weak',[39] 'If India is to win freedom the women must be awakened', and so on.[40] There were two versions of this. The weak version recommended to women no direct political participation, but a constructive role from within the confines of the home: 'India's wives and mothers will ... raise the future soldiers for Swaraj' in their homes which remain 'their principal realm'. The strong version said that this was not enough, women were not to be confined to their duties at home, they must 'carry the flag and enter the freedom struggle like their husbands and sons'.[41]

Some of this was mere rhetoric and too much can be made of it in terms of the deeper intentions of the nationalist leadership. Between intentions and outcomes there is often a mismatch in history. What we know of activists who were upholding the women's cause (for example, suffrage, child marriage, education, and similar issues) and also joined the ranks of the nationalists, does not suggest that they were co-opted to the detriment of the women's cause in some mysterious manner. On the contrary, it brought to them resources, networks and skills to advance that cause. It will be incorrect to hold a contrary view without taking into account the life and work of women like Jyotirmoyee Ganguly (1890–1945) or Sneha Sheela Chaudhuri (1886–1955) or Urmila Devi (1883–1956) and their peers of that generation. Moreover, a reduction of the multidimensional gender question to a one-dimensional perspective at times suffers from serious inadequacies.

The Four-Letter Word, 'Love'

Finally, let us turn from the public to the private domain and ask the question, did the years around the 1920s witness an attempt to redefine the gender relationship? The answer is that there was perhaps such an attempt. To begin with, one notices an explicit and recurring theme: love is demanded in conjugal relationships. Is it not remarkable that, as we noted earlier, in 1929 a forty-four-year-old lady, a veteran Congress worker, talks of such 'love' at a public meeting, attended by the Press, in Calcutta's Albert Hall? But Sneha Sheela Chaudhuri was articulating a thought that occurs in many unexpected places. One would, of course, expect it in contemporary literature, especially that of the 'new wave'; but it is also found, unexpectedly, in the works of highly conservative and traditional authors such as those of housewives' manuals and catechisms for Hindu women.

The literary journal *Kallol* (1923–9) brought into the domain of the literature of 'high culture' many hitherto untouched themes. A literary historian has tabulated and thematically analysed the fictional works in the journal; his conclusion is that 'discontentment with conjugal love' and 'illicit love' are major themes in the writings in that journal which spearheaded a new era in the 1920s.[42] In so far as thematic analysis is useful, limited as it is, it strengthens the point we have made earlier: there is in this period a confrontation between new sensibilities and established social institutions and values. The heroine of a novel published in 1927–8 in *Kallol* by its founder–editor, Dinesh Ranjan Das (1888–1941), says that love is not to be taken for granted by the husband, it has to be won. 'Conjugal rights you have had. If you expect more than that you have to win it in your life',[43] the heroine tells her husband. Another leader of this literary group, Gokul Nag (1894–1925), makes the emptiness of marriage without love the theme of his novel published in 1923.[44] Shortly before the appearance of *Kallol,* Naresh Chandra Sengupta's (1883–1964) novel published in 1920 depicted a married woman leaving her home in search of true love, a theme considered outrageously bold and disturbing at that time.[45] Needless to say, others before that had addressed the theme of love disturbing conjugal felicity. In a different way, Tagore's novel *Ghare baire* in 1915 had invited thoughts on the Bengali woman's home and the world outside and how they met and related. But, from 1923, the spurt of writings in *Kallol* marked the beginning of a widely shared trend. What attracted attention was that in the realm of high culture the *Kallol* group explicitly touched on the libidinous. A contemporary writer records that a Bengali author, probably Anurupa Devi (1882–1958), the granddaughter of Bhudeb Mukhopadhyay, said in her Address to a Literary Conference: authors who write of sexual love in the new fashion should have been eliminated at the moment of their birth.[46] This drastic remedy came from a lady who praised child marriage and was herself the object of strong criticism from the radicals.[47] There was a battle between old sensibilities and a new awareness about 'love', conjugal or otherwise, in literature. A number of cognate questions were raised by Sarat Chandra Chatterjee in his didactic writings and by others.[48] Jyotirmoyee Ganguly (1889–1945), daughter of the Brahmo leader Dwarakanath Ganguly, asked whether companionship in marriage was possible in a male-dominated society?[49] What remains of women's humanness if she is regarded as a machine to deliver sons?[50] Above all, was love consistent with inequality in the relationship between men and women?

Below the domain of high culture at a lower level of discourse, these questions were addressed by obscure authors of books to exhort and train the *bhadra mahilas* or aspirants desiring to rise to that station in life. In Mrs Nagendra Bala Mustafi's manual (1904) for the housewife, along with chapters on 'Herbal Medicines', 'How to Be Happy', 'Spiritual Uplift', and so on, there is a chapter entitled 'Love'.[51] A similar book (1925) by Dhar expatiates on 'love that in the West comes before marriage and among Hindus after marriage'.[52] Dhar says that the Hindu woman begins to love first out of a sense of duty and some other love blooms later. His image of an ideal conjugal relationship includes 'friendship among equals'.[53] Another didactic work, *Swamee-stree* (Husband–Wife, 1933), again has a chapter on 'Love'. In a book stuffed with advice against modern education, fall from chastity, vegetables to be avoided when stars so ordain in the Hindu calendar, and so on, the author talks of the four modes of a wife's relationship with her husband: as a partner, as a woman, as a friend, and as a 'spiritual' companion.[54] One can sense a search for a new language to negotiate with 'love' in conjugal life.

The 'love' these authors talk about is obviously of a rather special kind, somewhat 'spiritual', but they feel the need to bring it in. Sexual attraction (*kama*), P.K. Dhar (1925) ventures, may be present in the beginning but it becomes love (*prem*): do not forget, the husband tells the wife sententiously, the 'Hindu marriage is spiritual (*adhyatmik*)'. Mrs Nagendra Bala Mustafi (1904), twenty years earlier, held the same view, as we have seen. In fact, they held it as a self-evident truth that the women of this country were more 'spiritual' than their Western counterparts. On one occasion, Viceroy Lord Lytton made a rather nasty crack about Indian women—that they harass the police with false cases of abduction and rape. A Bengali daily editorialized under the rubric 'National Insult':

> In Lord Lytton's own country what is the standard of Ladies' chastity and dignity? The awful moral state of women in England—how women sell themselves in public parks, opera houses, dance halls, hotels, seaside resorts—has been lamented by the Archbishop of London himself.... In England are not the ties of matrimony becoming lax and likewise the social institutions built upon that basis.... Let Lord Lytton know that there is a difference of heaven and hell between the model of chastity among women of this country and that prevailing in the West.[55]

This was a stereotype that was very common in the early twentieth century discourse, and not so uncommon even later. It served to underline again the supposed 'spirituality' of some special kind of love in the Hindu conjugal relationship. That was a means of reconciling the affective relationship in the concept of 'prem' with traditional notions. The traditional ideas about conjugal relations continued to be articulated. The same P.K. Dhar who talks about love and friend-like relationship asks: Is it right for the wife to address letters to her husband as 'Lord of my heart' (*praneshwar*, a word made famous, let us recall, by Bankim Chandra Chatterjee in the first Bengali romance, *Rajsimha*, six decades ago)? No, the wife should address her letters 'To thy honoured feet (*sree-charaneshu*)'. Moreover, being an independent person is all very well, but the Hindu woman must not forget that modesty or reserve (*lajja*) is a trait she must not lose. And so forth. Thus the pendulum swings. There is a wavering between two paradigms, and an effort to reconcile opposites. These negotiations of a transition are qualified by the participation of women in the public sphere, initially in social reform type of initiatives and, increasingly, in politics,[56] partly but not wholly circumscribed by a kind of traditional patriarchalism. On the whole, the contemporary evidence we have surveyed leaves one with the impression that the discourse of gender was rather complex in the early years of the twentieth century and it anticipated the ambivalences characterizing middle-class thinking throughout the major part of the century.

Emergence of Women in Politics and the Public Sphere

In the 1920s and 1930s, the participation of women in political activities brought into existence a new dimension of the role of women, chiefly the women who were *bhadra mahila*. There were several ideological strands in the complex of ideas inspiring women's intervention in the public sphere and politics. Predictably, the Indian National Congress and the *biplabi* (militant nationalists) groups proved to be ideologically influential, followed later by Leftist ideologues of various hues, ranging from the mildly socialistic to the Communists of the International. Standing apart from these trends there was another kind of intervention by women in the public sphere, without any overt political affiliation—the women's education movement. It is neither necessary nor possible to chronicle here these developments; excellent studies in recent years have narrated the story and what may be useful to do here will be to raise a few questions about the nature of women's participation in public affairs and politics.

Perhaps the most interesting question is this: It has sometimes been said in recent times that participation in political activities did not confer agency on women; they were mere automatons directed by male leaders. How correct is that generalization? Very little evidence from the actual participants' observations and memories has been produced to establish that the women so engaged in political activity felt a lack of agency, that they failed to be true subjects. It is arguable that these later historical accounts ignore the *unintended consequences* of the induction of women into political activities by leaders far from being emancipationist in their outlook.[57] The political activities at least allowed women to get out of the domestic and into the wider sphere. Later, we shall look at evidence of women leaders contesting Gandhi's position and arguing that their place is not merely tending the hearth, debating whether 'conjugality is not just for procreation', asserting their 'right to every kind of work', and charging the Congress with a negligent attitude to their role in political work. We have instances of women's journals started by the Congress or its allies publishing trenchant critiques of the Congress under Mahatma Gandhi. There is also evidence of women's groups and associations initiated by men like Subhas Chandra Bose eliciting the support of certain women in public life who cannot be lightly accused of complicity in concealing patriarchalism under a façade of women's participation in politics. Probably it will be more correct to say that in the story of women's emergence in the public sphere one may see patriarchal attitudinizing in the early stage but the real story is the gradual erosion of patriarchalism and women gaining agency in the public sphere. Apart from this issue, there are interesting questions about the interface between the current political ideologies and the women's movement, or more appropriately their public associative activities. Were the specificities of women's approach to politics entirely determined by the ideological orientation of the parties to which women in active politics were affiliated, or distinct from it?

The overwhelming presence of the Indian National Congress was being challenged in Bengal politics in the 1920s and 1930s. In the early 1920s, the Congress began to make a dent in the traditional *bhadra mahila* cast of mind during the Non-cooperation Movement, but the

Congress was unable to bring them out into the public sphere in large numbers.[58] In 1921, when the movement was at its peak, C.R.Das's wife, Basanti Devi, courted imprisonment—a symbolic act widely reported, but the numbers involved in such activities were small. The agenda of action assigned to women in the movement was also limited: barring some occasional demonstrations of the kind Mrs Das was in, their task was to help male Congress volunteers organize boycott of foreign cloth and liquor shops. This action too met with an unexpected suspension after Chauri Chaura. Compared to 1920–1, a more generalized participation of women in Congress activities began in the late 1920s. Protests against the Simon Commission through a strike in Bethune College, participation of women in the Youth Conference chaired by Jawaharlal Nehru in a public park; a girl students' convention in Calcutta University leading to the foundation of the Chhatri Sangha by Kalyani Bhattacharya; the renaming of the All-Bengal Young Men's Association as Youth Association at the instance of Subhas Chandra Bose to allow women's membership; the foundation of the Mahila Rashtriya Sangha led by Latika Ghose under the auspices of the Congress; the public manifestation of women's participation in Congress activities in the form of a parade of a women's squad at the Calcutta session of the Congress—all that happened in a rush around 1928. In 1931, the Civil Disobedience Movement, under the Non-cooperation Movement earlier, attracted women's participation—for example, Dr Prabhabati Dasgupta, later a trade union leader, Indumati Goenka (noteworthy because she belonged to the conservative Marwari community), and Kalyani Das (Bhattacharya) of the Chhatri Sangha took part. However, after the heady days of the Salt Satyagraha and Civil Disobedience, the Congress agenda of action probably failed to excite the young radicals in the women's movement—most of them were attracted to the militant nationalists or *biplabi* or the Communist ideology in the 1930s. And Subhas Chandra Bose, a promoter of women's participation in Congress activities, was marginalized by the hardcore Gandhians in 1938–9, ultimately leading to his expulsion. Most important of all, the narrow social base of the women's section in the Congress was a weakness that could not be overcome, and the factional struggles between Bose, Jatindra Mohan Sengupta, and the Gandhians and the Anushilan and Jugantar factions which entered the Congress slowly exacerbated the many infirmities of the Congress in decline in the 1930s.

A moment of revival for the women's section in the Congress was the foundation of a journal in 1938, entitled *Mandira*. It was intended by the party bosses to promote the Congress' position, but it actually propagated an ideology more radical than that of the mainstream of the Congress. As we have seen earlier, the Congress in Bengal in the 1930s accommodated a great variety of political groups, including the *biplabis* who were brought in by Subhas Bose and Jatindra Mohan Sengupta—many in those groups were on a trajectory towards conversion to Leftist ideologies. Like its predecessor *Jayashree* edited by Leela Roy, in guiding *Mandira* editorially a few radical women, Kamala Mukherjee, Kamala Dasgupta, and their associates often departed from the Congress 'line' in taking a position in between the Congress, on the one hand, and the *biplabis* and the Left on the other. Edited by women and carrying mainly, though not exclusively women's writings, from 1938 to 1948, it followed a radical line which eventually attracted the party bosses' attention. They decided to appropriate the journal, appoint a man as editor in place of the women who had run the journal for ten years to make it a success. The rationale for the change, as stated by the new editor, was: 'Taking advantage of the liberal views of our colleagues, some [that is, editors] tried to steer it to an anti-Congress path'.[59] This criticism was the best compliment the women editors got. It is clear that a great degree of freedom was enjoyed by them in the past ten years. The credit for this goes chiefly to the group of women who edited and contributed to the journal in those years. There is little justification for representing them as mere instruments in the hands of the dominant male leadership in politics.

As we said earlier, side by side with the official Congress initiative in the domain of the women's movement was the *biplabi*, or revolutionary nationalist strand in that movement. It was ideologically distinct from the Congress's position, but the party had rather porous boundaries at that time and thus many mentors and activists in the *biplabi* women's group were in the Congress as well. A product of Bethune College and the first woman to earn an MA degree in Dhaka University, Leela (Nag) Roy (1900–0) was in the women's enfranchisement movement (1920), the organizer of the Dhaka Mahila Committee for flood relief work (1922), the founder of the women's political association Dipali Sangha (1923), the first woman to be admitted to the executive committee of a revolutionary nationalist organization, Shree Sangha (1926), the joint-leader of Shree Sangha with Anil Roy from 1928 to 1930, and the leader after the latter's imprisonment, as well as the founder-editor of an exclusively women's journal, *Jayashree* (1931). While the women's organizations the Congress sponsored were also engaged in political activities since the days of Subhas Bose, there were some distinguishing characteristics of the revolutionary nationalist women's organization. Shree Sangha was active throughout the year, not a thing conjured into existence for a Congress session or a particular action programme adopted for the time being by the Congress. Shree Sangha worked with women through the year—it ran a library, organized regular discussion sessions, trained activists physically and intellectually, prepared them for public leadership, and held up the idea that no political work was exclusively a male monopoly. The journal *Jayashree* announced its objective in the first number in April 1931: to 'inspire the spirit of patriotism and a fearless desire to serve the country among the women of Bengal'.[60] In fact, it was precisely at the time of the widespread repression and arrests following the Chittagong Armoury Raid in 1931 that the journal was founded 'to help us stay focused ideologically'.[61] It is abundantly clear that the British Police were aware of the ideological difference between the Congress and Leela Roy's group of women: they did everything possible to put her out of action. After the assassination of the District Magistrate of Dhaka by two young girls (December 1931), the Deepali Sangha was banned (1932), Leela Roy and a co-editor of her journal were arrested, and the journal was required to publish under such conditions imposed by the government that it folded up in 1935. It was in 1938, when Leela Roy came out of prison, that it was revived.

When one looks at the editorials and articles published in *Jayashree* and *Mandira*, one begins to appreciate that the radical women of the 1930s in Bengal had indeed prepared a road-map distinctly different from that of the nationalist political Establishment. For example, a Congress activist Bina Bhowmik, writes in 1939 upon release from jail:

> I could not believe my eyes when I read in the papers the other day that Gandhiji had said: 'We should pledge unconditional support to England. I shall not be able to stand the fall of Westminster Abbey'. I was never was so confounded in my life. Is this what he has taught us so far? ... Is Gandhiji joking with us now?[62]

Few Congressmen would have dared to challenge Mahatma Gandhi in this manner. Or again, Leela Roy writes in *Jayashree* contesting Gandhi's view expounded in *Harijan*. 'In my opinion', Gandhi wrote, 'it is degrading both for men and women that women should be called upon or induced to forsake the hearth and shoulder the rifle for the protection of that hearth.... The sin will be on the Man's head for tempting or compelling his companion to desert her special calling'.[63] Leela Roy boldly contested the notion that women's 'special calling' was tending the hearth. She wrote, in refutation of that view: 'Such [an] artificially constructed divide between the home and the world is absolutely unnecessary—all workplaces outside the house or inside should be equally accessible to both men and women and they should have equal rights in exercising their choice according to their disposition and needs'.[64] On issues specific to women, the radical woman intellectuals were often as anti-establishment as in politics. Sudhamayee Devi of Santiniketan, writing in 1932 in *Jayashree* on birth control, along with a parallel exposition of Margaret Sanger's views by the editor, presented the following view: 'It is true that procreation is the primary objective of marriage. But conjugality is not just for procreation. It is important to have a physical relationship for couples to feel attraction and love for each other ... to come closer to each other mentally. There is no harm in controlling birth as necessary for the purpose'.[65] Santi Sudha Ghosh questions in the pages of *Mandira* the Bengali social custom requiring women to wear vermilion, shell bangles, and the veil, and the Bengali women's willing compliance: 'Why should women alone be so concerned to flaunt their marital status when men are least bothered to wear any such signifier?' If the wife wears vermilion on the parting of her hair, why does not the husband also wear a symbol like that? 'Those who laid down such rules could easily have made it mandatory for men to declare their marital status on their person. But that is not so.... [I]t looks like those who govern society wanted to circumscribe a woman's life only around marriage'.[66]

The radicalization of the women associated with groups like these, affiliated to the Congress or the *biplabis* or to both, was accompanied by a slow infusion of ideas from the Left. The first editor of *Mandira* joined the Communist Party, the journal carried, during her time on it and later, writings of Leftist intellectuals like Hiren Mukherjee or Somnath Lahiri, along with writings of the *biplabis* of the Jugantar group and the Congress. The Leftist trend in *Jayashree* tilted the group towards the Forward Bloc which accommodated some Marxists and that journal too carried contributions from Left intellectuals like Gopal Haldar or Chinmohan Sehanobis along with critiques of Marxism by Anil Roy. Perhaps a certain degree of eclecticism or rather openness to ideas was natural at this time when boundaries were in a flux since the parties were undergoing reorientation. Hence the women's groups we looked at are best characterized not by party labels but by the central thrust within a diversity of ideologies—that central endeavour was to give voice to the women who were emerging into the public sphere, to enhance their political awareness, and to enable them to play their role in this sphere.

Finally, let us turn to an ideological battle altogether different from the other ones. That battle was in progress in the discourse of Muslim women's education. An iconic figure in this area was Begum Rokeya (1880–1932) who founded one of the earliest public schools for Muslim women in 1911, and a Muslim women's association, Anjuman-e-Khawatin-e-Islam, in 1916. Having been educated at home and encouraged by her husband, a proponent of women's education among Muslims, she was driven by the idea that the *zenana* education for women, in seclusion behind the *purdah*, must be replaced by regular institutional education. When she started her school with just eight girls and very limited resources, mainstream Muslim opinion was against sending girls to school. A typical conservative view in *El Islam* in 1919 went thus: 'The reality is that the Muslim girls must be educated in a manner appropriate for Muslim society.... For Muslim girls to go to school, riding to school, wearing chemise and dress, is not appropriate.... It is an education that warps their taste, and opens the gate to an undesirable lifestyle and lack of faith in religion'.[67] However, in the course of the next two decades defenders rallied around Rokeya. For example, one Feroza Begum wrote in *Saogat* in 1926:

> The greatest impediment to female education are the *mullahs*. Their view is that spread of female education will bring about the decline of the [Muslim] community.... They fail to give due regard to the fact that for want of real education, the woman is not the mistress of the house as she should be, nor adequate as a mother, nor a true counsellor and companion in life.[68]

Through the 1920s and 1930s there was a running battle between these two camps, but the conservatives were steadily losing ground. Rokeya Begum and the case of women's education became a major issue in the public sphere: the movement for the 'Emancipation of Intellect' led by Kazi Abdul Wadud in Dhaka University, the Muslim Sahitya Samiti of Dhaka, the journal *Saogat* edited by Ahmad Nasiruddin, the poet Kazi Nazrul Islam (editor of *Langal*, founded 1922), the future Communist leader Muzaffar Ahmad (editor of *Ganabani*, founded 1926), and so on. Thus the story of the much-debated public schooling of girls merges into the story of the rise of the Left in Bengal to which we shall turn later in these pages.

On the whole, the segment of Bengal's culture and society we have looked at suggests that the prolonged negotiation of traditional male hegemonism with new emancipatory ideas from the 1920s to the end of the 1940s is a complex story, replete with ambivalences, compromises, as well as spirited assertions of women's rights, and does not fit into the commonly accepted monotonic stereotype about an unqualified patriarchalism in the private as well as the public sphere. Even if the only outcome of this exercise is to alert us to the need to rethink those stereotypes, this exercise will have served its purpose.

Notes

1. Tagore's 'Streer patra' (A Letter from the wife) was published in *Subujpatra* in 1321 BS (or 1914 CE); the title of Sarat Chandra Chatterjee's 'Nareer mulya', published in the journal *Jamuna* in 1913, can be translated either as 'The Status of Women' or as 'The Worth of Women'.
2. I have found the following very useful on gender history: Tanika Sarkar, *Hindu Wife, Hindu Nation: Community, Religion and Cultural Nationalism* (New Delhi, 2002); Meredith Brothwick, *Changing Roles of Women in Bengal, 1844–1905* (Princeton, 1984); Ghulam Murshed, *Reluctant Debutante: Response of Bengali Women to Modernization* (Rajshahi, 1983); Himani Bannerji, 'Fashioning a Self: Educational Proposal For and By Women in Popular Magazines in Colonial Bengal', *Economic and Political Weekly*, Bombay (26 October 1991); Partha Chatterjee, 'The Nationalist Resolution of the Women's Question' in *Recasting Women: Essays in Indian Colonial History*, eds K. Sangari and S. Vaid (New Delhi, 1989); Malavika Karlekar, *Voices From Within: Early Personal Narratives of Bengali Women* (Delhi, 1991); Chitra Deb, *Antahpurer atmakatha* (Calcutta, 1984);

Sumanta Banerjee, 'Marginalisation of Women's Popular Culture in 19th-century Bengal', in *Recasting Women*, ed. K. Sangari (Delhi, 1989); Dipesh Chakrabarty, 'The Difference-Deferral of a Colonial Modernity: Public Debates on Domesticity in British Bengal', *History Workshop* 36 (1993); Srabashi Ghosh, 'Birds in a Cage: Changes in Bengali Social Life', *Economic and Political Weekly*, Bombay (25 October 1986); not many of these address the twentieth-century issues on which the most recent well-documented study is Sarmistha Dutta Gupta, *Identities and Histories: Women's Writings and Politics in Bengal* (Kolkata: Stree, 2010). While I found these writings illuminating, the following pages on the 1920s and 1930s are by and large based upon contemporary writings.

3. *Ananda Bazar Patrika*, editorial and report, 19 June 1929; the Youth Conference met at Kalia in Jessore, East Bengal; the editorial cited in the text is from the same source. [*Ananda Bazar Patrika* is hereafter cited as *ABP*].
4. *ABP*, 19 June 1929.
5. *ABP*, 21 June 1929, editorial 'Apatti keno'; *ABP*, 3 September 1929, editorial, 'Balya vivava virodh'.
6. Prafulla Kumar Dhar, *Strir sahit kathopakathan* (Conversation with a Wife) (Calcutta, 1332 BS, 1925 CE), p. 138.
7. Sreemati Nagendra Bala Mustafi, *Garhasthya-dharma* (Burdwan, 1904).
8. Dhar, *Strir sahit kathopakathan*, p. 160.
9. Priyanath Bose, *Griha-dharma* (Calcutta, 1934).
10. Nandalal Mukhopadhyay, *Swamee-stree* (Husband and Wife) (Calcutta, 1340 BS, 1933 CE), pp. 70–1. This was the second edition, the first having been printed sometime in the 1920s.
11. Mohammad Abdussalam, *Purdah-tattwa* (Theory of purdah) (Calcutta, 1331 BS, 1926 CE), a defence of the seclusion of women.
12. A.E. Porter, ICS, *Report on the Census of Bengal, 1931* (Calcutta, 1932), pp. 79–81.
13. P. Bose, *Griha-dharma*, pp. 9, 185.
14. Mustafi, *Garhasthya-dharma*, pp. 3–4.
15. Mohammad Abdul Rauf, *Basarey: Swami strir kathopakathan* (Conversations between Husband and Wife on the Nuptial Night) (Calcutta, 1923), p. 11.
16. Translations from Rassundari, Jnanada Nandini and Sarada Devi, by Malavika Karlekar, *Voices from Within: Early Personal Narratives of Bengali Women* (Delhi, 1991), pp. 116, 78, 106.
17. Mustafi, *Garhasthya-dharma*, p. 79.
18. Dhar, *Strir sahit kathopakathan*, pp. 7–8.
19. N. Mukhopadhyay, *Swamee-stree*, pp. 13–14.
20. Sir J.N. Sarkar's speech reported in *ABP*, 19 February 1927.

21. *Ananda Bazar Patrika*, editorial 'Naree shiksha', 19 February 1927.
22. P. Bose, *Griha-dharma*, p. 169.
23. *ABP*, 23 February 1929.
24. *ABP*, Report on meeting and speeches at Albert Hall, College Street, Calcutta, 12 January 1929.
25. The best account available is Sonia Nishat Amin, 'Women and Society', in *History of Bangladesh*, ed. S. Islam, (Dhaka, 1992), vol. II, ch. 19.
26. Dulali Nag, 'Fashion, Gender and the Bengali Middle Class', *Public Culture*, 3, no. 2 (1991), p. 16.
27. I acknowledge personal communication from Ms Malabika Bhattacharya.
28. Chitra Deb, *Thakurbarir andar mahal* (Calcutta, 1391 BS, 1984 CE), pp. 32–4; the sister-in-law mentioned above was the wife of Satyendranath Tagore, the first Indian ICS officer, who was posted in Bombay Presidency for years; his wife seems to have combined stylistic elements of the Parsi sari and the traditional Bengali style of wearing that garment to devise a new mode that was imitated first by Brahmo Samaj women and then by the rest of the middle-class Bengalis. I understand that recently doubts have been cast on this history of the origin of the modern style of wearing the sari.
29. *ABP* editorial, 'Janani o jaya' (Mother and wife), 12 January 1923.
30. *ABP*, editorial, 'Narir adhikar' (Rights of women), 21 August 1925.
31. Letter from Governor-General Lord Irwin and his Council to Secretary of State for India, Wedgwood Benn, 20 September 1930, para 29 on Female Suffrage.
32. Nanilal Bhattacharya, *Narir adhikar* (Rights of women) (Calcutta, 1925).
33. This was the resolution on the Swaraj Constitution passed by the All-India Congress Committee at Bombay in August 1931, D. Chakrabarty and C. Bhattacharya (eds), *Congress in Evolution: Congress Resolutions* (Calcutta, 1935), pp. 28–9.
34. *ABP*, 3 February 1929.
35. An example is Narayan Ray, 'Hindu uttaradhikar', *Bharati* XXX, no. 1 (1942).
36. *ABP*, 3 September 1929.
37. *ABP*, editorials on prevention of child marriage and resistance to it, 18 August 1929 and 3 September 1929; Report on Committee on Age of Consent, 10 July 1929.
38. *ABP*, 7 September 1929.
39. *ABP*, editorial on 'The Place of Women in the Freedom Struggle', 10 February 1923.
40. *ABP*, editorial on 'The Swadeshi Spirit and the Women of Bengal', 5 March 1928.

41. *ABP*, editorial on 'The Women's Call', 10 January 1924.
42. Debkumar Bose, *Kallol goshthir katha sahitya* (Calcutta, 1387 BS, 1980 CE).
43. *Deepak* by Dinesh Ranjan Das.
44. *Pathik* by Gokul Chandra Nag.
45. *Shubha* by Naresh C. Sengupta (I have drawn upon the discussion of these works in D. Bose, *Kallol goshthir katha sahitya*).
46. Achintya Kumar Sengupta, *Kallol yug* (Calcutta, 1950), p. 61; D. Bose's research suggests that Anurupa Devi made this remark at a literary conference in 1926, D. Bose, *Kallol goshthir katha sahitya*, p. 231.
47. See Anurupa Devi's writings in *Bharatvarsha*, contradicted in *Bharati* (Phalgun, 1330 BS), by Ushaprabha Sen, pp. 1046–53.
48. Sarat Chandra Chatterjee's 'Narir mulya' was approvingly discussed by Annada Sankar Ray in *Bharati* (Aswin 1331 BS).
49. Jyotirmoyee Devi, 'Narir pratibha', *Bharati* (1331 BS), pp. 796–801.
50. Abanimohan Chakrabarty, 'Narir katha', *Bharati* (1330 BS), pp. 752–7.
51. Mustafi, *Garhasthya-dharma*, ch. 15.
52. Dhar, *Strir sahit kathopakathan*, p. 14.
53. Dhar, *Strir sahit kathopakathan*, p. 27.
54. N. Mukhopadhyay, *Swamee-stree*, pp. 15–16.
55. *ABP*, editorial 'Jatir apaman' (Insult to the Nation), 8 August 1924.
56. Barbara Southard, *The Women's Movement and Colonial Politics in Bengal* (New Delhi, 1995).
57. Indeed the representation of women in politics as puppets under male subjection sometimes sounds like a parrot-cry irrelevant to early twentieth century Bengal; vide Susnata Das, 'Swadhinata sangrame banglar chhatri-samaj', in *Mukti sangrame banglar chhatra-samaj*, ed. Barun De (Calcutta, 1992), pp. 30–129.
58. We are indebted to the path-breaking work in this area done by Tanika Sarkar, 'Politics and Women in Bengal: Meaning of Participation', in *Women in Colonial India*, ed. J. Krishnamurty (New Delhi, 1989); Barbara Southard, *The Women's Movement and Colonial Politics in Bengal, 1921–1936* (Delhi, 1995); Bharati Ray, 'The Freedom Movement and Feminine Consciousness in Bengal, 1905–29', in Ray, *From the Seams of History* (New Delhi, 1995); and the latest, an empirically rich account by Sarmistha Dutta Gupta, *Identities and Histories: Women's Writings and Politics in Bengal* (Calcutta, 2010).
59. Arun Chandra Guha, editor, *Mandira* (Baisakh 1355 BS, 1948), cited in Dutta Gupta, *Identities and Histories*, p. 168
60. *Jayashree* (Baisakh, 1338 BS, 1931), cited in Dutta Gupta, *Identities and Histories*, p. 108.
61. *Jayashree* (Kartik, 1338 BS, 1931), cited in S. Dutta Gupta, *Identities and Histories*, p. 107.

62. Bina Bhowmik, in *Mandira* (Bhadra, 1347 BS, 1940); I owe this and the three following references and translation to S. Dutta Gupta, *Identities and History*, an invaluable survey of women's journalistic writings of Bengal; also see Sarmistha Dutta Gupta, *Pather ingit: Nirbachito sambad-samayik patra bangalimeyer samaj-bhavna* (Kolkata, 2007).
63. *Harijan*, 24 February 1940, cited in *Collected Works of Mahatma Gandhi*, vol. 71, p. 208.
64. Leela Roy, in *Jayashree* (Baisakh, 1347 BS, 1940), cited in Dutta Gupta, *Identities and Histories*, p. 101.
65. Sudhamayee Devi, in *Jayashree* (Agrahayan, 1339 BS, 1932), cited in Dutta Gupta, *Identities and Histories*, p. 115.
66. Santi Sudha Ghosh, in *Mandira* (Jaishtha 1345 BS, 1938), cited in Dutta Gupta, *Identities and Histories*, p. 154.
67. Sheikh Abdur Rahman, *El Islam*, V, no. 8 (1919), cited in *Samayik patre jiban o janamat, 1901–30* (*SPIJ*), ed. Nurul Islam (Dhaka, 1977), p. 23.
68. Feroza Begum, in *Saogat*, VII, no. 1 (1926), cited in *SPJJ*, p. 23.

3

AFFINITY AND ITS DENIAL

Caste and Community Identities

What keeps together the civilization of India? This question was a matter of deep concern for Bengali intellectuals in the early decades of the twentieth century. We have seen that Tagore himself lent his authority to a view of the integral unity of the civilization of *Bharatvarsha*; the poem 'Jana-gana-mana', he wrote in 1911, later to become the national anthem, put that idea in highly emotive terms. Not only did the agenda of nation building demand the postulation of 'unity within diversity', but the rise of a new Bengali patriotism also required its reconciliation with, and placement in, the discourse of nationalism of a wider ambit. Moreover, as the communal divide widened, and caste cleavages were manifested in the form of backward caste solidarity movements and electoral politics in the 1920s and 1930s, the question acquired a new urgency. Was Bengal a bundle of tribes and castes and religious communities tied together loosely by a common language? And, likewise, the bigger question was, what kept together the Indian civilization?

The artificial rhetoric of 'national integration' in the post-1947 period, the deadening hand of state-sponsored patriotism, and the boring predictability of critics who have worked out an equation between nationalism and one form or another of hegemonism, make it difficult to approach this question without a sinking feeling of getting bogged down in a rerun of what has been said too often and not too well on the politics of colonial Bengal. Instead of covering the same ground, we shall try to address some questions about the ground realities of social and cultural life underlying political history, in particular identity politics in the pre-1947 decades.

Crossing Community Boundaries

To begin with, let us look at the Census of 1931, acknowledged by demographers to be the most thoroughgoing enquiry in the twentieth century in Bengal till the Census of 1961.

The manner in which the census was conducted by the government may have exacerbated divisions within a population already divided into a large number of religious communities. A.E. Porter, ICS, directing the census operations in 1931, states in his report that instructions to the supervisors were as follows: 'Care should be taken not to enter Jains, Sikhs, Brahmos and Aryas as Hindus. If a man says he is a Jain or a Sikh he should be entered as such, even though he also says he is a Hindu'.[1] This policy was also followed in respect of tribals.

> It is the religious allocation of primitive peoples which presents the greatest difficulty. Their beliefs and those of groups included within Hinduism are alike often vague or vaguely understood, and Hinduism is sufficiently catholic to embrace them without notably adding to the incongruities and inconsistencies already existing in the body of tolerated belief and observance.... There is ... a natural tendency for Mundas, Oraons, Santals and similar primitive people to adopt Hindu practices ... and amongst both the Oraons and the Santals recent movements of religious reforms professedly tribal in character have shown the influence of Hinduism.[2]

The classification 'intended at the Census' was to keep tribal religions separate, but the tendency stated above (as well as the pressure of the Hindu *shuddhi* movement, trying to swell the numbers counted as Hindus amongst the tribals) made things complicated for the census officers. Incidentally, this census was bitterly contentious due to communal awareness of the political significance of the numbers to be recorded as Hindu or Muslim.

> The Census was taken at the end of a decade in which communal feeling had been more bitter between Hindu and Muslim than for many years previously and when no member of these communities could fail to be alive to the importance in Bengal of the numerical strength of

> his co-religionists in view of impending constitutional changes and the question of communal electorates. Numerous allegations were made on both sides during the process of enumeration that enumerators of one community were suppressing details of persons of the other community and fictitiously increasing the numbers of their own.[3]

Upon investigation, Porter found such charges to be insubstantial.

The interesting point is that despite this feeling among the politically aware, there continued to be an admixture of the cultures of the two communities at 'lower' levels. There are a number of significant observations on communities 'on the border of Hinduism and Islam'. We will cite some examples in Bengal in 1931. The Satya-dharma or Bhagwania sect had recruits from both Muslims and Hindus who did not intermarry but dined together; those formerly Hindu gave up *ahnik* and *sandhya* devotions, those formerly Muslim gave up *namaz* and the Ramzan as well as circumcision; both observed some Vaishnava rites and ceremonies, buried their dead, and declared themselves Hindu or Muslim as they pleased in the census. The Nagarchis of Bakarganj included people who read *kalma* at marriage and performed *jonacha* at death, but bore Hindu names, ate no food forbidden to Hindus, and worshipped Hindu gods. The *kirtaniyas* of Pubna and Mymensingh, commonly regarded as Muslims, were reportedly observing 'practices consistent with orthodox Hinduism'. The census also recorded the ambivalent position of the Chitrakars or Patuas of some western districts of Bengal. (This was also observed by me at Santiniketan in Birbhum district in the early 1990s.) They were in 1931 'generally classed as Muslims, make images and pictures of the Hindu gods and goddesses and do not practise circumcision or the burial of the dead'.[4] (To this day, their names are partly Muslim and partly Hindu and those I met declined to be classified as either.)

Numerically such groups were small. They appeared to be extreme cases of what was a more generally shared trend towards mutual acculturation across communal boundaries. Census Superintendent Porter observed in 1931:

> In many parts of the country the Muslim peasant is indeed tolerant of Hindu practices and joins to some extent in Hindu worship.... Inter-communal borrowing is not confined to the Muslims: the unsophisticated Hindu will render reverence to any manifestation of holiness without enquiring what religion it exemplifies, and *pirs* and *fakirs* or

> their memory receive veneration and offerings in many parts of Bengal. In Rangpur it is reported that Hindus will extend to elderly Muslims the gesture of touching the feet which is more an act of religious veneration than a punctilio of good manners.[5]

As examples of 'approximation of practices' Porter mentions common worship, irrespective of communities, of Sitala, Manasa, Satyapir, and so on. The latter deity, supposedly Muslim in origin, was worshipped by Hindus; Manasa and Sitala were goddesses to be propitiated to ward off snake-bite and smallpox. These were worshipped particularly if faith in them was reinforced by some crisis, for example, a smallpox epidemic. Sitala worship was 'almost universal and professing specialists of the disease, calling themselves *Kaviraj*, though Muslim, will admit to taking fees for the express purpose of propitiating the goddess'.[6] If we are to identify some old Bengali festivals as Hindu, then these too were adopted by the Muslims: for example, as reported from the districts, the brother's day and son-in-law's day (*bhai-phonta* and *jamai-shashthi*) in Jessore, the harvest festival (*navanna*) in Bogra, and offerings to the river in Rangpur and Jalpaiguri districts. On the whole, there were trends, even in the midst of communal tension in 1931, towards convergence of socio-religious practices 'in the country districts'. For this, greater credit must be given to the tolerance of the Muslim peasantry towards practices of their neighbours. This was the trend and it was sought to be reversed by religious revivalist movements from the 1890s. 'This approximation of practices is', A.E. Porter in the Census of 1931 recorded, 'discountenanced by the orthodox and efforts are made by preachers of both communities to purge away observances not consistent with strict communal bigotry…'.[7]

'The Hindu Social Order'

How did the Bengali Hindu world view accommodate all manner of people, tribes and castes, and other communities, in an overarching order? I shall use two contemporary informants, one well-known, the other less so: the anthropologist Nirmal Kumar Bose (1901–5) of Bosepara in Calcutta, and the Maharaja of Susanga of north Bengal, Bhupendra Chandra Sinha (1898–1975?). The memoirs written by the latter are an obscure but invaluable source. No one could be more of an establishment figure than him. Belonging to a family that acquired overlordship of lands on the northeastern frontier of Bengal in the early fourteenth century and became tributary chieftains under the Mughals and hereditary maharajas in the British regime, he was also the hereditary *kulapati* (caste chief) of the Varendra (north Bengal) Brahmans and for some time the president of the Bengal Brahman Sabha. Till he joined Presidency College, his had been a thoroughly traditional education as the *maharajkumar*, and he functioned at the head of local society till the zamindari was lost to the family. A few extracts from his memoirs will show how the highly variegated composition of the population, including Garos, Hajongs, and other tribal groups, and Muslim and Hindu peasant and higher castes in that part of the country was handled as tradition prescribed.

One of his earliest memories was of being

> brought to the court for a brief while to get my first lessons in courtesy to be offered to the local tenants as well as to dignitaries.... Some very elderly person would put questions to me as follows: 'Is the Maharajkumar in good health?' and I learned to answer 'As the Mighty Mother *Dashabhuja* has wished we are all well...'. The Muslim tenants would say, 'Is the Maharajkumar keeping good health through the blessing of Allah?' The reply from me would be, 'Perhaps the Mighty Mother and the Great Allah have kept you and your family in good health...'.[8] During the festivities of Diwali, Hajong boys from all villages used to come in masquerade and had the unique privilege of free access into the inner courtyard of the Raj Bari, where very strict purdah was observed [on other days].... The women would come to pay their respects to the Ranees on *Dussehra* day and used to receive from the hand of the Ranee betel, betel-nuts and *sindur* (vermilion) mixed with mustard oil'. The symbolic opening of the inner quarters of Raj Bari signified ceremonial recognition of the lower orders. The following account similarly suggests that there was an inclusive system recognizing all the categories, and at the same time a hierarchy that was inviolable. A hunt or shikar, was almost a weekly affair for this family. After each such shikar 'the venison of the male deer would be kept for the Raj Bari, priests of *Dashabhuja* temple, Brahman officers of the Estate, and *kulin* and other respectable Brahmans and Kayasthas. The does that had their throats cut according to the Muhammadan custom were distributed to Muslim *mahuts* [elephant keepers] and other Muslim employees. Boars were distributed among first the Sudra servants and then among *dhobis, malis, namasudras, majhis* [Santhals], Hajongs, Banais, Hodies and Garoes.[9]

It was a world view giving each caste or tribe or community a place in a traditionally recognized hierarchy. It included all these categories but it was also terribly exclusive at moments. 'When I was about nine years old, our old servant, a very correct upholder of old practices, ordered all the Muslims and lower caste Hindus, including the respectable merchants and tenure holders [tenants with occupancy rights], to clear out of the *verandah* before he served a glass of drinking water to me'.[10] Nevertheless, as a young man, before starting on a hunting expedition, Sinha would routinely make offerings at the *dargah* or shrine where Muslims worshipped, as well as sacrifice white pigeons as prescribed by the Garo headman to appease forest gods.[11] Such appeasement was 'a feature so common in our daily village life' no one questioned to which sect a *pir* (Muslim holy man) or a god belonged to. 'Nurtured from very young days in such an environment, I learnt to accept the position that the people of Susanga belonged to a single human family within which different groups had their own peculiarities of culture'.[12]

An intellectualized version of this world view is Nirmal Kumar Bose's. The impression he formed during his field trip among the Juangs in 1928–9 were confirmed by his studies in the next twenty-five years. 'We must analyse in depth the internal economic structure of Hindu society, the Aryan or Brahmanic culture system and broadly speaking the Hindus' *dharma* and civilization…'.[13]

> If we analyse carefully the culture of various tribal groups included within the Aryan social system, directed by Brahmanism, we observe that for centuries in India they have been gradually incorporated within the *varna* order, and consequently many of them have merged their identity into Hindu society in the wider sense and have enriched and expanded it. At the same time they have also gained to a great extent in that the ambit of their existence has enlarged.[14]

Bose was aware that from a certain orthodox Hindu point of view the culture of many of these tribal peoples was different; in fact, supposed to be inferior. But he contends that in the 1920s the popular view was the contrary; if the Juangs, for example, eat forbidden meat so do the 'England-returned' Hindus; if the tribals speak a strange language, the languages spoken in different parts of India are strange to Hindus of other parts; if tribals believe in other gods, then there is a similar diversity in the Hindu pantheon, and so on. This interesting argument concludes with the statement that, given such diversity in socio-cultural practices in different regions and communities within Hindu society, there can be no reason to refuse to consider different tribal groups as 'non-Aryan tribes within Hindu society'.[15] In a brief anthropological excursus into the variants of Holi and similar festivals in tribal areas and the Hindu core areas, Bose argued that it showed a connectedness between 'non-Aryan' and 'Hindu' elements of the population.

> We shall find numerous such examples if we examine the social festivals of many people whose religion is Hinduism. In places the ancient village deities are worshipped by outcaste *jatis*, and higher castes accept such a right of a non-Aryan priest.... If one analyses the rituals conducted by women of the family at the time of marriage ceremonies, in many castes it seems that the rituals of a time prior to the Brahmanic remodelling have survived in these women's rituals. These and customs and practices receive recognition from the Brahman priesthood as customs of the region or of the people.... Just as Hindu society is the synthesis of various peoples, Hindu religion is also the synthesis of different views and ways.[16]

The interesting point in Bose is that he does not say that this is how it should be but he says this is how it was and how it was perceived by people in India.

There is much that is debatable in Nirmal Bose's exposition, in particular his unquestioning acceptance of the 'Aryan' category, but it illustrates a point of view that was not uncommon among those who perceived the 'Hindu social order' as an integrative force in India, particularly among the nationalists. Bose was, of course, active in the nationalist movement, and Maharajkumar Sinha was not. We have chosen these two as exemplars of a trend of thinking that provides a paradigm in which the Hindu social order accommodating diversity is given a centrality. There was another model that dispensed with the Hindu part, although a good deal of that discourse often had 'Bharatvarsha' standing in as a surrogate for Hindu India. The Upanishadist Brahmo in Tagore did not offer a Hindu vision of India.

> We see that the aim of Bharatvarsha has always been to establish unity amidst differences [or diversities], to bring to a convergence different paths, and to internalize within her soul the unity of the severalty,

> that is to say to comprehend the inner union between externally perceptible differences without eliminating the uniqueness of each element.... Bharatvarsha has endeavoured to tie up diversities in a relationship. If there be genuine differences, it is possible to accommodate in its appropriate place such differences. You cannot legislate unity into existence. Elements which cannot assimilate need to be recognized and put in their appropriate separate places ... Bharatvarsha knew the secret of this mode of unification ... Bharatvarsha limited the conflict between opposing and competing elements in society by keeping them separate and at the same time engaged in a common task that brought diverse elements together....[17]

We have extracted and translated this rather long passage because this statement of 1902 was unique in its insightful exposition.

In so far as a Hindu social order acquired a centrality because of its newly found integrative virtues, the legal and institutional aspects ought to be taken into account. In law who was a Hindu, and to what extent was the ideal Hindu social order—encapsulated in the varna and caste system—recognized in law? To illustrate the relevance of that question: under British Indian law, was admission to or being part of Hindu society as open as Nirmal Bose suggests and, from the legal angle, is each caste group looked upon as a component of one integrated order in Hindu society? These questions are important because British Indian law not only disabled or enabled social institutions to function in the manner they thought fit (caste associations, temple trusts, religious institutions, and so on), but also helped frame their self-image as well as the image of the Hindu social order in a broad sense.

The legal historian Marc Gallanter has answered some of these questions with reference to a mass of court cases in the late nineteenth and early twentieth centuries. It seems that under British Indian law it was easy to be a Hindu, and difficult to escape being a Hindu. 'Heterodox practice, lack of belief, active support of non-Hindu religious groups, expulsion by a group within Hinduism—none of these removed one from the Hindu category, which included all who did not openly renounce it or explicitly accept a hostile religion'.[18] A case in 1903, *Bhagwan Koer vs Bose*, established that actively promoting another religion was no bar; another case in 1946, *Chungu Manjhi vs Bhabani Majhan*, established that it was sufficient that a tribal group acknowledged themselves as Hindus and adopted some Hindu social usages, notwithstanding retention of non-Hindu usages; a case in 1928, established that being expelled or outcaste was no bar to claiming Hindu status; in a case in 1934 the court decided that reconversion to Hinduism did not require in law proof of formal abandonment of another religion. Thus Hinduism was indeed a rather catholic sort of religion in the eyes of the law.

The other point that Gallanter makes is that the view that usually prevailed in the British Indian courts of laws was that each caste was 'a component in an overarching sacral order of Hindu society. Hindu society is seen as a differentiation but integrated order in which the different parts may enjoy different rights, duties, privileges, and disabilities; these are determined by the position of the caste group in relation to the whole'.[19] There developed 'the notion of a single articulated Hindu community' including various caste groups—and borderline cases like those cited earlier—each with its privileges and disabilities were part of Hinduism 'seen as a unified order'. Incidentally, the caste order within the *varna* system was so much taken for granted that its extension to non-Hindu communities was acceptable to the courts of law. A case in 1895, *Abdul Kadir vs Dharma*, elicited an observation from the Court that caste comprises 'any well-defined native community governed for certain purposes by its own rules and regulations' and was not confined to Hindus. 'Here we find that the autonomous caste group is recognised not only among Hindus but also amongst Muslims, Parsis', and so on, though these groups are not placed in a *varna* order, and cannot claim rights which Hindu castes 'derive from a place in a larger Hindu order'.[20]

To sum up, the British Indian legal system reinforced the claim of a Hindu sacral order to its integrative function in the context of great diversity of caste groups, tribes, and communities, and allowed a place in that order to virtually any individual or group that did not explicitly abandon the Hindu faith. That the law pushed this line (unfortunate from the point of view of secularism) meant a measure of legitimacy to the principle of integration that the anthropologist N.K. Bose, among others, spoke of. It was a principle that recognized the affiliation of each part to the whole social order, on the basis of some undefined affinity with the whole. But some uncomfortable questions remained: for instance, given the fact that hierarchization was a necessary element in the system and inequalities were inherent, how would the system handle claims to equality that would inevitably come with social evolution? Moreover, how did a 'Hindu' sacral order, effective as it might have been at one time in binding together diverse elements, accommodate the majority of the population—Islamic in faith—in a part of India like Bengal? What would be the consequences of denial of affinity? We shall return to these questions later.

How Was Bengal Imagined?

Some anthropologists in our times have also raised the question as to how was an idea of a unified civilization sustained in India though it was extended over a large, politically and socially divided subcontinent. Thus, Robert Redfield, in the course of his very innovative theoretical work in the 1950s on primary and secondary civilizations, defined the major task of anthropologists in India to be the study of the social organization of tradition.[21] His work with Milton Singer exploring the continuous interaction between peasant society and the Great Tradition through countrywide networks with nodal urban centres was seminal. Bernard Cohn and McKim Marriott pushed forward the exploration into the rural 'networks' of relationships and denser nexus of relationships that they called 'centres'. They raised questions that have not yet been adequately addressed with specific reference to Bengal.[22] The regional and supralocal reach of rural networks (of trade, marriage, pilgrimage, political contacts, and so on) varied from region to region, and the nodal centres and 'hinge groups' mediating transmission of trade were, of course not uniformly effective. How effective were the networks in Bengal to endow it with unity and make it a part of the subcontinental network?

What was the concept of Bengal in the imagination of the traditional Bengali mind? And what sort of unity was attributed to Bengal, other than the obvious one, the language? Mukundaram Chakrabarti's poetic narrative *Chandi mangal* of the early seventeenth century was prefaced by the praise of various gods and goddesses; as a routine, like other poetic texts of those times, Mukundaram begins with a *dik-bandana* (literally, worship of the quarters of the compass) which is as follows.[23] He mentions the presiding deity at each major pilgrimage centre or smaller temple sites in different directions; there are a greater number of these examples in the south of Bengal because when he wrote he was in the present district of Midnapore, having migrated from his native village in Burdwan. He begins with major centres beyond Bengal: Neelachal in Orissa, Vrindavan, Ayodhya (*Ayodhyae bandibo thakur Sri Ram*), Gaya, Prayag, Dwaraka, Hastinapur, and Varanasi. Then the poet mentions serially the temples and deities within his knowledge in Bengal, ranging from major centres like Kalighat to lesser temples and sites of pilgrimage like those in Bikrampur, Kharagpur, Teotia, Damanya, Chandrakona, Tamralipta, and so on.[24] Similarly, *Ray Mangal*, written in 1723 CE by the poet Hari Deb Sharma of the present-day district of Howrah, has a *dik-bandana* listing places of pilgrimage; this has a more limited range not going beyond Puri and Vrindaban. What is interesting here is the inclusion of *pirs* revered by Muslims. Thus, along with Mahamaya or Jagannath, you have Dafar Khan Gazi of Tribeni or Sarenga Saheb.[25] Like Mukundaram, Hari Deb was thoroughly rural and derived income from cultivation. In 1770, there appeared a detailed account of the pilgrimage of a raja to Hindu sacred sites up the Ganga to Varanasi.[26] This was the Raja of Bhukailas whose elder brother was the *dewan* (agent) of Harry Verelst, Governor of Bengal for three years after Robert Clive's departure in 1767. It is possible that Verelst had engaged the Raja to visit towns on and near the Ganga and report on the local notables, landed magnates, and others. Thus it was possibly a dual mission, political intelligence work and pilgrimage. The account of the raja's pilgrimage includes Calcutta, Nadia, Hooghly, Patna, Tikari Prayag, Varanasi, and so on, and the important personalities and sacred sites he visited. This long narrative poem called *Teertha mangal* shows the wider range of the network accessible to the rich and resourceful, while village poets like Mukundaram or Hari Deb Sharma knew a pilgrimage circuit within Bengal and probably heard or read of greater all-India pilgrimage centres in the heartland around Benaras. These three works were written around 1604, 1723, and 1770. In the nineteenth century, the tradition continued and by then even a poor person could travel great distances due to better transport. A recently discovered narrative poem describes the pilgrimage to and education in Varanasi of a poor Brahman boy of the district of Jessore, Mahananda Bandyopadhyay (1854–1912); the young pilgrim and the author of the poem happened to be the father of Bibhuti Bhushan, the author of *Pather panchali*.[27] Mahananda was a *kathak*, that is, a reciter of the scriptures, *tirtha-mahatmya* (lore of pilgrimage centres), poems, and stories. They played an important role in mediating between the Sanskritic tradition and the common people who had no access to that language, the scriptures, or to distant places of pilgrimage.

We have taken a great deal of trouble to establish a few facts about pilgrimage in Bengal as an example of the pattern of the network that promoted awareness of *a larger ideal space*, beyond the limits of the rural quotidian life experience. This ideal whole could be Bengal as defined by sites sacred particularly to the Bengalis, and it could be a Bharat of sacred imagination. If this was true of the seventeenth, eighteenth, and nineteenth centuries, did it also apply to the twentieth? Surajit Sinha and Baidyanath Saraswati led an anthropological team to inquire into the sacred complex of Kalighat in Calcutta in the 1960s. The shrine was managed by Bengali *sevayat*s (serving devotees, actually managers and co-sharers in the earnings of the shrine). Priests from Orissa and north India also helped pilgrims and were known as *sathi*s (companions). The shrine was part of a network of fifty-one *shakti* worshippers' shrines, many of them in eastern India, and most of the pilgrims were Bengali. But the random sample checked by the investigators included people from distant parts of India up to Punjab, Gujarat, and Tamil Nadu. 'Co-participation as pilgrims, however, does not bring the linguistic communities too close to each other, for the pilgrims visit the temple as socially and culturally isolated clusters. All, however, share a common integrative feeling of visiting an important Hindu shrine'.[28]

Granted that the evidence we have gathered of the Bengalis' pilgrimage circuit exemplifies the integrative function of certain supra-local networks and nodal urban centres connecting the Great Tradition with the tradition of lesser communities, a question remains. Would not integration by that process exclude those who had a different Great Tradition? Islam in Bengal was a co-sharer in a separate stream of the Great Tradition. There may be cultural admixture of the Islamic and the Hindu at a popular level, but would the superior clarity and definition of Great Tradition at the 'centres' allow it? We meet the limits of the civilization's integrative capacity in so far as it is conceived in terms of the sacred.

The Denial of Affinity

We have seen that the discourse of a unifying integrative hierarchized social order was effective to some extent in certain social and cultural practices in the life of Bengal. To look upon that discourse as no more than a part of the ideologization accompanying the nation-building enterprise is inadequate in cultural and historical terms. At the same time, its inclusive aspects, drawing in tribes and assigning caste positions in a hierarchical order, had its flip side: an exclusive tradition, however latitudinarian its definition might have been. Thus the inevitable question, what of Islam? And, again, what if a tribe or a caste did not accept the superordinate and subordinate relationship implicit in the Hindu sacral order? And how was a civlizational unity, limited as it was, to be translated into political unity in the struggle against the colonial state and the formation of its successor state in the future? We shall get back to these questions when we look into the political story. For the present we limit ourselves to the processes within civil society.

We met the Maharaja of Susanga earlier and saw how he conceived of and actually took part in the replication of a Hindu social order that sought to make room for tribes and castes and communities in an ethnically variegated tenantry he inherited. Abul Mansur Ahmed (1898–1979) was an almost exact contemporary of the Maharaja and spent his early years in a village in Mymensingh district, not far from Sinha's Susang. Abul Mansur's traditional maulvi family, which had Faraizi connections at one time, were tenants under the Hindu zamindari of Muktagachha. Delving into his childhood he recalls the *naib* (agent) of the landlord addressing him as *tui* ('you' in either a derogatory or an intimate way) and he, in turn, also addressing the latter as *tui*. His grandfather admonished him saying an elderly person should be addressed properly as *apni* ('you' honorific). Mansur's answer was, 'Why does the *naib babu*, younger to you and my father, address you as *tumi*?' (*tumi* is less respectful than *apni*).[29] The question was unanswerable, for Muslim tenants were routinely addressed with scant respect by the landlords, their agents, and other gentrified Hindus.

> Not only did the Hindu landlords address Muslim tenants as *tui* out of lack of respect, not only did they neglect to offer such Muslims a seat in their offices or sitting-rooms, but also their agents, relatives, brahman priests or cooks, Hindu lawyers and doctors and the lot of them looked down upon Muslims as *prajas* [tenants or subjects] and lower in social rank. This pattern had nothing to do with the landlord–tenant relationship. It was the pattern of the Hindu–Muslim relationship.... Thus in practical life in Bengal, Hindus and Muslims were two separate societies, ethnic groups and self-contained communities.[30]

Nirmal Chandra Bhattacharya (1896–1986), son of a small landowner in Faridpur district in East Bengal, records in his memoirs the distinctions maintained in the *cutchery* (estate office) in seating arrangements: upper-caste Hindus on the carpet, lower-caste Hindu traders and tenants on mats, the Muslim tenants and occasionally specially unfortunate Hindu tenants on the bare floor. As a Brahman child, Nirmal was not unaccustomed to observing caste restrictions, but he could learn, only upon enquiry from *gomastas*, the reason why particular seats were for particular men in the *cutchery*.[31] Abul Mansur Ahmed also recalled, sixty years later when he wrote his memoirs, that even in the folk-theatre (*jatra*) performances 'the bhadralok were seated, and the Musalmans were given standing room only'.[32] In the Muslim mind the resentment against this abominable social discrimination was exacerbated by a sense of 'fall from a glorious state'. For example, Maulvi Ghulam Qadir, in his address to the Anjuman-e-Ulema's annual all-Bengal conference in 1915 asks: 'Where is that kingdom, where is that kingly status?... The descendants of those who had at one time the monopoly of positions of nawabs, subedars, chiefs of the army, magistrates and judges, are now beggars on the streets, menial guards at the door, cooks, orderlies, coolies and labourers'.[33]

Terms of opprobrium applied to Muslims by Hindus were numerous. A Muslim writer in the monthly *Al Islam*, edited by Maulana Akram Khan (1868–1968), observes in 1917:

> Hindu zamindars in their *cutchery* treat with extreme discourtesy the Muslim tenants.... The less said about ordinary Hindus' behaviour the better, the sweetest term they have for Muslim is *neray* [literally shaven headed, and used abusively for Muslims]. We often hear the Hindus present say this when a group of Muslims board a steamship or a railway compartment: 'Oh God, a bunch of *nerays* have come in'.... If one wishes to bring amity in this country, this is the sort of thing one should put a stop to.[34]

Sometimes there was no conflict but merely an abyss of ignorance between the two communities. Nirad C. Chaudhuri, who spent the major part of his youth in Kishorganj in East Bengal, writes of his first contact with Muslim theologians while he was secretary to Sarat Chandra Bose: 'One day, I saw a procession of Muslim divines trooping into Sarat Babu's house; I was quite familiar with the modern Muslim dress, but had no idea that these learned Muslims wore different clothes.... We, the educated and urban Bengali Hindus, ... did not even imagine that such persons existed in Bengal'.[35] Not all educated and urban Bengali Hindus can confess to ignorance easily, but ignorance about Muslims is perhaps easier for them to admit.

These may be particularly unfortunate examples of the 'amicable' relations in everyday life between the Hindus and Muslims in the first three decades of the twentieth century. But one could easily multiply such examples. And there could be parallels from the opposite side that would reinforce the impression these instances produce of the root of the problem lying outside of the public and political sphere in day-to-day social transanctions. This applied equally well to the 'lower' vis-á-vis the 'higher' castes. It now appears incredible that as late as 1928–9 the fact that a Namashudra (a cultivator and 'untouchable' caste) accidentally touched a Brahman priest outside a temple led to incidents that provoked a *satyagraha* for 261 days; this happened in Munshiganj in Dhaka district and eventually the right of Namashudras to enter the temple was secured.[36] At a 'higher' level, consider the Saha trading caste. Nripendra Chandra Banerji (1885–1949) recalls a social blunder he made in 1907 or thereabouts. While serving as a college teacher in Sylhet he accepted the invitation of the founder and patron of the college, a big zamindar with the title of Raja.

> I was invited to dine one evening by the Raja and I accepted the invitation with gladness—it was a mark of courtesy.... What was my surprise next day to be told by my colleagues and also by a nice oldish gentleman who was a man of influence and the District Judge's right hand man that I must not say anything about my having dined with the Raja—for he was a Saha, while I was a Brahmin! And if anybody asked me about it, I must conceal the fact of the dinner as absolutely and utter blatant falsehood, denying that I had any invitation to the Raja's house at all! If I did not do that, I ran the risk of being ostracised by the Hindu community of Sylhet.[37]

Banerji was saved from this terrible fate by the offer of a job in Presidency College, Calcutta, and thus being able to leave the scene.

Whether it is inter-caste or inter-communal relations that we consider, this *exclusion principle in the private sphere* was probably the most important of all causes of conflicts in the public sphere. Those conflicts varied over time cyclically but the incivility of mutual exclusion in private social transactions was a constant factor. Tagore insightfully commented that after years and decades of exclusion of Muslims from social relationships of any kind 'one day we summon them and say "We are brothers, you must also pay the price of imprisonment and death"'. That cannot conjure unity into existence. This was written in 1926, a few days after the assassination of Swami Shraddhananda by a Muslim.[38] In 1931, Tagore reiterated the point and squarely equated casteist divisiveness with communalism.

> Clannish exclusiveness has entered the bones of our social practices, and yet we are surprised when in politics we fail in our effort to include some people. It has been reported that these days in some places the Namashudras, without compunction, joined the Muslims in the anti-Hindu disturbances. Should we not stop and think why they were lacking in sympathy, *why this denial of affinity*?[39]

In many other essays Tagore said over and again that for this reason, political unity was unattainable.

The Namashudras mentioned by Tagore were a so-called untouchable caste that had a strong identity movement aimed at raising their status. The Bhumij were a tribe incorporated gradually into the Hindu social order and undergoing a social mobility movement. We select these two case studies, both well researched, for they show a contrast despite some similarities—one tends towards a protest movement and the other conforms to Sanskritization.

The Bhumij: A Case Study

The Bhumij, a southern offshoot of the Munda tribe, spoke Bengali since the early 19th century, and almost exclusively Bengali since the 1880s. In Barabhum (in Manbhum district in Western Bengal) they formed a set of exogamous totemistic subdivisions although they had almost forgotten their totems when H.H. Risley surveyed the tract in the 1880s; they 'profess to be Hindus'.[40] In the late 19th century, an aspiration to be regarded as Rajput-Kshatriyas was limited to a few prosperous landed families, but from the turn of the century the bulk of the caste members also shared this aspiration. What were the means of raising their status? (*a*) Abstention from social drinking of liquor, and from taking chicken—a taboo for good Hindus; (*b*) proscription of group dancing by women, widow remarriage, and junior leviration;

(*c*) initiation by gurus into Vaishnavism or its variants, worship of Hindu gods, and employment of such Brahmans of the 'fallen' category as were willing to perform rites of passage for Bhumij families.

In this Sanskritization process, the advent of holy men played an important role. First came Srinath, a Vaishnava guru, in 1897, and then a Bhumij holy man, Kishtodas Sadhu, in 1914. The first brought into use symbols like Vaishnava sect marks, sacred basil (*tulsi*), and enjoined some abstentions and austerities. The second preached a more permissive and liberal faith. Then, in 1921, 'a rumour spread that a new king had appeared on earth who forbade wine, meat and fish of any kind'; three or four years later 'the name of this new Raja finally came out as Gandhi Mahatma' and it was further revealed that, apart from those abstentions, use of home-spun thread was a requirement.[41] In the meanwhile, scriptural proofs in favour of Bhumij status as a Hindu caste of the Kshatriya *varna* were being collected. Finally, the chief of a federation of forty-nine village *panchayats* (councils) called a meeting in 1935 to formally set up the Bhumij Kshatriya Samiti which cited those scriptural proofs and the 'rituals, festivals, religious practices' being observed by the Bhumij to claim, on an organized basis, Kshatriya status. In 1935–6, the chief and the *panchayats* almost assumed magisterial powers to supervise social practices and to punish infractions. In the 1940s, Jaipal Singh's Jharkhand Party began to influence the Bhumij people and thus the older Sanskritization aspirations were overlaid by new ones.

This account by the anthropologist Surajit Sinha, showed typical traits of similar social mobility movements among the Kurmi or Kurma-Kshatriyas, Pod or Paundra Kshatriya, and Bagdi or Byagra-Kshatriyas in the western part of Bengal in the same period.[42] In the case of the Bhumij, however, certain traits came out more clearly. First, in the process of incorporation of a tribe into the caste order, the class factor was important; the superior landholders (*tarafdars*) among the Bhumij could obtain the services of Brahmans in rituals and even marry into more established Rajput castes. The bulk of the Bhumij population, called Nagadi, were less successful in this regard. Secondly, resentment is as much a part of mobility endeavours as the desire to emulate the 'superior' Hindu castes' practices, that is, abstention from eating chicken or drinking liquor, or proscription of women's participation in group dance, and so on. 'How are they any better?' is a question underlying the proposition, 'Let us behave as they do'. Thus Sanskritization was not inconsistent with an aggressive competitiveness. Resentment against exclusion found expression in both of these ways. The pamphlets, speeches, and so on, reported by Sinha, can be read both as an articulation of protest and a desire for promotion in the *varna* order.

Thirdly, the 'Hinduization' of the Bhumij meant the excision of their 'tribalness'—they lost their language, their totemistic inner organization, their traditional social practices, and so on, in the course of the nineteenth and twentieth centuries. The Census Report of 1931 on Bengal contains an unusual subsidiary tabulation of tribal languages actually spoken at that time. The question put to tribal persons was whether they could 'speak the tribal language as mother tongue or subsidiary language'. Of 85,000 Bhumij, about 9.75 per cent could speak that language and only a few among them, about 4,000, declared and spoke it as their mother tongue; the rest habitually spoke Bengali.[43] This was true of some other tribal groups that had moved ahead in Hinduization.

In some tribal groups, thirty to ninety per cent were unable to speak the original language; there was, in later times, resentment due to the fact that they had lost their own culture and this had political consequences, particularly in north Bengal, in terms of resistance to hegemonization. (One could feel it in the air in Bhumij country in the 1960s, for example, in Barabhum in Purulia district of West Bengal which I visited with Sinha, the anthropologist.) Let us turn back from these anticipations of the future to the 1920s and to the other case study we plan to look at, the Namashudras of East Bengal.

The Namashudra Caste

The Namashudras, originally known as Chandals and assigned a low ritual status as untouchables, were mainly cultivators settled on land reclaimed from marsh and jungle in the districts of Bakharganj, Faridpur, Jessore, and Khulna. Nirmal Kumar Bose noted their 'claims to Brahman status' in their caste journals and tracts from at least 1908, along with their efforts to change some social customs to approximate those of higher castes.[44] But, unlike the Bhumij, on the Namashudras there is no complete anthropological research one can draw upon. There is, however, Sekhar Bandyopadhyay's excellent historical study thoroughly documenting the development of the Namashudra identity and protest movement.[45] The landmarks in this course of development are reported to be as follows: In 1872, a protest against disabilities imposed by the caste system (that is, untouchability, being denied services of barbers and washermen, refusal by any except 'fallen' Brahmans to perform their rituals, and so on), a social boycott and 'no-work campaign' directed against high-caste Hindus, ends in failure. In 1881, begins a series of 'uplift meetings' and conversion to a variant of Vaishnavism, called the Matua cult, repudiating casteism under the leadership of its preceptor, Harchand Thakur, and his son, Guruchand. In 1902, the establishment of the Namashudra Hitoishini (welfare) Samiti in Dhaka leads to the formation of the Bengal Namashudra Association ten years later. In 1906, disillusionment with 'high-caste' political leaders of Bengal and expectation of favoured treatment, on a par with British policy towards Muslims, leads Namashudras to oppose the Swadeshi anti-partition agitation. In 1911, after twenty years of petitioning and memorializing, the census authorities delete Chandal in favour of Namashudra as an appellation for this caste. In 1917, is held the first meeting in Calcutta to demand 'a share of power' in the impending 1919 Government of India Act, that is, caste representation. In 1922, the British authorities in Bengal initiate a policy of special dispensation to recruit to government service Namashudra and similar backward castes. In 1921, 1923, and 1926 elections to the Bengal Legislature generally prove the inability of Namashudra candidates to win in constituencies where the caste predominates, but nomination by the government to the legislature secures Namashudra representation. In 1922, the Namashudra Association unanimously resolves that the Non-cooperation Movement against the British government is detrimental to the interests of the Namashudra community. In 1928, the pro-zamindar bias of the Hindu Swarajist–Congress leaderships of Bengal becomes evident in the Bengal Legislature deliberations on the Tenancy Bill, and the Muslim and backward caste leaders unite in stoutly opposing this reactionary bias. In 1929–30, Namashudra Association leaders reject the National Congress stance on every political question by welcoming the Simon Commission, by rejecting dominion status for India, and by opposing the Civil Disobedience Movement.

We cannot for the present follow the further developments of Namashudra politics. The story till the end of the 1920s tells us several things. First, the construction of a new identity for an oppressed social group, in this case untouchable, seems to be a difficult process because effective struggle against social disabilities needs political support and that could be obtained at a price: the supplicant group must be willing to be co-opted. Having opted out of the nationalist mainstream, the Namashudra leadership were, increasingly, pushed into a position of dependence vis-á-vis the British authorities while their relationship with the Muslim League veered between alliance and dependence. A backward social group like the Namashudras lacked the necessary *social capital*, that is, access to network with established institutions—political or otherwise, organizational capacity, and the necessary educational base for that, communication on a scale beyond the local level; in short, the whole range of civil skills and resources needed to push forward their agenda in a system of constitutional politics. Secondly, in so far as such social capital came into existence within the Namashudra community, it became the collective monopoly of a handful of leaders who gradually began to benefit materially from their position as brokers in the political co-optation process. Sekhar Bandyopadhyay, in his searching study of that political history, comments that from the beginning of the 1930s this leadership had started to forget their peasant followers; 'the demands which they raised more frequently were for more educational facilities, employment opportunities and special constitutional rights. They were, in other words, in pursuit of concessions that could only serve their sectional interests'.[46]

The third point that emerges is the failure of an agenda of class action to develop from out of a welter of feelings of indignation and resentment and humiliation. The Namashudra leadership appeared to foster a caste rather than a class consciousness, although these could have merged. The upper-caste Hindus were not only the social oppressors but also, as landlords, the economic exploiters of the Namashudra peasant. But, barring some isolated protests of the spontaneous type at the local level, no sustained class action was undertaken, or even projected, by the leadership. In 1928, Namashudra and Muslim share-croppers joined hands in one sub-division of Jessore district to demand two-thirds of crop-share instead of the customary half; but their move to boycott Hindu landlords and to leave their lands uncultivated fizzled out since the share-croppers were unable to hold out for more than one season and they were also harassed by legal proceedings.

Adrienne Cooper, in her study of the share-croppers' struggle in Bengal, cites evidence of a contemporary observer that it was 'a spontaneous movement'.[47] This interesting episode, anticipating the Tebhaga Movement under Left leadership, was not part of any sustained programme of anti-landlord struggle of the Namashudra caste leadership. They limited their intervention to rhetorical gestures and moving or supporting amendments to a Tenancy Bill and, as legislators, occasional trips `to study rural conditions' at a time when the movement was strong in the 1930s. Only 0.89 per cent of Namashudras had rental income; there were, of course, many types of intermediate interests. One cannot say whether vested interests of the leadership explain their failure to mount any significant share-croppers' or peasants' agitation on the ground, despite plenty of speeches voicing resentment against the Hindu landlords. Taj-ul-Islam Hashmi, in his study of the 'communalization of class politics in East Bengal', remarks: 'It is quite interesting that instead of fighting their immediate landlords, who were not among the least oppressive, the lower peasantry—mostly Muslim and some Namashudra—were chiefly mobilized against the more distant Hindu zamindars, mahajans and bhadralok'.[48] While the Namashudra peasant or share-cropper sporadically rose against the landlords (boycott, rioting, looting), to their leadership the target seemed to be not the landlord per se but the upper-caste *bhadralok* who happened to be the 'superior landlords'.

The role of the colonial state in lending its authority to the ordering of 'superior/inferior' castes through the census enumeration system has often been commented upon: G.S. Ghurye and M.N. Srinivas have pointed out how the Census livened up the caste spirit and touched off cyclically a race to promote castes in the rank order.[49] One of the earliest objects of the Namashudra caste organizations in Bengal, from 1891 to 1911, was to secure a change in nomenclature in the census from Chandal to Namashudra. Not only was the late-nineteenth-century colonial state thus play-acting as a Hindu raja but, in a later phase in the 1920s, it also assumed the role of dispensing social justice and promoting the interests of particular castes of which Namashudra was one. Hindu Nationalist leaders reacted to it fairly early. Ambika C. Mazumdar (1851–1922), a close associate of Sir Surendranath Bannerjea and the President of the Indian National Congress in the Lucknow Session in 1916, and Aswini Kumar Dutt

(1856–1923), a pillar of the Congress in East Bengal from 1886 till his death, belonged to Faridpur and Barisal respectively. In these and contiguous areas in the days of the Swadeshi movement they tried to address Namashudras' demand for social justice through district-level associations—for example, to persuade barbers and washermen to serve Namashudras. But this was not a conspicuous success; the social prejudices were more enduring than nationalist sentiments.[50] On the other hand, the government had within its power concrete things to offer to Namashudras: jobs in government, representation in district governance, and in the Bengal legislature by election or nomination. Mahatma Gandhi's well-known commitment to the uplift of untouchables failed, just as Mazumdar and Dutt had failed earlier. To the Namashudra caste leaders

> the nationalist movement was really to further the interests of the wealthy upper caste bhadralok. How Guruchand [a Namashudra leader] explained the situation to his disciples may be worth mentioning here. In an average educated high caste family, he mentioned, usually one brother would be a lawyer, the second a clerk, while the third a trader. So, while the lawyer brother would leave the court and join the Non-Cooperation Movement, the clerk would retain his job to maintain the family, while the businessman brother would actually make profits by selling *khadi*. Hence the Namashudra peasants, who had no connection with the officer, courts or trade, should not be a party to this game.[51]

Thus the Namashudras' non-participation in the Non-cooperation and Civil Disobedience Movements was practically secured. But whatever the calculations of the leaders might have been, Sekhar Bandyopadhyay remarks, the common peasants among them were less aware of the material prospects of loyalty to the government, nor 'concerned about the concessions their leaders were demanding'.[52] Unlike the Namashudras, the Bhumij peasants were influenced by the Congress, and much more so, the Mahishya peasants in Medinipur. The Namashudras constitute an extreme case. Non-participation in the nationalist agitation in their case was by design whereas in other instances it occurred by default, due to inadequate mobilization and passivity.[53] Such non-participation was not necessarily a vote for the British Raj from these peasant castes, nor against nationalism, as some would have us believe.

The most significant thing about the Namashudra caste and the Bhumij tribe/caste is not so much their politics, but their relationship with the social order in which they were historically placed. On the one hand, we have an offshoot of the Munda tribe in the process of being drawn into the Hindu social order in a region on the margins of Bengal and, on the other, a caste positioned for centuries in the heartland of Bengal within a hierarchy of ritual statuses, trying to break away from it.

Inequality and Integration

The mainstream anthropologists' approach in India has justly been criticized for its 'caste-centred' bias, to the exclusion of class.[54] However, in so far as anthropological research gives some concrete referents for the disembodied notion of the unifying genius of Indian civilization, it has its uses. We have particularly paid attention to Nirmal Kumar Bose because he was a contemporary observer who specifically addressed the question of the integration of tribes and castes into the 'Hindu social order'. In that scheme of things, the case of the Bhumij people fits, a little loosely, but the recent history of the Namashudras does not—they were a pre-eminent example of fission rather than fusion.

Finally, these two case studies allow us to reflect on two more issues. Both of them show that at least till the early decades of this century social disabilities mattered a great deal. There is a commonly shared impression that the contrary was and is true in Bengal. How did such an impression form? Perhaps part of the answer lies in the findings of anthropologists about the caste composition of villages in Bengal. On the basis of the Census of 1911, M. Marriott estimated the number of ethnic groups in the villages in different regions of India; he found that the average number of ethnic groups or castes living in villages in the Bengal delta was two to five, whereas it was nine in the Upper Ganga delta and fourteen in Coromandel in present-day Tamil Nadu. A village with few ethnic groups is unlikely to have as elaborate a system of inter-caste relationships as a multi-ethnic village with many more castes in face-to-face situations in daily life.[55] It may be inferred from this that villages with many castes, as in north India or Tamil country in 1911, were more visibly stratified and segmented than villages with fewer castes as in Bengal.[56] The estimated mean population in each 'effective village community' studied by Marriott was also lowest in Bengal (189), compared to north India or the upper Ganga Valley (414) and Coromandel (813). In short, Bengal had smaller villages with fewer castes in each; the visibility of caste distinctions was low; it did not, however, mean that it was any less real.[57]

Another question is whether dissatisfaction with a position in a hierarchical sacral order meant that some modern egalitarian ideology was gaining ground? Perhaps the answer is in the negative. The Bhumij social mobility movement was geared to attaining Kshatriya status. The entire organized Namashudra initiative began with a claim to being 'better than' Shudras. There were claims to Brahman origin. In both cases, emulation of upper-caste social practices is noticed. The Namashudras continued to be divided into endogamous subcastes and these were also hierarchized, the cultivators being put at the top; commensality between Namashudra sub-castes was forbidden (except in Khulna district). The Bhumij also were stratified in their own reckoning into three strata according to the degree of sanskritization and divided into clans that began to bear Brahmanical names in place of Mundari ones.[58] This picture is too complex to allow us to say that egalitarianism inspired these social mobility or 'self-respect' movements. There were, however, resentments against inequality in so far as it entailed social disabilities and humiliation. That is clearly the positive aspect, at least in the case of the Namashudras.

In fact, casteism had eaten so deep into people's minds that even the relatively egalitarian philosophy of Islam was affected in Bengal. Although in its Semitic form Islam was commonly supposed to have been democratic, in Bengal it was far from that due to contamination by the caste system. In the sixteenth and seventeenth centuries, there is evidence in *Kabikankan chandi* that caste-like distinctions divided Muslims. However, compared to caste-ridden Hindu society, Muslims appear to have had a unity graphically brought to life in one line in the sixteenth-century poet Ruparama's *Dharma-mangala*: 'ek ruti paile hazar mian khaye' (a thousand Muslims would share one piece of bread).[59] In the twentieth century, unity founded on egalitarianism, at least as an idea, brought to the Muslims a spirit unknown in the Hindu community. Status-based stratification, as between Hindu *bhadralok* and the rest, was nevertheless undeniable. One of the best sociological analyses of Muslim politics in the pre-1947 decades states:

'It is interesting that many Muslims, especially the educated well-to-do ones, claimed their alien origin.... An Aryan or Semitic descent was considered superior in all respects among the local people.... "Last year I was a Jolaha (weaver), this year I am Shaikh, next year if prices rise I shall be a Syad" as the saying goes in the region'.[60] Thus the *ashraf*, or the cultured, noble, or genteel people, liked to distinguish themselves from the *atraf* or *ajlaf* or 'low-born rustics'. An anthropologist studying Muslims of rural Bengal in 1969 noted the replication of the Hindu categories *bhadralok* and *chhoto-jat* (low born) that were basically concepts created by the *bhadralok* themselves. The *ashraf* among Muslims included persons claiming to be of Syed, Sheikh, Pathan, or Mughal origin; the lower stratum of *atraf* or *ajlaf* comprised the rest of the Muslims, the commoners.[61] However, while this maintained a social distance, 'interaction between these groups is not built up systematically into a set of hierarchic relationships as with the Hindu'. This is because of the egalitarian content of the Quran and also because 'the upper and the lower status groups do not usually live in the same village'.[62] Like the Brahmans, the Syeds did not plough the land, and they along with the Pathans were roughly endogamous groups; within the *ashraf* there was rivalry over claims to superiority, and there were also tendencies towards vocational heredity as in Hindu castes, and so on. At the same time there was a tendency in the community to emphasize 'the difference between themselves and the Hindus in order to maintain their social identity and cultural boundaries'.[63]

That was the picture in Muslim villages in West Bengal in 1969. Let us return to the 1920s.

> In this country ignorant and uneducated Muslims, in imitation of their Hindu neighbours' caste distinctions, have been creating caste divisions among themselves. This is because of the fact that having lived side by side with Hindus for centuries, Hindu influence has penetrated in Muslim society.... Moreover, those who have recently converted from the Hindu religion to join Muslim society are trying, on account of their generations-old tradition of casteism, to introduce caste distinctions in egalitarian Muslim society.

Thus wrote Mohammad Yakub Ali, BA, a former headmaster of a secondary school, in 1927. This little book on caste division among Muslims pointed to the fact that the Census recorded eighty groups such as Sheikh, Syed, Mughal, Pathan, or Darzi (tailor), Dhoba (washerman), Fakir (mendicant), Jolah (weaver), and so on. Yakub Ali commented:

> Jolah, Kalu (oil-presser), Chasha (farmer), and so on, which are appellations indicating occupation, used as caste names by non-Islamic (*vidharmee*) people, are being used in Muslim society.... A section of Muslims, steeped in the dark of ignorance, refrain from social relations with Muslim fish-traders out of a contempt for that trade, though the Quran praised it.... It has sometimes been seen that Muslims, proud of their ancestry, who patronized Muslim students drove them away when it became known that they were sons of farmers, *nikaris* [fish dealers], *jolahs*, or *kalus*.[64]

In 1927, when this was written, vocational heredity was strong.

It seems that the notions of superordinate and subordinate relationships was ingrained in Bengali Hindu culture. The Muslims could not escape the contagion despite the strength of egalitarianism in early Islam. Endogamy and an elaborate kinship system made the castes or caste-like groups enduring and auto-replicatory. Research in the post-1947 period by Ralph Nicholas, A. Ostor, or Ronald Inden reveals the centrality of kinship in Bengal's culture.[65] It is the most important axis in social interactions.[66] Not only is this system in Bengal very elaborate—it is reported that Bengali kinship terminology includes 200 lexemes (which explains Bengali impatience with vague English words like 'cousin')—but kinship relationships also involve a 'hierarchical love relationship'.[67] Love among equals was rare in terms of kinship. According to Inden and Nicholas: 'While Bengalis have valued egalitarian love relationship, the predominant stress in Bengali culture has been placed on hierarchical form of love', where *sneha* and *bhakti* (roughly, affection and respect) are basic concepts. We need to reflect on this a little. This is borne out by daily experience in Bengal, and amply in literary fiction. While a Bengali is ready to extend to acquaintances and strangers, kinship terms like *bhai*, *dada*, *didi*, *mashi*, and so on (brother, elder brother, elder sister, aunt), it is done selectively on the basis of some status criteria and usually implies a relationship within a hierarchy. Inden and Nicholas's observations raise a question. Was a pattern of hierarchising affective relationships so imprinted on the individual mind, in the family and kin group, that it also patterned the public sphere relationship between collective entities like castes and communities? It is a question to ponder.

To sum up, we point out that in attempting to understand the social and cultural roots of identity politics in Bengal we have drawn upon contemporary observers' reports and anthropological research to form some tentative conclusions. There were tendencies towards approximation or convergence of certain socio-religious practices observed by Hindu and Muslim communities, but there was also a contrary pull of orthodoxy. There was an inclusiveness in the Hindu social order as imagined in early twentieth century Bengal, but it was a highly hierarchized order that assigned a low place to the lower castes and non-Hindus. There had been in the sacred imagination of the traditional Bengali mind a notion of Bengal as a unity in relation to a larger ideal space called Bharatvarsha, but the translation of the notion into Hindu practices, for example, the pilgrimage circuit, excluded Muslims. We have seen the blatant denial of affinity with other communities in the Hindu *bhadralok* attitude and behaviour. There were rhetorical gestures towards unity in the public sphere but in the private sphere there were unacceptable social practices based on notions of inviolable boundaries and superordinate–subordinate relationships; that pattern showed up not only in relation to the Muslim community but within the Hindu community as well as in the relationship between upper and lower castes or tribal groups. Thus we see a bundle of contradictions and in the following pages we shall note the interplay between them in Bengal politics. Perhaps the battle for unity was lost in the private social sphere, in the quotidian life from childhood onwards, long before it was lost in the public sphere.

Notes

1. A.E. Porter, ICS, *Report on the Census of Bengal, 1931* (Calcutta, 1931), ch. 11, p. 381.
2. Porter, *Census of Bengal, 1931*, p. 383.
3. Porter, *Census of Bengal, 1931*, p. 384.
4. Porter, *Census of Bengal, 1931*, ch. 11. Also Muhammad Enamul Haq, *A History of Sufism in Bengal* (Dhaka: Asiatic Society, 1973); this outstanding work of scholarship was published about forty years after it was written as a Ph.D. thesis at Calcutta University under the supervision of Suniti Kumar Chatterjee; see particularly chapter 12, 'Popular Islam'.

5. Porter, *Census of Bengal, 1931*, p. 390, and M.E. Haq, *Sufism in Bengal*; Asim Ray, *The Islamic Syncretic Tradition in Bengal* (Dhaka, 1983) is the most authoritative study in this area.
6. Porter, *Census of Bengal, 1931*, p. 390.
7. Porter, *Census of Bengal, 1931*, pp. 390–1; a contrary trend prevailed in Calcutta where there was greater rigidity in the Muslim community studied by Kenneth MacPherson, *The Muslim Microcosm: Calcutta, 1918–36* (Wiesbaden, 1974). On the role of the *maulvis* in 'separating' the two communities in the nineteenth century, see Rafiuddin Ahmad, *The Bengal Muslims, 1871–1906: A Quest for Identity* (Delhi, 1981).
8. Maharaja Bhupendra Chandra Sinha of Susanga, *Changing Times* (Calcutta, 1965), p. 15.
9. M.B.C. Sinha, *Changing Times*, pp. 111–12, 21.
10. M.B.C. Sinha, *Changing Times*, p. 30.
11. M.B.C. Sinha, *Changing Times*, p. 29.
12. M.B.C. Sinha, *Changing Times*, p. 30.
13. Nirmal Kumar Bose, *Hindu samajer gadan* (The Structure of Hindu Society) (Calcutta, 1949), vide p. 17; the book has recently been translated into English by André Béteille.
14. N.K. Bose, *Hindu samajer gadan*, p. 57.
15. N.K. Bose, *Hindu samajer gadan*, p. 14.
16. N.K. Bose, *Hindu samajer gadan*, pp. 74–5; Verrier Elwin wrote an interesting pamphlet, about the same time as Nirmal Kumar Bose wrote his book, arguing that 'the aboriginals of peninsular India profess a religion of the Hindu family ... they should be classed as Hindus at the time of the Census'. Elwin recommended that the Christian missionaries leave the tribal people alone and some day the tribals might have 'their honoured place as Kshatriyas in the Hindu social system'. V. Elwin, *Religious Banditry* (Delsi: All-India Arya Dharma Seva Sangha, 1947). I am indebted to Joseph Bara for drawing my attention to this.
17. Rabindranath Tagore, 'Bharatvarsher Itihas' (The History of India), *Bangadarshan* (1309 BS, 1902), revised and reprinted in 1905 and 1908; vide 'Itihas', pp. 10–11.
18. Marc Gallanter, 'Religious Aspects of Caste: Legal View' in *South Asian Politics and Religion*, ed. D.E. Smith (Princeton, 1966), p. 299. The cases mentioned in the text above are cited by Gallanter: case of 1903 in 30 1.A.249; 1946 in AIR Pat. 218; 1928 in *R.D. Morarji vs Admr. General of Madras, AIR 1928, Madras 1929, 1283*; 1934 in *Durgaprasad Rao vs I. Konan, AIR, Mad. 630.*
19. Gallanter, 'Religious Aspects', p. 278.
20. Gallanter, 'Religious Aspects', pp. 284, 288–9; *Abdul Kadir vs Dharma, 20 BOM, 190* (1895). According to Gallanter, the 'sacred order' model

was replaced by the 'associational model' and the 'sectarian model' by the adoption of the Indian Constitution in 1951.

21. Robert Redfield, *Peasant Society and Culture* (Chicago, 1955); Redfield and Milton Singer, 'The Cultural Role of Cities', *Economic Development and Cultural Change*, (1954): 53–73; M. Marriott, 'The Little Communities in an Indigenous Civilization' in *Village India*, ed. Marriott (Chicago, 1955); M. Marriott and B.S. Cohn, 'Networks and Centres in the Integration of Indian Civilization' *Journal of Social Research*, I (1958): 1–9, reprinted in B.S. Cohn, *An Anthropologist among Historians and Other Essays* (Delhi, 1987), pp. 78–87; Surajit Sinha, 'Coexistence of Multiple Scales and Networks of a Civilization in India' in *Scale and Social Organization*, ed. F. Barth (Oslo, 1978), pp. 122–32.
22. An exception is Surajit Sinha's programmatic statement 'Complex Religious Institutions and the Study of Indian Civilization' in *Research Programmes in Cultural Anthropology*, ed. S. Sinha (Simla, 1970), pp. 87–95.
23. Kabikankan Mukundaram Chakrabarti probably wrote his *Chandi mangal* around 1603–4 CE; Sukumar Sen attributed it to the mid-sixteenth century; according to the latest view, this wrong dating was due to a misplaced *pushpika* (colophon); see Khudiram Das, *Kabikankan chandi* (Calcutta, 1987) pp. xxii–xxiv; 'Dik Devata Bandana', *Kabikankan chandi*, pp. 275–6.
24. It appears from Das's edited text, *Kabikankan chandi*, that 'Dik bandana' does not occur in some manuscripts, although it is part of the major manuscripts collated; it is also possible that 'Dik bandana' was added by another contemporary poet or copyist, but that leaves my argument unaffected.
25. Hari Deb Sharma, *Ray mangal* (MS in Visva Bharati, Santiniketan), edited by Panchanan Mandal in *Sahitya prabeshika* (Visva Bharati, 1960), pp. 7–8, and 'Introduction'.
26. *Teertha mangal* (1770) by Bijoy Ram Sen has been published by Bangiya Sahitya Parishad, and commented upon by Suprasanna Bandyopadhyay, *Itihasasrita bangla kavita 1751–1855* (Calcutta, 1361 BS, 1954 CE), pp. 34–9.
27. I am indebted to Gautam Bhadra for this reference to the MS discovered by him and published in *Yogasutra*, October 1993, Calcutta.
28. Surajit Sinha, 'Kali Temple at Kalighat' in *Cultural Profiles of Calcutta*, ed. S. Sinha (Calcutta, 1972), pp. 61–72.
29. Abul Mansur Ahmad, *Amar dekha rajnitir panchas bachhar* (Fifty years of politics as I saw it) (Dhaka, 1995), p. 5.
30. Ahmad, *Rajnitir Panchas Bachhar*, p. 126.
31. Nirmal Chandra Bhattacharya, *Bismrita bangla* (Calcutta, 1997), ch. 2. I have used the Anglo-Indian terms which are to be found in the *Oxford English Dictionary* (*OED*); some of these words would be spelt differently if one followed Bengali pronunciation, for example, *cutchery* in *OED* would be *kachhari*.

32. Ahmad, *Rajnitir panchas bachhar*, p. 14.
33. Address by M.G. Qadir at the third conference of the Anjuman-e-Ulema at Chittagong, 1915, reprinted in S.K. De, *Anjuman-e-Ulema-e-Bangala, 1913–19* (Calcutta, 1992), p. 92.
34. Ahmad Ali in *Al Islam*, III, no. II (1324 BS)
35. Nirad C. Chaudhuri, *Thy Hand, Great Anarch! India 1921–1952* (London, 1987), p. 469.
36. Buddhadeb Bhattacharya, et al. (eds), *Satyagraha in Bengal, 1921–1930* (Calcutta, 1977), pp. 159–84; Nripendra Chandra Banerjee, *At the Crossroads* (Calcutta, 1950, 1974), pp. 190ff. Banerjee led the temple entry movement.
37. Banerjee, *Crossroads*, pp. 69–70.
38. Rabindranath Tagore, 'Swami Sraddhananda' in *Pravasee* (1333 BS), reprinted in Tagore, *Kalantar*, p. 319.
39. Rabindranath Tagore, 'Hindu-Musalman' in *Pravasee* (1338 BS), reprinted in Tagore, *Kalantar*, pp. 326–7.
40. H.H. Risley, *The Peoples of India* (Calcutta, 1915), p. 75. Our main source on the Bhumij is Surajit Sinha 'The Bhumij Kshatriya Social Movement in South Manbhum', *Bulletin of the Department of Anthropology*, VIII, no. 2 (1959): 9–32.
41. S. Sinha, 'Bhumij Kshatriya Social Movement'.
42. S. Sinha, 'Bhumij Kshatriya Social Movement', pp. 30–1.
43. Porter, *Census of Bengal, 1931*, ch. 10.
44. N.K. Bose, *Hindu samajer gadan*, pp. 140–2.
45. Sekhar Bandyopadhyay, 'A Peasant Caste in Protest' in *Caste and Communal Politics in South Asia*, eds S. Bandyopadhyay and S. Das (Calcutta, 1993), pp. 145–90; Sekhar Bandyopadhyay, *Caste, Politics and the Raj, Bengal 1872–1937* (Calcutta, 1990); Sekhar Bandyopadhyay, 'Caste and Society in Colonial Bengal: Change and Continuity', *Journal of Social Studies* (28 April 1985).
46. Sekhar Bandyopadhyay in Bandyopadhyay and S. Das (eds), *Caste and Communal Politics*, p. 169.
47. Adrienne Cooper, *Sharecropping and Sharecroppers' Struggles in Bengal, 1930–50* (Calcutta, 1988), p. 117; on the role of the Bengal Provincial Kisan Sabha in the Namashudras' struggle in the Tebhaga Movement, see pp. 140, 214, 256.
48. Taj-ul-Islam Hashmi, *Peasant Utopia: The Communalization of Class Politics in East Bengal, 1920–47* (Dhaka, 1994), p. 43; on *bhadralok* opposition to the social mobility and enfranchisement of Namashudras, pp. 100–1.
49. On G.S. Ghurye, M.N. Srinivas, and B.S. Cohn's views on the census and caste ranking, see B.S. Cohn, 'The Census, Social Structure and

Objectification in South Asia' in Cohn, *Anthropologist among Historians*, pp. 241–2.

50. Sekhar Bandyopadhyay in Bandyopadhyay and Das (eds), *Caste and Communal Politics*, p. 163.
51. Bandyopadhyay and Das (eds), *Caste and Communal Politics*, pp. 163–4.
52. Bandyopadhyay and Das (eds), *Caste and Communal Politics*, p. 164.
53. Cf. Sumit Sarkar, 'The Conditions and Nature of Subaltern Militancy: Bengal from Swadeshi to Non-Cooperation' in *Subaltern Studies*, III, ed. R. Guha (Delhi, 1984).
54. Pradip Kumar Bose, *Classes in Rural Society: A Sociological Study of Bengal Villages* (Delhi, 1984).
55. M. Marriott, *Caste Ranking and Community Structure in Five Regions of India and Pakistan* (Deccan College, Pune, 1960).
56. S. Sinha, 'Coexistence of Multiple Scales', p. 126.
57. Gouranga Chattopadhyay, *Ranjana: A Village in West Bengal* (Calcutta, 1964) shows that caste solidarity remained intact, and possibly increased in the 1950s.
58. S. Sinha, S. Sinha, 'Bhumij Kshatriya Social Movement', pp. 9–13; Bandyopadhyay, 'Peasant Caste in Protest', pp. 150–1.
59. Anima Mukhopadhyay, *Satero sataker radh benglar samaj sahitya* (Calcutta, 1990), pp. 80–1, on evidence from Mukundaram and Ruparam's *Dharma Mangal.*
60. Hashmi, *Peasant Utopia*, p. 34.
61. Ranjit K. Bhattacharya, *Muslims of Rural Bengal: Socio-cultural Boundary Maintenance* (Calcutta, 1991), pp. 31–8.
62. Bhattacharya, *Muslims of Rural Bengal*, p. 33.
63. Bhattacharya, *Muslims of Rural Bengal*, p. 61.
64. Mohammad Yakub Ali, *Musalmaner jatibhed* (Casteism among Muslims) (1927), extracts in N.K. Bose, *Hindu samajer gadan*, pp. 143–7; I have not been able to access the original work.
65. Ronald B. Inden and R.W. Nicholas, *Kinship in Bengali Culture* (Chicago, 1977); apart from Akos Ostor's well-known work on kinship and ritual in Bengal, also see his *The Play of the Gods* (Chicago, 1980).
66. Suraj Bandopadhyay shows that kinship was more important than class in rural social interaction; 'Exploring Boundaries of Social Interaction in Rural Areas: Village, Kinship, Caste and Class' (mimeo, Indian Statistical Institute, Calcutta, 1984).
67. Inden and Nicholas, *Kinship in Bengali Culture*, p. 87.

4

THE LOGIC OF FISSION

Muslim Identity and Its Contestations

The growth of a new Bengali Muslim identity was part of the process of a redefinition of Bengal in the 1920s and 1930s. In India, the rise of Bengali Muslim identity consciousness in the early decades of the twentieth century is often looked upon from an adverse point of view, for it is identified as the precursor of communalism. Is such identity consciousness of necessity potentially communalist? In current historiography there is an overwhelming emphasis on communal conflict, communal ideology and propaganda leading to such conflict, and communal tension providing the *casus belli* for the conflict. Is a monotonic depiction of Hindu–Muslim relations as perpetually inimical historically accurate? Do the actions in the public sphere—the conferences of the communal parties, the sonorous speeches and resolutions intoned in their gatherings, the elections they fight—explicate exhaustively the communal divide, as we historians often assume in our narratives, or do we need to look at the private sphere, the quotidian life experiences and everyday transactions at the interface between individuals of the two communities? We shall try to address these questions here, leaving the political chronicle for a later chapter.

The vast and ever-growing academic writings on communalism are characterized by three features. First, the focus has been on the political and public sphere, that is, on the political parties—the Muslim League, the Hindu Mahasabha, and the Congress, the political leaders who were spokesmen of explicitly anti-Hindu or anti-Muslim propaganda and ideology, and the government interventions exacerbating the communal divide. This stress exclusively on the public sphere has led to the neglect of *social transactions* in people's quotidian lives where, we will argue, lay the roots of the breaches between communities. As we shall see in the following pages, the manner in which members of different communities related or did not relate with one another (for example, commensality, social entertainment, and associative patterns); the encounters with a communal divide embedded in memories of childhood experiences and schooldays; the tropes that were part of conventional language embedding prejudices not consciously thought of (for example, *neyray* for Muslims, *Chandal* for Namashudras); the communal referents in language (that is, 'Musalmani Bangla'); the modes of address (for example, *tui* for low-caste persons and for *atraf* Muslims); intolerance regarding forbidden food (for example, Muslim prejudice against pork eaten by some Hindu lower castes and tribes and, of course, Hindu prejudice regarding beef, not to speak of finer points like *halal*); community-wise and caste-wise clustering of houses and settlements in villages and sometimes in towns; the separation of low-caste and high-caste or Hindu and Muslim hostels in schools and colleges (for example, not only in Dhaka but also in Calcutta, let alone *mofussil* towns); the day-to-day face-to-face interactions—these and many other things taken for granted constituted a cultural milieu that divided communities more effectively than resolutions of the League or speeches in the Congress sessions or the political pacts made and unmade by leaders. That is the bottom line in this chapter. In this and the previous chapter we have emphasized this cultural milieu of private spaces and quotidian social transactions; these seem to be part of the history that is *remembered*, distinct from the *history* that usually gets written and which is concerned with political acts in the public sphere.

Moreover, another common stereotype also merits re-examination: the *maulvi* as the villain of the communal story from the Hindu perspective. Aijaz Ahmad has made an interesting point on the problem with this stereotype: 'It is one of the great paradoxes of modern Indian history that traditions of Islamic piety, from [Abul Kalam] Azad to the Deoband *ulema*, eventually found their way into composite cultural and political *nationalism;* theories of modernization, as taught in the British or pro-British institutions, from Lincoln's Inn to Aligarh, begat, on the other hand, communal *separatism*'.[1] Aijaz Ahmad looks upon Azad as typical of the first trend, and Jinnah of the second. In Bengal, if one looked instead at, for instance, Maulana Akram Khan and Humayun Kabir their misfit with this observation is obvious. But the point of the remark remains valid: the stereotype of the traditional intellectual being *necessarily* 'separatist' is very dubious. Consider, for instance, the fact that Maulana Maniruzzaman Islamabadi (1875–1950) of Chittagong, as we shall see later, meets Swami Shraddhananda, a leader of the Hindu *shuddhi* and revivalist movement, at the Khilafat Conference in Delhi in 1919 and with his letter of introduction visits the Gurukul school in Hardwar—and this is said to have inspired Islamabadi to found an Arabic university on similar lines. In this curious situation do we infer that traditionalists of both the communities shared a common outlook equally illiberal and communalist, or is it an evidence of a liberal openness on the part of the Maulana and the Swamiji? The nuances of the traditionalists' discourse will be missed in casting them in latter-day stereotypes.

Thirdly, a feature of the extensive literature on communalism both in India and in Bangladesh is the isolation of the Hindu–Muslim relations to the exclusion of the network of other relationships that are also characterized by a struggle for identity assertion. If we perceive in Hindu–Muslim relations an increasing consciousness of 'separateness', that was one of several such perceptions of separateness in respect of other communities. This is why we have interpolated the Muslim voice along with that heard from other sections of Bengali society in the previous pages on perceptions of unity and self-definition of separateness. To isolate the Muslim grievances out of many imparts a disproportionality to our perspective. There is a stereotype, popularized in Indian films, portraying the obstreperous younger brother breaking up the happy joint family under the protective care of the big brother. Although many historical narratives would later portray the big brother, Hindu-dominated Congress, playing such a role vis-á-vis the Muslim League in Bengal in the 1940s, the communal imbroglio was not quite like that. Isolating the Muslim question tends to lend credibility to that scenario. It is useful to bear in mind that Muslim identity was not the only one that was threatened. Consider, for instance, the fact that in the 1920s tribal identity was being submerged. For example, of the Bodos living in Bengal in 1931, more than 31 per cent were unable to speak their language; of the Gurungs (from Nepal) 80 per cent had lost their language, and of the Kukis, 77 per cent.[2] Consider the fact that the Census of 1931 also tells us that the percentage of population enumerated as followers of 'tribal religions' decreased by 60.5 per cent between 1921 and 1931, while that of Muslims increased by 9.1 per cent, and of Hindus by 6.7 per cent. This cannot be explained as the work of Christian missionaries because in terms of absolute numbers, the 'tribal religion' category declined by 3.2 lakh and the Christian category increased by only 0.4 lakh. In 1921, 1.81 per cent of Bengal's population was put in the 'tribal religion' category; in 1931, it fell to 1.04 per cent. We do not know how much of this decline was due to conversion to Islam. But certainly the Hindu Mission and the Provincial Hindu Sabha tried 'to secure a return as Hindus of all members of primitive tribes' according to A.E. Porter, ICS, chief of the 1931 Census operations in Bengal.[3] Infringement of tribal cultural identity later exacted a price, in terms of separatist movements. Similarly, hegemonization of depressed castes such as the Mahishyas led to their alienation from the mainstream of Hindu *bhadralok* politics. Upper-caste hegemony remains a notable feature of the Bengali Hindu community.

In short, to ignore these specificities of the 1920s and 1930s and to extrapolate today's tropes of communalism will be, therefore, plainly inadequate. Finally, there is also an implicit assumption made too often about the 'monolithic Muslim mind', a stereotype that is questionable. Among others, Tazeen M. Murshid has criticized this stereotype very insightfully.[4] She has pointed to the irrelevance of such an essentialization of the complex Muslim discourses in two ways: first, by establishing the changes over time in her study of the changefulness 'of identity formation which was constantly being rearticulated against an "other"'. Second, she shows the contending coexistence of values, essentially inconsistent with each other in the discourse of the Bengali Muslim intelligentsia—in particular a 'persistent tension between a religious and a secular outlook'. This rejection of a monolithic interpretation of a so-called 'Muslim mind' in Bengal should lead us to qualify a good deal of writings on the communal question that depict Hindu–Muslim relations as perpetually inimical by focusing disproportionately on the incidents of communal conflict.

Assertion and Contestation of Identity

The expression of a new personality, a new consciousness of the Muslim community, often took the form of certain contrapositions vis-á-vis the Hindu community. Such a contraposition was not necessarily inimical in intent; it was a device to assert an autonomy of identity. For example, Abdul Karim (1863–1943), an alumnus of Presidency College and Inspector of Schools in the Bengal Education Service, writes in 1903: 'Our neighbours and brothers of the Hindu faith have left us so far behind on the road to progress that they laugh at us. Everyone in the world is progressing, all are trying to push forward their own people and country. Are we alone to remain inert?'[5] By the 1920s, the tone is more critical of the Hindus. Sometimes, no doubt, the rhetoric of communal politics surfaces in that discourse. 'At present', an essayist in *Muslim Darpan* writes in 1926, 'the Hindu is the wealthy zamindar. You are a peasant under him; he has money, you are the borrower; he is the lawyer and advocate, you are the client; he is the judge in the law court, you are in the dock…'.[6] Some intellectuals, as we shall see later, made a genuine effort to combine an assertion of the Muslim identity with a strong message of inter-communal harmony that would be based upon mutual respect. But it seems that the latter element, an attitude of respect, was very widely perceived to be wanting in the Hindu *bhadraloks*' social interactions—or lack thereof—with the Muslim community. Of the major sites of inter-communal discord vis-á-vis the Hindu community, this was what the Muslim spokesmen highlighted in their newspapers and journals. There was a very strong reaction against the social behaviour of the Hindu *bhadralok* in everyday life, and this was about the private domain beyond politics and public issues. Secondly, the Muslim intellectuals and thought-leaders began proudly to assert their '*Bengali* Muslim' identity on the one hand in their interface with Hindus and, on the other, with the pan-Islamist sentiments that spread in the course of the Khilafat movement. These were linked later by many Bangladeshi historians with the *Mukti juddha*, the movement for the independence of Bangladesh. Third, along with that identity assertion in linguistic–territorial and religious terms, there were material factors such as lack of access to formal education, disproportionately small representation in the government services, exclusion from prominent positions in civil society institutions, the concentration of landownership in the hands of upper-caste Hindus, and so on, that created a perception of the Muslims being deprived and disadvantaged in comparison with the Hindu community. These are perceptions that recur over and again in the 1920s and 1930s in the news media owned and controlled by the Muslim middle class. Let us look at some of these writings to understand the multifaceted process of identity assertion in those decades.[7] It is unfortunate that in translation we lose the flavour of those writings.

As regards the first of these trends in perception regarding Hindu–Muslim associative patterns, or lack thereof, in the private domain, we have to concede that our focus on that in this work is against the received wisdom; historiography by and large ignores the private domain while focusing on events in the public sphere and processes in which the state and politics are central. And yet we choose to prioritize the private domain because there is much to learn there about the prevailing cast of mind. In 1917, the well-known Bengali Muslim poet Siraji wrote an essay on the identity of the Bengali Muslims.

> From their childhood our children learn from the Hindu school teachers and textbooks, over and again, that the Bengali Muslims are descendants of the low castes and of untouchable Hindu castes.... Having been taught thus, the inheritors of the world famous and world-conquering—the Arabs, Iranians, Turks and Pathans ... are incapable of entertaining thoughts of their national (*jatiya*) glory and superiority.[8]

A few years later, *Islam Pracharak* carried an interesting essay on the social distance between the two communities. The few Muslims who receive education see in all public spheres only the Hindus: 'Hindu zamindar, Hindu magistrate, Hindu clerks, Hindu advocates and barristers, Hindu police officers...'. This creates a conviction that the Hindus are a superior people and then the Muslim middle classes try and find a space for themselves in the proximity of the Hindu *bhadralok*. However, 'the *babus* [Hindu *bhadralok*] still look upon them with contempt. Their touch will spoil the water in their *hookah*—Muslim contact will contaminate their bodies, their couches, etc.'[9] In other words, whatever the cross-community relationship and associative patterns in the public domain, in the private domain there were unsurpassable barriers. Again, in 1917, we see Ahmed Ali's long statement on the social status of Bengali Muslims: 'In the offices of the Hindu *zamindars*

Muslim peasants are treated with contempt.... The treatment meted out to Muslim peasants is much worse than that to Hindu peasants'.[10] Further, apart from the Hindu *zamindar*, 'the behaviour of the common Hindus on public roads, railways, steamboats, and in markets shows contempt and derision directed towards Muslims'. Unlike the Hindus, 'the Muslims are not allowed to sit on the mat when they go to the office of the Hindu *zamindars*'.[11] The author asks, in the days after the end of the Khilafat and Non-cooperation Movements: 'The last few years we have heard morning and night the message of unity loudly proclaimed, but how far have our Hindu brethren progressed towards brotherhood or unity? Have they given up their "touch-me-not" attitude ... their exclusive notions?' Even the approach of a Muslim to close proximity caused offence to a Hindu, for example, to avoid consequent 'defilement', the latter would throw away drinking water. It was not unlike the monstrous belief in untouchability in Hindu society. The famous author Mir Musharaf Husain wrote half in jest of this painful phenomenon: 'What is the Hindu–Muslim discord about? Is it not like some absurd disputes in the family, among neighbours, in idle men's gatherings, about inconsequential things...? You consider one side of the banana leaf pure, we think it is not. If I go near the couch on which you are sitting, you think that something has gone wrong with the water in your *hookah*!'[12] Long after Musharaf Husain, the situation remained unchanged. From the early twentieth century, there was strong Muslim reaction to such treatment. The resentment grew stronger still, and we shall return to this theme later when we look at childhood experiences recorded in memoirs of this period.

The second major feature of Muslim Bengali identity formation in the 1920s seems to be a strident assertion of Bengaliness, vis-á-vis Pan-Islamism, on the one hand, and a perception of Hindu hegemonism on the other. About this time, the Khilafat movement, endorsed by Mahatma Gandhi, brought pan-Islamist ideas to a salience it had never enjoyed before. Along with that, there was an Islamic consciousness that often found expression in contradistinctions with other religions, particularly Hinduism. The contradistinction with the latter acquired an edge when the Arya Samaj, the '*shuddhi* movement' in north India, disputes about census classifications, and enumeration of the two religious communities, and so on, occurred in the 1920s and 1930s. An opinion leader in Bengal, Maniruzzaman Islamabadi writes in

Al Islam in 1920: 'If the Khilafat is in danger, it is a great loss to Islam and ruination for the Muslims.... Muslims have been compelled to resort to non-cooperation.... We must stop cooperating with the British to the extent possible'.[13] While Khilafat comes to hold a central position in their thoughts, there were also differences and debates between sections of Muslim intellectuals and opinion-leaders. On the one hand, some of them would accord priority to the cause of Khilafat. *Islam Darshan* editorializes in 1921: 'Every Muslim must remember that to us Islam comes first and the country next; religion first and after that comes the land of our birth'.[14] On the other hand, there was a contrary view that prioritized India's freedom. According to *Soltan*'s editorial outlook in 1923:

> Those who are for Khilafat, those who are anxious to preserve the land sacred [to Islam], those who desire independence for Egypt and Iraq, those who are well-wishers on the side of the Khilafat and Constantinople, must realize that in the first place we have to try and gain India's freedom in order that those countries' interests and the cause of religion may be advanced.[15]

Apart from this dichotomy, the other notable feature of the 1920s was a great emphasis on the purification and consolidation of Islam in India. It was a response to a new religious consciousness that figured in the discourse of Khilafat, on the one hand, and on the other a reaction against activities of the Arya Samaj and the *shuddhi* (purification and re-conversion to Hinduism) movement. Some of the notions of purity of religion and traditions appeared in attitudes to small things in quotidian life, for example, objection to the use of the Gandhi *topi* by Muslims, or prefixing a Muslim name with 'Sree'. The editorial view of *Islam Darshan* was that the Gandhi *topi* was 'against Islamic religious principles'. The use of *Sree* in place of *Janab* was 'contrary to Islamic customs' on account of its association with Hinduism.[16] Or, again, there was protest against the fact that the number of holidays declared by the government for Muslim festivals was not in proportion to the Muslim population.[17] Generally, however, more important issues were addressed. The community was alerted against the 'net of stratagems adopted by people like Swami Shraddhananda to convert Muslims to the Arya faith'.[18] In particular the conversion of about fifteen thousand Muslims in Rajputana in 1922–3 was condemned.[19] The call of

'Tanzim' was broadcast, especially to Muslim youths, and they were asked to unitedly prepare themselves physically and morally, bearing in mind 'the unity that was achieved by the earliest [Arab] Muslims'.[20] Needless to say, symbolic things like the song 'Vande Mataram' were to be rejected as infringement of Muslim identity. 'The mixture of the *kalma*, *Allah-o-Akbar* in praise of the one and only *Allah*, with the Hindu hymn to Mother India in the song *Vande Mataram*' was beyond doubt sinful in the eyes of Islam.[21] In fact, the journal *Shariat-e-Islam* was of the view that let alone singing that Hindu song, 'according to the prescription of the *shariat*, even to utter *Vande Mataram* is utterly forbidden for a Muslim'.[22] Further, slogans in support of political leaders were frowned upon: 'We have nothing against Mr Gandhi. But we do not think it is permissible for a Muslim to proclaim praise of any human being'.[23] This opinion of an authoritative journal, *Islam Darshan*, was possibly an extreme and isolated position, because the supporters of Khilafat or Muslim League often raised adulatory slogans for their leaders.

While on the one hand such *external* infringements and inroads into the Muslim self were thus resisted, the 1920s and 1930s also witnessed a campaign to combat *internal* threats to the purity and integrity of Islam through internal purification. In this regard, religious as well as socio-cultural practices were on the agenda of Muslim opinion-leaders. Ismail Hussain Siraji, the famous author and an ideologue of Bengali Muslim cultural revival, notes the 'influence of *Hinduani*' (that is, Hindu-like behaviour) in the Muslim community: 'Many Mosolman's make a vow to [the deity] Kali. On the day of the *Lakshmi-puja*, in many Mosolman households everything short of worship of the image is done to celebrate the day. Among the womenfolk the customs and rituals of *Hinduani* are widely prevalent'.[24] *Raoshan Hedayet*, a journal expressing views of conservative Muslim religious thinkers and supposed to be affiliated to the Hanafi school, observed a couple of years later:

> Many Mosalmans innocently celebrate' all the Hindu *pujas* and they 'join in the boat race, the horse race, feasts with relatives, the village fair, visits to prostitutes, games and gambling; it looks as if it is their *puja*, and apart from these disgusting pastimes forbidden by the *shariat*, they also pay cash for the *puja* to the zamindar, along with their rent payment'.[25]

Apart from these 'reprehensible' popular recreations, it was reported that these Muslims 'were in the habit of using charms and swearing in the name of [Hindu deities] Kali, Durga, the deity at Kamaksha, etc., and all of that means that they are losing their *Iman*, they are becoming *kafirs*, and they are ensuring their descent into hell'. An authority no less than Maniruzzaman Islamabadi held the view that in the form of reverence for the *pirs* the Hindu custom of idol worship had crept in among the devotees. 'Have we not made the grave of every *pir* an idol for worshipping?.... Not only men, but thousands of women go to the *dargahs* of the *pirs* on the occasion of *urs* or to seek a boon.... It is incumbent upon us to protest against these worshippers of gravestones, *pirs* and *dargahs*'.[26]

Among the Muslim theologians there were, of course, disputes between sects at loggerheads with one another, for example, the conflict between the Hanafi and Muhammadi schools of thought; but commentators like Islamabadi or Siraji were concerned not so much with these internal differences but the departure from Islam as they saw it. Many of these critics blamed the *maulvis* and this was a strand of criticism going back at least to the early twentieth century. Mohammad Maniruzzaman wrote in 1903: 'If our society can be made free of the influence of *maulvis*, *mullahs* and *pirsahibs*, there will be greater possibility of social progress'.[27] Two decades later, a contributor to *Saogat*, a renowned liberal journal, wrote of the '*Mullah* group' in Bengal that they were solely concerned with '*purdah* [seclusion of women], beard, their vestments [special headgear and dress distinguishing their vocation] ... their parochialism, their vested interests, their limited outlook'.[28] On commencing publication, *Islam Pracharak* editorially stated that its agenda was to address the problem of unIslamic practices among 'the simple god-fearing illiterate Muslims who constitute the bulk of the community'.[29] It was observed that among such people reverence for *fakirs* was increasing day by day, even as the behaviour and teachings of the *fakirs* were 'no better than' those of *kafirs*; the simple peasants, denied the benefits of religious teaching, counselling, and leadership, 'fall into the trap and are fast moving towards hell'. It was further pointed out that 'educated persons do not support' *fakirs* and their deceptions, but simple folk are 'caught in the maze' of false religious beliefs. *Islam Pracharak* later sponsored an organization, the Bengal Islam Mission, to propagate a 'pure and authentic' Islamic faith.[30]

Last of all, let us note that the various attempts to excise impurities brought in by popular religion did not include the status of women. One finds occasional references, for example, to iniquities suffered by wives due to polygamy[31], to the abuse of the custom of *talaq*,[32] and to the evils of the *purdah* system,[33] and so on. But nothing was done by Muslim legislators to initiate legislation in respect of marriage under Muslim personal law.

In contemporary Hindu society as well there was a lively discussion in the 1920s and 1930s of the need for reforms. This was partly an extension of late-nineteenth-century social reformism. Moreover, it was also a response to Mahatma Gandhi's exhortations regarding eradication of untouchability, the Arya Samaj and Hindu Mahasabha's missionary activities, and the debate on the Sarda Act (1929), all of which gave rise to new issues.[34] But the Hindu discourse on socio-religious reforms was different in that it was not powered by the sense of urgency of a community embattled whereas the Muslim journals of those times suggest that there was such a sense of urgency in that community.

The third factor that shaped the Bengali Muslim identity assertion was their perception that they were unfairly disadvantaged in material terms. This perception was justified more often than not. In the civil services, partly due to unequal access to education, the Muslim community was hugely under-represented. They had the memory of having had, in the pre-British period, privileged access to the official language (although that was limited to the *ashraf* stratum of the community), and hence government service. Connected with this was the grievance that the Muslims did not benefit from the spread of 'English education' and were therefore out of the reckoning for government services. As regards the business world, there were as few entrepreneurs in the Muslim community as there were among the Hindus. But in the professions, particularly in law and medicine, the Hindu community's disproportionately large share of success was conspicuous. Further down the social scale, the obvious fact that sprang to the eye was the exploitative relationship, particularly in eastern Bengal, between the *zamindars*, of whom the overwhelming majority were Hindus, and farmers and tenants of whom the majority were Muslims.

A Japanese historian of agrarian relations in Bengal, Nariaki Nakazato, has remarked that the economic and the social dimensions of rural transactions under the *zamindari* system were inseparably intertwined. The payments exacted for Hindu festivals clearly exceeded the legal economic rights of the landlord. No doubt, as Rafiuddin Ahmad has shown, in the nineteenth century syncretic tendencies at the level of popular beliefs were in evidence and that social situation might have been viewed as a an excuse justifying taxation of non-Hindus for Hindu festivals. However, in the early twentieth century there was strong resentment against forced participation in 'idolatrous' festivals, as well as against the economic burden.[35] In rural areas this addition, *abwabs*, to the rent burden was a major grievance mentioned in the contemporary newspapers. Apart from the *abwabs*, another common grievance was the pressure exerted by Hindu *zamindars* on their Muslim tenants in respect of *qurbani* (sacrifice). The prescription of the cow sacrifice was widely accepted in Muslim society while the proscription of cow slaughter was a strong tenet in Hinduism. Informal coercion by Hindu *zamindars* to prevent cow sacrifice was often reported in Muslim journals.[36] Some observers, aware of the strength of Hindu sentiments, recommended a compromise, and suggested the performance of the sacrifice 'out of public sight'.[37] But, as inter-communal relations worsened, the compromise did not work and conflict on this question was both cause and consequence of bitter conflicts. In 1926, when communalism, in particular riots in Calcutta and Dhaka, deeply affected the mental environment, one notices Muslim resentment against Hindu rural artisans as well: 'Your rice bowl is made by the Hindu potter, your plough is made by the Hindu *kamar* [ironworker] ... your cooking utensils are made by the Hindu *kansari* [brassworker], your sweetmeats are made by the Hindu *moira* [sweetmeat maker], you go to the Hindu *napit* [barber] ...', and so on. This is, of course, a middle-class journalist's view.[38] How far the Muslim peasant entertained such resentment against Hindu members of his own class is difficult to establish. But the class factor vis-á-vis the *zamindars* was beyond doubt overwhelmingly strong in shaping the mentality of the Muslim rural masses. In a later chapter, we shall return to this theme.

Muslim grievances finding expression in the newspapers were preponderantly middle-class ones. Topmost was the disproportionately small number of Muslims in government service. In 1903, it was reported that while there were 529 Hindus in the position of deputy magistrate, there were only 76 Muslims; the corresponding numbers were 343 and 18 in the case of *munsiffs* (civil servants a grade below deputy magistrates), and 85 and 4 in the superior positions of sub-judge and judges of various courts.[39] A moment's calculation will show the ratio of Muslims in these three categories: 12.5 per cent, 5 per cent, and 4.5 per cent. The policy of the British Indian government to advance Muslim education, and to correct this disproportion and the administrative changes that followed the partition of Bengal during 1905–11, slightly improved the share of Muslims in government jobs.[40] Reportedly, in 1924 the Muslim share was 25 per cent in executive positions and 6 per cent in judicial positions.[41] This too was far short of what the Muslims desired: the complaint was that of about Rs 7 crore spent on salaries of provincial government servants '6 crore and 35 lakh are swallowed by the Hindus', though Muslims should have got more than half of the total expenditure. A contributor to *Al Islam* writes in 1917: 'Apart from government service, in the self-governing institutions created by the government, e.g. municipalities, district boards, local boards and the offices of chairman, vice-chairman, etc., the Muslims scarcely have any share'.[42]

The crux of the problem of unequal recruitment to government jobs was unequal access to education. It was obvious that 'without education in English, education remains incomplete', but there was a conservative opinion that English education was *kafiri*. 'Lord Bentinck's time saw the abolition of Persian in the courts of law.... Our mind was a prisoner of the superstitious prejudice that English was a *kafiri* language, that English learning leads to *dozaq* [hell]. But life's struggle and the necessity of earning a livelihood made us realize that those ideas were wrong'. 'There are some heads of family who ... declared that English learning [*kafiri ilm*] was to be eschewed. They wanted religious education, but if you get educated in the madrasa, you cannot earn a living. As a result a new type of *madrasa* has been started where English education is permitted'. These reports of 1903, 1907, and 1926 indicate the initial problem, a matter of attitude.[43] To their credit, Muslim intellectuals carried on a tireless fight against that attitude towards learning English. But progress was slow.

According to the General Report on Public Instruction of the provincial government, up to 1905 Calcutta University had produced only 713 Muslim graduates, that is an average of only 15 a year.[44] Equally discouraging was the fact that till 1905 entry into professional education was very limited: only 5 Muslims attained the Bachelor of Medicine degree and 168 the Bachelor of Law degree. Thanks to the Dhaka Medical School, from the 1920s there was greater Muslim participation in medical education. As regards general education at college level, there was an improvement in the 1920s; in 1930, we have an estimate of Government colleges all over Bengal showing about 15.2 per cent Muslim enrolled undergraduates, whereas the percentage was below 8 in 1912–13.[45] Needless to say, small relative improvements did not satisfy the aspirations of the leaders of the Muslim middle classes who were demanding participation in education proportional to the population. The education question and the whole scenario—the sense of deprivation, the grievances, the resentments that found expression in the Muslim journals of those times—reveals to us an impatience that developed in the 1920s and 1930s. There was the impatience of the latecomer trying to catch up with those who had begun the race before them. To those ahead this appeared to be unseemly haste. But let us not forget that many Englishmen also saw Indian aspirations to independence in a similar light.

The core of the problem of the exclusionary world outlook was pointed out by Rabindranath Tagore with his usual clear-sightedness in 1926, a year that saw much communal violence. He recalled that when he first entered the office of the *zamindari* of the Tagore family he saw that there was a carpet for some visitors to be seated, and there was no carpet for some visitors—in that part of the room the carpet was rolled up. When he asked why that was so, the *zamindari* officials explained the difference: 'This custom is an old one. The Muslims have accepted it and the Hindus too know of it. The portion uncarpeted is for seating Muslims, the carpeted portion is for others'. Tagore recalls that experience and writes that after having for years and years treated the Muslims like that, after having rolled up the carpet lest they sit on it, comes a day when we are fighting the British Government and now

> we call upon them and say, 'We are brothers, you must make sacrifices like us, you must be ready for prison or even death'. And then we see on the other side red fez caps and hear the words 'We are different'. We say with surprise what is the problem, are you not with us in national matters? The problem is the rolled-up carpet, *that gap* from long ago. That is not a trivial thing.[46]

Tagore goes on from the image of the rolled-up carpet to elaborate on the theme of many of his writings: 'If men are neighbours, but they have no relationship, or there is only a warped relationship, or one demanded only by necessity—if that is so, catastrophe awaits us'. Tagore believed that this distance from the Muslim community was only one of many manifestations of the amazing capacity of Hinduism in the modern period to create barriers between castes and communities and peoples. Tagore believed that although India at one time welcomed all peoples and cultures, from the middle ages when brahmanism acquired a centrality, Hinduism built for itself 'a system of barriers. Its nature was to forbid and to exclude. The world never saw such a neatly constructed system against assimilation of any kind. This is not a barrier only between Hindus and Muslims. People like you and me who want freedom in conducting our life are also impeded and imprisoned'.[47] That was a statement he made in 1922 and the next year, in another essay, Tagore wrote that the principle of exclusion operating in Hinduism against castes and communities and all 'out-siders', contrasted sharply with the propensities of the Muslim community. Muslims were no doubt intolerant towards the *kafir*, but at the same time there was a readiness to usher into Islam all external elements, except *kafirs*, and to bind the community with a bond of equality in theory. 'The Musalmans' original principles of their religious community are such that a deep-seated unity has developed in their community, while the Hindu social prescriptions have created disunities within'.[48] Thus, to Rabindranath Tagore, the absence of unity between the Hindus and Muslims should be viewed in the larger perspective of the historical traditions of those communities, not merely as a matter of political negotiation. The long run of history has shown the correctness of this approach.

In voicing such ideas, Tagore was not alone, but he was certainly in a small minority. In the Muslim community as well, there were men like the great scholar Muhammad Shahidhullah, spokesman of a small minority working against the current of Muslim opinion that tended to focus upon divisive issues. 'I believe we shall unite in the domain of culture. As long as the Muslims remain ignorant of Hindu culture, and Hindus likewise about Islamic culture, there can never take place a meeting of minds. I am for that kind of unity and at the same time I concede that everyone has the right to propagate his religion'.[49]

He projected literature as the *milan mandir*, the temple of unity. 'Bengali literature will be the eternal temple of the unity of Hindus and Muslims. The literary creations of the Hindus and Muslims are but two chambers in that temple ... neither is the exclusive preserve of the Hindu and Muslim literatures. Many Hindu authors ... have contributed to Muslim literature'.[50] He pointed out that many Bengali authors were unaware of this unifying role their writing should play. In this connection he touched upon an important subject, the textbooks in use in the 1920s and 1930s. Some textbooks for children 'strike at the root of national unity'. They focus only on great personages and episodes of Hindu history, the Hindu children are taught 'no one is greater than the Hindus', while Muslim children begin to believe 'we are a lesser people, no great person belonged to us'. Such teachings in schoolbooks 'plant the seeds of ruination'.[51] Muslim authors, he said, failed in this respect compared to Hindu writers. Likewise, they failed to effectively reply to the misrepresentation of Muslims in Indian history. Is it enough, Shahidullah asked, to just abuse Bankimchandra? Where are historians like Jadunath Sarkar or Akshay Kumar Maitreya among Muslims? The poet Kazi Nazrul Islam displayed his usual boldness in his writings, in *Ganavani*, a Leftist journal edited by the Communist leader Muzaffar Ahmed.

> It is possible to tolerate Hinduism and Islam, but their fetishism about the sacred beard and the sacred tuft of hair on the head [*tikitwa, daritwa*] is intolerable, because that is what causes conflict. That tuft of hair on the head is not Hinduism, it is the priests' signature. That beard is not Islam, it is the Mullah's sign.... The fight is between them, not between Hindus and Muslims.[52]

That was written at a critical moment, when the Dhaka communal riots took place. He also wrote at this time: 'The cry of the mortally wounded did not matter a jot to the masjid, nor did the stone deity in the temple respond. Only the blood of innocent men left its mark on those edifices'.[53] Consider the courage of conviction of a relatively obscure intellectual, Sadat Ali Akhand, who used to write in *Saogat*, an exceptionally liberal Muslim journal: 'The Bengali Muslims have forgotten the fact that Islam is a religion, it is not a nation—and therefore they are proclaiming to the world that they are an Islamic nation. They think that "nation" and "religion" mean the same thing'.[54] He said that in modern times in all Muslim countries the national identity had overcome the religious affiliation. 'To re-enact the Crusades and Jihad today is impossible'.

It is instructive to bear in mind that words such as these from this author, or Nazrul Islam, or Shahidullah were published in Bengali Muslim journals in the 1920s, even though they constituted a small minority compared to the mainstream view we have outlined earlier. In the last years of the 1920s, the minority began to challenge the Establishment views in the Buddhir Mukti Andolan (Movement for the Emancipation of the Intellect). Kazi Abdul Wadud (1894–1970) and his literary society, the Muslim Sahitya Samaj, founded in 1926, played a significant role in this regard. Further, the foundation of the University of Dhaka, as we have noted in an earlier chapter, marked an advance into a new era in the intellectual history of the Muslim community. Wadud, then on the faculty of that university, gathered around him luminaries like Muhammad Shahidullah, Abul Fazal, Abdul Qadir, and others who expressed a secular and radical point of view contra the conservative Islamist approach. Wadud who later in 1935 made a combative statement on *Hindu–musalmaner virodh* ('The Hindu–Muslim Conflict'), became the spearhead of a concerted critique of Muslim conservatism, particularly in so far as it related to the nationalist movement and inter-communal harmony. Recently, Muhammad Shah and Tazeen M. Murshid have made excellent studies of the new trend; instead of reproducing their conclusions, let us look at one radical journal to instantiate the new thought trend that was encapsulated in the motto of the journal *Shikha* ('Flame') published by the Muslim Sahitya Samaj of Dhaka from 1927 to 1932: 'Where knowledge is constrained, when the intellect is inert, there can be no freedom'.[55]

Shikha carried essays that questioned the basic premises of establishmentarian conservatism. 'There are *madrasas* in Calcutta, Dhaka, etc., for religious education. Education in *madrasas* is not enough for livelihood.... But we seem to have decided that we do not want literature, history, geography, mathematics, philosophy, and science, and that it is enough to get a religious education'.[56] 'To reform the Muslim education system we should first of all abolish training in alien languages like Arabic, Persian, Urdu, and close down all *madrasas*, new and old, and switch to the school and college system.... What do we need *madrasas* for?.... No education at all may well be better than the warped education [*kusiksha*] of the *madrasas*'.[57]

> It has been reported that in Bangladesh there are even to this day many Muslims who are ashamed to admit that Bengali is their mother tongue. It amounts to saying that as *sharif* or high-born Muslims they cannot accept it as their mother tongue.... Everyone knows how futile was their propaganda to pass off Urdu as the language of the rural people of Bengal.[58]

Music in the vicinity of mosques was a perpetual cause of inter-communal conflict, and an essay in *Shikha* argues:

> One of the shortcomings in our community is an inimical attitude to our Hindu neighbours. Conflict among neighbours should be eschewed.... The fuss made by parochial Muslims about music before a mosque is not something worthy of support.... No doubt it is not easy to accept that, but how does it make it sinful for us? Is it not the case that Hindus play the music, not us Muslims?[59]

A long-standing dispute in Islamic law has been that about the theologists' dictum against legitimacy of Muslims taking interest on money given on loan. A contributor to *Shikha*, pointing out that Muslims were quite marginal in business and industry and displayed little entrepreneurial talent, recommended: 'Given the economic crisis Muslims are facing, at present it would be better to enter the business of money-lending at interest rather than to remain paupers and beggars'.[60] In these and many other matters *Shikha*, as a medium for the Emancipation of Intellect Movement, took a position that was against the grain of established conservative wisdom. The journal lasted only five years. However, the significance of the voices of dissent like those of Nazrul Islam, Muhammad Shahidullah, Kazi Abdul Wadud, or the *Shikha* is to demonstrate that the stereotype of a monolithic communal mind often ascribed to the Muslim community is incorrect. Along with the mainstream trend of opinion we have outlined on the basis of contemporary journalism, we find that there was also this voice of dissent, the voice of the emancipated intellect.

Childhood Experiences

Our brief survey of the writings in Muslim journals touches the fringes of the major issues around which a new Muslim discourse nucleated in the 1920s. One major issue of those days was *madrasa* and school education and textbooks for children. That was but natural. Childhood experiences in forming personality could be decisive. We have earlier laid stress on such experiences. It seems probable that in educated Muslim families the stress on religious instruction was greater than in Hindu families in a similar social position. This might have been due to the fact that imparting religious instruction and teaching Arabic were inextricably associated. Abul Hashim was born in a highly educated family of civil servants and landowners in Burdwan district in 1905; his mother's father was a classmate of Bankimchandra Chatterjee and his great-grandfather was a subordinate judge in the days of the East India Company. Although the family was exposed to Western education and culture for at least three generations their children went through a traditional system of training. 'Muslim pupils—before they were taught Bengali, English, arithmetic, etc., were invariably taught to read the Quran and the rules of namaz.... My education began with lessons in reciting the Quran with correct pronunciation and offering namaz'.[61] Special care was taken in this family, as in almost all upper-class families, to teach correct Arabic pronunciation. (Bengali mispronunciation was disdained and Professor Nurul Hasan used to say that till his youth some Bengali families would send their sons to Aligarh or other north Indian Muslim centres of learning so that their 'speech was not spoilt'.) Hashim, after this training under a reputed *maulvi* from the Deoband School, went to a Muslim students' hostel, founded by his father in the Burdwan Maharaja's country house, and supervised by a *maulvi*.

Abul Mansur Ahmed (1898–1979) was brought up in a village remote from urban influence in Mymensingh district in a family far less exposed to English education than Hashim's. The elders in this family were influenced by the Faraizi movement and later the Wahabi movement. Apart from lessons in the *maqtab*, the Muslim children's minds were shaped by the stories and poems recited or read from chapbooks, that is, popular literature in the form of poorly printed ballads and tales, often from the low-end publication hub in Calcutta known as *Bat-tala*. The first verse that Abul Mansur memorized as a child was: 'If Allah wills, O Brother, I will go to Lahore/There I shall fight the holy fight (*jihad*) with the Sikhs/I shall be a *ghazi* if I win, and a *shahid* if I die/I shall give my life to keep the *tauhid* alive'.[62] Abul Mansur has described vividly the formative role of the chapbooks, *punthis*, *jihadi risala*, and also romances and religious lore recited by the literate for the benefit of the unlettered and small children. The message of these chapbooks was not necessarily anti-Hindu, but it helped instilled in children consciousness of a specific religious and historical tradition that was far from being inclusive. At the same time, consider the fact that in his schooldays Abul Mansur repeatedly encountered Hindu domination, as soon as he passed from the *maqtab* and moved on to middle and high school. In high school, he recalls, out of thirty-five teachers only one was Muslim, and that too because he taught Persian.[63] What was worse, the school celebrated Hindu *puja* on its premises but year after year permission to hold *Id Milad* was refused. Abul Mansur's experience may be compared to the shameful episodes decades ago during Mir Musharaf Husain's (1848–1911) schooldays. He was compelled to dress in *dhoti* and *chaddar* in Krishnagar high school and not only did he have to discard pyjama and the Muslim long coat but his skull cap was burnt by his classmates.[64] Hossain also noticed the predominance of Hindu deities and scriptural injunctions and stories in the 'English' schools and commented that this is what compelled Muslim students to go to *madrasas*. Other examples are not hard to come by and it is important to bear in mind the long-term effects of such childhood experiences. This is a factor ignored by historians. But perhaps these childhood memories were more important than the propaganda in formal political forums historians focus upon.

Let us turn to school textbooks.

> Every school has a common room. The books placed there are all by Hindu authors and full of anti-Muslim sentiments. Then the textbooks used in the classes are based on assorted stories from the *Mahabharata* and the like and some are writings by anti-Muslim writers like Bankim. Every now and then Hindu teachers and students address Muslims as *Mosla, Mleccha, Yavana, Neray*....

Thus wrote *Al-Islam*, the journal run by the Anjuman Ulema-e-Bangala, in 1920. Three years earlier, the outstanding scholar Mohammad Shahidullah wrote in the same journal an article on 'Our Literary Poverty':

> The first thing we need is textbooks for Muslim boys and girls.... [The child] reads in his textbooks ... only stories about Hindu great men. Naturally, the impression is formed in his mind that we, the Muslims, are an inferior race, we have no great men amongst us. Such books

> deprive the [Muslim] child of his identity. Hindu children read those books and think, no one is greater than us.... Thus national unity is destroyed right at the beginning.

About the same time, the poet Ismail Hussain Siraji (1880–1931) wrote:

> Our children usually study works of history by anti-Muslim authors', taught by anti-Muslim teachers. If one reads any one of these books one would see that great care has been taken to root out, erase and cut out all that was glorious in the Muslim period.... From their childhood, impressionable children, far from entertaining national pride and respect, develop contempt and disrespect for their own people.[65]

In reaction to this perception, new books from the Muslim point of view began to be written, and the British authorities encouraged this through the Textbook Committee; moreover, in the 1920s, the recruitment policy began encouraging entry of Muslims into the Education Department of the Government of Bengal. In the Hindu perception the new textbooks were communal: a typical editorial in the *Ananda Bazar Patrika* on 'Communalism in Education' alleged the infusion of Muslim communalism in textbooks approved recently.[66] Thus textbooks became a very contentious issue.

History as a Site of Contestation

As usual, history became the major site of contestation. The construal of the history of Bengal and of India in the hands of Hindu historians was identified as communally biased. Maulana Mohammad Maniruzzaman Islamabadi (1875–1950) tried to redress the balance in his book on Musalman civilization in India published in 1914; he blamed English historians more than the Hindus; the latter, he surmised, adopted the prejudices of English civil servants against their predecessors, the Muslim rulers.[67] Curiously, the historical question whether Bengali Muslims were converts from the lower order of Hindu society assumes importance. That Muslims were such converts was the view of the report on the Census of 1872. H.H. Risley in *Tribes and Castes of Bengal* (Calcutta, 1891) ethnographically supported this view. Khondkar Fazl-e-Rabbi, the Dewan of Murshidabad, wrote a book in Persian, later translated into English, to contest this;

Kazi Abdul Wadud (1894–1970) in his perceptive analytical essay on Hindu–Muslim relations in 1935 devoted a good deal of space to the consideration of the question.[68] Perhaps it assumed importance not only because it was related to the origins of Muslims but also the *ashraf–atraf* hierarchy.

However, these were of academic import: what really engaged Muslim attention was their representation in the flood of historical fictions and dramas in Bengali. Bankimchandra Chatterjee was held guilty on many counts by Muslim critics: did he not portray Mir Kasim, the Nawab of Bengal, as a traitor, Muslims in general as profligate and cruel, Muslim women as immoral and 'immodest?'[69] Particularly the portrayal of Muslim women falling in love with Hindu men was resented vehemently. A writer in *Al-Islam* in 1915 states that Muslim women in Bankim's fiction 'are not acceptable to us'. An author introduced as Sofia Khatun, BA, writes in the journal of the Muslim Literary Society in 1922 that there was a deep prejudice and preconception in the depiction of Muslim women falling madly in love with Bankim's Hindu heroes.[70] More generally speaking, the representation of Muslim women by Hindu novelists and playwrights was attacked. The most strident of these critics was the poet Siraji. An example:

> The Muslim *padshahs* are dug out of their marble tombs and in novels and poems shown as terrible, autocratic, monstrous, profligate, and so on, and in plays likewise, to receive Hindu spectators' applause in the theatre halls of Calcutta and the mofussil.... The princesses who were sheltered in the impenetrable harem are being dragged out of their sanctuary and opium-eaters' imagination depicts one of them as the lover of ... [adjectives omitted] Shivaji; another woman as infatuated with some [adjective omitted] Rajput; and another as the mistress of some Hindu serf—and these things are enacted to dispense immaculate pleasure to the theatre-hall spectators.[71]

Among the playwrights Dwijendra Lal Roy's (1863–1913) popular 'historical' plays were specially singled out by Muslim critics: the portrayal of Shah Jahan and Nur Jahan or that of Muslim rulers in general in his plays on the fall of Mewar and the life of Rana Pratap and some Hindu heroes, alienated Muslim sentiments.[72] To put before the Muslim readers another history of Islam became the focal point of the creative writings of Maniruzzaman Islamabadi (1875–1950), Kaikobad (1857–1951) [the pen name of Mohammad Kazem Ali Qureshi],

Ismail Husain Siraji (1880–1931), and the more academic writings of S. Wajed Ali (1890–1951) or Abdul Karim (1864–1953).[73] An interesting feature of all their works, except Abdul Karim's, was a pan-Islamist vision, going beyond Islam in Bengal or India to the global role played by the Islamized people at one time, ranging from the Moorish conquest of Spain to Aurangzeb's India.

Increasing Access to Higher Education

Another and a broader issue was the correct perception of the Muslim intelligentsia that a Hindu monopoly in the sphere of education impeded the advancement of the Muslim community. Although the first partition of Bengal of 1905 was annulled, some major steps were taken by the British authorities from that decade to address the undoubted imbalance in participation in formal education. The problem that should have been addressed was the low level of literacy. Only 5 per cent and 5.7 per cent of the Muslim population was literate, according to the censuses of 1921 and 1931 respectively, as compared to 14.1 per cent and 14 per cent of the Hindus. But it was secondary and higher education that engaged the attention of the Muslim middle classes and the government. Special aid for Muslims by way of scholarships, setting up Muslim hostels, appointment of Muslims as teachers and inspectors in the Department of Education, promotion of private and government colleges in the eastern districts, and the announcement in 1911 of the government's resolve to set up Dhaka University—all these marked an era of expansion of educational opportunities in East Bengal between 1905 and 1911. This expansion had two characteristics. First, an overwhelming stress on higher education; in 1906–11 the increase in enrolment was 42 per cent at primary, 158 per cent at secondary and 407 per cent at college level in East Bengal.[74] Overall enrolment of Muslims increased by 46 per cent while that of Hindus increased by around 30 per cent.

In the alternative stream of Muslim education, the *madrasa* system, major reforms were initiated in 1915 by the government, at the instance of the provincial Muslim Educational Conference. Except for the old Calcutta Madrasa, founded in the days of Warren Hastings, all the government *madrasas* switched to a modernized syllabus. From 1919, the Dhaka Madrasa, among other institutions, began to teach undergraduate classes in Islamic studies, that is, it functioned as a college; and from 1922 there began, under governmental orders, reservation of seats for Muslims in some vocational courses, for example, teachers' training and engineering. Muslim dissatisfaction with the admission policy in Presidency College eventually led to the foundation in 1926 of its Muslim counterpart, Islamia College, at the initiative of Fazlul Huq. On the whole, the 1920s represented a period of remarkable growth in Muslim education; in the years 1921–6 the number of Muslims enrolled in educational institutions at all levels increased by 29.4 per cent.

The foundation of Dhaka University (1921) is another landmark. In the beginning, the vested interests around Calcutta University looked upon it as an infringement of its monopoly and alleged that in course of two decades a communal ambience was established in the new university. At the same time, the new university initially was regarded by many, Hindu and Muslim, as a welcome initiative to build on lines other than the pattern of Calcutta. Calcutta University was primarily an examining body with affiliated colleges; graduate studies departments were added on later. Recalling his Dhaka days Naresh Chandra Sengupta said: 'I hoped that I would be part of an effort to build a teaching and residential university. I had an opportunity to help build such a university. But that ideal of the university was soon demolished', and he blamed the communalization of education attendant upon the Montagu-Chelmsford constitutional proposals coming into operation.[75] Sengupta served Dhaka University between 1921 and 1924 as the head of the Law College; Ramesh Chandra Majumdar, the historian, recalls that Sengupta was the first Provost of Jagannath Hall and his assistant and successor was Ramesh Chandra. More notably, Sengupta started a literary society in Dhaka University which is sometimes regarded as the point of origin of the *Kallol* era.[76] If the communal count is at all meaningful in the context of academic appointments, the number of Hindus among teachers was overwhelmingly large. According to a recent study, in 1921 only 8 out of 60 teachers were Muslim, and of the 26 readers and professors only 4 were Muslim. In 1935–6, out of 124 teachers only 24 were Muslim. Among students the ratio was 5 Hindus to 1 Muslim in 1921, and 3.5 to 1 in 1937.[77] That such statistics of communal distribution were collected and were and are being scrutinized with care in Bangladesh even today suggests a particular orientation: the bias in favour of Hindus in Calcutta University was to be corrected in Dhaka. A distortion caused by an historical accident was to be countered by design. This was reflected in the organizational and controlling bodies which ensured heavy weightage of Muslim representation under the Dacca University Act of 1920. A Bangladesh historian writes in 1992, after pointing to the culture of the Muslim Hall in Dhaka University—compulsory prayers, Sunday Quran classes, discussion meetings on Islamic religion and culture, the dress code requiring north Indian *achkan* and cap: 'In the eyes of the Muslims of Bengal, Dhaka with its Muslim Hall was the only seat of higher education where they constituted a majority community and could establish their cultural identity free of Hindu condescension and intellectual arrogance'.[78]

Language as a Site of Contestation

In the process of cultural redefinition, 'Musalmani Bangla' became a contested symbolic issue. As Suniti Kumar Chatterji points out, Persian words in Bengali vocabulary were numerous in the eighteenth century, the result of interaction between Persian and Bengali languages since the thirteenth century. Persian influence, almost entirely lexical, declined in the nineteenth century but the language remained a source for vocabulary in legal, administrative, fiscal, and matters relating to the state. In the colloquial language of Calcutta of the mid-nineteenth century, as in Kaliprasanna Sinha's *Hutom Penchar Naksa*, the percentage of Persian words was about 7, while in the standard Bengali dictionary of 1916 the proportion was only 3.3 per cent, a total of about 2,500 Persian words.[79] A much larger percentage of Persian or Urdu words were used in the legends of Muslim saints and romances produced in the nineteenth century in the tradition of *punthi* literature, printed in crude printing presses in Calcutta, somewhat like the chapbooks in England.[80] This genre of literature was scarcely taken notice of by the elite of Bengal, Hindu or Muslim. Adverse Hindu reaction set in when college-educated Muslims began writing Bengali with a liberal sprinkling of Urdu words in the early decades of the twentieth century. This Hindu reaction took two forms: ridicule of the new 'Musalmani Bangla' used in standard journals and literary works by Muslim authors, and, secondly, a drive towards the Sanskritization of Bengali to differentiate it from the other stream. As usually happens in a communal tussle, each such action produced a reaction, equal and opposite. Some Muslim literary journals accepted the description and styled their usage as 'Musalmani Bangla'[81] Thus on the one hand there developed a spiralling trend towards Urduization and on the other towards Sanskritization. The literary journals in the 1920s and 1930s controlled by Hindu intellectuals lampooned Musalmani Bangla. This kind of humour, ranging from ingenious satires on 'Urdoskrita', that is, a hybrid of Urdu and Sanskrit, to the most abominable ethnic jokes, seems to have been welcome to the Hindu Bengali readership of the day.[82]

On the other side of the fence, Muslim literary men identified Muslimness with the use of Persian and Arabic words. Maulana Mohammad Akram Khan (1868–1968), in his Presidential Address to the Third Muslim Literary Conference in 1918, said that 'in the interest of the special identity of our religion' Muslims could not do without using such words.[83] He was an important intellectual, editor of two influential journals *Muhammadi* and *Daily Azad*, elected to the Legislative Assembly in 1935, and to the presidentship of the Bengal Muslim League between 1941 and 1951. There were many Muslim intellectuals who echoed Akram Khan's views, sometimes in stronger terms, and there were others who differed. Sheikh Habibur Rahman (1890–1961), a poet and assistant editor of *Muhammadi*, wrote in 1921: 'Hindu writers are trying to exile Muslim words out of Bengali literature. Do my Muslim brothers want to exile Hindu words in retaliation?'[84] His answer was 'no', except when there was something directly contrary to Islamic beliefs. Almost all Muslim literary journals rejected Sanskritized Bengali of recent vintage, enriched with 'bones picked up from the graveyard of a dead language', as one of them put it.[85] It was said that many Bengali words had Hindu idolatory inherent in them and at least one Muslim journal issued instructions to the prospective authors that their writings would be rejected unless those were free of 'un-Islamic words'.[86] Syed Ismail Husain Siraji of Sirajganj town in Pabna district of East Bengal, writes in 1923 that Arabic and Persian were languages of the brave and borrowing from them would impart masculinity to Bengali which 'the Tagoreans, in their attempt to make it sweet, have rendered weak and sickly, unfit to be a model for Muslims'.[87]

There were men like Dr Muhammad Shahidullah (1885–1969) who tried to rise above the communal debate. A great linguist (who was, incidentally, rejected as a student by Hindu *pundits* at Sanskrit College, Calcutta, despite having graduated with Sanskrit Honours) and the author of major works of research on Bengali language and literature, Shahidullah made a plea in 1929 for 'the living language' and to save it from the Sanskritist fanatics on the one hand and, on the other, the inventors of 'Arabic-Persian-Urdu-Bengali kidgery'.[88] Such words of moderation fell on deaf ears.

An interesting argument sometimes advanced by Muslim authors was that authenticity called for words commonly used within the Muslim community.[89] 'Srijukta Mohit Lal Majumdar and some like-minded litterateurs have objected to such Arabic and Persian words.... [But] if you do not use them, local colour [sic] will be incomplete....'[90] Mohit Lal Majumdar (1888–1952) was often criticized by the Muslim media. He was, ironically, a teacher at Dhaka University from 1928 to 1944, after having served as a schoolteacher for many years. The author of several books of poems and a competent literary critic, he also wrote rather bitter polemics against 'Muslim Bangla' under various pseudonyms.

Apropos of the debate on so-called Muslim words, there was also a controversy about dialect variations. The use of the 'spoken language' as distinct from the traditionally used 'chaste' or literary language occasioned the controversy. Pramatha Chaudhuri and his literary magazine *Sabuj Patra*, among others, first attracted attention by using the language spoken in or near Calcutta. Their critics, particularly Muslim authors from East Bengal, questioned the smug assumption that the Calcutta dialect was the best suited to be the standard language for literary writings. 'If such a dialect is used, this Calcutta dialect would be incomprehensible in Chittagong, and the Sylhet dialect would be impossible for the Calcutta people to follow', writes the journal *Al Islam* in 1915.[91] Another journal in 1921 condemns 'Pirali literature' (a reference to Tagore's clan), 'low-class argot', and 'peculiar verb declension' in the Calcutta dialect.[92] (The verb declension referred to here is the use of *gelem*, *pelem*, and so on, in place of *gelam*, *pelam*—the normal form). The attack on the use of spoken language in literature merges with opposition to the presumption of using a Calcutta dialect. On the other hand, Syed Wajid Ali (1890–1951) writes in 1928:

> Of the many spoken languages we have to accept one as the model, there is no other way.... The language spoken in West Bengal is relatively cultured and pleasing to the ears compared to the dialect of other parts.... So it is very natural that the language spoken in West Bengal is becoming the language of educated sections in Bengal and the language of literature.

Wajid Ali belonged to West Bengal, to be exact, the district of Hooghly.[93] And he also belonged to a background similar to Pramatha Chaudhuri's: graduation from Cambridge, admitted to the English Bar, distinction in judicial service, success as a barrister in the Calcutta High Court. On certain matters, at least aesthetic ones, there was perhaps a like-mindedness among the elite, whatever their differences might have been in other matters.

Lastly, what was the view of Rabindranath Tagore, the final arbiter? He addressed the question of Musalmani Bangla most directly in an address to a literary conference in 1926 and argued eloquently against the imposition of Urdu for that was like 'throwing out one's mother to spite one's brother'. At the same time, he condemned the Hindu partisan spirit that criticized the 'Musalmani Bangla' language.[94] He believed that literature and culture were the realms where Hindus and Muslims might unite—'Some make the mistake that politics is the arena' for uniting them, but that is a mistake. 'It is our good fortune that we have a common ground—our language and literature. Exchange in that sphere is not fractured by communal differences'. The meeting of minds in that common ground should bring about a unity that politics by itself could not achieve. But how long could language and literature unite people whom politics divided?

A Battle Lost?

Access to education, rival interpretations of history, contestation of communal stereotypes in fiction, textbooks as means of ideologization, Muslim children's perception of a hostile ambience in Hindu-dominated schools, attachment to traditional education dispensed by the *maqtab*, and so on, and language itself were on the agenda of the Muslim intelligentsia in the cultural sphere—and, for the present, we are concerned only with that and not the political agenda. The larger objective was to assert a *Muslim identity*. Was it necessarily and exclusively to be defined in religious terms? And even if it were so defined, would it of necessity entail political separatism?

In the 1920s these questions were being answered in different ways by Muslim intellectuals. Even among the *maulvi*s there were thinkers who could not be identified as votaries of communal separatism or a 'two-nation' theory, though some could. The Anjuman Ulema-e-Bangala, which was active from 1913, owed its inspiration to the Deoband School and it played an important role in mobilizing Muslim public opinion in favour of the Khilafat movement. Among its leaders were men like Dr Muhammad Shahidullah and Maulvi Maniruzzaman Islamabadi who cannot by any stretch of imagination be called anti-Hindu; on the other hand, it also included men like Maulana Akram Khan who, after a phase of accommodation, for example, during the Khilafat movement, eventually adopted an aggressive communal approach.[95] What was the social composition of the Anjuman? My analysis of the list of delegates we have of the third conference of this Anjuman in 1918 shows that of about 340 delegates less than 160 were *maulvi*s, 28 were in the legal profession though holding the title of *maulvi*, 56 were *zamindars*, 60 were government employees, and 40 or so were traders.[96] No doubt *maulvi*s formed the head and front of the Anjuman and their main programme of action was to promote Islamic consciousness, 'to make Musalmans true Musalmans' in accordance with the Anjuman's constitution. It is also true that some of the objects of their attack were perceived as 'Hindu influences' against true Islam, for example, visits to the shrines of *pirs*, music or dancing at weddings, child marriage, caste-like hierarchies, and so on. The Anjuman Ulema-e-Bangala wanted to establish what it conceived as the Islamic way of life among the common Muslim peasants and tribals who were 'half-Islamized'.[97] The members tried to emulate the social role of those whom Richard Eaton[98] has described as 'the religious gentry' at the time of the early expansion of Islam in medieval Bengal, though their position in terms of theological dogma appears to be different.

In the 1920s and 1930s *maulvi*s were mostly poorly paid teachers in schools and *madrasas* and recipients of meagre support from religious trust properties. They were close to their fellow villagers and the people's only conduit of communication to the wider world. Most of the *maulvis* could be described as intellectuals among the villagers and villagers among the intellectuals. If in the 1930s most of them lacked the clarity of Abul Kalam Azad, they also lacked the single-mindedness of Mohammad Ali Jinnah. There is no evidence that till the 1940s they were a homogeneous force working against the unity of Bengal.

In short, the battle for unity across the communal divide was not yet lost in the 1920s. There were among Muslim intellectuals a good number prepared to support that cause.[99] From 1918 to 1923 the journal published by the Bengal Muslim Literary Society and edited by Dr Shahidullah and M. Muzammal Haq generally aimed at preserving communal harmony. This was also the aim of *Muslim Bharat*, again edited by Haq, in its brief life of eighteen months, 1920–1. The literary monthly *Saogat*, started in 1918, had the longest life among Muslim literary journals; M. Nasiruddin the editor, became the nucleus of a group that included liberal writers. More radical but ephemeral was *Naba Yug*, a daily which lasted only a year, 1920–1. It was patronized by A.K. Fazlul Huq and edited by the young communists, Muzaffar Ahmed, and Kazi Nazrul Islam. Then followed *Dhumketu*, 1922, edited by Kazi Nazrul Islam, who gave full-throated support to Hindu–Muslim unity and to the cause of ending India's political subjection. *Soltan* (1923) in the new series, aiming to advance the Khilafat movement and communal amity, was edited by Maulana Maniruzzaman Islamabadi. The weekly *Langal* was started in April 1925 and later merged with *Ganabanee* in August 1926; the second was edited by Muzaffar Ahmad, and the first by Nazrul Islam—both propagated socialism and combated communalism. As we have seen earlier, Kazi Abdul Wadud took the lead in founding in Dhaka in 1926 the Muslim Sahitya Samaj with 'freedom of the mind' as the stated objective; this group brought out the journal *Shikha* for five years from 1927, to fight obscurantism and promote rational criticism of contemporary society.

No doubt, there were identifiable Muslim communalist organs as well, just as there were Hindu ones. Maulana Mohammad Akram Khan (1868–1968) who lived long and wrote a great deal, edited at different times various journals from 1908 onward; his most influential phase was as editor of the monthly *Mohammadi* from November 1927. He edited the pro-Khilafat newspaper *Sevak* (from 1921) and the non-political *Al Islam*, but his claim to fame was as the chief progenitor of Muslim identity consciousness, eventually pointing towards separatism.[100] Numerous ephemeral journals must have also played that role along with the chapbooks, tracts, *punthi* literature in print, and so on, of the kind mentioned by Abul Mansur Ahmad.[101] Rafiuddin Ahmad has focused attention on the solidarity mobilization achieved by the rural *mullahs* in the late nineteenth century.[102] There was a qualitative difference between that and the kind of separatist political agenda of Maulana Akram Khan and his like in the decade leading to the Partition of 1947. To bring back the purity of Islam was, after all, in part a response to the Hindu *shuddhi* and *sangathan* movements; it was thus a natural interactive process that generated indigenous Bengali Muslim consciousness about 'purity' until the separatist political agenda was handed down from above by the central all-India Muslim leadership. Till that crucial moment in the development of Bengali Muslim consciousness, options had been open. Our conclusion in this regard is in accord with Suranjan Das's in his study of communal riots in Bengal from 1905 to 1947:

> At one historical juncture religious loyalties could cut across all forms of class and sectional consciousness, while on other occasions ethnic, regional, class or linguistic identities might transcend religious bonds.... Several possibilities were thus open for the convergence of popular identities with organised politics. In the specific configuration of Bengal's social, economic and political conditions, a predominantly communal form would develop only in the 1940s.[103]

Polarization was already in evidence from 1926 when communal riots occurred—but the outcome of the brief survey we have made is clear: a new cultural consciousness in the Muslim community was developing but there was till the late 1930s an openness to views that offered alternatives to the 'two-nation theory'.

Chitta Ranjan Das made a very insightful statement in 1917 that went against the grain of the common Hindu *bhadralok* perception of Bengali Muslim consciousness as 'anti-national' *ab initio* and of necessity. C.R. Das's argument was that 'the spirit of nationality spoke among the Mahomedans' at the time of the Swadeshi movement, although the articulate Musalmans were generally opposed to that movement and supportive of the partition of 1905. 'If the Swadeshi movement was the first step in our national self-consciousness so far as Hindus are concerned, I say it was equally the first step of Mahomedan self-consciousness. Its appearance was against the Nation but its reality was in our favour'. In his speech as President of the Provincial Congress Conference in 1917, C.R. Das conceded that there was 'disunion' between the two communities but it was only the result of 'interested machinations of a few self-seekers'. He asked those who 'boast of our Hinduism' to give up 'false pride of birth and breed' and to cooperate with Muslims and lower castes 'and only then your labours will be crowned with success'.[104] Paul Greenough, in a study of Das's politics, makes a perceptive observation that Das's 'unruffled acceptance of this [Hindu–Muslim] conflict as an inevitable, even desirable, development, stemmed from his sophisticated understanding that conflict sometimes serves to forge an encompassing unity between combatants'.[105] Thus C.R. Das undoubtedly looked realistically upon the development of Muslim consciousness as an inevitable and, indeed, a positive development. Failure to negotiate with that reality was not peculiar to Bengal, but it cost Bengal and Punjab more dearly than any other part of India.

To reject what C.R. Das called Muslim 'self-consciousness' and to identify that as communalism was a part of this failure. Gopal Haldar in Muslim-dominated Noakhali recalled and analysed the failure in 1923–5:

> In reality the nationalism on which our political consciousness was founded—built from the days of Rajnarayan Bose and Bankim [Chattopadhyay]—the roots of that nationalism were in question. The more the Muslim educated middle-class increased in number and acquired consciousness of economic and political matters, the more were they alienated by the nature of Hindu nationalism.... If on the basis of India's composite culture a composite nationalism had been evolved from the beginning, perhaps there would have been no opportunity for a third party to play a divisive role.... No doubt Rabindranath [Tagore] had realized that the history [of India] was one of an endeavour to reach unity in diversity. That endeavour was incomplete.... What this country needed most of all was Atheism.[106]

Gopal Haldar might have been unaware at the time that Tagore felt the same urge to preach atheism. It was an untypical urge in Tagore and his speech on these lines remains unknown because it was never included in his published works, not even in the thirty volumes of

Collected Works. In deep disgust, after having witnessed the communal riot in Calcutta in 1926, Tagore spoke these unremembered words for atheism on 21 April 1926 at Santiniketan:

> The essential truth inherent in religion has to be tested in all its aspects just as one tests scientific knowledge.... The slightest inertia in this matter will allow all kinds of untrue superstition, narrow communal feelings, meaningless rituals, all manner of dark filth to pile on the throne of Religion to suffocate and kill Religion.... Straightforward atheism is preferable to this terrible thing, the delusion of religiosity. If India burns to ashes this mockery of religion and truly embraces atheism, if India searches for the genuine religion and genuine atheism, then India will be born anew. I do not see any path other than beginning anew by burning in the fire of atheism all perversions of religion.[107]

Tagore certainly was no atheist, but he spoke of scientific rationality in an unusual moment of anguish during the communal riots of 1926. But the rationality Tagore spoke of was never to be sufficiently internalized in Bengal's culture to stop or even slightly check the avalanche of communal discord. Since the end of the Bengal Renaissance, that was one of the underlying texts of the palimpsest of Bengal history on which Sir Cyril Radcliffe inscribed his signature in 1947.

Notes

1. Aijaz Ahmad, 'Azad's Careers: Roads Taken and Not Taken', in *Islam and Indian Nationalism: Reflections on Abul Kalam Azad*, ed. M. Hasan (Delhi, 1992), pp. 167–8.
2. A.E. Porter, ICS, *Report on the Census of Bengal in 1931* (Calcutta, 1932), p. 387.
3. Porter, *Census of Bengal in 1931*, p. 383.
4. Tazeen M. Murshid, *The Sacred and the Secular: Bengali Muslim Discourses, 1871–1977* (Delhi, 1995).
5. Abdul Karim in *Islam Pracharak* V, nos 7–8 (1903).
6. Mohammad Ilias, in *Muslim Darpan* II, no. 1 (1926).
7. We are deeply indebted to a collection of writings in Bengali Muslim journals published by the Bangla Akademi of Dhaka, Mustafa Nurul Islam (ed.), *Samayik patre jiban o janamat, 1901–1930* (Dhaka, 1977), cited hereafter as *SPJJ*.
8. Siraji, 'The Identity of the Bengali Muslims', *Al Islam* III, no. 4 (1917), *SPJJ*, p. 153.

9. Ibn-e-Aj, in *Islam Pracharak* VIII, no. 8 (1908), *SPJJ*, p. 70.
10. Ahmad Ali, in *Al Islam* III, no. 11 (1917), *SPJJ*, p. 289.
11. M. Sirajul Haq, in *Raoshan Hidayat* II, no. I (1925), *SPJJ*, p. 264.
12. Musharaf Husain, in *Kohinur* I, no. 3, 1899, *SPJJ*, p. 255.
13. M. Islamabadi, *Al Islam* VI, no. 10 (1920), *SPJJ*, p. 214.
14. Editorial, *Islam Darshan* II, no. 11 (1922), *SPJJ*, p. 215.
15. Editorial, *Soltan* VIII, no. 4 (1923), *SPJJ*, p. 216.
16. M.A. Hakim, *Banga-nur* I, no. 3 (1920), *SPJJ*, p. 154.
17. M. Elahi Baksh, *Soltan* VIII, no. 48 (1924).
18. M. Serajul Haq, *Raoshan Hidayat* II, no. 7 (1926).
19. Siraji, *Soltan* VIII, no. 14 (1923), *SPJJ*, p. 156.
20. Editorial, *Dainik Taraqqi* I, no. 1 (1926), *SPJJ*, p. 159.
21. Abdul Wadud, in *Islam Darshan* I, no. 4 (1920), *SPJJ*, p. 244.
22. Editorial, *Shariat-e-Islam* III, no. 11 (1928), *SPJJ*, p. 245.
23. Editorial, *Islam Darshan* II, no. 6 (1921), *SPJJ*, p. 245.
24. Siraji, in *Soltan* VIII, no. 17 (1923), *SPJJ*, p. 127.
25. Editorial, *Raoshan Hidayat* II, no. 11 (1926), *SPJJ*, p. 128.
26. Islamabadi, *Al Islam* IV, no. 10 (1918), *SPJJ*, p. 130.
27. M. Maniruzzaman, in *Islam Pracharak* V, nos 9–10 (1903), *SPJJ*, p. 117.
28. Syeduddin Khan, in *Saogat* VII, no. 2 (1929).
29. Editorial, *Islam Pracharak* I, no. 1 (1891), *SPJJ*, p. 129.
30. M. Raoshan Ali Chowdhury, in *Islam Pracharak* VI, nos 1–2 (1904).
31. 'Terrible Torture of Women in Muslim Society', *Islam Pracharak* V, nos 7–8 (1903), *SPJJ*, p. 82.
32. M. Akram Khan, in *Masik Mohammadi* I, no. 3 (1927), *SPJJ*, p. 86.
33. Mrs M. Rahman, notable as a rare piece of writing by a woman, *Saugat* VII, no. 1 (1929), *SPJJ*, p. 76.
34. For instance, editorials in *Ananda Bazar Patrika*, 5, 7, 8, 10, and 11 April 1922.
35. Nariaki Nakazato, *Agrarian System in Eastern Bengal, 1870–1910*, Calcutta, 1994, ch. 10; Rafiuddin Ahmed, *The Bengal Muslims, 1871–1906: A Quest for Identity* (New Delhi, 1981), pp. 56–9.
36. For example, Habibur Rahman, in *Islam Darshan* V, no. 2 (1925), *SPJJ*, p. 223.
37. For example, Ahmed Ali, in *Al Islam* III (1917), *SPJJ*, p. 288
38. Mohammad Ilias, in *Moslem Darpan* II, no. 1 (1926), *SPJJ*, pp. 157–8.
39. *Navarur* I, no. 4 (1903), *SPJJ*, p. 276
40. Zaheda Ahmad, 'State and Education', in *History of Bangladesh*, ed. S. Islam, (Dhaka, 1992), vol. III, p. 129.
41. *Islam Darshan* IV, no. 3 (1924).
42. Ahmad Ali, *Al Islam* III, no. 11 (1917), *SPJJ*, p. 289.

43. *Nabanur* I, no. 11 (1903); *Islam Pracharak* 8, no. 11 (1907); *Shakha* I (1926), *SPJJ*, pp. 5, 8, 10.
44. *General Reports on Public Instruction*, of the Government of Bengal, in M. Shamim Firdous, *British Policy on Education and Muslims in India* (Calcutta, 2013), p. 10.
45. Firdous, *British Policy on Education and Muslims*, pp. 14–18.
46. Rabindranath Tagore, 'Swami sraddhananda', *Pravasi* (1926), reprinted in *Kalantar* (Calcutta, 1937, new edn 1993), p. 319.
47. Rabindranath Tagore, 'Hindu–Musalman' (1922), *Kalantar* (1993), p. 313.
48. Rabindranath Tagore, 'Samasya', *Pravasi* (1921), *Kalantar* (1937, reprint 1993), p. 239.
49. Muhammad Shahidullah, in *Soltan* VIII, no. 2 (1923).
50. M. Shahidullah, in *Saogat* VI, no. 10 (1929), *SPJJ*, p. 414.
51. M. Shahidullah, in *Al Islam* II, no. 2 (1916).
52. Kazi Nazrul Islam, in *Ganavani*, 2 September 1926, *SPJJ*, p. 266.
53. Nazrul Islam, in *Ganavani*, 26 August 1926, *SPJJ*, p. 286.
54. Sadat Ali Akhand, *Saogat* VI, no. 5 (1928).
55. Muhammad Shah, *In Search of an Identity: Bengali Moslems, 1880–1940* (Mellen Press, 1996); Murshid, *The Sacred and the Secular*.
56. Anwarul Qadir, in *Shikha* I (1927), *SPJJ*, p. 10.
57. M. Ahmed, *Shikha* I (1927), *SPJJ*, p. 15.
58. T. Ahmed, in *Shikha* I (1927), *SPJJ*, p. 323.
59. A. Qadir, in *Shikha* I (1927), *SPJJ*, p. 272.
60. R.A. Ahmed, in *Shikha* (1927), *SPJJ*, p. 304.
61. Abul Hashim, *Amar jiban o bibhag-purva bangladesher rainiti* (Calcutta, 1988), pp. 22–3.
62. Abul Mansur Ahmad, *Amar dekha rajnitir panchas bacchar* (Dhaka, 1995), pp. 1–5.
63. A.M. Ahmad, *Rajnitir panchas bacchar*, p. 21.
64. M.M. Hossain, *Amar jibanee* (Calcutta, 1908–9), vol. I, pp. 164–5, 254, 286, cited in Mohammad Shah, 'Social and Cultural Basis of Bengali Nationalisms' in *History of Bangladesh*, ed. Islam, vol. III, p. 777.
65. M. Idris, 'Kaifiyat', *Al Islam* V, no. 2 (1920); M. Shahidullah, 'Amader sahityik daridyata', *Al Islam* II, no. 2 (1916); Siraji, 'Itihas charchar abashyakata', *Al Islam* II, no. 5 (1916)—all in *SPJJ*, p. 24ff.
66. *Ananda Bazar Patrika*, 2 December 1933, p. 4, editorial, 'Shikshae sawpradayikata'.
67. M.M. Islamabadi, *Bharate musalman sabhyata* (Calcutta, 1914).
68. Kazi Abdul Wadud, *Hindu musalman virodh* (Calcutta, 1935), pp. 12–17.
69. These were comments on Bankimchandra Chatterjee's *Chandrasekhar, Durgesh-Nandini*, and *Anandamath* in *Al Islam* III, no. 2 (1324 BS);

Islam Pracharak V, nos 9–10 (1310 BS); *Soltan* VIII, no. 17 (1330 BS)—all in *SPJJ*, pp. 351–6.

70. A.N. Chowdhury, 'Banga sahitye musalman ramanir sthan', *Al Islam*, I, 1, 1322 BS; Sophia Khatun, 'Bangla sahitye anudarata', *Bangiya Musalman Sahitya Patrika* V, no. 4 (1329 BS)—all in *SPJJ*.
71. S.A. Mohammad Ismail Siraji, in *Islam Pracharak* V, nos 11–12 (1310 BS), *SPJJ*, p. 356.
72. For example the criticism of D.L. Roy's *Mebar Patan*, *Rana Pratap*, *Nurjahan*, and *Shahjahan* by S.M. Akbaruddin, in *Al Islam* II, no. 9 (1323 BS); *Al Islam* II, no. 10 (1323 BS)—all in *SPJJ*, pp. 261, 367–8; this critic was generally liberal minded and secular in outlook.
73. For the chronology and biographical details of Muslim personalities I have used, for want of a dictionary of national biography of Bangladesh, Jafar Alam, *Bangladesher smaraneeya baraneeya* (Indian ed., Calcutta, 1995).
74. This and the following statistics of Muslim participation in education have been collected by Zaheeda Ahmad, 'State and Education' in *History of Bangladesh*, ed. Islam, vol. III, ch. 20.
75. Naresh Chandra Sengupta, *Yuga parikrama* (Calcutta, 1961), vol. I, p. 9.
76. Sukumar Sen, *Bangla sahityer itihas*, vol. IV, p. 254.
77. Z. Ahmad, State and Education', pp. 136–7.
78. Z. Ahmad, State and Education', p. 138.
79. Suniti Kumar Chatterji, *The Origin and Development of the Bengali Language* (Calcutta, 1926), vol. I, pp. 201–23.
80. *Bat-tala* literature, of both Hindu and Muslim authors, comprises a class of publication scarcely studied; two recent studies are by Sumanta Banerjee and Gautam Bhadra.
81. Hamid Ali uses the term in *Basana* II, no. 1, (1316 BS), perhaps the earliest known (AD 1909).
82. Haladhar Bhar (pseudonym of Mohit Ghosh), 'Urodskrita pracharinee sabha', *Sanibarer Chithi* (1339 BS).
83. M. Akram Khan, *Bangiya Musalman Sahitya Patrika* I, no. IV (1325 BS), *SPJJ*, p. 333.
84. Sheikh Habibur Rahman, in *Islam Darshan* II, no. 8 (1328 BS), *SPJJ*, p. 336.
85. Editorial, *Soltan* VIII, no. 9 (July 1923), *SPJJ*, p. 349.
86. *Raushan Hidayat* II, no. 9 (1333 BS); *Soltan* VIII (31 December 1923), *SPJJ*.
87. Siraji, in *Soltan* VIII (13 August 1923), *SPJJ*, p. 338.
88. M. Shahidullah, *Muazzin* II, nos 1–2 (1336 BS), *SPJJ*.
89. Editorial, *Muslim Bharat* I, nos 5 (1327 BS), *SPJJ*, p. 334.
90. Editorial, *Muslim Bharat* I, nos 5 (1327 BS), *SPJJ* p. 335.
91. S. Ahmad, *Al Islam* I, no. 10 (1322 BS), *SPJJ*, p. 344.

92. *Islam Darshan* II, no. 9 (1328 BS), *SPJJ*, p. 345.
93. S. Wajed Ali, 'Bengali musalmaner sahitya samasya', *Masik Muhammadi* I, no. 7 (1335 BS), *SPJJ*, p. 346.
94. Rabindranath Tagore, 'Sahitya sammelan' (1333 BS) in *Sahityar pathe, Rabindra Rachanavalee*, vol. XII, p. 506.
95. Sunil Kanti Dey, *Anjuman-e-Ulema-e Bangala, 1913–19* (Calcutta, 1992), pp. 1–32.
96. Dey, *Anjuman-e-Ulema-e Bangala*, pp. 102–15.
97. M. Islamabadi in *Al Islam* (1327 BS), pp. 63–5, cited in Dey, *Anjuman-e-Ulema-e Bangala*, pp. 28–9; Shahidullah was to be sent to Assam on a proselytizing mission by Islamabadi, but funds to pay him a subsistence allowance were unavailable, Dey, *Anjuman-e-Ulema-e Bangala*, p. 31.
98. Richard M. Eaton's *The Rise of Islam and the Bengal Frontier, 1204–1760* (University of California, 1993) contextualizes the role of the Muslim 'religious gentry' in the agrarian order in Bengal and the growing centralization of authority; in the late 19th century there was a shift away from the openness characteristic of the early Sufis in Bengal. On the spread of Islam a work of equal value has not received attention—M. Emanul Haq's *A History of Sufism in Bengal* (Dhaka, 1975).
99. I have depended on the ownership and publication data of Muslim periodicals in Nurul Islam, *Sambadpatre jiban o janamat, 1901–1930* (Dhaka, 1977), pp. 427–1, and *Bengali Muslim Public Opinion as Reflected in the Bengali Press, 1901–1930* (Dhaka, 1973), both invaluable sources.
100. Amalendu De, *Bangali buddhijibee o bicchinnatabad* (Calcutta, 1991), pp. 224–6.
101. A.M. Ahmad, *Rajnitir panchas bacchar*, ch. 1.
102. R. Ahmad, *The Bengal Muslims, 1871–1906*; Soumitra Sinha, *The Quest for Modernity and the Bengali Muslim, 1921–47* (Calcutta, 1995); Hosainur Rahman, *Hindu–Muslim Relations in Bengal, 1905–47* (Bombay, 1974), a doctoral dissertation supervised by Nirmal Kumar Bose; Tanika Sarkar, 'Communal Riots in Bengal' in *Communal and Pan-Islamic Trends in Colonial India*, ed. M. Hasan (Delhi, 1981); Chandi Prasad Sarkar, 'Bengal Muslim Politics, Society and Culture during the Khilafat and Non-Cooperation Movements', *Bengal: Past and Present* 107 (January 1984); Suranjan Das, *Communal Riots in Bengal, 1905–47* (New Delhi, 1975).
103. S. Das, *v*, p. 25.
104. C.R. Das, *India for Indians: Speeches. October 1917–February 1921* (Madras, 1921), pp. 62–3; *Deshbandhu Chitta Ranjan: Brief Survey of Life and Work. Provincial Conference Speeches, etc.* (Calcutta, 1926), citied in Paul Greenough, 'Death of an Uncrowned King', mimeo, Iowa University, 1984, pp. 18–23.

105. Greenough, 'Death of an Uncrowned King', p. 22.
106. Gopal Haldar, *Rupnarayaner kule* (autobiography) (Calcutta, 1978), vol. II, pp. 145–7.
107. This unusual sermon was delivered by Rabindranath Tagore at Santiniketan on 21 April 1926; it was reproduced in *Pravasee* in June 1926, from notes made by Kshitimohan Sen; on the historical context, see Sabyasachi Bhattacharya, 'The Archaeology of a Poem', *The Telegraph*, Calcutta, 20 August 1993.

5

GANDHIAN POLITICS AND ITS ALTERNATIVES 1920–35

Historians of the nationalist movement usually locate Gandhian politics at the centre of the narrative from 1919 and other lines of political action are judged in relation to it. To decentre the story and to shift the focus is not easy but it is essential to enable us to understand the 1920s as well as the long-term trends in Bengal. Mahatma Gandhi carried all before him in a tidal wave in most parts of India from 1920. *But in Bengal there were a number of alternatives to Gandhism that made the political tide run through many channels*. These alternatives ranged from revolutionary nationalism wedded to violent means, to the constitutionalism of the far right which questioned the boycott programme, not to speak of the Communist and other Leftist movements. Wherever in India such alternative political paths were well established, large sections of the politically active did not follow the Gandhian line to the exclusion of all others, although they lent support to it at times. The Maharashtra region was a prominent example, and this applied to Bengal as well for two reasons. First, some of these alternatives were more deeply entrenched positions in Bengal because of the early politicization of this region. It was quite unlike the situation in regions where Gandhi's movement *began* the process of politicization. Second, the institutions and the networks in the public sphere were more complex in Bengal than in some other parts of the country where civil society was relatively less developed in terms of voluntary associative activities of the proto-political kind. (If one disaggregates the picture to look at different parts within Bengal, the same generalization can be sustained.) From the late nineteenth century, Bengal, particularly urban Bengal, was endowed with a strong tradition of public activities in numerous voluntary associations that had not only their cultural and social agendas but also functioned as catchment areas for political activists to whom work in the public sphere was not necessarily identical to that for the Congress under Mahatma Gandhi.

The outcome was that in Bengal the following acquired by the Gandhian Congress in periods of mass movement at the turn of the 1920s and the 1930s was substantially lost to the contrary pulls, for Gandhian politics was looked upon in Bengal as *one of several possible alternatives*. Swings away from Gandhi's Congress, in terms of public sympathy and participation of the politically active, strengthened Chitta Ranjan Das's Swaraj Party during 1923–5, the *biplabis* or revolutionary nationalists during 1923–5 and 1930–5, and from the 1930s the Leftist following of M.N. Roy and Muzaffar Ahmed who held throughout an independent course of their own.

Party politics apart, at the ideational level Gandhian politics was questioned in Bengal in a fundamental way in the 1920s. Rabindranath Tagore entered into a debate with Mahatma Gandhi. While they were completely in accord on many issues and were closely in touch through correspondence since Tagore's renunciation of knighthood in protest against the Jallianwallah Bagh massacre, Tagore found that the agenda of the Congress in 1920–1 fell short of his expectations. Gandhi responded sharply to the criticism and there ensued a debate between May and October 1922 in *Modern Review* and Gandhi's journal, *Young India*. 'The movement which has now succeeded the *swadeshi* agitation [of 1905–8] is ever so much greater and has moreover extended its influence all over India', wrote Tagore.

> Previously the vision of our political leaders had never reached beyond the English-knowing classes.... Nothing resembling self-sacrifice or true feeling for their countrymen was visible. At this juncture Mahatma Gandhi came and stood at the cottage door of the destitute millions, clad as one of themselves, and talking to them in their own language. Here was Truth at last. So the name of Mahatma, which was given to him, was his true name.[1]

But while paying the Mahatma this and many other tributes, Tagore thought that his noble concept of *satyagraha* was being abused by politicians as if it was a mere political stratagem. They had converted Gandhi's message into a mindless *mantra* and thus strengthened bigotry and inertia. Apart from this objection to an instrumentalist view of *satyagraha*, divested of its moral core, Tagore also posed the question as to what was the rationale for boycott of schools and colleges when there was no alternative educational system. Tagore himself was the severest critic of the British-sponsored educational system, but the question remained: 'Our students are bringing their offering of sacrifice to what? Not to a fuller education, but to non-education'. Such a programme could not be sustained for long, and in this matter Tagore proved to be right.

Moreover, Tagore was sceptical of the *charkha* and the burning of foreign cloth as the panacea for India's problems. He questioned 'the magical formula that foreign cloth is impure' and that spinning is a sacrament; the question 'belongs mainly to economic science' but to talk in terms of sin and impurity is to replace the rationality of economics with a moral dictum. The objection here is not so much to the substantive point about foreign manufactures, but to the Gandhian terms of discourse, the use of moral language in place of the economic. And Tagore also asked a pertinent question: How long would it be possible 'to hide ourselves away from commerce with the outside world?'[2] Finally, Tagore was apprehensive that an isolationalist obscurantism might develop if India, obsessed with the 'sins' and shortcomings of Western civilization, failed to take a broader view of human civilization as a whole. He might have seen seeds of this obscurantism not so much in Gandhi himself as in the mind and words of the self-proclaimed Gandhians.

Gandhi's reply to this critique was that he could not agree that his followers had fallen victim to bigotry, though to slavishly mimic his message would be truly abominable bigotry. As regards boycott of educational institutions, that was fully justified for they 'rendered us helpless and godless'.[3] On the *charkha* question he reiterated, 'I consider it a sin to wear foreign cloth. I must confess I do not draw a sharp or any distinction between economics and ethics'.[4] On the question of Gandhi's views on the machine and 'the materialism of the West' the battle was not fully joined at this time. We shall follow in a later chapter the continuation of this debate. On the whole, the differences between Gandhi and Tagore revealed in the debate in the 1920s a fundamental chasm between two philosophies and Tagore's position raised a resonance in some minds.

On the other hand, Tagore faced extremely hostile criticism from the Gandhians in Bengal. Scurrilous poems and spoofs lampooning him were published in Bengali newspapers. For example, according to an editorial in the *Ananda Bazar Patrika*,

> The *charkha* movement has been revealed to the Poet's intelligence as a hoax.... Only an extraordinary genius can say such an extraordinary thing.... The ludicrous opinions of the Poet may appeal to those who live in a dream world, but those grounded in the soil of the country ... will, no doubt, feel that the poet's useless labours are sad and pitiful.[5]

And the press statement of a well-known Bengali Gandhian says that Tagore 'is unfit to be a priest at the sacred sacrificial rites (*yajna*) for freedom.... Few have won accolades of the world equal to what Rabindranath has won and he deserved them. But why should he be aggrieved if he does not get accolades which he cannot claim in other spheres?'[6] Harsh words, and about a man who was already something of a Bengali icon.

Thus a great contestation for the Bengali mind was in progress in the 1920s between Gandhian politics and its critics. That is not to say that Mahatma Gandhi was under attack. Tagore implicitly made a distinction between Gandhian *politics* and Gandhism in the broader sense. In raising questions about the trend of Gandhian politics—and later the ways of the Congress in the 1930s—Tagore represented a strand of thinking that would not be deterred from looking hard at all alternatives. A multiplicity of alternative politics was nurtured in Bengal due to early politicization and a strong tradition of public sphere activities in the form of voluntary associations of all sorts.

There were parts of India where the Indian National Congress virtually began public associative activities; in other parts there were such activities but these were limited to caste mobility movements or religious sectarian congregations. Among the few regions in India where there was a long tradition of institutionalized activities in the public sphere, through societies registered under the Registration of Societies Act of 1860 or through less formal associations, Bengal was one.

Within the constraints of a colonial system where Indians were members of a subject race rather than citizens vis-à-vis the state, public associative activities built a civic tradition, social networks facilitating coordinated action, and eventually a capacity for aggregation of public interest at levels beyond the immediate locality and group. These activities in the realm of civil society, far from the bastions carefully controlled by the colonial state, created a social resource that had a political potential, namely an organizational and coordinating capacity in individuals and groups that enabled them eventually to participate in political activity.[7]

In the emergence of a public sphere and in developing this kind of social resource, the late nineteenth century witnessed a beginning. 'The responses of the common people to the policies of the government—the almost spontaneous meeting in the *bazaar*, the deputation of the elders to the *sarkar*, the memorializing and petitioning about grievances' formed, then, one end of the spectrum. At the other end were 'tightly knit and highly organized groups, each more or less homogeneous in terms of economic interests and pursuing objectives specific to those interests' such as *zamindars*' and traders' associations. In between, typologically speaking, was another kind of associative activity that comprised heterogeneous interests, in a coalition of mutual accommodation, pursuing philanthropic or social reformist or cultural agendas of their own. None of these were 'political' activities but 'the efforts to organize opinion, to publicize grievances or demands, lobbying, and so on—these are exercises that limber up the political mind. The consequences of such activity extended far beyond the immediate arena of action'.[8] This late-nineteenth-century scene forms the background to the proto-political and explicitly political activities of the early twentieth century.

In Bengal in the first decades of this century, the richness of civic life in terms of associative activities is well known. Those located in Calcutta figure prominently in that history, for example, the Dawn Society (1902) founded by Satish Chandra Mukherjee, or the Swasthya Akademi (1904) founded by Sarala Devi, or the Atmonnati Samiti (1897) of Wellington Square. That there were also similar social initiatives in the *mofussil* as well is often forgotten: the Suhrid Society (1902) of Mymensingh, Bandhab Sammilanee (1902) of Chandernagore, Swasthya Kendra (1904) of Changripota in the 24 Parganas,

Swadesh Bandhab Samiti (1905) of Barisal, and so on. Such voluntary associations were engaged in a wide range of activities—*akharas* or gymnasia for physical exercise, 'moral instruction', literary studies, and social work (*jana seva*, a new concept). The focus of activity could change over time; for instance, a founder-member of the Anushilan Samiti describes how it began in March 1902 as a Boxing Club and took on programmes of self-instruction in *biplabi* (revolutionary nationalist) ideas and, when the police woke up to what was happening, transformed itself for a while into the Bengal Young Men's Zamindari Cooperative Society![9] Associations inclined towards revolutionary nationalism were driven underground during 1907–9 due to enactment of new laws and rigorous application of old ones in reaction to the Swadeshi agitation; these societies turned away from their public sphere activities or began to look upon them as a facade to cover their secret ones. But other voluntary associations continued with their social and cultural agendas and in the process laid out a recruiting ground for political workers; they maintained the vitalizing link with their public—limited as it was mainly to the middle class *bhadralok*—that secret societies were bereft of.

These voluntary associations were nodal points in a social network that generated an organizational capacity and a civic tradition we must not ignore, though the activities of many of them may appear rather banal and unexciting compared with bomb-making by secret societies or fiery speeches at Congress meetings. The associative activities in the public sphere served as a nursery where a 'hundred flowers bloomed', although many wilted soon. In this chapter we shall consider (*a*) Gandhian politics and its alternative in the Swarajist agenda of Chitta Ranjan Das; (*b*) alternatives to the Gandhian path proposed by the *biplabi* or revolutionary nationalists; (*c*) the agenda that emerged in Left politics and began to challenge the hegemony of the Gandhian Congress.

The Gandhian Congress and the Swarajist Alternative

In 1921–2, the Non-cooperation Movement swept all before it in Bengal. Tagore wrote that it was as if Mahatma Gandhi stood at the cottage door, and as soon as 'true love' appeared at the country's door 'it flew open.... At the touch of Truth, the pent-up forces of the soul are set free'.[10] To understand this victory in the battle for the mind of the people it is not very illuminating to offer a list of places and dates. Instead we propose to consider the personal narrative of one individual touched by the political tide.

Nripendra Chandra Banerji (1885–1949) born in a middle-income Brahmin family in Dhaka district was thiry-six years old and a teacher in the Government College at Chittagong town in 1921. His autobiography contains a rare first-person account of the impact of the Non-cooperation Movement on the ground. Nothing except good results in examinations and a reputation for teaching in good colleges, including Presidency College at Calcutta, distinguished him at the time as out of the ordinary. He had been 'morally and mentally attuned' to respond to Gandhi's call to resign government service and to boycott colleges like the one he served—indeed he had listened to Gandhi's speeches with admiration at the Nagpur Congress ('this man cuts us all out, I said to my own mind'), but there were other considerations as well: 'I was ruminating how I could pull on without any income. I was then earning about Rs 700 monthly'.[11] That was a great deal of money in 1921 and he had many dependants. Reflecting on the experiences of his generation, he goes on:

> The lessons of 1905–19 had been seared into our hearts and brains: we had passed through peaceful constitutionalism, underground terrorist coups, widespread boycott of British goods and institutions.... We had seen the revolutionary movement and struggle of Bengali youthful elements who had the hardihood to sail uncharted seas for years, without much visible support from the country's masses, for the masses were as yet absolutely disorganized and young Bengal dreamt of a forcible seizure of power by a small minority—a dream that could never come true....[12]

To such a person, Gandhi at Champaran (1917) and then at the Nagpur Congress (1920) with his 'tremendous power and drive' and his ability to communicate with masses of people, appeared as the man of the hour. Banerji was mentally preparing to burn his boats, resign his job and join the Non-cooperation Movement when Chitta Ranjan Das, at the head of the movement in Bengal, visited him at Chittagong. Banerji told Das that while his heart was with the Congress he was worried how he could do without a salary; Das, who probably earned per hour what Banerji earned in a month, said he too had wrestled with the same question but had decided to 'take the leap he had to take, in faith and in scorn of consequence'. The two men talked for hours and it was midnight when they broke off. Banerji wrote in his autobiography,

> I kept awake till the small hours of the morning and had not the courage to tell even my wife who was by my side that I was resigning and that she and the children and the family must perforce prepare for a life of great hardship and uncertainty.... I wrote out a simple letter of resignation.... With this note I saw C.R. Das at about 6 in the morning.[13]

Thus, in March 1921, Banerji took the plunge, no easy task for a *bhadralok*.

He forthwith joined the newly formed District Congress Committee. Jatindra Mohan Sengupta, a prosperous barrister and his European wife, Nellie, had already been converted by C.R. Das; Sengupta became the president and Banerji second in command. The DCC included the head of the Chittagong town Sikh *gurdwara*, a *swamiji* who had resigned his job at an engineering college to become a monk and a labour leader, a Bengali Hindu entrepreneur who set up the first Indian bank in Chittagong, a local Muslim leader, and a sprinkling of pleaders in the local court of law. The District Congress Committee was aided by a band of young lawyers, schoolteachers (including the future *biplabi* or revolutionary, Surya Sen), local journalists, and Hindu and Muslim students. The District Congress's mode of agitation was to send a group of district-level leaders to each village, to open each meeting with patriotic songs, to talk about *satyagraha* as a method, and to collect money for the *Swaraj* fund and recruits for the party. Altogether one lakh members were thus enrolled.[14]

As this movement gathered pace it became involved in popular causes other than those originally on the agenda (propagating the *charkha* and boycott of government institutions). The labour force of the Chittagong branch of the British-owned Burmah Oil Company organized a union with the active help of the *Congressi babus*, including Banerji. The ringleader, close to Banerji, was dismissed by the oil company. Banerji and two other district committee members encouraged the labourers to go on strike; what was considered sensational was the *babus* 'fraternizing with them and sitting down to dine in the open with ordinary coolies'. The strike was a success and the British manager settled for a compromise. This incident was followed by a more well-known popular movement. During 1921 Congress workers' propaganda had encouraged a belief among the tea garden labourers in Assam that Gandhi Raj was at hand. There was a mass exodus of several thousand labourers from Assam towards Chandpur, the rail and steamer head on the Meghna River joining Assam to the rest of India. At the request of the European owners and managers of tea gardens the assembled labourers at Chandpur were dispersed by means of baton- and bayonet-charges.

> The news of the atrocity reached Chittagong, and I immediately ordered a fortnight's boycott of the law courts. All approaches to the town by road or river were controlled by our volunteer guards and no litigants could reach the town.... The subordinate officials everywhere were with us or for us: so no clash occurred anywhere.... Soon after [J.M.] Sengupta and myself conferred with some Indian employees of the Assam Bengal Railway—and formed a very loose Railway Union.... A small piece of paper on which J.M. Sengupta wrote out his directive for a general strike was carried from railway centre to railway centre and after 48 hours, the entire Indian Staff had practically struck work. The entire Railway from Dibrugarh and higher up down to Chandpur was paralysed and very soon the Steamer agency men at Chandpur, Barisal, Narayanganj and Goalando, the main riverine ports, also followed suit.... Our plain object was to paralyse the entire administration by a General Strike all over the country....[15]

When matters reached this point, alarm bells began to ring in higher quarters. 'The Calcutta Congress coterie did not see eye to eye with Sengupta and myself with regard to the Railway and Steamer Strikes (which had now become practically one unified movement) and would do nothing to rouse the East Bengal and East Indian Railways'. Moreover, all the District Congress funds were exhausted to pay allowances and doles to distressed workers on strike 'and some of the office *babus* took our strike money and then betrayed the cause'. The railway company refused to enter negotiations for they were not worried about loss. (British capital, exclusively used to build railways, enjoyed a government guarantee against loss.) C.F. Andrews and C.R. Das came down to 'ease the situation'. The 'European bloc' (presumably British business interests and the bureaucracy) had realized that it was 'a revolutionary political strike and not an ordinary labour strike'. And Banerji writes that 'we found later ... Gandhiji was not thinking as yet in terms of such a revolution'. In the meantime, 'a few of our boys in despair took to violent ways', for example, derailment of goods trains by sabotage. Banerji was summoned to Calcutta where, in the presence of Gandhi himself, he was chastised by the provincial leadership 'because Congress work in Bengal in their view had been deflected from constructive paths by our Chittagong strikes and large funds had been used up'. Eventually, Gandhi decided to go with Banerji to Chittagong and he met the strikers, the Indian Merchants' Chamber, and Congressmen. 'There was a meeting of the Congressmen and railway strikers when Gandhiji strongly advised immediate calling off of the strike' and the District Congress Committee decided accordingly forthwith.

Soon after this, in September 1921, Banerji was tried and sentenced to imprisonment for one year.

> I was asked either to execute a bond of good behaviour and offer abstention from further speech-making, or go to jail for a year with hard labour. Naturally I preferred jail-going.... One grey-bearded Muslim peasant began to weep and cried out in extreme anguish of soul: Even such men are being put in jail by the Britishers! .... [This was] a tribute from the masses—the oppressed and exploited peasantry for whom the fight had really been launched.[16]

It is instructive to read Banerji's memoirs and its many details because they tell us about the transformation that a man like him underwent in a few months, from March to September 1921, and how the local movement which a few like him initiated almost acquired a momentum of its own regardless of the original agenda of action. The pattern is the same in some parts of Medinipur district which vied with Chittagong in the Non-cooperation struggle. Between 1921 and 1923, Satkaripati Roy and a few Congressmen led a political agitation among *adivasis* and peasants in the Jungle Mahals of Medinipur. The Congress targeted the British-owned Midnapur Zamindari Company. In the first round of this fight, the strike by *adivasi* labourers working for the *zamindari* company and the tenants' refusal to cultivate land, forced on the company a compromise with the Congress leaders on terms suggested by those leaders through the mediation of the British magistrate. In an oral testimony later, Roy claimed that during the agitation the Congress performed functions of the government—registering land transactions, running the post office, setting up granaries where people put in their surplus paddy, and so on.[17] Roy and Congress *babus* also had the Santals vowing to abstain from alcohol in deference to Gandhi Maharaj, to boycott foreign cloth, and even to protest against the export of rice by local *zamindars* that was depleting local food supply. The movement "acquired its own dynamism and autonomy" within a few weeks when, in January 1922, Santals on their own began to organize raids on *haats* (marts) to destroy foreign cloth. The local Congress leaders disapproved of this as well as any conflict with *zamindars* other than the British Zamindari Company. The post-Chauri Chaura decision to call off the Non-cooperation Movement might have been opportune for those who disapproved of such autonomous and uncontrolled popular participation. It seems that even after this, in the middle of 1922, there was another wave of *adivasi* protest in which the Congress leaders were completely marginalized: this was on the issue of restoration of forest rights to *adivasis*.[18]

On the other hand, in another part of the same district of Medinipur, the Congress leader B.N. Sasmal led a highly controlled and measured protest against taxation levied by the Union Board of Contai. In January 1921, under the Bengal Village Self-Government Act, union boards began to be formed in rural areas. While apparently a good thing that village self-government was being introduced by the minister of the department concerned, that is, Sir Surendranath Banerjea, it was actually only a means of legitimizing local taxes through a partly nominated and partly elected local body. The newly formed union boards did not have the authority to refuse to tax themselves or to tax themselves according to local needs; the District Magistrate was the final authority in that matter. Moreover, the latter continued to control the village employees, especially the *chowkidar* (guard) while the union board paid their salaries. Nor was there any guarantee that the taxes collected would be expended locally. The resentment against this system was shrewdly used by B.N. Sasmal to launch a campaign as a part of the Non-Cooperation agitation. From June 1921, Sasmal began to organize local businessmen at *bazar* meetings and landholders and farmers in rural meetings, first to memorialize the government and then, from August, to refuse to pay union board taxes. Attachment of movable property was the penalty for non-payment of local taxes; this punishment was accepted by about 4,000 households in Contai by October 1921 and about 31,000 more were awaiting this punishment but they still refused to pay the tax.[19] The idea of attaching movable property was, of course, to auction it to recover the tax that had not been paid. But this proved impossible because while government went around attaching and seizing items of property—to the musical accompaniment of conch shells blown by villagers peacefully submitting to the loss of assets—the attached goods could neither be taken away nor sold in auction. Carters to a man refused to carry the attached goods and no one offered bids for them in auctions—such was the extent of popular support for the 'tax strike'. S.N. Ray, ICS, Joint Magistrate, reported: 'B.N. Sasmal, who after standing as a candidate for the Bengal Legislative Council had turned non-cooperator … was quick to seize the opportunity to appear in the role of a champion of the people's rights and their spokesman. Here was an admirable opportunity to form a combination to thwart government and to strengthen his own influence'.[20] Ray went on to say that to enforce tax payment was 'neither possible, without an enormous staff, nor politic' because people were peaceful and even respectful but there was 'beneath it all a stubbornness'. The English District Magistrate of Medinipur pointed out that even when loyal members of local boards wanted to pay taxes, they 'have at length been overpowered by the social boycott that has been brought to bear on them'.[21] It is interesting to see that even the Magistrate thought it was not 'fair to leave it to the District Officer' to deal with the Non-cooperation agitators; there should be 'government orders as to how to deal promptly with anyone who goes around preaching civil disobedience in the form of non-payment of taxes'. It suggests a lack of confidence at the top of the district administration in the face of the Non-cooperation Movement at its height. The outcome of all this was that the union boards in Medinipur were dissolved, and attachment of property for non-payment of tax ceased. Sasmal kept control over the movement throughout and allowed no violence by his caste-brothers of the locally dominant Mahishya caste. He won the battle without any aid from the Provincial Committee of the Congress (indeed they recommended in February 1922 cooperation in respect of local self-governance). Thus a local issue which S.N. Ray said threw 'these people into the hands of the non-cooperators'[22] provided the power while the format of non-cooperation provided the track on which a movement was pushed ahead very effectively. Sasmal became one of C.R. Das's district satraps.

While Chittagong and Medinipur were the two major centres of the Non-cooperation agitation, the third, obviously, was Calcutta. Then, as now, this city was the theatre for staging spectacles that would influence the rest of Bengal as well as the locus of interaction of the all-India leadership with the provincial leadership. Having overcome at the Nagpur session of the Congress (1920) C.R. Das's initial scepticism, Gandhi's call for non-cooperation evoked a good response in Calcutta. Already, the Khilafat link had brought to Gandhi a following among Bengali Muslims; particularly important was the opening of the 'National' *Madarsa* in the Chitpore area in Calcutta; this was followed by similar institutions in Mymensingh, Hooghly, Chittagong, and Dhaka. From the beginning of 1921, Calcutta led again in the boycott of government educational institutions and—to a lesser extent—in joining the national schools and colleges. Reportedly, in February 1921, out of 103,000 students about 11,000 joined the boycott.[23] The boycott of the law courts, led by C.R. Das himself at enormous cost to his private fortunes, no doubt, became a moral example to some who had been hesitant about taking the plunge and resigning government jobs. An impact on the morale of the movement was also made by the courting of arrest by elite women, including the wife of C.R. Das. Finally, in 1921, Calcutta also led Bengal in staging a massive *hartal* (general strike) to boycott the government's arrangements to welcome the Prince of Wales. However, one scheme designed in Calcutta fell flat in parts of Bengal—a 'jute boycott' to deny supplies to British-owned jute mills—not all farmers would give up a profitable crop.[24]

A Hegemony Contra the Colonial State

> The profound patriotism of Mahatma Gandhi blessed this country like the waters of the Ganga.... Bengal too was touched by that sacred stream. Here too people's power (*gana sakti*) was awakened for a while. But did we, the educated *bhadralok* succeed in guiding it? ... We failed, that is why this lassitude, this lack of the vital spark in the country.[25]

In thus editorializing, the *Ananda Bazar Patrika* expressed sentiments typical of the 1920s: on the one hand, a new regard for 'people's power' and, on the other, the old *bhadralok* mindset arrogating to itself the directive role. The political scene we have witnessed till now shows the tussle between these contrary pulls within the Non-cooperation Movement. Many observers have said that this is the contradiction within the Congress, that it advanced mass consciousness at some junctures and 'back-pedalled' at other times.[26] However, it is a big question whether one can at all talk of Congress doing this, that, or the other. It may be more useful to think of the Congress as a stage and not as an actor. If one looks at the ground level of action in the Non-cooperation Movement, at Medinipur or Chittagong, the Congress emerges as a site of negotiation between (*a*) a 'national' agenda devised by Gandhi's Congress, and (*b*) other 'local' agendas demanding the politicians' intervention if they wanted to garner popular support. The Congress was where negotiations took place between these agendas and the programmes of action differed from place to place since the national agenda was mediated through local agendas.

This way of looking at it may also be true of negotiation between interests of classes or political aggregates, or even of political parties. Gandhi's alert political sense must have noticed the diversities under the Congress umbrella and he seems to be thinking of the Congress as a forum allowing representation of divergent views. Early in 1920, he wrote in *Young India* that the Congress 'cannot be kept any longer as one party organization if it is not to have seceders from it on increasing scale from year to year. Measures must be devised whereby all parties can be presented on it and the annual assembly can retain its truly national character'.[27] And again, 'the Congress must, if it is to serve the country, more and more tend to represent not one view but many'.[28] In April 1920, the idea seems to have crystallized further: after accepting the position of President of the Home Rule League he issued a statement: 'I do not consider the Congress as a party organization, even as the British Parliament, though it contains all parties ... is not a party organization'.[29] In June 1921, Gandhi wrote in *Young India*: 'The Congress represents the whole nation and may therefore have every type and all parties', while the Working Committee represented the majority opinion.[30]

Thus Congress was being represented not just as a political party but a conglomeration of political formations ranging from voluntary associations (including those started by Gandhi, but not exclusively those alone) to full-fledged political parties (such as the Swaraj Party in the early 1920s). Likewise, it was represented in the social and economic arena as something of an arbitration forum, supposedly not a partisan in conflicts of interests or of classes. This idea accorded with Gandhi's notions of conflictless class relations. In 1921, Gandhi wrote repeatedly on this theme in his propaganda organ, *Young India*. Although the Non-cooperation Movement was on, he wrote, 'There is no non-cooperation going on with capital and capitalists'; they are bound with labour by mutuality of interests, he maintained and exhorted millworkers 'to identify themselves with the interests of the mill owners'.[31] Gandhi suggested a familial relationship between labourers and employers: 'There is only one royal road before you, viz., to elevate workmen by creation between the two parties [that is, labourers and employers] of a family relationship'. This was contrasted with the European class relationship where 'they fight to the bitter end'.[32] He conceded that workers justly 'regard themselves as being chiefly instrumental in enriching their employers' and that 'in the struggle between capital and labour, it may be generally said that more often than not the capitalists are in the wrong box'.[33] He also conceded, while writing of the European-owned tea gardens (which were affected by the labour agitation mentioned earlier), that such interests 'based on injustice' were 'supported mainly by brute force but not by people's goodwill'. Nevertheless, the principle of non-violence was sacrosanct.[34] 'It would be suicidal if the labourers rely upon their numbers or brute force, i.e. violence'; they should, Gandhi recommended, 'take their stand on pure justice and suffer in their person to secure it…'.[35] His concept of non-violence led him to the rather singular conclusion that on the occasion of a strike 'an employee who gives himself leave uses violence, for he commits a criminal breach of contract of his service'.[36] He was particularly wary of the potential of violence in 'political strikes' in association with the Non-cooperation Movement; thus he characterized as 'criminal disobedience' Bombay mills strikes boycotting celebrations of the visit of the Prince of Wales on 17 November 1921.[37]

All of these writings appeared in 1921 during the Non-cooperation Movement. Given this approach, it was but natural that the Congress would be represented as a body that included comfortably the employee and the employer, labour and capital, and so on. In the late 1920s this notion was generally propagated (in part as a response to the emergence of the Left). For example, the Maharashtra Provincial Congress adopted a resolution in 1927: Congress should be 'taking upon itself the duty and the responsibility of reconciling as far as possible the growing conflict of different interests in India'.[38] In Bengal, similar views were voiced about the same time: 'The Congress is the main agency for the unification of the nation: the Congress will unite under its flag all the people of all classes in India by providing equal protection of interest to all'.[39] (On this impossible promise, the Communist leader Muzaffar Ahmad wrote in 1928: 'What will be the *kidgery* system' that will unite 'the tiger and the goat', that is, the exploiter and the exploited?[40] But we shall come to that later.)

The Congress was thus projected as a forum for the expression of a wide range of political views, perhaps even a conglomerate of parties if so needed, and as an arbitrator between conflicting interests in society standing above the conflict—that is to say, as if it were the State. Hence Congress would claim *a hegemonic position countervailing the colonial state*. Thus the multiplicity of agendas and the crosscurrents within local, provincial and national leadership were not just the outcome of specific conjunctures in the course of the Non-cooperation Movement but the outcome of deeper-seated demands of a project to claim a hegemony that could challenge the colonial State in the long run.[41]

C.R. Das and the Swarajist Alternative

This chapter began with the objective of examining the lineaments of Gandhian politics and the alternatives to that path in Bengal in the 1920s and early 1930s. Three of these alternatives demand our attention: the militant nationalism of the *biplabis*, the ideology of the Left of various hues and, for a while, the Swarajist alternative devised by Chitta Ranjan Das. Let us first look at the latter. A careful study of the speeches of C.R. Das suggests that in the brief period of about eight to ten years as a leader, he always moved on a trajectory of his own—sometimes moving close to Gandhi's position, sometimes far away from it, but consistently autonomously. Das sailed into provincial leadership on the crest of a wave of regional patriotism at the Provincial Conference of 1917, as we have seen in an earlier chapter. He also rode the wave of a new generation entering politics; this generational change was probably as important as the supposed continuity of the 'extremist' tradition that brought on to his shoulders the mantle of

Bipin Chandra Pal. We have also seen that the replacement of the older generation of Moderate leadership, represented by Sir Surendranath Banerjea, was accomplished fairly quickly.

In the agitation against the Rowlatt Bill in 1919, Gandhi's and Das's paths by and large converged. Das made his mark in the agitation which was strong enough to cause police firing and the killing of eight persons in Calcutta. At the Amritsar session (1919) of the Congress, Das and Gandhi clashed on the question of cooperation with and participation in the constitutional processes initiated by the Montagu-Chelmsford Reforms: Gandhi wanted to work the Reform Scheme while Das would have none of that. Das adopted a practice never seen before, moving his resolutions already drafted in Calcutta and introducing them well ahead of the moving of official ones. Gandhi moved amendments watering down Das's acerbic resolution rejecting the reforms. A patch-up of a compromise was to resolve that 'the people will so work the Reforms [this is what Gandhi desired] as to secure an early establishment of full responsible Government [this is what Das demanded]'. 'The resolution was a triumph neither for Das nor for Gandhi exclusively. It was a triumph for both.... By that time it was clear that the stalwarts of the Indian Congress could not see eye to eye'.[42]

The next few months saw Das and his radical stance outflanked. Gandhi pressed for non-cooperation while Das was put in the position of a defender of cooperation. By August 1920, Gandhi had begun touring the country campaigning for non-cooperation and the Congress met in a special session in Calcutta in September 1920 to consider this turnaround. Gandhi's resolution recommending non-cooperation was passed (1886 delegates for, 884 against) and Das's amendment basically recommending deferral of non-cooperation was not accepted. Three months later, the usual December session of the Congress met at Nagpur. The Bengal contingent was divided between those who (led by J.L. Banerji) supported Gandhi's line, and those who had doubts about it. The latter supposedly included delegates sponsored by Das so as to reverse the decision of the Calcutta session. The unexpected happened. C.R. Das himself moved the resolution supporting Gandhi's programme of non-cooperation and it was, of course, passed.

This convergence of Das's and Gandhi's 'general line' mystified many at that time. It transpired that Das was converted by Gandhi over a long discussion they had the night before the open session began.

Later, in his autobiography Gandhi recalled making some amendments to the draft at the instance of C.R. Das. Moreover, Das's request to be allowed to move the non-cooperation resolution was accepted by Gandhi. The slogan 'Swaraj within one year' won over not only Das but even the revolutionary nationalists from Bengal. One of them writes in his memoirs: 'My friends went to the Nagpur Congress to support Chitta Ranjan [Das] against Gandhi. They came back in the train of Chitta Ranjan having accepted Gandhi's lead.... Gandhiji's promise of Swaraj within a year inflamed them. "One year, only one year"...'.[43] These were some of the reasons why Das changed his line. Finally, there is the usual explanation of Chitta Ranjan's conversion: Gandhi's charismatic personality.

Be that as it may, the so-called conversion could have also been a part of Das's own strategy of uniting politically active elements in Bengal politics. Das's constituency was the younger generation of political activists and they wanted action in response to British obduracy and to avenge Jallianwallah Bagh. The *biplabis* or revolutionary nationalists read the 'Swaraj within a year' slogan as an ultimatum. They were willing to buy *ahimsa*, on trial so to speak, and agreed to hold their horses for one year. Later some of them returned to their terrorist methods, but some remained within the Congress fold. These highly committed young men and women were useful in Bengal politics as a counterweight to the cent per cent Gandhians. Das's mutually supportive relationship with the Anushilan and Jugantar groups of revolutionaries proved useful in many ways. Except for Bipin Chandra Pal, most of the leaders senior to Das in the Congress such as Aswini Kumar Dutta (1856–1923) and Byomkesh Chakraborty (1855–1929) had opted already for non-cooperation in the Calcutta session. Finally, the link between Khilafat and non-cooperation provided Das with a bridgehead towards cooperation with the Muslims, a vital gain in a province where they commanded numerical majority. In place of the usual 'conversion' theory, an explanation in terms of strategic advantage is equally plausible.

Once C.R. Das accepted the programme of non-cooperation—indeed, he was eloquent in the open session of the Congress as the mover of the resolution—he put his heart and soul into it. The extent of the impact of non-cooperation in Bengal was partly due to his leadership. But his greater achievement was less in the limelight—building up the party machine. This has not been fully investigated by historians yet: the organizational network of the Congress extending downwards to the district level and beyond. The few district-level studies we have suggest that Das's method was (*a*) to pick up local level leaders and to invest them with his authority and support, or (*b*) to despatch 'emissaries' to the districts, carefully selecting such Congresspersons in Calcutta. The first of these methods was effective in Murshidabad district for example.[44] There, the District Congress Committee was set up formally in 1921 under the chairmanship of Braja Bhushan Gupta; he was persuaded by C.R. Das, during one of his visits to Berhampore, to accept this charge—a shrewd choice because Gupta was already well known locally as the secretary of the Murshidabad Association, a member of the Berhampore Bar since 1897 and, in part, as the financier of Congress activities in the district. The other method was suited to areas where Congress politics was virtually unknown; thus, for instance, Satkari Roy was sent to work in the Jungle Mahals and neighbouring Bankura and Singhbhum by C.R. Das in early 1921.[45] Roy, in turn, chose as his lieutenant a briefless lawyer and these Congressmen took an active part in *adivasi* peasant movements against landlords, particularly the English-owned Midnapur Zamindari Company in 1921–2. Then there were Calcutta Congressmen who had links with one district or another and these were hand-picked by Das and areas were, so to speak, farmed out to them. For example, Birendra Nath Sasmal belonged to the Mahishya caste, dominant in Medinipur district, and he had worked in that district to provide relief to flood victims in 1913 and 1920; C.R. Das chose him to lead the Congress in Medinipur and he was successful in linking local issues and grievances with the wider political strategies of the provincial party.[46]

Likewise, Jatindra Mohan Sengupta was 'put in charge' of Chittagong district, Anil Baran Ray of Bankura district, and Someshwar Choudhury of Rajshahi district. These young leaders came to form the backbone of C.R. Das's party machine and they were personally indebted to him.[47] Seizing the opportunity of the Khilafat alliance with the Non-cooperation Movement, C.R. Das also built links with a new Muslim leadership, for example, Akram Khan in 24 Parganas, Ashrafuddin Ahmed Chowdhury of Tipperah, and Abdullah Baqui of Dinajpur.

This party machine, and loyal district-level leaders, gave C.R. Das the political clout not only to conduct the non-cooperation campaign effectively in Bengal, but also to offer an alternative when his path again diverged from that of the Gandhians in 1922.[48] This time, the divergence was far enough to lead to the formation of a separate body, the Swaraj Party. After a tumultuous year of non-cooperation when the Congress session met in Ahmedabad at end of 1921, the president-elect was C.R. Das but he was in jail (arrested on 9 December 1921). He was still in prison when the Chauri Chaura incident precipitated Gandhi's decision to call off the Non-cooperation Movement in February 1922. When Das was released from jail, after six months, in August 1922, Gandhi was in jail. The bitterness generated by the withdrawal of non-cooperation by Gandhi had abated. The new issue facing the Congress was the difference within the party on the feasibility of Civil Disobedience: a committee reported on that question and it showed up differences on the question of 'Council entry'. Were members of the Congress to boycott provincial legislative councils or not? At their meeting in Calcutta at C.R. Das's residence on Russa Road, the AICC wrestled over this question for five days in November 1922 and failed to form a consensus. In December 1922, the Congress session in Gaya saw the schism nearly coming to a split in the party. C.R. Das was again president at this session. A faithful Gandhian, Pattabhi Sitaramayya wrote later that Das and Motilal Nehru, in favour of Council entry, represented 'those that worked politics on the intellectual and material plane'; ranged against them were the Gandhians [Gandhi was in jail] who 'raised politics to a spiritual level', inspired by Gandhi whose absence 'in flesh and blood made no difference'.[49] Thus Gandhi's presence in the Congress was not corporeal but nonetheless no less real! This spirit influenced the so-called 'no-changers', that is, those who did not want a change in the status quo and wished to continue with boycott of the Legislative Councils, whereas the 'pro-changers' were led by C.R. Das and Motilal Nehru, strongly supported by delegates from Maharashtra and Bengal. The 'no-changers', headed by C. Rajagopalachari, commanded a majority at the Gaya Congress; Das resigned his presidentship, and the Swaraj Party was brought into existence by Motilal and Das. This victory of 'no-changers' was illusory: at its meeting in Allahabad (February 1923), the AICC worked out a compromise that was tantamount to surrender to the 'pro-changers'; feathers were ruffled and the 'no-changers' began to resign their membership of the AICC or Working Committee, and finally a special session of the Congress met in September 1923 to resolve the internal conflict. Abul Kalam Azad, the president, designed a formula that confirmed the victory of Das and Motilal's 'pro-changer' party. The Congress resolved to 'suspend all propaganda against entering the Councils' and to permit 'such Congressmen as have no religious or other conscientious objections' to enter the Legislative Councils through the impending election.[50]

Thus C.R. Das and Motilal Nehru won a difficult battle. Why did Das stake his all, including the presidentship of the Congress, to push forward the 'Council entry' programme? On the face of it, that was a tame programme, constitutionalist in tone and far from being satisfactory to the radicals in Bengal. The explanation offered by Gandhians has been that he was keen on entering a course of action that would 'shut to the sideline of legislative activity' the Non-cooperation Movement.[51] Even if we suppose that is how it was, why did the Bengal leader want that? The only explanation seems to be in terms of the political situation in that Presidency. Das declared that 'Council entry' was a means of wrecking the system from within. The Swarajists' manifesto issued by Das and Motilal Nehru from Allahabad in February 1923 declared the strategy: 'Speedy attainment of Dominion Status', to contest elections to Legislative Councils to push for 'legitimate demands' in the Council and, if the government, as expected, remained unresponsive, 'uniform, continuous and consistent obstruction within the Council'. This programme was Das's response to the situation in Bengal since the withdrawal of non-cooperation by Gandhi. The revolutionary nationalists, or so-called terrorist *biplabis*, whom Das had persuaded to give non-violent non-cooperation a trial, were up in arms against inaction and lassitude since the withdrawal of the movement in February 1922. The upper-middle class elements with political ambitions saw that despite the boycott of the elections to the Legislative Council (November 1920) the Council had been formed and Sir Surendranath Banerjea, Abdur Rahim, or P.C. Mitter were ministers while the followers of C.R. Das languished in a political wilderness. To satisfy these Congressmen itching to enter electoral politics, council entry was a good idea. But, on the other hand, would that not be too tame a programme for the revolutionary radical youth? It would not, if 'Council entry' was perceived as a tactic for wrecking the system from within.

That such political calculations led C.R. Das deliberately to evolve a new line and form the Swaraj Party is not my contention, but it is possible to argue that his decision suited the circumstances pretty well. 'The boycott of the legislature', wrote his trusted lieutenant Subhas Chandra Bose later, 'as conceived by the Calcutta Congress in 1920, had proved to be a failure. While nationalists had kept away from the legislatures, undesirable persons had captured these bodies. According to Deshbandhu [C.R. Das], the vantage points in a revolutionary fight should not be left in the hands of the enemy'.[52] To capture the Councils and to 'keep up a systematic opposition to the members and agents of the government' were better tactics. This new line, presented by Das as president of the Congress at Gaya, was not acceptable to the 'no-changers' led by Rajagopalachari. Das wanted the freedom to 'work separately' while being 'within the Congress' and this was granted, as we have seen, to allow the Swarajist group to fight the elections to the Councils.

Thus Das and Motilal forced the installation of an alternative to the line that was preferred by the Gandhians and had been till then formally the Congress position. Das's next step was to establish this alternative line in the Bengal Provincial Congress Committee. Among the middle-rank leaders he recruited for support were Tulsi Goswami of the landlord lobby, Nalini Ranjan Sarkar from the business world, Bidhan Chandra Roy and Sarat Chandra Bose who were leaders in their respective professions of medicine and law, Bhupati Mazumdar who was a doyen among the revolutionary nationalists as a leader of the Jugantar group, and Maulana Akram Khan who was a Muslim communal leader drawn into the mainstream as a Khilafatist. Thus a whole range of political elements were brought together by Das, and he was able to put his own supporters in controlling positions in the Bengal Provincial Congress Committee.

At the end of 1923, this group was very successful in the elections to the Legislative Council and the time had come to carry out the promise made in the Swaraj Party manifesto regarding their objectives as an Opposition within the Council.[53] The refusal of the Council to grant salaries to the ministers of the government (March 1924) was a great coup. This was a spectacular defiance of Governor Lytton: in the hope of cowing the Opposition, the Governor himself appeared in the Council chamber and harangued the Swarajists, but they, by a majority, denied salary to his ministers. A few months later, grants proposed by the government were rejected by the Swarajist majority in the Council (August 1924). The ministers had to resign and the Governor prorogued the Council *sine die*. Thus Das's declared aim of exposing the hollowness of the dyarchy constitution set up in 1919, and to 'wreck the Council from within', was partly achieved.

As an Opposition in the Legislative Council, Das's followers acquired a visibility that helped build a command over the public mind. This political gain was inaccessible to them earlier, though the boycott at that time might have secured moral satisfaction. An even greater political gain was the capture of many municipal and local bodies through elections. Ironically, it was Sir Surendranath Banerjea, the Minister for Local Self-Government, who facilitated this by enacting a new law allowing preponderance of elected members over official and government-nominated members. The most spectacular achievement was the capture of the Calcutta Corporation in the election of March 1924 by the Mayor C.R. Das, Chief Executive Officer Subhas Chandra Bose, and Deputy Mayor Shaheed Suhrawardy. Khadi-clad councillors and aldermen brought about changes: not merely in renaming public places after national heroes, but also in orienting the health and sanitation department to pay more attention to non-European quarters of the city, in setting up a new education department under K.P. Chattopadhyay, in switching to Swadeshi supplies for the municipality, and in making new appointments favouring political sufferers and neglected minorities. A staunch Congressman, Nripendra Chandra Banerji also noted wryly that the Swarajists found the Calcutta Corporation useful 'to strengthen the coffers of the party'.[54]

Did C.R. Das fail to deliver?

While these were C.R. Das's achievements in 1923–5 his failures also were undeniably evident by 1925. The failure–not for want of any effort on the part of C.R. Das—that was fatal for Bengal was the collapse of the so-called Bengal Pact. To resolve Hindu–Muslim friction, Das had committed himself to designing an understanding, not clearly spelt out but hinted at during the Legislative Council election, over sharing of government jobs, and seats in the Council. Much to the chagrin of many Hindu Swarajists and Congressmen, in December 1923 he spelt out the plan, immediately named the 'Bengal Pact' by the media. Das considered the Hindu–Muslim Pact so important that he confided to Aurobindo, in a conversation they had in 1923, that he would not be happy if the British departed from India before the resolution of the communal conflict.[55] At the next Provincial Conference (June 1924) Das managed to have this accepted, aided by his more secular-minded supporters and by Muslim leaders who had been drawn in by the Khilafatist cause earlier. The three main provisions of this plan were: (*a*) representation in the Bengal Legislative Council would be on the basis of population, Hindu and Muslim, with separate electorates; (*b*) representation to local self-government bodies would be on the basis of *60:40 = Muslim:Hindu* in Muslim majority districts, and *40:60 = Muslim:Hindu* in other districts, and (*c*) government jobs would be apportioned on the basis of the formula *55:45 = Muslim:Non-Muslim*, provided that till this percentage distribution was attained by specially facilitating Muslim recruitment, a ratio of *80:20 = Muslim:Non-Muslim* would be maintained in recruitment.

This was a very far-sighted initiative taken by C.R. Das. But the possibility of a rapprochement between the two communities was negated by the Hindu middle class who were up in arms against the Bengal Pact. The controversy damaged communal amity immensely: Muslims were aghast as the *Amrita Bazar Patrika* accused Das of 'selling Bengal to the Muslims' while *Ananda Bazar Patrika* described the Pact as Muslim aggression against Hindus.[56] On the other hand, conservative Muslim opinion was impatient with Das for not delivering quickly what he had promised. For instance, Al Faruq wrote in *Islam Darshan* that 'between his words and action there is a discrepancy'.[57] Liberal Muslims like Abul Mansur Ahmed felt later that this was a great opportunity, irrevocably lost, to establish Hindu–Muslim amity.[58] The concession wrested by Das from his unwilling following was lost due to a short-sighted opposition. His opponents bided their time till his forceful personality was removed from the scene. Within a year of his death, the Bengal Congress Committee, backed by the central leadership, reneged on the Pact, putting paid to C.R. Das's efforts.

Secondly, Das also failed to satisfy the revolutionary nationalists or *biplabis*. They expected that he would, as promised in the election manifesto, bring about the release of detenus and political prisoners—most of them *biplabis*—imprisoned without trial under an antiquated law (Regulation III of 1818). The Swarajists in their first few days in the Legislative Council moved and carried by majority a resolution demanding release of such prisoners. There also began a public agitation on the issue. The government's refusal to concede this demand once again exposed the hollowness of the constitutional concessions made by the British India government. But it also exposed the ineffectiveness of 'Council politics'. Former revolutionaries, brought into the mainstream of politics by Das, became despondent and restive. By the middle of the 1920s, some of them reverted to their earlier tactics of terrorism.

Thirdly, the experience of C.R. Das's politics in 1923–5—when he was chief of the Bengal Congress, the Corporation of Calcutta, and the Swarajists—left dissatisfied a good number of Congressmen. Take for instance Nripendra Chandra Banerji who had joined Congress and the Non-cooperation Movement at the instance of C.R. Das. From the year 1923, Banerji distanced himself from Das, as did Dr Prafulla Ghosh and the old Gandhians. Banerji later wrote in his memoirs, 'C.R. Das was an astute politician and, inch by inch, he began to shake us up and enrol men from our party into his group and ended by capturing the Provincial Congress Committee'.[59] To men like Banerji, Das was a politician but Gandhi the true statesman—a view *Ananda Bazar Patrika* repeatedly asserted. Another middle-level leader, Birendra Nath Sasmal of Medinipur, had been won over by Das to his side; but he was now pushed aside from provincial leadership, he complained in his memoirs. There was a new breed of leaders with 'money power' and high social status, like Nalini Ranjan Sarkar or Bidhan Chandra Roy or J.M. Sengupta. Sasmal said that 'politics had become a sorry pastime for the unscrupulous rich'.[60] While it was to the credit of Das that he built the Congress party machine, money and graft began to play a role in party politics. Nirad C. Chaudhuri recalled in his autobiography that by the late 1920s the Calcutta Corporation had entered a course of 'steady descent into inefficiency and graft. The last had reached such proportions when I went to work for it that the popular name for the Calcutta Corporation was Calcutta Chorporation'.[61] It was ironical that Das, an exemplar of self-sacrifice, was unable to control self-aggrandizement in the party machine he built.

Finally, what of the incipient Left? C.R. Das's slogan, 'Swaraj for the masses' (September 1922) had encouraged a vague populist sentiment.

He was careful to stipulate that Swaraj 'should be for all—the masses, the middle-classes, and the upper classes—so long as there are different classes'.[62] Despite the limitations of such a supposedly class-neutral approach, the Swarajist Manifesto issued by Das and Motilal Nehru contained a promise that raised expectations, a promise in the form of a desire for 'helping the labour and peasant organizations throughout the country'.[63] Prior to this Das had occasionally acted as a typical 'outsider' leader in relation to some labour organizations,[64] for example, he was chairman of the Advisory Board that set up the All-India Railway Employees' Union (1920); in the railway and steamer strike in 1921 in eastern Bengal Das had issued a circular to all local Congress committees to help strikers since they were actually non-cooperators; and the names of his trusted lieutenants J.M. Sengupta and Subhas Bose adorned several trade union bodies.[65] Sengupta was a member of the 'Labour Committee' appointed by the Congress by a resolution passed in the Gaya Session (1922) over which C.R. Das presided.[66] However, the Left increasingly became convinced, according to M.N. Roy, that the Swaraj Party represented 'bourgeois nationalism', that it did not 'stand for a democratic revolution'.[67] This analysis by Roy in 1926, a few months after Das's death, was preceded by the foundation of the Labour Swaraj Party of the Indian National Congress on 1 November 1926. This party, founded by Kazi Nazrul Islam and Hemanta Kumar Sarkar, formed a nucleus for those who, disillusioned with the Swarajists, turned to a more radical direction. Muzaffar Ahmed joined it in January 1926 and it was renamed Peasants' and Workers' Party of India in February 1926. His group's umbilical chord with the Congress and the Swaraj Party was snapped.[68]

In the final analysis, the question is whether C.R. Das indeed presented an alternative to the Gandhian path? He himself never failed to assert allegiance to the Congress, and the Swarajists were acknowledged by the Congress as an integral part of the party. There were differences between Gandhi and Das—more often between Gandhians and Das—but were they deeper than tactical differences?

These differences, we have argued, arose from Das's rootedness in Bengal politics, although he played a role in the national arena and was fully responsive to politics beyond Bengal. The logic of Bengal politics led him to explicitly make a departure from the majority view of the Congress and to set up the Swaraj Party. This was his response to the need to forge a unity between Congressmen keen on 'Council politics', revolutionary nationalists who wanted a programme to overcome the rejection by Gandhians, Muslims who wanted recognition of their claims in the matter of representation in legislature and share of jobs, and an incipient Left that wanted to put workers' and peasants' demands on the politicians' agenda. This unity of irreconcilables was achieved for a while. And it was needed at a time when inaction and lassitude had set in after the withdrawal of the Non-cooperation Movement by Gandhi. Whether in the long run the unity could be sustained had C.R. Das's career run a longer course is difficult to guess. What seems certain is that Das addressed political problems in Bengal and to the extent that the Gandhians' prescriptions did not help address those problems he rejected them and tried to frame an alternative. He was the last leader in Bengal for many decades to chart a path for himself and to participate in the central decision-making processes of the Congress disregarding consequences of dissent.

It is ironical that after having emerged in 1917 as a radical critic of the Moderate leadership of Surendranath Banerjea's generation, Das at the end veered towards a position that was perceived by many as too 'compromising' and moderate. His last public statement, the Presidential Address at the Provincial Conference in Faridpur in May 1925, was seen even by a devoted follower, Subhas Bose, as 'rather tame', a plea 'for a compromising attitude'. It was seen as a position 'satisfactory to the authorities with whom Deshbandhu [Das] was engaged in negotiating'.[69] The negotiations Bose refers to were rumoured to be discussions with Governor Lytton; nothing transpired in them, but we have evidence from Das's daughter that parleys did occur.[70] Was Das willing to settle for peace and power?

Das's friend and biographer P.C. Ray is of the view that in this last speech Das 'struck altogether a new note and invited the government to meet him halfway ... a gesture which surprised both his friends and his enemies'.[71] What did Das actually say? The crucial passage was this: 'I must make clear my position—and I hope of the Bengal Provincial Conference—that provided some real responsibility is transferred to the people there is no reason why we should not cooperate with the government'.[72] On that basis there was a possibility of settlement: 'It is not possible to lay down the exact terms of any such settlement at the present moment, but if a change of heart takes place and negotiations are carried on by both sides in the spirit of peace, harmony and mutual trust, such terms are capable of precise definition'. This need not be seen as surrender to the government. But they are the words of a man willing to settle as if he was in a hurry. Was the thought of impending death at the back of his mind? Or the threat of the dissolution of the unity he had engineered? His private letters about this time suggest that he was perhaps at the end of his tether. He wrote to a personal friend on 9 June 1925 from Darjeeling where he was recuperating from illness.

> I am in great difficulty ... having given to the Swarajya Party practically [all] I had, I cannot meet my expenses and may have to return before I have recovered my health. It would be a pity not so much for my sake, as my life is practically finished, but for the country which requires all my energy in 1926.[73]

Chitta Ranjan Das died seven days later at the age of fifty-five.

Civil Disobedience and the Decline of the Congress

After C. R. Das's death, the Bengal Congress entered the doldrums. The Congress was immobilized by ferocious faction fighting among the middle-level leaders Das had recruited, there were communal riots from 1926 debilitating the nationalist Congressmen, and there was none of the stature of Das representing Bengal in the national forum. John Gallagher has suggested that in the 1930s in Bengal the Congress was definitely in decline.[74] The party, he says, failed to make the Civil Disobedience Movement a success, particularly in East Bengal; its organization weakened in the post-C.R. Das years and there were only 6 out of 150 district sub-divisions with Congress Committees; the Calcutta politicians were out of touch with the *mofussil* districts and with caste leadership among Mahishyas or Namashudras; and the alienation of Muslims from the Congress was growing. In some respects Gallagher was wrong. He fails to give due weight to the fact that Bengal provided the largest number of people arrested in the Civil Disobedience movement, 1930–1, and also accounts for the highest incidence of violence. This is by no means evidence of failure of the movement, though it might have been more fragmented than it was in regions where the Congress's organization was superior, for example, Gujarat or Andhra.[75]

What is perhaps an equally important index is that in the decade that followed Civil Disobedience, there was an increasing flow of migration into the Congress, particularly after the last terrorist outburst in 1934. The Swarajist alternative to Gandhian politics that we have examined earlier seemed to have been exhausted by 1934. In the 1930s, not only the *biplabis* but also erstwhile Swarajists and many socialists sought in the Congress a place for themselves. Thus, far from declining, the party could be said to be acquiring more political space.

At the same time, there is some sense in talking of a decline and Gallagher was not altogether wrong. It became evident in the late 1930s, and was basically a failure of the Bengal Congress to forge an agrarian programme and a bridgehead into the Muslim electorate. Both of these are failures of the *bhadralok* cast of mind to which the Congress leadership remained captive. Further, the factional struggle between the lieutenants of C.R. Das, between the Anushilan and Jugantar groups in Congress, between Calcutta leaders and district chieftains and, finally, between the central 'High Command' and the Bengal provincial leadership, manifested themselves from time to time in the 1930s to diminish the Congress as a political force. There were also the earliest signs of 'corruption' within the Congress, chiefly in the form of the role of 'money power' in electoral politics. Some of these features we shall discuss in a later chapter, but the most salient fact that springs to the eye is that the Congress was weaker than ever in Bengal and its only strength was that there was no alternative. Thus, the picture in Bengal is rather different from that commonly projected in respect of India as a whole. In Bengal, it is not exactly a story of a steady progress of Congress through stages from 1905–7, to 1921–2, to 1930–1 and on to 1942 and 1947. Nevertheless, a general perception of exhaustion of alternatives put Congress at the head of politically active forces in the 1930s in Bengal, including many uncommitted to the Gandhian tradition in the Congress.

The weaknesses and the strengths of Congress are best examined in the light of what was happening on the ground. The best is Hites Ranjan Sanyal's study of Medinipur district where the strength of the national movement became legendary.[76] From his account it seems that we can divide the 1930s into four phases. The first was from April 1930 to March 1931 when the Gandhi–Irwin Pact was fashioned. The anti-Salt Act movement was a great success for three reasons:

(*a*) The Medinipur estuarine region had been manufacturing salt till the British India government prohibited it in 1878; now an ancient right was seen to be a cause worth fighting for. The Gandhi–Irwin agreement eventually conceded the right to make salt for consumption as well as for sale within twelve miles of place of manufacture. (*b*) The sub-divisional Congress committees and the village-level Congress units had been working on the *khadi* programme from 1921 to 1930; though its economic benefit was marginal, it provided an organizational base extending right to the lower levels, with the latter units capable of functioning autonomously. (*c*) A kind of autonomy was displayed in village-level activities. In Kanthi and Tamluk, the Salt Act was openly violated without the aid of Congress volunteers. Likewise a 'no-tax campaign' began in June 1930; this soon shaded off into a 'no-rent' campaign, without Congress endorsement.

The second phase, from the suspension of the Civil Disobedience Movement in March 1931 to its resumption in December 1931, witnessed a *bhagchasi* or sharecroppers' agitation, without any support from the official Congress. Sharecroppers, who had recently defied the police to make salt, now defied *jotedars* to secure half-shares of paddy and hay, liquidation of outstanding debts, and abolition of illegal cesses. The sharecroppers boycotted cultivation of *jotedars*' lands and the latter evicted the cultivators. During the sowing season in the middle of 1931, the clashes in Khejuri Thana compelled the Sub-divisional Congress Committee members to negotiate a settlement which made some concessions to sharecroppers, with the consent of *jotedars*.

The third phase began in December 1931 when the Civil Disobedience programme included non-payment of *chowkidari* tax, boycott of foreign goods and liquor. This movement was soon officially called off by Congress but in most other parts of the Bengal there had scarcely been any movement to call off. In Medinipur, however, in some places there was a 'no-rent' campaign on the ground that rent contributed to revenue payment by landlords to government; in other *thanas* the sharecroppers' agitation spread again, parallel to a staunch campaign on Congress lines.

In the fourth phase, from May 1934 to 1939, the trends in the previous periods crystallized: (*a*) The sharecroppers' agitation became more militant; for instance, they took away the 50 per cent crop share they claimed without the *jotedars*' consent; a milder method was to boycott the *jotedar* socially and economically and refuse to cultivate his land. By the end of the 1930s the entry of the Kisan Sabha, including many politically workers inclined towards communism, intensified the struggle. (*b*) The movement of tenants against *zamindars* also began in Tamluk thana in 1937–8 mainly on the issue that *zamindars* collected a cess, *tahuri*, for maintenance of drainage channels but failed to perform that function. Village-level Congress workers participated in this movement and, by 1939, almost all of Tamluk thana was affected by an agitation against payment of *tahuri*, and even rent, if *zamindars* failed to maintain drainage works. (*c*) It appears from Hitesh Sanyal's chronicle that the Congress in Medinipur was increasingly divided both vertically and horizontally. Horizontally, because the superior leaders in the sub-divisional and district level, such as Satis Chandra Samanta, Nikunja Bihari Maiti, and Ajoy Mukherjee,

> remained neutral leaving such campaigns (sharecroppers' and tenants') to lower-level organizers but also cautioning the peasant agitators against violence.... The old veterans of the earlier movements perhaps realized that if the mass base of nationalism was to be preserved such agrarian agitations could not be avoided. But it was also apparent that since 1921 rich landowners had been chief suppliers of resources to the Congress, and they had carved out an important position in the Congress machinery. Some of the Congress leaders may have formed patronage links with the *jotedars*. As such, they could not extend full support to the egalitarian logic of the lower peasants' struggle....[77]

(*d*) Finally, there was also a vertical split. Some Congress workers were charged with violence in course of the agrarian agitation and expelled. Some remained nominally in Congress but worked with the Kisan Sabha Communists who formed a base in eastern Medinipur in 1939. Some other Congress workers went over to the Forward Bloc founded by Subhas Bose in 1939.

While the Medinipur story typically displays the wide range of political actions that were witnessed in the 1930s, in most parts of Bengal the range and intensity were more limited. Well-documented studies of the Mahishbathan salt satyagraha (24 Parganas district), the Brikutsa tenants' agitation (Rajshahi district), Arambagh Settlement Boycott (Dhaka district)—all of which occurred in 1930–2—exemplify one or another of the features which we notice in Medinipur.

The last one of these *satyagrahas* was an unusual one for two reasons: It was an agitation to allow the entry of 'low'-caste Namashudras into a 'high'-caste temple, initiated by a *swami* of the Hindu Mahasabha. It was resolved, after the failure of top Congress leaders like J.M. Sengupta, at the intervention of local 'upper'-caste women, *bhadramahilas*, who forced their entry into the temple to clear the way for the Namashudras.[78] Some agitations in 1930–1 had methods and objectives identical with those declared by Gandhi. The Mahishbathan agitation was personally led by Satish Dasgupta who had been named chief organizer of the salt *satyagraha* in Bengal, along with Patel in Gujarat, Rajagopalachari in Madras, and so on.[79] The Arambagh agitation was led by Prafulla Chandra Sen at the instance of the District Congress Committee of Hooghly; the object here was to observe a *hartal* and to prevent revenue settlement operations that would put new exactions on both *zamindars* and tenants.[80] The government gave in.

The Brikusta *satyagraha* was an interesting instance of a Muslim tenants' agitation, against a Hindu *zamindar*, under the leadership of an upper-caste Hindu Congress leader in a Muslim majority district. The grievances were the usual ones—illegal cesses exacted by *zamindars*, enhancement of rent in violation of regulations, and so on. The Muslim tenants chose a Hindu Congress worker, P.C. Lahiry, as their spokesman and a 'no-rent' campaign ensued. The arrest of Congress workers did not deter the peasants, nor did other attempts to detach the Muslim peasants from their leaders, who happened to be Hindus.[81] During the peasants' agitation, the seizure of their property by the government failed likewise and, in fact, at auctions villagers refused to bid in protest against the seizure. Eventually the intervention of the District Magistrate put an end to the *zamindars*' malpractices. The Gandhian Nirmal Kumar Bose said that the District Magistrate's intervention in favour of tenants at the end won their admiration;[82] be that as it may, the intervention came after a long period of unsuccessful repression. The Muslim peasants' trust in Hindu Congress workers was remarkable in this agitation; as we shall see in a later chapter, this trust became a thing of the past with the intrusion of communalism in the late 1930s.

Episodes like this Rajshahi agitation (or the Tripura and Jalpaiguri 'no-rent' agitations) contrast sharply with the dismal pictures one gets of Congress leadership at the higher, that is, provincial, level. The Civil

Disobedience movement in Bengal was under divided leadership; the Subhas Bose faction, at that time controlling the official BPCC or provincial council appointed one committee to conduct the campaign, and another committee was formed by his rival, J.M. Sengupta, and some senior leaders. Gandhi writes to Satish Dasgupta in 1930, half in jest: was he the 'Dictator' of one faction or two?[83] While factionalism impeded the Congress, blind pursuit of the party line impeded the Communists. The reversal of the 1922 position in the Sixth Comintern Congress of 1928 meant insulation of the 'true' Communists from 'reformist' nationalists. Some Left elements, for example, in Kisan Sabha, cooperated with Congress but not the hardcore Communists. The Meerut Conspiracy Case arrests and trials lopped off the top leadership and incapacitated the Communist Party for a while. After the general strike in jute mills in 1929, partly under Communist leadership, there was no big industrial action except for the abortive GIP Railway Strike in 1930. Strikes were unlikely to work under the Depression conditions from 1929 onwards. This hampered the younger Communist leaders like Somnath Lahiri and Abdul Halim. The ban on the Communist Party in 1934 was also a factor. A positive gain for the Communist movement was the influx into its fold from the ranks of the *biplabis* or revolutionary nationalists. However, the Communist veterans retained a certain scepticism towards them. Of the *biplabis*, Muzaffar Ahmed later wrote in his autobiography that they 'studied Marxism–Leninism in prison and joined the Communist Party.... But a great problem is that these terrorist revolutionaries think even now that they alone are the revolutionaries ...'[84]

The Congress gained more political space with the waning of revolutionary terrorism, while the Left was not yet a challenge to it. Its problems were within. The series of Round Table Conferences yielded one result which the majority of Bengal Congress leaders perceived as a disaster: Ramsay MacDonald's Communal Award. A middle-level Gandhian leader expressed an opinion commonly held, at least among Hindu Congressmen: 'Imperialists hatched an Anglo-Muslim pact behind Gandhiji's back, in a sense double-crossed him, and later evolved the infamous Communal Award and Special Electorates, by which India was divided into religious and communal camps and the fate of India ... was sealed for a generation'.[85] The split within the party on this issue was precipitated by the Congress's decision 'neither to accept nor to reject' the Award. The formation of a separate Congress Nationalist Party at a meeting in Calcutta convened by Pandit Madan Mohan Malaviya affected Congress's unity in Bengal more than anywhere else. In the Legislative Assembly elections, the new National Congress did very well, the old Congress rather poorly. In December 1934, the Congress Working Committee at its meeting in Patna considered the plea from Bengal for a reconsideration of the Communal Award; the decision was that reconsideration was impossible, for the Congress's declared policy 'had been overwhelmingly endorsed by the country at large'.[86] Thus began a long period of discord between the Bengal Congress and the High Command. Worse was to follow: the walkout of the Muslim delegates en bloc at the Bengal Provincial Congress Conference in 1935 when the BPCC resolved against the Communal Award. Thus, Congress in Bengal by 1935 was splintered and alienated from the central leadership. It was destined to tread a path that would be asymptotic to the trajectory to be followed by the numerical majority, the Muslims of Bengal, as well as many of the 'lower castes' who had been spurned by the *bhadralok* for generations. The Congress in Bengal, indecisive and unable to cope with the rising flood of communalization of politics, became a victim of the politics of exclusion it had created as a system.

Revolutionary Nationalism: an Alternative?

When Gandhian politics came to Bengal it encountered an alternative outlook that the *biplabis* offered. As we have already noted, those who were known to the British India police as 'terrorists' in Bengal in the early twentieth century were commonly called *biplabis* or revolutionaries in the Bengali language to distinguish them from other nationalists. We shall interchangeably use this Bengali description and its English equivalent, 'revolutionary nationalists'. The history of the *biplabis* is obscured by some amount of popular mythification, on the one hand, and negligence of the historians on the other. A sort of revolutionary romanticism has led to the accretion of many myths around some heroic figures among the *biplabis*. And, since they lost out in the 'Transfer of Power' in 1947, they have been virtually erased from the history sponsored by the political establishment. There is another problem. In enquiring into the history of the revolutionary nationalist activities one is confronted with many versions of what happened, as in Akira Kurosawa's film *Rashomon*. Here were secret societies each working on the principle that the less each individual knew of the others in it the better. The police reports, despite the enormous efficiency of the British India intelligence gathering system, often exaggerated the potentials of these societies as a threat to the empire, while they belittled the individuals involved in them. The personal narratives of the participants are useful in understanding their mindsets and their perceptions of political alternatives, but not necessarily as sources one can exclusively rely on.[87]

It goes without saying that the endeavour of the revolutionary nationalists in the long run ended in an impasse. And yet the *biplabi*s occupy such a space in the Bengali historical imagination that it would be silly to regard it as irrelevant in an effort to understand the Bengali mind in the twentieth century. There is a great deal in the revolutionary or 'terrorist' stream in the history of nationalism that is difficult to understand. Did the participants really believe that individual acts of violence, in isolation, against an overwhelmingly strong imperial power had any chance of success? Since such a belief seems impossible for many of those who took part in it, why did they engage in a pursuit of the impossible? Why did this path of revolutionary violence appeal to the Bengali mind while it failed to enthuse many equally patriotic men and women in most other parts of India, with the prominent exceptions of Punjab and Maharashtra? Why does revolutionary violence, despite setbacks and failures, recur cyclically, for example, the waves during 1906–8, during 1923–5, during 1930–3? From what sources deep inside Bengal was the impetus renewed over and again? We shall try and answer questions such as these rather than offer a blow-by-blow account of the acts of 'terrorism' of the *biplabi*s.

To begin with, let us consider three personal narratives by contemporary observers or participants: Nirad C. Chaudhuri (1897–1999) who was an observer completely detached from the revolutionary movement, Gopal Haldar (1902–93) who was a participant-observer on the fringes of the movement, and Rakhal Chandra Dey (1900–2002) who was at the core of a *biplabi* group and was condemned to life imprisonment in 1926 in a bomb case.

To Nirad Chaudhuri 'the Bengal revolutionary movement' was 'an explosion of nationalist passion' unfortunately in the form of 'half-baked militarism.... My disapproval of violence in politics was due to the knowledge that Bengali violence would be invariably feeble and ineffectual. I was not ready to admit that a set of feckless young men would become effectual simply because they had become hysterical'.[88] The murder committed by the *biplabi* Gopinath Saha in January 1924, Chaudhuri felt, should not have received support from C.R. Das for that was tantamount to committing 'Bengal to political violence in its lowest form, political murder'. Or, again, the Chittagong Armoury Raid by the *biplabi* group led by Surya Sen in April 1930 horrified Chaudhuri: 'I knew too much about military matters to think that any armed insurrection could be carried out by Bengalis, or to ignore what the armed forces could do against any such attempt.... Yet all educated Bengalis were in sympathy with the revolutionaries'.[89]

While Chaudhuri kept a distance from the revolutionary group, Haldar participated in one such in Noakhali in the 1920s, though he remained in the margins. His sympathy is clear:

> After Bardoli 1922 the active edge of the Congress programme was lost. The movement collapsed.... The elders among my comrades in the older revolutionary groups became followers of Deshabandhu [C.R. Das].... They were not wholly satisfied with that. But the collapse after Bardoli demanded means of keeping alive political activity and Das's politics provided it. That was a challenge to the British. At the same time, through their secret ways why not let the revolutionary nationalists' efforts also go ahead? ... I felt a compassion for them though, as I got to know more and more of the pros and cons, I saw the limitedness of their vision and I despaired. My intention was to merge myself with them and to move with them towards the wider sphere of mass action....[90]

Haldar was thus torn between the alternatives posed by the paths of political action open to men like him in the 1920s, till his arrest in 1932. His doubts about the revolutionary path became stronger over time and eventually he veered to the Left and the Communist Party. While the Congress offered for a while, during 1920–1, the possibilities of bringing in the masses into the movement, after 1922 it seemed to offer only two ways—'the charkha circle and the Council chamber'—neither acceptable to Haldar. On the other hand, revolutionary nationalists

> did not even have the possibilities, however limited, of a mass movement. Hence the circle treaded repeatedly, political murder, murder of spies,

> efforts to procure small arms, armed robbery to get money to procure arms, court cases to be fought, more robbery to pay for court cases—this was the vicious circle in which *Anushilan* and *Jugantar* groups spent most of their energy.[91]

And if you turn to a committed revolutionary, Rakhal Chandra Dey, who was sentenced to life imprisonment in the Andamans for his involvement in the Dakshineshwar bomb case (1925), you get a third perspective. Unlike the other two memoirs above, Dey's is a highly passionate account of his commitment to the cause. 'Sarva-swarupe, sarveshe, sarva-shakti samanvite, bhayebhah trahi devi…'.[92] (Give us freedom from fear, Devi, thou art all-powerful, ruler of all, ubiquitous in all that exists….) This deity merges with the author's motherland. Recruited at Chittagong by Surya Sen—who later led the Armoury Raid of 1930—Dey worked as a volunteer in the Non-cooperation Movement in 1920–1. From 1922, he progressed from being a gymnasium enthusiast, a social worker, and Non-cooperation volunteer to close involvement with gun-running, bomb manufacturing, and an aborted scheme to go to Japan to arrange supply of arms; he was arrested at a bomb-making den near Calcutta in 1925 while Surya Sen was able to evade the police.

> We did not think much of the anaemic nationalism of Gandhiji. The armed struggle for independence such as that led by Mazzini or Garibaldi seemed a more attractive and a real struggle. The youth were beginning to talk of an armed insurrection…. Some people said that the ground must be prepared for a mass movement before an armed insurrection. But the youth were impatient. We split on this question.

The avowed objective of armed *insurrection* was partly due to doubts about the efficacy of *individual* actions leading to 'political murders' to remove particular police officers, magistrates, and so on. Dey recognized, later in life when he wrote his memoirs in 1974, that impulsive youthful spirit and intoxicating passion for self-sacrifice were not enough, one needed 'to control these forces towards a goal', for want of that, 'our revolutionary struggle eventually disintegrated into oblivion'.[93] Dey, during his Andamans days, was attracted to Gandhism, while many of his fellow prisoners became Communists. But Dey remained steadfast in his admiration for Surya Sen and the martyrs of the noble struggle that failed.

There can be no doubt that a great many observers like Nirad Chaudhuri, or youths like Gopal Haldar on the fringes of the revolutionary societies, or even those deeply into the movement like Dey, saw during or soon after their encounter with revolutionary nationalism that its agenda of action was not feasible under the prevailing circumstances. And yet, wave after wave, young men and women threw themselves into this endeavour for almost three decades, from 1906 to 1935. How do we account for it? One gets the glimmering of an answer in various personal narratives of the revolutionaries. For example, Ganesh Ghosh writes of the declaration of Independence after the Chittagong Armoury Raid (1930): 'It was known to the rebels that this [the proclaimed independence] could not last very long. In the next forty-eight or seventy-two or ninety-six hours large British forces would inevitably come ... and obliterate the rebels...'. He said the main aim of the revolutionaries was to deliver a blow to the British administrative machinery, to proclaim an independent government and 'to die defending it'.[94] Even though they knew that 'the momentary "liberation" of a small part did not mean India's liberation', they took up a 'programme of insurrection and death at that time in the then condition of India with the aim of setting an example ... to inspire the youth'. Pradyot Kumar Bhattacharya who was sentenced to death for the assassination of the magistrate of Medinipur (1931) carried a message in his pocket, in anticipation of death: 'May this sacrifice awaken India'.[95] Many other men, before execution or at their trial, made similar last statements. In fact, in the first major 'bomb case' in Bengal (1908–9) Barindra Kumar Ghosh, brother of Aurobindo, made such a full statement in court on the growth and objectives of his group that it caused problems for the defence lawyers; Ghosh said his intention was to reveal all to his countrymen so that the people would 'lose the fear of death'.[96] Gopal Haldar, in his memoirs of that period, says that among the revolutionaries many admitted that the terrorist actions of a few individual might not achieve independence, but 'maximum sacrifice by a few would induce the many to make at least a minimum of sacrifice'.[97] Thus a symbolic value was attributed to spectacular acts of violence. In fact, these need not necessarily be acts of violence—witness the self-sacrifice of Jatin Das, the revolutionary who fasted in Lahore jail for sixty-four days till his death on 13 September 1929 to draw attention to the ill-treatment of political prisoners. Das was acclaimed by all revolutionary groups and by the Bengali people. The point was exemplary and fearless defiance of the ruling power so as to create an impact upon people's consciousness. This appears to be the most plausible explanation of the cycles of revolutionary actions in the foreknowledge of failure and death or severe penalties.

Nirad Chaudhuri offers some other explanations that appear less plausible. First, this 'infatuation with violence', according to him, had its origins in the *Sakta* faith, the worship of power in the Mother Goddess. 'Even those upper-caste Bengalis who had lost their Hindu beliefs retained the psychological predisposition. The followers of Gandhi in Bengal were mostly Vaishnavas' who were attuned to his doctrine. He also suggests that predisposition to violence was due to 'Bengali violence in social life. The Bengali gentry were given to a sort of blood feud resembling the vendetta of the Corsicans'.[98] It is true that *Sakti*, the Mother Goddess, appears frequently in terrorist writings right from 1906 and we have also seen an example in Rakhal Dey's memoirs. But this was a rhetoric of personification of *Desha-matrika*, the country iconized as the Mother. How deeply this influenced the choice of political alternatives is an open question. There is no evidence that Gandhi's Bengali followers were mostly Vaishnavites. Moreover *Sakti* worship was the prevailing faith in many other parts of India that did not witness terrorist violence. As for Corsican-style blood feuds, this was a part of the culture of the semi-feudal landlord class in many other parts of India which, again, saw no terrorist violence. However, Chaudhuri may be correct in suggesting a cultural predisposition against violence among staunch Vaishnavites. In Bengal this applies with lesser force than other parts like Gujarat or Rajasthan because it was not uncommon in Bengal to worship both Sakti and Vaishnav deities often coexisting with family deities and in sacred places. More convincing than Chaudhuri's explanation is, perhaps, the hypothesis offered by Sudhir Kakkar about the 'obsession with manliness' and the construction of a *sanyasi* icon, endowed with spiritual heroism as a means of assertion of masculinity.

Another explanation of terrorism in Bengal commonly offered is that, as Chaudhuri says, 'the Bengalis had read about the Carbonari, Nihilists, and Anarchists in Europe, and in the Twenties they had become fanatical admirers of the Irish terrorists'.[99] This is perfectly true. Likewise, Chaudhuri is correct in rejecting the pseudo-economistic explanation of terrorism:

> a very shallow theory was current from the very first that the revolution movement was due to unemployment in the Bengali middle class.... It is necessary to show the falsity of the theory, all the more so because all British and American historians of today who were writing on this period of Indian history and on this subject, have nothing else to go on except the mistakes of the British epigone and myth-making of the Indian nationalists.[100]

He argues, from his personal experience, that 'those who had problems of livelihood had no time for revolutionary activities' and those who engaged in such activities were from well-to-do homes with no problem of livelihood. Moreover, he recalls that when the recruits came into the movement they were between the age of fourteen and eighteen, when the question of employment did not arise. It is true that teenagers of the upper-middle class were recruited as if, as one of the recruits to Anushilan Samiti in 1911 remarks, it was part of extra-curricular school activity. This insignificant recruit records in his memoirs how he was drawn into Anushilan with three other classmates in Faridpur Zilla School, as a courier and custodian of secret papers, and then drifted out of the secret society when, three years later, he joined Presidency College in Calcutta.[101] Probably the lives of many people were thus briefly touched by revolutionary nationalist groups at an extremely young age. Like the Anushilam Samiti, the Jugantar group also recruited schoolboys. John Hunt who later rose to fame by scaling the Everest, was seconded from the British Army to the Bengal Police to work in the District Intelligence Branch in Chittagong district soon after the Armoury Raid (1930) by Surya Sen's group. He recalls that 'many young Jugantar Party members were being recruited from the High Schools of Bengal and were in some cases among the most promising pupils'.[102] To sum it up, Nirad Chaudhuri seems to be correct when he says that the recruits to the so-called terrorist societies were from an age-group and a background where the 'problem of livelihood' did not explain their political attitude and behaviour.

Three Waves of Biplabi Activity

'One man's terrorist is another man's freedom fighter', writes John Hunt in the memoirs we have cited earlier.[103] Likewise, in the perception of the revolutionary nationalists the acts of terrorist violence against the government were also the sacrament of love for the country. Of the various factors we have considered, the one that seems most important is the national revolutionaries' objective of making a public statement through their secretly organized action, so as to arouse the patriotism of their countrymen. It is difficult to say whether their outlook was universally accepted in Bengal. But gradually, over time, one notices a very wide acceptance of that view, even among those who did not join the revolutionary nationalist movement.

A pattern was set in the first wave of *biplabi* action and we need to go back a little to take a look at that. The first wave began in the form of societies like the one led by Aurobindo Ghosh, and as revolutionary propaganda through the journal *Jugantar* in 1906, and finally took the shape of terrorist action around 1906–7 (for example, the attempted assassination of the Dhaka District Magistrate, cases of political *dacoity* or robbery, the attempt to blow up a train to kill the Lieutenant Governor of Bengal, Andrew Fraser). In April 1908, eighteen-year-old Khudiram Das and another associate took two lives but failed to kill the Muzaffarpur District Magistrate. Early in May 1908, six centres of terrorist activities in Calcutta were raided by the police leading to the arrest and trial of the brothers Aurobindo and Barindra Kumar Ghosh and thirty-four of their comrades. The trial in the famous Alipore Bomb Case (1908–9) saw Chitta Ranjan Das, as yet an impoverished and obscure lawyer, emerge into the limelight in their defence. The trials had an unintended consequence. The publicity made a great impact and installed the revolutionary nationalists as heroic figures in the public mind.

A notable feature of this early phase was ideological propaganda on revolutionary nationalist lines in their journals: Brahma Bandhab Upadhyay's *Sandhya*, Bhupendra Nath Datta's *Jugantar*, and Aurobindo Ghosh's *Bande Mataram*. They were forced to cease publication in 1907–8. The Prevention of Seditious Meetings Act in 1907, and the amendment of the Indian Penal Code in December 1908, imposed severe restrictions on public associations and activities. The government was now empowered to declare any association illegal and mere presence at a meeting of an association so declared became a punishable offence; the government also acquired the power to confiscate all assets of such an association and, in 1909, to confiscate the printing press and to take other penal measures against seditious newspapers. These measures drove the revolutionary nationalists underground. Earlier, they had carried on many public activities—organizing 'gymnasium clubs', literary circles and libraries, and social services in their locality—along with the core group's secret work. Curiously, both police reports and romanticization of terrorist heroism tend to see these public activities as a facade, or a 'front'. Actually, it was much more than a front for it not only provided a link with people who would have nothing to do directly with secret terrorist activities, but also a recruiting ground for youths willing to undertake such endeavours. Thus two notable consequences of governmental reaction to revolutionary nationalism were to push them from their public into 'underground' activities and, through public trials, to elevate them to a heroic status in the public eye.

In the decade 1908 to 1918, there are police reports of numerous cases of 'political *dacoity*'; the term *dacoity*, defined as 'gang-robbery' in the *Oxford English Dictionary*, is described in Article 396 of the Indian Penal Code as robbery with the threat or use of violence by five or more persons. The adjective 'political' signified the composition of the gang; as distinct from professional criminals, *swadeshi babus* comprised these gangs. The objective was also political in the sense that the loot collected was to be used for procuring explosives and arms for terrorist action. In fact, on some occasions these political *dacoits* left behind a receipt specifying the value of the loot collected and a promise that, after Independence, the looted property would be restored to the owner.[104] In crime statistics the distinction between such actions and ordinary crime is difficult to make, particularly in the unsolved cases. However, according to police reports there were eighty-four such political dacoities in Bengal between 1908 and 1917.[105] About two-thirds of these occurred in the east Bengal districts. In western Bengal the arrest of Aurobindo Ghosh and other leaders involved in the Alipore Bomb Case was a blow to the organization. Terrorist activities continued but in a somewhat acephalous state. Along with the political *dacoities* there were also a number of political assassinations, most often targeting minor officials and suspected traitors or police informers: altogether forty-seven such cases were recorded between 1908 and 1918.

It is instructive, in order to understand this phase, to look at the political career of M.N. Roy (1887–1954), then known by his original name, Narendra Nath Bhattacharya. He was one among the younger people who were coming up into a leadership role. Expelled from school for having tried to organize a meeting to honour Surendranath Banerjea (there was a government order against student participation in such meetings), he drifted into the Anushilan Samiti which sent him to work in a relief camp for the famine-stricken in Orissa in 1907. Roy is reported to have written journalistic pieces in *Jugantar* shortly before it ceased publication, and was involved in at least two dacoity cases; trial proceedings of the Howrah Conspiracy Case (1910) charged him and forty-three others of conspiracy to 'deprive the King Emperor of the sovereignty of British India' and of 'dacoities carried out by *bhadraloks* with the object of securing funds for the conspiracy'.[106] After about a year awaiting trial, Roy and others were released for want of sufficient evidence. He established contact with the German Consul to obtain arms supplies but the outbreak of World War I brought that effort to naught. In February 1915, Roy was one of the gang that looted cash from the British managing agency Byrd and Company in Calcutta; arrested, he jumped bail. Soon after, in April 1915, and again in August of the same year, Roy went to Batavia as an emissary, disguised as Revd. C.A. Martin, to obtain German arms. He failed and, in the meanwhile, learnt of the death of his *guru*, Jatin Mukherjee, in an encounter. Roy sailed to San Francisco and to fame in the Communist International. For men of his strategic instincts and breadth of vision no further useful political activity was possible in Bengal in this phase of revolutionary nationalism.

From 1919 to 1923, there were few terrorist actions. The Non-cooperation Movement generated the hope of an alternative path. There was a tacit understanding that the terrorists would hold their horses and give the Gandhian way a trial. A sort of agreement was explicitly discussed between Gandhi and Bhupendra Kumar Datta (representing Bengal revolutionaries, in so far as any one person could represent their diverse groups) in Nagpur in 1920. Datta writes that he promised Gandhi that the revolutionaries would 'follow your [Gandhi's] leadership, work for the Congress, and not for our own programme', but after a year the *biplabis* would have the right to return to their own methods should the Congress fail to win *Swaraj*.[107] It is useful to recall here that Gandhi spoke of 'Swaraj within a year' at this time: '*Swaraj* will be established in India before next October', Gandhi wrote on 23 February 1921. But then he also, wisely, enunciated the need to fulfil some preconditions; these included complete avoidance of violence, Congress organization in every village, a *charkha* in every home, removal of untouchability, Hindu–Muslim unity, and so on.[108] It was quite a list! At any rate, the upshot was that the Bengal revolutionaries gave up violent means for the time being. The experience of mass contact deeply influenced some of them and these stayed in the Congress. Simultaneously, the efforts of C.R. Das, as mentioned before, forged a unity in which there was space for Anushilan and Jugantar group members. Unfortunately, this also sowed the seeds of factionalism in the Congress.

By 1923, the revolutionary nationalists began to go back to their old ways. The second wave of political dacoities began: two in Chittagong and two in and near Calcutta in 1923. In 1924, a celebrated political incident was Gopinath Saha's (his actual name, according to trial records, was Gopimohan Saha) attempt to assassinate the chief of Calcutta Police and a bete noire of the terrorists, Charles Tegart. Due to mistaken identity, another Englishman was killed; Saha, before being sentenced to death, expressed regret for having killed an innocent man ('Not all Englishmen are my enemies') but he hoped that 'each drop of my blood' would sow the seed of liberty in each home in India. Far from that happening, a controversy ensued between his sympathizers and the Gandhians who condemned Saha's action. The Bengal Provincial Congress Committee passed a resolution which, while 'denouncing and dissociating itself from violence', expressed appreciation of Saha's ideal of self-sacrifice, 'misguided though it is'. C.R. Das proposed an endorsement of this view in the AICC meeting at Ahmedabad while M.K. Gandhi opposed it, since any infringement of the principle of non-violence was unacceptable to him. There were seventy-eight votes for Gandhi and seventy for Das; Gandhi regarded this narrow margin as tantamount to his defeat in that national forum. (Gandhi faced much criticism on this occasion and the next time such an issue came up six years later he allowed due honour to Bhagat Singh and also pleaded with the government for his life.) The Saha case was followed by detection and exposure of several bomb-manufacturing workshops in Calcutta and some district towns (1925–6) and the conspiracy at Kakori, near Lucknow, in which nine revolutionaries from Bengal were involved (1925).

The third great wave of revolutionary nationalist activity came in 1930–5. Unlike the Non-cooperation days, the Civil Disobedience Movement did not bring about a truce with Gandhians requiring suspension of the use of violent means; in fact, sometimes the revolutionaries were heard to shout, during action, 'Mahatma Gandhi ki jai!' It was as if two different paths were being followed at the same time although the revolutionaries were doubtful of the chances of success by non-violent means, while Gandhians—never known for entertaining doubts—had none at all as to the unethical nature of violent means. In April 1930, Surya Sen's group raided the Armoury in Chittagong. In August, both the Inspector General of Police in the Intelligence Bureau and the Chief of Police were shot dead in Dhaka. In December 1930, three young men stormed the headquarters of the Bengal government at the Writers' Building to kill the Inspector-General of Prisons. Soon surrounded by policemen, Badal (Sudhir) Gupta took potassium cyanide, Binoy Basu died of wounds inflicted on him in the ensuing gunfight, and Dinesh Gupta was sentenced to death. In the Dhaka incident, Binoy Basu had escaped. In the Chittagong raid, there was prolonged action on both sides, as we shall see later. The years 1931–3 witnessed several political assassinations: three district magistrates in Medinipur District, one after the other; a judge in Calcutta, reputed to be biased against political prisoners; the Magistrate of Comilla District (killed by two schoolgirls, the first incident of its kind); four police officials of middle rank, as well as half a dozen suspected police informers. This list excludes many other attempted political murders intended as retribution. Among these, a memorable incident was the attempt by a student, Vina Das, to shoot the Governor of Bengal while he was performing the role of chancellor at the Calcutta University convocation in 1932.

In this last wave of militant activity, the raid on the Armoury at Chittagong was a little unusual. To begin with, it was conceived as an armed insurrection to form an independent government as a symbolic act—unlike the individual actions against targets of political assassination. The schoolteacher who took the lead, Surya Sen (1894–1934), named his group the Indian Republican Army and proclaimed the formation of a Provisional Revolutionary Government.[109] He seems to have known full well that it could not last: in fact, immediately after the proclamation he remarked, 'What can we do with our muskets against the enemy's machine guns?' Likewise, what could he do when the British army reinforcements came in response to a wireless message from the ship in Chittagong Port? How could the temporary advantage of a surprise attack be sustained against an overwhelmingly superior enemy? One of Surya Sen's lieutenants writes that the discouraging answer to these questions was known to their 'War Council', but their aim was to become to their countrymen exemplars of fearless martyrdom.[110] Theirs was, as they put it, a 'death programme'. Therefore, to find fault with their tactics and shortcomings, as Nirad Chaudhuri did, is to miss the point. In planning and execution there were indeed many shortcomings.[111] It was a mistake not to anticipate quick transmission of the news of their action through the wireless from the ship in the port, thus the point of destroying the telephone and telegraph system was lost. (Once again, as in 1857, the technological advantage belonged to the British, thanks to their communications system.) Again, capture of the armoury proved useless because there was no ammunition for .303 rifles, though there were many guns. The planned action in the European Club took place at a wrong time; upon entry, the attackers found it deserted. A group of seventy-eight comrades undertook the entire task, while the British brought in large army units within two days, drawing from the Eastern Frontier Rifles, Surma Valley Light Horse, and later the 8th Gurkha Rifles.[112] The group's food supply was obviously inadequate even for the brief period they defended the hillock they occupied from 18 April when, after the attack on the armoury, they dispersed in small groups. Finally, they were within range of machine-gun fire on the hillock, while the British army units were beyond the range of Sen's musket-bearing comrades. Despite this unequal contest when Sen's comrades dispersed it was tougher for the British. Of the two main groups, one was apprehended months later in September 1930 and Surya Sen and some others evaded arrest till February 1933. A small unit from the latter group made a terror attack on the Chittagong European Club in September 1932 under the leadership of Pritilata Waddedar who committed suicide after completion of the mission. Sen was betrayed to the police by a Hindu *zamindar* and executed in January 1934.[113]

The fact that evasion of arrest was possible for the *biplabis* for such long periods suggests that they enjoyed support from the villagers among whom they sought shelter and escape routes. The memoirs of the participants of the Chittagong action contain plenty of evidence of this; the Muslims of the district, an overwhelming majority, as well as Hindus did not cooperate with the British army and police operations. The sole example of betrayal was that of Surya Sen—a reward of Rs 10,000 was promised by the government for his capture—and generally the terrorists received shelter from the common people. John Hunt, the military intelligence chief leading the capture operations, writes that it was necessary to adopt a 'drastic policy of counter-terrorism whose purpose was to weaken the influence of the party [that is, the 'terrorists'] especially in areas where it moved freely, harboured by cowed population among whom they also were winning young recruits'. Hunt says that a 'deliberate programme of harassment' was adopted by the 8th Gurkha Rifles for 'it was hoped that local people would be deterred from sheltering them in future'.[114]

In other parts of Bengal too, there appears to have been strong sympathy for the revolutionaries, though it was often a passive sympathy. While there is no doubt that the revolutionary activists were recruited from the *bhadralok* class—which in itself spans a very wide income range from very low level to opulence—it is difficult to agree with the amateur sociologism that is critical of the 'narrow social base' of the revolutionary nationalists.[115] It is possible that in some places the local Congress leaders stood firmly against terrorist methods, as in Medinipur: but even there assassination of three district magistrates was sympathetically received by the people as actions that 'supplement other activities carried out in the name of the Congress' during the Civil Disobedience Movement.[116] Due to fear of reprisal by the government, middle class or popular support took peculiar forms; for instance in Murshidabad district, a citadel of the Anushilan Samiti from the early 1920s, the Berhampore Bar Association resolved to boycott lawyers (except the officially appointed Government Pleader) who accepted prosecution on behalf of the police; this meant punishment to some Bar Association leaders from the High Court.[117] While it is true that programmatically the revolutionary nationalists did not address the kind of class issues the Communists did later, the fact that in the 1930s they were rapidly drawn into Communist consolidation suggests that theirs was not a narrow middle-class political vision. For example, virtually the entire local leadership and cadre of the Communist Party, formed in Faridpur district in 1939, came from the Anushilan and Jugantar groups of revolutionaries;[118] this also applies, in lesser measure, to the districts of Murshidabad, Jessore, and Khulna.[119] Unfortunately, we do not have enough district-level and local studies of politics on the ground. The evidence we have till now does not show that the nationalist revolutionaries were denied popular support; it is true that they did not interact with the Muslim section of the population, their greatest weakness. The fact that they were exclusively Hindu groups was commented upon by people as far apart as Abul Kalam Azad and Muzaffar Ahmed. But the Congress too was not spectacularly successful in that area from 1935 onwards. The terrorist actions were regarded by the common man as heroic deeds that helped restore the self-respect of a defeated nation. But the problem was that the possibility of popular participation was precluded by the very nature and methods of revolutionary nationalism. This is where Congress scored and revolutionary terrorism languished in an impasse.

An interesting feature of the *biplabi* mentality was that though they were limited in the range of their contacts in the 1920s with regard to the politics of the rest of India (with the exception of Punjab), at the ideational level they escaped becoming provincially parochial. While their language and rhetoric and values were ineluctably those of the Bengali *bhadralok*, they looked beyond Bengal to a concept of nationhood that eschewed regional sub-nationalism. For example, Surya Sen and his group called themselves the Indian Republican Army, or IRA (unlike Subhas Bose's Bengal Volunteers), they thought that to attack the European Club in Chittagong would be a way of 'avenging Jallianwallah Bagh', the IRA badge they devised was the map of India, and they raised the Indian National Congress tricolour after burning the Union Jack at the Chittagong Armoury.[120] One can dismiss all these as mere gestures but this attempted communion in imagination with India as a whole was an important part of Bengal's effort, from C.R. Das onwards, to define Bengal's identity within Indian nationhood.

Finally, what was the legacy left behind by the revolutionary nationalists? Their path appealed to the heart of Bengal but it was rejected by the best of minds. In folk song and folk theatre (*jatra*), in fictional writings, in rumours and tales, the *biplabis* passed into the realm of legend. At the same time, many opinion makers in Bengal were critical of them. Among them, C.R. Das was particularly important. While he empathized with *biplabis* emotionally, defended them as a lawyer free of charge when he was a practising barrister, wanted them to join the Swaraj and Congress parties—his ultimate judgement was against their approach and methods. His press statement of August 1924 and his last presidential speech at the Bengal Provincial Political Conference were unequivocal:

> I ask these young men who are addicted to revolutionary methods, do they think that the people will side with them?.... I appeal to the young men of Bengal who may even in their heart of hearts think in favour of violent methods, to desist from such thought, and I appeal to the Bengal Provincial Conference to declare clearly and unequivocally that in its opinion freedom cannot be obtained by such methods.[121]

Rabindranath Tagore, likewise could not endorse the *biplabi* agenda of action though he expressed compassion and, indeed, admiration. From 1908 onwards his judgement remained firmly against their approach for he considered it futile since a few individuals' willingness to sacrifice themselves was not enough to bring about a political awakening of the people.

> Where there is no politics, a political revolution is like taking a short-cut to nothing.... These impetuous youths offered their lives as the price of their country's deliverance; to them it meant the loss of their all, but alas, the price offered on behalf of the country was insufficient. I feel sure that those of them who still survive must have realized by now [Tagore writes in 1921] that the country must be the creation of all its people, not of one of its fragments alone. It must be the expression of all the people's heart and mind and will.[122]

Two famous novels reflect the contestation in the Bengali mind between the *biplabi* point of view and the dissenters. Sarat Chandra Chatterjee's *Pather dabee* (The call of the road, 1926) and Rabindranath Tagore's *Char adhyay* (Four episodes, 1934). In the first, Sarat Chandra fuelled the fire of revolutionary romanticism: an improbably heroic revolutionary leader, a network of revolutionary operations spreading up to China and southeast Asia, preparations for armed insurrection, spies and traitors, the works. The racy romance was proscribed by the government and secured for it immediate popularity, the novel being secretly passed from hand to hand. When Sarat Chandra requested Tagore to appeal to the government to lift the ban, Tagore refused on the ground that Indians should take upon themselves consequences of defying the government and not expect tolerance.[123] The book was not one of Sarat Chandra's best from the literary point of view, but it was more than just a racy romance. A conflict of ideas is portrayed subtly. Apurba, the main male protagonist, a typical *bhadralok* intent upon securing for himself a good job and a comfortable life and, at the same time, open to the sentimental appeal of wordy patriotism, is exposed to *biplabi* ideas; his middle-class limitations are devised as a counterpoint to the heroism of the revolutionary. In the manner of some pre-1917 Russian novelists, Sarat Chandra posits a debate, imbricated in the narrative. On the one hand, the middle-class hesitation to commit oneself to active involvement in the revolutionary movement is expressed:

> India's civilization at one time propagated to the world the message of peace.... Power against power, violence against violence, might against might, that goes back right to the age of barbarism. Is there nothing beyond and nobler than that?.... It is not only futile to challenge the might of a world power, it is lunacy.... If the Indian Government undertakes fundamental constitutional reform, the revolutionary programme will become irrelevant.

These are some of the thoughts of Apurba and persons like him, sentimental patriots and infirm in commitment. With this is juxtaposed contrapuntally the *biplabi* mentality:

> Those who have come from a distant land to rule over the country of my birth, to take away my manhood and my self-respect and my platter of rice—do they alone have the right to take my life and I have none? What is ethical about it? .... Reform is tantamount to burnishing the thing [the British India government], not throwing it out. It is a design to make tolerable what is an enormous crime which has become intolerable.... The self-respect of a man is his manhood.... We [revolutionaries] have no home, we have not a thing we can call our own, and foreigners have made laws to deny us any shelter in our own land—we go about like wild beasts seeking shelter.... See the impotence of a nation in chains and on its knees....[124]

While Sarat Chandra's novel powerfully conveyed a certain mindset that accounted for the cyclical recurrence of the *biplabi* theme in Bengal, Tagore's novel *Char adhyay* (1934) implicitly contested the basic premises of that mindset. It was a searing portrayal of the revolutionary secret society, on the one hand, and, on the other, an episode of love between two persons caught in that turbulent milieu. Tagore wrote a *kaifiyat* (explanation) later that he had intended the portrayal of the political background to be no more than a background, the real story is that of love and, therefore, a piece of creative writing should not be read as a political tract.[125] Nevertheless, neither did Tagore hide his political views nor did his readers miss them in the novel. They were impossible to miss because of the intensity of the reflections on the experience of a member of a revolutionary group voiced by the main male protagonist, Ateendra: 'I have murdered the human nature that was within me, the worst of all murders.... I live in fear of the dark ghost of my own soul'.[126] Earlier, Tagore had questioned the practical feasibility of the *biplabi* agenda, but in this novel in 1934 it is the ethical aspect he focuses on. In his preface to the novel, later discarded, Tagore wrote of this in an elliptical fashion: he recalled the story of a brilliant contemporary of his, Brahma Bandhab Upadhyay, who met him at the end of his life of revolutionary activism, only to mutter a hasty confession, 'Rabi-babu, I have fallen to the depths'.[127] This preface and the novel did not endear Tagore to the Bengal revolutionaries. Prior to this, Tagore had made his criticism abundantly clear in the novel *Ghare baire* (1916) in his depiction of a revolutionary leader; Tagore's sympathies were not with the leaders but with the innocent youth who were instruments they manipulated.[128] In his political essays, Tagore spoke on the same lines, for example, the essay 'Call of Truth' in 1921 cited earlier in these pages. In 1908, during the first wave of *biplabi* activity in Bengal, Tagore had written, metaphorically, against 'the narrow short-cut' of violent methods nurtured in secrecy, as opposed to 'the wide public thoroughfare' of politics with greatest possible participation.[129]

And yet, Tagore could not deny compassion and, indeed, admiration to the valiant failure of the *biplabis*. Their endeavour 'touches the heart' despite the 'inevitability of failure ... it is in human nature to try the impossible', he writes in 1908. And further: 'We have nourished it in our minds, our writings, and in our personal involvement in one way or another.... The consequent responsibility and its woes must be acknowledged by the Bengali people'.[130] In another essay (1908), he elaborated on the theme: it is understandable that when 'the passion to avenge abasement burns in the heart of the victim' there is an impatience that demands action here and now. It was in his poems, however, that Tagore gave the finest expression to such thoughts.[131] Not only on occasions when their action stirred his mind, for example, the death of the hunger-striker Jatin Das in Lahore Jail (1929), but also at the express request of revolutionaries he wrote some memorable poems. His poems adorned the first number of the journal of the Anushilan Samiti, that of the Jugantar group, and again the first number of *Langal* [The Plough] brought out by the poet Nazrul Islam and the Communist leader Muzaffar Ahmed in 1925.[132] The most famous of these poems was the one written in 1931, addressed to political prisoners in Buxar Jail: 'They cage the bird, but they cannot cage the song...'. It seems that Tagore, critical of the programme of *biplabis*, at the same time felt an empathy with what he called 'the radiant spirit that illuminates even the futility' of their effort.[133] In this Tagore, reflected an ambivalence of the Bengali mind in his times.

Politics of the Left

Of the three alternatives to the Gandhian Congress we have considered—the short-lived Swarajist alternative, the *biplabi* or revolutionary nationalist path, and the Left—the latter appeared to be less important in that age, but in hindsight and in the light of the development of the Left in the post-1947 period, we can appreciate its importance in Bengal history. However, we must bear in mind the fact that in the politics of those times the Left was only one of several paths that men and women saw in their historical context. Moreover, contrary to a sedulously propagated narrative, within the Left the Communist Party of India (CPI) represented only one strand among many. The Left was a broad spectrum containing many groups professing ideologies akin to but not identical with one another. Perhaps a third point needs to be made: between the so-called Left and the Congress the boundary was porous so that individuals and groups freely went into and out of these political affiliations; as for the *biplabis*, the nature of their secret organization meant strong boundary maintenance, but in the

1920s and 1930s increasingly there was interpenetration. We have noted earlier the affiliation of some *biplabi* groups to the Congress from the days of the Non-cooperation Movement onwards, as well as the conversion of *biplabis* to some version of the Leftist ideology from the 1930s. Satinath Bhaduri in his novel, *Jagari*, very sensitively explores the coexistence of different political ideologies in depicting the chief protagonists of the novel—the father a Congressman, a son drifting towards the Congress Socialist Party, and another son uncompromisingly committed to Communism.

The Ideological Arena

Communism was far more influential as an ideology than as a political party in the pre-independence decades. Writings in contemporary journals, newspapers, and books have been surveyed by Sipra Sarkar and the picture that emerges is roughly as follows: The attitude of the nationalist press was far from being inimical in the 1920s. Ramananda Chatterjee greets with enthusiasm in 1917 the Bolshevik Revolution and recalls Rammohun Roy's jubilant admiration for the revolution in France in 1830.[134] C. R. Das's journal carries in 1920 articles by the *biplabi* Upendra Nath Bandyopadhyay in praise of the socialist revolution.[135] The *Bangiya Musalman Sahitya Patrika* publicizes the laudable egalitarianism of Bolshevism.[136] Professor Benoy Sarkar of Calcutta University draws attention to the theoretical contributions of Karl Marx and Friedrich Engels.[137] Editors of the *Ananda Bazar Patrika*, firm Congress supporters, heap praise on 'Lenin the Great' in an obituary in 1924.[138] Parallel to the traditional nationalist opinion, one can discern another current, a new Left not yet known by that appellation. The journal *Samyavadi* declares in 1924 that Islam had anticipated the egalitarianism of the socialists.[139] The future Communist Party leader Muzaffar Ahmed expounds the doctrine of class struggle in the new journal *Langal* in 1926.[140] His friend and colleague, the poet Nazrul Islam, translates the song 'International' for the first time into Bengali in 1927.[141] A new Leftist journal, *Ganavani*, in 1926 opens a campaign to propagate the message of class struggle: the 'spiritual nationalist leaders and soft-minded labour leaders' are chastised for their absurd belief that 'in this sacred land there is no class struggle'.[142]

Rabindranath Tagore's visit to the USSR in October 1930 and the *Letters from Russia* he published marked the beginning of a new and more complex discourse of socialism. On the one hand, Tagore was optimistic about the possibility of a social order that aimed at equality, the effort to incorporate in the new polity previously marginalized nationalities conquered by Tsarist Russia, and the prospect of the elimination of a leisure class living on the labour of the unprivileged. On these matters, he spoke with enthusiasm. On the other hand, Tagore saw reasons to be cautious—for instance, he heard 'rumours of the cruelty of the present administration', the suppression of free discussion of economic policies, and the fact that 'many persecutions were taking place in Russia'. He suspended judgement on a basic issue: 'Time is not yet to say whether the [Soviet] economic doctrine is completely valid'. With a mixture of appreciation and caution he wrote in 1931: 'My only fear is that in a scripture-ridden and priest-led country [India], the natural bent of our ignorant mind is towards accepting a foreign dictum as biblical truth. Guarding ourselves against this danger, we must say that a doctrine can be tested only by its application: the end of the experiment is not yet'.[143] While sounding a note of caution, on the whole Tagore appreciated the principles of the Russian revolution even if some of the practices of the new regime were open to question. Like Sidney and Beatrice Webb, he saw there the possibilities of building 'a new civilization', he wrote to his secretary Amiya Chakrabarty in 1935.[144]

In the 1930s there developed a lively debate on the issues raised by the Russian experience and Marxist theory. On the one hand, there were strong critics like Soumen Tagore who saw in Stalin's Russia in 1930 a 'dogmatism and a cult' that was against the original spirit of Communism.[145] Likewise, Nalini Kanta Gupta, a *biplabi* who became Aurobindo's chief disciple at Pondicherry, saw in 1931 a grossly mechanistic materialism in Bolshevism.[146] Manabendra Nath (Bhattacharya) Roy, after his expulsion from the Communist International in 1928 was a major critic of Russian policies and the ideas of the Sixth International; a brilliant polemicist, he had some of his writings translated into Bengali.[147] The Gandhian sociologist Nirmal Kumar Bose pointed to the conflict between the Communist doctrines and Gandhian political practice.[148] Between these critics and the defenders of Marxism there developed a running battle. On the other side were intellectual stalwarts like Bhupendranath Datta (Swami Vivekananda's brother), Susobhan Sarkar, Dhurjati Prasad Mukherjee, Dhirendra Nath Sen, Hiren Mukherjee, Gopal Haldar, Bhabani Sen, and others. It is pointless to compile a long list of names. The essence of the story was that a contestation was on for the mind of Bengal and the Left was becoming a strong contender.

From June 1941, after Hitler attacked the USSR, the Communists adopted the 'People's War' line, that is, the view that the character of the World War had changed in that it was no longer simply a fight between imperialist powers, but a war against the vanguard of the world Communist movement. This stand isolated them and provided to the anti-Communist forces propaganda ammunition for years to come. Legitimacy accorded to the party by the British Indian government in July 1942 in consequence of the new position of the CPI did not help to gain popularity. Worst was to follow from August 1942 when the Communist Party opposed the Quit India Movement. Bhabani Sen's tirade in the Communist journal *Jana-juddha* was typical of the CPI position in 1942: 'This country is about to fall prey to the Japanese fascists and the patriots in this country, unable to see the path to liberation, are misled and are becoming puppets in the hands of the Fifth Column'.[149] Songs were sung by Communist Party cadres in praise of Russia at war:

> Each home in Russia's cities is ready for the fight
> To liberate the world they try with all their might.[150]

The reaction to this position was clearly enunciated by Humayun Kabir, a Congress intellectual inclined towards socialism:

> It is questionable whether the present war is a People's War. Stalin has declared often enough that the present war is to defend the Soviet state.... Russia has joined the war because Germany did not abide by the Non-Aggression Pact between Stalin and Hitler. If Hitler had kept his promise then Russia would have remained uninvolved in the war.... It is difficult to see the war Soviet Russia is fighting as a war for the liberation of mankind or for furthering the cause of people's rights.... Stalin has concluded a pact with the British imperialists that includes a promise not to interfere in the internal issues of the empire. The chief internal issue in the British empire is freedom of India and other colonies.[151]

Thus, Kabir concluded, the agenda of Soviet Russia was defensible from their own pragmatic point of view, but did not include liberation of the oppressed peoples of the world, hence there was no question of thinking on the lines of a 'People's War'.

Despite the generally adverse reaction to the notion of People's War and non-participation in the Quit India movement, intellectuals inclined towards Communism found common ground with other Leftists and even the firmly non-Communist nationalists in anti-fascism. A public demonstration of this was the Anti-Fascist Writers' and Artists' Association conference in December 1942 which attracted not only Left intellectuals but also many writers and artists who were distant from the communist ideology. Some of the foremost creative writers and artists worked with that Association in the next few years.[152]

Industrial Labour and the Left

Parallel to the contestation for the mind of Bengal, a contest was on in the industrial workers' movement. In the 1920s, leadership was in the hands of non-Communist personalities but by the end of the 1930s Communists seriously challenged that leadership. Broadly, one can see three phases in the industrial labour movement in Bengal in this period: the first till 1929 was dominated by the Non-cooperation and Khilafat Movements and their aftermath, and the second between the general strikes of 1929 and 1937 was the period of the World Depression. The third was characterized by the steady decline of the Congress and the rise of the Left leadership in trade unionism. The Left also figured prominently in the history of peasant movements, but the politics of agrarian relations forms part of another chapter in this book.

Regarding the history of industrial labour in Bengal, research has been by and large limited to the jute industry on the periphery of Calcutta and our knowledge is as yet very limited in respect of those employed in the railways, river and sea transport, tea in north Bengal, steel and engineering industries, chemical manufactures, and so on. In the jute industry the three distinctive characteristics of the labour force were that (*a*) unlike Bombay, Kanpur, or Madras, the participation of the local population was very limited; (*b*) there were many more single migrants than migrant families; and (*c*) the third characteristic, diminution of female employment, was shared with almost all industries in twentieth-century India except tea plantations. As regards Bengali presence in the jute mill labour force, there were exceptions like the old mill established in the nineteenth century, Fort Gloster, which employed 4,000 local Bengalis and 2,000 immigrants from other provinces in the 1920s. But in the industrial belt as a whole the overwhelming majority in almost all mills were immigrants from Bihar, the United Provinces (that is, present-day Uttar Pradesh), and Orissa.[153] The steady flow of millworkers cyclically returning to their village homes was a subject of extensive comment in the report of the Royal Commission on Labour in India, for they saw in it the characteristics of a labour force that was comprised of half-peasant and not wholly industrially committed workers. A number of labour historians, for example, Dipesh Chakrabarty, emphasize the importance of the pre-capitalist background jute mill workers came from and their continuing links with that world in shaping their social consciousness;[154] on the other hand, there is a strong trend among historians on the Left to underline heavily the instances of class consciousness and protest movements among the industrial workers. The immigrants, oftener than not, left their families behind in the village home. The women left behind were also part of an economically active population and they supplemented the low wages received by migrant members. They thus played a crucial role in the survival strategy of the household, as well as in the social reproduction of labour that the capital–labour relationship required.[155] Samita Sen, in a path-breaking work on women jute-mill workers, has estimated that the proportion of women in the industry declined from about 20 per cent in the late nineteenth century to 12 per cent in the 1940s. There was hierarchical job segregation in the factory, differentiating male and female workers—the latter were assigned labour-intensive and low-paid work. To date, few historians have explored the interface between gender and class because, it has been said, they feel 'a discomfort with categories like gender that are potentially divisive of class'.[156] Be that as it may, there is evidence that the women workers did not shrink from participation in protest movements alongside male workers. Moreover, as Chitra Joshi has argued in a different context, in the working-class family gender relationships inevitably changed when women of the family were industrially employed.[157]

In the early phase of the industrial workers' movement in India, the Left was marginal compared to the leadership they called 'petty-bourgeois reformists'. The latter founded the All-India Trade Union Congress (AITUC) under the patronage of the Indian National Congress: Lala Lajpat Rai was the president at the first AITUC session in Bombay (31 October 1921) and among those present were Motilal Nehru, Vithalbhai Patel, Annie Besant, M.A. Jinnah, and others While the 'reformist' N.M. Joshi was the leading trade unionist in that assembly, the future Communist leaders S.A. Dange and R.S. Nimbkar were among the student volunteers. A conspicuous absentee was Mahatma Gandhi who personally disapproved of the idea, though the Congress was happy to appropriate this attempt to reach out to industrial workers. While this was the scene at the all-India level, in Bengal the chief characteristics of the first phase of the 1920s were different:

1. The participation of Bengal trade unions was quite small in that first AITUC conference as compared to that of Bombay and Madras. Bengal was represented by only a few unions of seamen, railway workers, press workers, and so on. However, it was represented by Chitta Ranjan Das as the President of the AITUC at the third and fourth conferences at Lahore and Calcutta in 1923 and 1924 respectively. The trade unionists in Bengal were unable to institute any permanent organization of the kind N.M. Joshi or R.R. Bakhale had set up in Bombay. In the wake of the Non-cooperation Movement there were some dispersed strikes—in particular the East Indian Railway strike of February 1922 which ended in defeat for the workers who had to face armed police in Asansol and firing in Burdwan.
2. It was not the National Congress but the Swarajists who initially provided leadership to industrial labour in Bengal. Chitta Ranjan Das was interested in expanding his labour links even before he set up the Swaraj Party. He was involved in organizing the All-India Railway Employees Union (1920), while his lieutenants, Subhas Bose and J.M. Sengupta, lent their names to the central committees of some major trade unions. In 1922, as president of the National Congress, C.R. Das appointed a Congress Labour Committee with Sengupta as a member. At a lower rung of leadership Swarajists drew upon the organizing ability of Mrs Santosh Kumari Gupta.

Recent research also reveals that along with the Swarajists the Khilaftists claimed a stake in labour leadership since there were many Muslim workers in the jute mills.

3. The third development that occurred in this phase was the growth of the Workers' and Peasants Party (WPP) from 1928. The Communists in the new party had a strategic schema, while the earlier labour leaders were limited to tactics as and when a strike occurred in an individual mill. The new WPP set up the Bengal Jute Workers' Union which mentored affiliated trade unions in local trade unions in many mills. A similar strategic vision is evident in the policy of the WPP to collaborate with non-Communists like Sibnath Mukherjee or Dr Prabhabati Dasgupta, accommodating them in a broad-based front.

The rise of the Communists in the trade unions caused alarm bells to ring in the Intelligence Department of the police and it was not fortuitous that three Communist trade unionists in the Bengal jute mills were arrested and put on trial in the Meerut Conspiracy Case along with S.A. Dange and others in 1929. Another strategic initiative of the Communists was the ideological campaign in Bengali. Muzaffar Ahmed edited *Ganavani* from 1926; in fact, there were also parallel endeavours in *Sramik* edited by Mrs Santosh Kumari Gupta and *Majdur* edited by Kutubuddin Ahmed. This campaign on class lines set apart the Left from the Congress which was tied to the Gandhian philosophy of a non-conflictual capital–labour relationship under capitalists as 'trustees'; in fact, Gandhi was on record stating on several occasions that even the civil right of going on strike was in moral terms reprehensible as an act of 'violence'.[158]

The next phase of the labour movement in Bengal—1929 to 1937—saw the rise of the Left which included not only Communist leaders like Muzaffar Ahmed, but also the M.N. Roy followers known as 'Royists', the Forward Bloc and the Congress Socialist Party. The two chief features of this phase were (*a*) the impact of the World Depression of 1929–35 and (*b*) the transition of trade union organization from localized and dispersed unionism to federative structures that made it possible to hold an industry-wide general strike. The World Depression reduced the global demand for jute products and the India Jute Mills Association (IJMA), dominated by British capitalists and managers, tried to ride through the crisis by reducing production and labour costs. This naturally meant worker retrenchment and reduction in wages. The government estimated that about 83,000 workers were retrenched between 1929 and 1934 and in the same period wage cost was reduced by over 25 per cent by working only one shift instead of two. Thus conflict between unions and management was endemic in this period; at the same time, because of Depression the entire labour market was tight and workers had to be cautious about going on strike for fear of losing their jobs and facing prolonged unemployment.

One of the ways of reducing wage costs was to increase the number of hours of work and this was the strategy adopted by the IJMA. In July 1929, all jute mills were instructed by the IJMA to increase hours of work from 54 to 60 per week; this is, of course, wage reduction by other means and it led to a series of industrial mill strikes and eventually a general strike. The unprecedented participation of almost all jute mills in and near Calcutta seems to have unnerved the IJMA and the notice in respect of increase in hours of work was withdrawn. Another important outcome of the strike was that the negotiating parties, IJMA and the Bengal Jute Workers' Association, signed an agreement to ensure that mill owners would not object to the formation of trade unions.

After this temporary victory, the workers faced a different strategy on the part of mill owners. Instead of the industry-wide management policy of July 1929, owners of each individual mill retrenched workers slowly and steadily and that is how, as we have noted earlier, more than eighty thousand workers were retrenched. There were strikes in individual jute mills and in the cotton mill industry, the most notable was the Kesoram Cotton Mill strike in 1935 involving almost 5,000 workers for about six months. Bengal led the rest of India in unionizing workers: in 1933–4 the number of trade unions in Bengal, Bombay, and Madras was 54, 44, and 38 respectively, and in 1937–8 the corresponding figures were 172, 72, and 54. The ratio of unionized workers to total workforce would have been a better index but that is not available. In Bengal, unionization was a strong trend in the railways, shipping, jute mills, ports, electricity and tramways. The Depression-induced unemployment curbed, as we have noted, workers' readiness to go on strike. But, by 1937, matters had reached a tipping-point for them. A series of strikes in individual mills coalesced into a general strike of jute workers from February to May 1937, involving 225,000 workers. The demands, predictably, were cessation of retrenchment and restoration of wage cuts. The central strike committee was a coalition of Leftist and other trade unions. Among the leaders of the strike were the Communist leaders Muzaffar Ahmed and Bankim Mukherjee, as well as some non-Communist Left leaders like Sibnath Banerjee. The situation was favourable because the Depression was over and the mill management was known to be making profit. Another factor in the situation was that although the Left was nowhere near gaining power, the formation of the government of the Krishak Praja Party under Fazlul Huq raised expectations in 1937. The Congress, in opposition in Bengal from 1937 to 1947, happily castigated Fazlul Huq's government and the predominantly British mill-owners for their failure to meet the workers' demands. In fact, it was a rare instance of the Congress Working Committee passing a resolution in support of the workers on strike and against police repression of workers.[159] Eventually, the strike committee negotiated with Chief Minister (then called Prime Minister) Fazlul Huq to reach a negotiated settlement that marked the end of a strike that had already collapsed due to factionalism among the Leftist leaders and the influence of communal politicians over the Muslim jute workers.

In the third phase of the industrial workers' movement in this period, the phase from 1937 to 1947, there were two prominent trends: (*a*) The Left emerged as the strongest among the contenders for leadership in the labour movement; on the other hand, it was a difficult time for the Communists because their adoption of the so-called People's War line did not make them very popular. (*b*) The second trend was the decline in the real income of workers under inflationary conditions during the Second World War. As regards the economic situation, suffice it to say that due to the War the index of profit (base year 1939 = 100) in the jute industry went up to 344.4 in 1941, 351.1 in 1942 and stood at 327.6 in 1945, but the real wages of workers declined considerably. We have India-wide wage indices showing that real wages of industrial workers slightly increased (base year 1939 = 100) to 103.7 in 1941 but thereafter the War-induced inflation steadily reduced real income of workers to 74.9 in 1945. The industrial worker's monetary income increased throughout this period, but the consumer price index (base year 1939) rose at a higher rate, eventually to reach a maximum of 269 in 1945. The British India government took great care to keep industrial production attuned to war-time requirements. For the jute industry and other industries in and near Calcutta the policy was to prevent industrial disturbance by ensuring payment of Dearness Allowance and arranging food ration in selected urban areas. The other aspect of the same policy was to suppress working class protest by various legal measures: the infamous Defence of India Rules allowed coercive recruitment of labour for government purposes, the National Service Ordinance of 1940 enabled the government to punish "troublemakers" in war-related industries in special tribunals outside civil judicial authority, and the Essential Services Maintenance Ordinance (later known as ESMA) of 1941 further strengthened the above-mentioned coercive measures.

As a result, despite the fall in real income of workers, there was no general strike or large-scale action by workers. There were dispersed and localized strikes, and the sole and abortive attempt in 1939 to organize a general strike took place before Bengal was drawn into the vortex of the war. Factionalism was rampant within the Left, and it destroyed the Bengal Jute Workers' Union in 1931. The Communist leadership, active earlier in the Worker's and Peasants' Party and later the Communist Party, founded a new federative body, Bengal Chatkal Mazdoor Union in 1937. However, from June 1941 the Communist Party position in respect of 'People's War' in response to the German invasion of the USSR, and thereafter their position on the Quit India Movement isolated them considerably. Moreover, as we shall see in a later chapter, the spread of communalism affected almost all civil society institutions in the 1940s and the trade unions were no exception. There were two other aspects of the industrial labour movement that were discouraging. The trade unions waxed and waned over the need for strike action as and when issues came up; in the early 1940s, after many years of trade union activity, there were only sixteen registered unions and three thousand members.[160] Trade unions as permanent bodies were exceptions rather than the rule at that stage. Second, the leadership was monopolized by 'outsiders', that is, non-working class individuals of the *bhadralok* status in society and thus the proletarians who, in theory, were to be the vanguard of revolutionary transformation were hegemonized by middle-class leaders. This characteristic had important long-term implications for the Left movement. There were, no doubt, working class leaders of middle rank and on the factory floor, but the rise of the Left did not bring about at the top a leadership proletarian in origin.

Notes

1. Rabindranath Tagore 'The Call of Truth', tr. of 'Satyer ahvan' in *Pravasee* (Kartik, 1326 BS or AD 1919), reprinted in *Kalantar* (Calcutta, 1937), cited in Sabyasachi Bhattacharya (ed.), *The Mahatma and the Poet: Letters and Debates between Gandhi and Tagore, 1915–1941* (Delhi, 1997), p. 76.
2. Rabindranath Tagore, 'The Cult of the Charkha', *Modern Review* (September 1925), in S. Bhattacharya (ed.), *The Mahatma*, p. 10.
3. M.K. Gandhi, 'The Poet's Anxiety', *Young India*, 1 June 1921; S. Bhattacharya (ed.), *The Mahatma*, pp. 65–8, and 'Introduction', pp. 4–21.
4. M.K. Gandhi, 'The Great Sentinel', *Young India*, 13 October 1921.
5. *Ananda Bazar Patrika* [hereafter cited as *ABP*], 19 August 1925.
6. Khitish C. Dasgupta in *ABP*, 20 April 1928.
7. A social resource, within the parameters of what Antonio Gramsci termed the Civil Society, can be of use only when the public sphere develops and this is perhaps what Tagore is talking about in his comments on the 'public' and the 'private' in the essay I cited in the Introduction earlier. Rabindranath Tagore, *Rabindra Rachanavalee*, vol. IX, p. 613.
8. Sabyasachi Bhattacharya, *Financial Foundations of the British Raj* (Simla: IIAS, 1970), pp. xix–xi, 274.
9. 'Memoirs of Satish Chandra Basu (1874–1948)' in Bhupendra Nath Dutta, *Bharater dwitiya swadhinata sangram* (Calcutta, 1949), pp. 179–94.
10. Tagore, 'The Call of Truth'. Apart from the sources mentioned in notes below, I have found the following useful for putting together an account of Bengal politics in this part of the book: J.H. Broomfield, *Elite Conflict in a Plural Society: Twentieth-Century Bengal* (Berkeley, 1968); Buddhadeb Bhattacharya, *Satyagrahas in Bengal, 1921–39* (Calcutta, 1977); Bidyut Chakrabarty, *Local Politics and Indian Nationalism: Midnapur, 1919–44* (Delhi, 1997); Joya Chatterji, *Bengal Divided: Hindu Communalism and Partition, 1932–47* (Cambridge, 1994); Partha Chatterjee, *Bengal, 1920–47: The Land Question* (Calcutta, 1984); Gautam Chattopadhyay, *Bengal Electoral Politics and Freedom Struggle, 1862–1947* (New Delhi, 1984); Suranjan Das, *Communal Riots in Bengal, 1905–1947* (New Delhi, 1991); L.A. Gordon, *Bengal: The Nationalist Movement, 1876–1940* (New Delhi, 1979); Rajat Kanta Ray, *Social Conflict and Political Unrest in Bengal, 1875–1927* (New Delhi, 1984); Tanika Sarkar, *Bengal 1928–1934: The Politics of Protest* (New Delhi, 1987), and works of Bengali fiction too numerous to mention.

11. Nripendra Chandra Banerji, *At the Cross-roads*, with an Introduction by Nirmal Chandra Bhattacharya (Calcutta, 1974), p. 125. In order to capture flavour of real-life experience in personal narratives, I have tried the method of presenting and reflecting upon experiences recorded by a few individuals in different contexts, for example, Nripendra Chandra Banerji, Nirad C. Chaudhuri, Abul Hashim, Abul Mansur Ahmed, Gopal Haldar, M.A.H. Ispahani, Muzaffar Ahmed, and Syama Prasad Mookerjee.
12. Banerji, *At the Cross-roads*, p. 119.
13. Banerji, *At the Cross-roads*, pp. 125–6.
14. Banerji, *At the Cross-roads*, pp. 133–5.
15. Banerji, *At the Cross-roads*, p. 137; the subsequent quotations in this paragraph in text are from the same source, pp. 137–9.
16. Banerji, *At the Cross-roads*, p. 139.
17. Swapan Dasgupta, 'Adivasi Politics in Midnapur, 1760–1924' in R. Guha, *Subaltern Studies*, IV (New Delhi, 1985), p. 126.
18. S. Dasgupta, 'Adivasi Politics', pp. 129–30.
19. B.N. Sasmal's statement in *Amrita Bazar Patrika*, 21 October 1921, cited in Buddhadeb Bhattacharya et al. (eds), *Satyagrahas in Bengal 1921–1939* (Calcutta, 1977), ch. 2.
20. S.N. Ray, Report of 1 November 1921, Local Self-government Dept., Local Boards Branch, f. no. L. 2-4-5(1), A-36/43, July 1922, reprinted in B. Bhattacharya et al. (eds), *Satyagrahas in Bengal*, pp. 29–43.
21. A.W. Crook, Deputy Magistrate to Commissioner, Burdwan Division, 3 November 1921, in B. Bhattacharya et al. (eds), *Satyagrahas in Bengal*, p. 26.
22. Report of S.N. Ray, ICS, Jt. Magistrate, 1 November 1921, reprinted in B. Bhattacharya et al. (eds), *Satyagrahas in Bengal*. Details of Sasmal's activities have recently become available in the work of Swadesranjan Mandal, *The Cracked Portrait of a Patriot: Desapran Birendranath Sasmal, 1881–1934* (Instt. of Historical Studies, Calcutta, 2012).
23. Reported by Chandi P. Sarkar in Barun De (ed.), *Mukti sangrame banglar chhatra samaj* (Calcutta, 1992), p. 137.
24. Home (pol.) confidential, F.395/1924 W.B. & P., cited in Ranjit K. Ray in B. De (ed.), *Mukti sangrame*, p. 27; also see Rajat K. Ray, *Social and Political Unrest in Bengal, 1875–1927* (New Delhi, 1984).
25. *ABP*, editorial, 11 July 1922.
26. S. Dasgupta, 'Adivasi Politics', pp. 126–7; Sumit Sarkar, *Modern India* (Delhi, 1985), p. 221.
27. M.K. Gandhi, 'The Congress', *Young India*, 7 January 1920.
28. M.K. Gandhi, 'The Reform Resolution in the Congress', *Young India*, 14 January 1920.

29. M.K. Gandhi's statement in P. Sitaramayya, *The History of the Indian National Congress* (Madras, 1935), p. 326.
30. M.K. Gandhi, 'The Working Committee', *Young India*, 29 June 1921.
31. M.K. Gandhi, 'Wages and Values', *Young India*, 6 October 1921, report on Gandhi's speech at the Ahmedabad mill workers' meeting; also *Young India*, 29 June 1921.
32. M.K. Gandhi in *Nav Jivan*, 8 June 1921.
33. M.K. Gandhi, 'Strike', *Young India*, 16 February 1921.
34. M.K. Gandhi, 'Assam Coolies', *Young India*, 8 June 1921.
35. M.K. Gandhi, *Nav Jivan*, 8 June 1921.
36. M.K. Gandhi, 'Strikes', *Young India*, 1 December 1921.
37. M.K. Gandhi, 'A Deep Stain', *Young India*, 24 November 1921.
38. Resolution of Maharashtra PCC Executive Committee, 3 April 1927, AICC Papers, file no. G-39 (III)/1927, Nehru Memorial Library; see Sabyasachi Bhattacharya, 'Swaraj and the Kamgar: Congress and the Bombay Working Class, 1919–31' in *Congress and Indian Nationalism*, eds R. Sisson and S. Wolpert (Berkeley, 1988), pp. 223–49.
39. *Atmashakti* (Calcutta), 24 August 1928.
40. *Ganavani*, 30 August 1928; this was the official organ of the Bengal Workers' and Peasants' Party.
41. S. Bhattacharya in R. Sisson and S. Wolpert (eds), *Congress and Indian Nationalism*, and 'The Intelligentsia in Colonial India', *Studies in History* I (January 1979), pp. 89–104.
42. Sitaramayya, *History of the Indian National Congress*, p. 305.
43. Gopal Haldar, *Rupnaryaner kule* (Calcutta, 1988), vol. II, p. 74.
44. Bishan Kumar Gupta, *Political Movements in Murshidabad, 1920–47* (Calcutta, 1992).
45. S. Dasgupta, 'Adivasi Politics', pp. 124–30. Satkaripati (also spelt as Satcowri Pati) Roy was interviewed in course of the Nehru Museum oral history programme of research and the transcript is Dasgupta's source.
46. Bidyut Chakrabarty, 'Local Politics and Indian Nationalism: Midnapur, 1919–1944' (New Delhi, 1997), ch. 2; H.R. Sanyal, 'Congress in South-western Bengal: The Anti-Union Board Movement in Eastern Medinipur, 1921', in *Congress and Indian Nationalism*, eds Sisson and Wolpert, pp. 352–76.
47. Bidyut Chakrabarty, *Subhas Bose and Middle-Class Radicalism* (London, 1990), pp. 8–9, 184.
48. I have depended for the following account on Prithwis Chandra Ray, *Life and Times of C.R. Das* (London, 1927); Ray (1870–1928) was a journalist and Congress worker from 1905 till his death, and a personal friend of Das. R. Sen and B.K. Sen (eds), *Deshbandhu Chitta Ranjan* (Calcutta, 1926)

contains the standard collection of his speeches, and for the period 1917 to 1920, C.R. Das, *India for Indians* (Madras, 1921). Barring Paul Greenough, 'Death of an Uncrowned King', mimeo, Iowa University, 1984, a Ph.D. thesis of Calcutta University, is the only academic work on Das: D.K. Chatterjee, *C.R. Das and the Indian National Movement* (Calcutta, 1965).

49. Sitaramayya, *History of the Indian National Congress*, p. 423.
50. D. Chakrabarty and C. Bhattacharya, *Congress in Evolution: A Collection of Congress Resolutions* (Calcutta, 1935), p. 111.
51. Sitaramayya, *History of the Indian National Congress*, p. 426.
52. Subhas Chandra Bose, *The Indian Struggle, 1920–1942* (Calcutta, 1964), p. 78.
53. On the activities of the Swarajists, see Sachin Dutt, *Deshapriya J.M. Sengupta* (Delhi, 1983); Sengupta was considered to be the leader of the Swarajist Party after Das's death. Also see G. Chattopadhyay, *Bengal Electoral Politics*, ch. 5.
54. Banerji, *At the Cross-roads*, p. 155.
55. This information is based upon the account given by Peter Heehs, *Nationalism, Terrorism, Communalism* (Delhi, 1998), pp. 114–15; the biographer of Aurobindo, Heehs, is quite an authority on his subject and the report is backed by Aurobindo's private correspondence. According to Heehs, Aurobindo disagreed with Das for he thought that concessions to Muslims were not an adequate response to the communal problem.
56. *ABP*, editorial, 'Hindu Musalmaner Milon', 9 May 1924; Abul Mansur Ahmad, *Amar dekha rajnitir panchas bacchar* (Dhaka, 1995), p. 35.
57. *Islam Darshan* IV, no. 5 (1331 BS), in Mustafa Nurul Islam (ed.), *Samayik patre jiban o janamat, 1901–1930* (Dhaka, 1977).
58. Ahmad, *Rajnitir panchas bacchar*, pp. 39–40.
59. Banerji, *At the Cross-roads*, p. 144.
60. Sasmal's remark is recorded by Banerji, *At the Cross-roads*, p. 171.
61. Nirad C. Chaudhuri, *Thy Hand, Great Anarch! India, 1921–1952* (London, 1987), p. 379.
62. *Amrita Bazar Patrika*, 5 November 1922; also his Amraoti statement, in D.K. Chatterjee, *C.R. Das and the Indian National Movement*, ch. 4.
63. *Times of India*, 2 May 1924; *Source Material for History of Freedom Movement* (State Archives of Maharashtra, Bombay, n.d.), vol. VI, p. 223.
64. S.N. Gourlay, 'Nationalists, Outsiders and the Labour Movement in Bengal during the Non-Cooperation Movement' in *Congress and Classes*, ed. Kapil Kumar (New Delhi, 1988), pp. 34–57.
65. Rajat K. Ray, *Social and Political Unrest*, p. 279, on the supposed 'spontaneous rising of the entire population specially of the lower classes'.
66. The Labour Committee of the Congress met infrequently and achieved nothing; this is evident from the All-India Trade Union Congress Papers

(Nehru Memorial Museum & Library), F.I., Correspondence between C.F. Andrews and N.M. Joshi; also see *Selected Material on History of the Freedom Movement*, vol. VI, p. 188; S.A. Dange's scathing remarks on the non-functioning committee, Statement of the Accused, pp. 773–5, in the Meerut Conspiracy Case Papers (P.C. Joshi Archives, JNU).

67. M.N. Roy, *The Future of Indian Politics* (London, 1926), pp. 64, 75.
68. Muzaffar Ahmed, *Amar jiban o bharater communist party*, vol. I (Calcutta, 1984); Gautam Chattopadhyay, *Communism and Bengal's Freedom Movement, 1917–29* (New Delhi, 1974); Aditya Mukherjee, 'The Workers and Peasants Parties, 1926–30', in *Studies in History* III, nos 1–2 (1981), pp. 1–44. A well-documented work, unavailable in English, is Amitabha Chandra, *Abibhakta banglaye communist andolan* (Calcutta, 1992), although it contains occasional exaggerations, for instance, the Kishorganj agitation of 1930, pp. 98–103.
69. Bose, *The Indian Struggle*, p. 109.
70. Aparna Devi, *Manush Chittaranjan* (Calcutta, 1928), p. 77.
71. P.C. Ray, *Life and Times of C.R. Das*; Naresh Chandra Ghosh, *Chittajayee Chittaranjan* (Calcutta, 1971), p. 327.
72. N.C. Ghosh, *Chittajayee Chittaranjan*, pp. 333–4.
73. C.R. Das to Hemendra Dasgupta, 9 June 1925, in N.C. Ghosh, *Chittajayee Chittaranjan*, p. 356.
74. John Gallagher, 'Congress in Decline in Bengal, 1937–39', in *Locality, Province and Nation: Essays in Indian Politics, 1870–1940*, ed. Anil Seal (Cambridge, 1973).
75. Sumit Sarkar, *Modern India: 1885–1947* (1983), pp. 301–2; also see his 'The Logic of Gandhian Nationalism: Civil Disobedience and the Gandhi–Irwin Pact, 1930–31', *Indian Historical Review* (July 1976). With due deference to his authority it may be submitted that the evidence produced by Hites Ranjan Sanyal on Medinipur might qualify Sarkar's judgement that the rural *bhadralok* eschewed 'no-rent calls' and that *jotedar*–sharecropper relations also remained outside the sphere of Congress theory and practice (Sumit Sarkar, *Modern India*, p. 303).
76. Hites Ranjan Sanyal, 'Congress Movements in the Villages of Eastern Medinipur', in *Asie du Sud: Traditions et Changements*, ICNRS, no. 582 (Paris, 1979), in *Chaturanga* 38th year, Calcutta, 1383 BS, and in Gyanendra Pandey (ed.), *The Indian Nation in 1942* (Calcutta, 1988). Field investigation and collection of oral evidence distinguish Sanyal's effort from other similar works.
77. Sanyal in G. Pandey (ed.), *The Indian Nation in 1942*, pp. 37–8.
78. B. Bhattacharya et al. (eds), *Satyagrahas in Bengal*, pp. 159–84.
79. B. Bhattacharya et al. (eds), *Satyagrahas in Bengal*, pp. 185–205.

80. B. Bhattacharya et al. (eds), *Satyagrahas in Bengal*, pp. 217–21.
81. B. Bhattacharya et al. (eds), *Satyagrahas in Bengal*, pp. 206–13.
82. N.K. Bose, *My Days with Gandhi* (Calcutta, 1972), p. 165.
83. Gandhi to S. Dasgupta, 17 March 1930, *Collected Works of Mahatma Gandhi*, vol. XLII, p. 89.
84. Muzaffar Ahmed, *Amar jiban o bharater communist party*, vol. II (Calcutta, 1988), pp. 393–4.
85. Banerji, *At the Cross-roads*, p. 199.
86. Sitaramayya, *History of the Congress*, p. 1004.
87. The convoluted story of the *biplabi* or militant nationalist movement in Bengal is available most clearly in the Intelligence Bureau reports of the Bengal Police now published in the excellent collection of documents edited by Amiya K. Samanta, *Terrorism in Bengal: A Collection of Documents on Terrorist Activities, from 1905 to 1939* (Governmentt of West Bengal, Calcutta, 1985), vols I–VI.
88. N.C. Chaudhuri, *Thy Hand, Great Anarch!* pp. 287, 290–1. The works I found useful on the theme of revolutionary nationalism or terrorism are: Peter Heehs, *The Bomb in Bengal: The Rise of Revolutionary Terrorism in India, 1900–10* (Delhi, 1993) and a classic, Sumit Sarkar's *The Swadeshi Movement in Bengal, 1903–1908* (Delhi, 1973), on an earlier period; in Bengali some participant-observer accounts are by Bhupendra Nath Datta, *Bharater Dwitiya Swadhinata andolan* (Calcutta, 1949); Upendra Nath Bandhyopadhyay, *Nirvasiter atmakatha* (9th edn., Calcutta, 1976); Bhupendra Kumar Rakshit Ray, *Bharate shasastra biplab* (Calcutta, 1970); Jadugopal Mukhopadhyay, *Biblabi jibaner smriti* (Calcutta, 1982); Satish Pakrashi, *Agnijuger katha* (Calcutta, 1971); Subodh Kumar Lahiri, *Biplabe pathe* (Calcutta, 1950). The political scientist Buddhadeb Bhattacharya edited a useful collection, *The Freedom Struggle and the Anushilan Samiti* (Calcutta, 1979), and likewise the reminiscences in B.D. Mukhopadhyay and S.P. Datta (eds), *Indian Republic Army: Chattagram Biplab* (Calcutta, 1995).
89. N.C. Chaudhuri, *Thy Hand, Great Anarch!* pp. 289, 287, 317.
90. Haldar, *Rupnarayaner kule*, vol. II, pp. 256–7, 269.
91. Haldar, *Rupnarayaner kule*, vol. II, p. 275.
92. Rakhal Chandra Dey, *Bandir jiban smaranika* (Jalpaiguri, 1974), p. 11.
93. R.C. Dey, *Bandir jiban*, pp. 23–4.
94. Testimony of Ganesh Ghosh, in Sachindranath Guha (ed.), *Chattogram biplaber bahnisikha* (Calcutta, 1974).
95. Ramesh C. Majumdar, *Bangladesher Itihas*, vol. IV, p. 282.
96. Bhupendra Nath Dutta, *Bharater dwitiya swadhinata sangram* (India's Second War of Independence) (Calcutta, 1949)., pp. 88–9.

97. Haldar, *Rupnaryaner kule*, vol. II, p. 284.
98. N.C. Chaudhuri, *Thy Hand, Great Anarch!* pp. 290–1; Sudhir Kakkar, *The Inner World* (New Delhi, 1981); and Indira Chaudhury-Sengupta, 'Reconstructing Spiritual Heroism: The Evolution of the Swadeshi Sannyasi in Bengal' in *Myths and Mythmaking*, ed. Julia Leslie (London, 1996), pp. 124–43.
99. N.C. Chaudhuri, *Thy Hand, Great Anarch!* p. 292.
100. N.C. Chaudhuri, *Thy Hand, Great Anarch!* p. 313.
101. Nirmal Chandra Bhattacharya, *Bismrita bangla* (forthcoming), ch. 4.
102. John Hunt, *Life Is Meeting*, cited in Mukhopadhyay and Datta (eds), *Indian Republic Army*, pp. 67–75. I have not been able to check the source of this extract.
103. Hunt, *Life Is Meeting*, pp. 20–4.
104. An example: the 'Finance Minister, Bengal Branch of Independent Kingdom of United India' issues a receipt for money taken in a Jugantar group dacoity in Howrah in 1916, to the effect that 'Rs. 9,891 - 1 anna - 5 pies have been received by this office ... God willing, upon achieving our objective, we shall return all the money with interest'. This is cited by R.C. Majumdar, *Bangla desher itihas*, vol. IV (Calcutta, 1982), p. 220. This is, of course, not so much an example of ethical standards but evidence of the terrorists' faith in their mission.
105. Majumdar, *Bangla desher itihas*, vol. IV, ch. 10 contains statistics of incidence of terrorist acts.
106. Samaren Ray, *The Twice-Born Heretic: M.N. Roy and Comintern* (Calcutta, 1986), pp. 25–30, citing *Calcutta Weekly Notes*, vol. XV, p. 596; M.N. Roy himself wrote later, in *Independent India*, of his contact with Khudiram Das.
107. Bhupendra Kumar Datta's memoirs in Mukhopadhyay and Datta (eds), *Indian Republic Army*, pp. 4–8.
108. M.K. Gandhi, *Young India*, 23 February 1921.
109. Binod Bihari Chowdhuri who took part in the Chittagong insurrection wrote later that Surya Sen modelled his IRA on the Irish Republican Army; Mukhopadhyay and Dutta (eds), *Indian Republic Army*, p. ix.
110. Ganesh Ghosh cited in Majumdar, *Bangla desher itihas*, vol. IV, p. 296.
111. N.C. Chaudhuri, *Thy Hand, Great Anarch!* pp. 294–9, provides a detailed critique of the tactical errors.
112. On the numbers involved, I have depended on Judgement, Armoury Raid Case no. 1, p. 70, cited by Asha Das in Mukhopadhyay and Dutta (eds), *Indian Republic Army*, pp. 9–27; the list seized from Ganesh Ghosh by the police contained fifty-four names; later memoirs mentioned a larger number, probably exaggerated.

113. Binod Datta assumed presidentship of the IRA and managed to evade arrest till August 1941; John Hunt mentions Datta in his memoirs as a 'legendary figure' with many 'fantasies' imagined about him. Mukhopadhyay and Dutta (eds), *Indian Republic Army*, p. 81.
114. Hunt, *Life Is Meeting*, p. 21.
115. While in Chittagong popular support in the form of connivance with terrorists is beyond doubt, in Midnapore no such support is found except among the urban *bhadralok*; for example, Bidyut Chakrabarty, *Local Politics and Indian Nationalism: Midnapur, 1919–1944* (Delhi, 1997), p. 112. Thus a lot of local variation in this respect is beyond doubt; in any event, the tactics of the terrorists themselves precluded any easily observable signs of popular support.
116. Bishan Kumar Gupta, *Political Movements in Murhsidabad, 1920–47* (Calcutta, 1992), pp. 74–6.
117. Amalendu De, 'Formation of the Communist Party in Faridpur' in *National and Left Movements in India*, ed. K.N. Panikkar (Delhi, 1980), pp. 266–98.
118. B.K. Gupta, *Political Movements in Murhsidabad*, pp. 86–91; A. Chandra, *Abibhakta banglaye communist andolan*, pp. 111–25.
119. Ananta Singh reminisces in *Agnigarbha chattogram*; Asha Das in Mukhopadhyay and Datta (eds), *Indian Republic Army*, p. 11.
120. C.R. Das, *India for Indians*, p. 280; in 1926 M.N. Roy in *Future of Indian Politics* (Calcutta, 1926, 1971, p. 50) commented that Das's Faridpur speech shows how much he was a member of the propertied classes, opposed to revolution.
121. Tagore, 'The Call of Truth', in S. Bhattacharya (ed.), *The Mahatma and the Poet*, p. 74.
122. Rabindranath Tagore to Sarat Chandra Chatterjee, 27 Magh, 1333 BS, in Chinmohan Sehanobis, *Rabindranath o biplabi samaj* (Calcutta, 1985), p. 125
123. Sarat Chandra Chatterjee, *Pather dabee* (Calcutta, 1920) in his *Collected Works* (Calcutta, 1977), vol. I, pp. 107, 173–7, 180–6.
124. The obvious contrast between *Pather dabee* and *Char adhyay* has been commented upon by many, most notably by Sehanobis, *Rabindranath o biplabi samaj*, and Tanika Sarkar, 'Bengali Middle-class Nationalism and Literature' in D.N. Panigrahi (ed.), *Economy, Society and Politics in Modern India* (New Delhi, 1985). Tagore's 'Kaifiyat' appeared in *Pravasee*, reprinted in *Rabindra Rachanavalee*, vol. VII, pp. 744–6.
125. Tagore, *Char adhyay*, in *Rabindra Rachanavalee*, vol. VII, ch. 4.
126. Tagore's preface to *Char adhyay*: 'I felt that he [Upadhyay] had come solely to say these few heartbreaking words. He was then a captive of his

own activities, there was no way he could escape'. *Rabindra Rachanavalee*, vol. VII, p. 744.

127. The ends and means question and the tragedy of noble souls mixed in inescapable circumstances of their own making is a major theme in the novel.
128. Rabindranath Tagore, 'Path o patheya', *Bangadarshan* (1335 BS, AD 1908), *Rabindra Rachanavalee*, vol. X, pp. 447–56.
129. Tagore, 'Path o patheya'.
130. Rabindranath Tagore, 'Samasya' (1335 BS, AD 1908), *Rabindra Rachanavalee*, vol. X, p. 472.
131. Tagore, 'The Call of Truth', in S. Bhattacharya (ed.), *The Mahatma and the Poet*, p. 74.
132. Sehanobis, *Rabindranath o biplabi samaj*, pp. 107, 110, 119.
133. Rabindranath Tagore, *Kalantar*, in *Rabindra Rachanavalee*, vol. 24, p. 326.
134. Ramananda Chatterjee, in *Prabasi*, Baisakh, 1324 BS, 1917, in Sipra Sarkar and Anamitra Das (eds), *Bangalir samyavad charcha* (Calcutta 1998) (hereafter cited as BSC), pp. 27–30
135. Upendranath Bandyopadhyay, in *Narayan*, Asadh, 1327 BS, 1920, in *BSC*, p. 37
136. Abul Hussain, in *Bangiya Musalman Sahitya Patrika*, Sravan, 1328 BS, 1921, in *BSC*, p. 42
137. Benoy Sarkar, *Naya banglar gorapattan*, 1324 BS, 1932, in *BSC*, p. 73
138. *ABP*, editorial on 'Lenin the Great', 16 Magh 1330 BS, 30 January 1924, in *BSC*, p. 61
139. Editorial in *Samyavadi*, Bhadra 1331 BS, 1924, in *BSC*, pp. 69–70
140. Muzaffar Ahmed, in *Langal*, 25 February 1926, in *BSC*, p. 80
141. Nazrul Islam, 'Antar-national sangit', in *Ganavani*, May Day 1927, in *BSC*, p. 90
142. Editorial, *Ganavani*, 27 September 1926, in *BSC*, pp. 84–6
143. Rabindranath Tagore, *Russiar chithi*, 1931, tr. into Engliah as *A Letter from Russia* by S. Sinha (Visva-Bharati, 1960), pp. 12, 60, 110–14, 117. I have also drawn upon a recent work, Sabyasachi Bhattacharya, *Rabindranath Tagore: An Interpretation* (New Delhi, 2011), pp. 161–4.
144. Rabindranath Tagore to Amiya Chakrabarty, 7 March 1935, in *BSC*, p. 170
145. Soumendranath Tagore, *Biplabi russia* (Calcutta, 1930).
146. Nalini Kanta Gupta, *Bolsheviki*, 1931, in *BSC*, p. 122.
147. M.N. Roy's speeches translated by K. Bhattasali in *Manabendranath rayer baktritabali* (Calcutta, 1937).
148. Nirmal K. Bose, in *Desh*, Poush, 1342 BS, 1935, in *BSC*, pp. 192–7.
149. Bhabani Sen, in *Janajuddha*, 15 December 1942, in *BSC*, pp. 347–9.

150. Benoy Ray, in *Janajuddha*, 6 October 1943, in *BSC*, p. 377.
151. Humayun Kabir, in *Chaturanga*, Aswin 1350 BS, 1943 AD, in *BSC*, pp. 369–76. Later, the CPI admitted its error, for instance, Gangadhar Adhikari: 'The negative attitude of the Party to the Quit India struggle ... did considerable damage to the Party.... Our People's War slogan ... isolated us from the anti-imperialist militants in the national movement and seriously damaged our mass base'. G. Adhikari, *New Age*, 6 February 1966, in A. Farooqui (ed.), *Remembering Dr Gangadhar Adhikari: Selection from Writings* (Delhi, 2000), pp. 199–200.
152. The anti-Fascist intellectuals' movement had at its core Subhas Mukhopadhyay, Bishnu Dey, Susobhan Sarkar, Sukanta Bhattacharya, and others, but also as fellow-travellers, avowedly non-Communist individuals like Buddhadeb Bose, Tarashankar Banerjee, Abu Syed Ayyub, Jamini Roy, and many others. The best account of this trend is by Amit Gupta, *Crises and Creativities: Middle-Class Bhadralok in Bengal, 1939–52* (Calcutta, 2009), pp. 118–24.
153. Fort Gloster Mill deployed in 1905 about 4,000 Bengali workers and 2,000 non-Bengali and the proportion was the same in 1928. Amal Das, *Urban Politics in an Industrial Area: Labour Politics in Howrah, 1850–1928* (Calcutta, 1994).
154. Dipesh Chakrabarty, *Rethinking Working-Class History: Bengal, 1890–1940* (Delhi, 1989).
155. Samita Sen, *Women Labour in Late Colonial India: The Bengal Jute Industry* (Cambridge, 1999).
156. Samita Sen, 'Gendering Class: Wives and Workers in the Jute Industrial Economy', in *A Case for Labour History: The Jute Industry in Eastern India*, eds Arjan de Haan and Samita Sen (Calcutta, 1999), p. 198.
157. Chitra Joshi, *The Lost Worlds of Labour* (New Delhi, 2003).
158. Sabyasachi Bhattacharya, 'Swaraj and the *Kamgar*: Indian National Congress and the Bombay Working Class, 1919–31' in *Congress and Indian Nationalism: The Pre-Independence Phase*, eds Richard Sassoon and Stanley Wolpert (Berkeley, University of California Press, 1988), pp. 223–49.
159. *Indian Labour Year Book, 1946*, Government of India, 1946, p. 166, cited in Sukomal Sen, 1971, p. 300; I have also drawn upon the richly documented study of labour politics in the jute industry in this period by Nirban Basu in De Haan and Sen, *A Case for Labour History*.
160. Parimal Ghosh, 'A History of the Colonial Working Class, India: 1850–1946' in *Economic History of India*, ed. B.B. Chaudhuri (Delhi, HSPC, 2005), vol. VIII, part 3, p. 685.

6

THE POLITICS OF EXCLUSION 1936–46

If one looks at the pattern of politics of the decade preceding 1947 some features spring to the eye. First, the policy of mutual exclusion followed by the leaders of the Hindu and Muslim communities in all public spaces—not just in the state apparatus but in every possible institution in civil society—tore apart the socio-political fabric of Bengal. Second, the efforts on the part of the regional Bengal leadership to exclude the central leadership (and vice versa), as well as the effort of each fraction of the regional party to exclude the other fractions from any share of power created a conflict that diminished effective action on the part of the Congress. The Muslim League also had its share of local *versus* centre and inter-fractional conflicts, but possibly to a lesser extent. Thirdly, politics in Bengal inevitably reflected a social situation verging on the breakdown of the moral order that had been the basis of civic and political relationships. Bengal's experience of an unprecedented level of inflation and a totally new phenomenon of the black market during World War II, the deaths of several millions in the countryside and also in the streets of Calcutta during the Famine of 1943, communal riots like those in Dhaka (1941) and Calcutta (1946) which bordered upon ad hoc civil war—these were the more obvious and visible elements in this scene of which politics formed a part. Viewed from the perspective of later times, all these add up to a crisis in the decade after 1936 which appears to be crucial in the history of modern Bengal. Our aim in this chapter will be to trace these patterns in Bengal's society and polity rather than to provide a blow-by-blow chronicle of what happened. However, a chronological framework is necessary to begin with.

Under the Government of India Act of 1935, elections to the provincial legislatures were held at the end of 1936. In Bengal, the election yielded decisive majority for none. Congress emerged as the largest single party with 43 of the 48 'general seats', that is, unreserved, 6 of the 30 Scheduled Caste seats, and 5 of the 8 labour seats, or a total of 54 members in a Legislative Assembly of 250. The next largest group of 43 were Independent candidates from the separate electorate for Muslims. The third and fourth positions belonged to M.A. Jinnah's Muslim League (39 elected members) and A.K. Fazlul Huq's Krishak Praja Party or KPP (36 elected) respectively. There are slightly different estimates of electoral success due to differing perceptions of party affiliations of Independents. They walked over to one party or the other, mainly the League or the KPP. Abul Mansur Ahmed, a KPP leader, observes: 'In our country, especially among the Muslims, at that time the party system and party loyalties had not yet crystallized.... It was seen that after elections were fought it was uncertain how many were elected from which party. It was seen that a lot of Independent members found it opportune to join one of the two parties', that is, the League or the KPP.[1]

Despite this fluidity of affiliations, the governing facts of the situation in 1937 were that (*a*) there were 121 reserved Muslim seats, none of which the Congress contested and (*b*) by winning over Independents to their side by various means, the League increased its strength from 39 to 60, and the KPP from 36 to 58. In the circumstances, there were three possible scenarios. First, that either the League or KPP blocs plus some Scheduled Caste members and 29 European and Anglo-Indian members could together command a thin majority with a bit of assistance from politically uncommitted quarters. The second scenario could be either the League or the KPP in alliance with Congress securing a majority. But there was naturally no question of a League–Congress alliance, and as for a KPP–Congress alliance, the question was answered in the negative by the Congress High Command. This was probably a mistake, as we shall see later. Scenario number three would be KPP and League members joining forces, but immediately after the bitter electoral battle between two Muslim parties such an alliance or merger would have been difficult to forge. Of these three scenarios, the first and the third yielded results leading to formation of ministries in the period 1937–47. Fazlul Huq tried to lay out the second scenario immediately after the election, but the obduracy of the Congress leadership defeated him. He, therefore, resorted to the first.

The ministry Fazlul Huq thus formed in 1937—comprising his KPP in alliance with the Muslim League and supported by the Scheduled Caste and European lobbies in the legislature—lasted till 1941. But it did so at the cost of the emasculation of his KPP and the growth of Muslim League hegemony. First, he could only keep two members of his KPP in the ministry, Huq himself and another; the able secretary of KPP, an aspirant for ministership, was excluded. Second, many of the election promises of the KPP had to be abandoned to keep the *ashraf* and upper class Muslim legislators happy; this was fatal for the KPP which had capitalized on rural grievances they promised to redress. Thirdly, Huq paid for the support he needed from Muslim legislators in another way: though he was still president of the KPP, he was pressured into joining the Muslim League in October 1937.

Although the achievements of the Huq ministry were not negligible, particularly in the areas of tenancy reform and alleviation of rural indebtedness, he failed to get much mileage out of these. The Muslim League tended to get the credit—and the Congress, in opposition, the discredit—while the KPP was not satisfied that it was getting by way of legislation and ministerial power all that it had hoped for. In fact, Huq, an admirable man in some ways, was rather changeful and made too many compromises. Right in the beginning of Huq's tenure, Governor of Bengal John Anderson writes to Viceroy Linlithgow in a secret report: Huq is 'very reasonable'; he has agreed to exclude from the ministry 'a lieutenant of his own', the KPP secretary, who happens to be a 'person of extreme views'.[2] What was reasonableness to the Governor was opportunistic compromise to Huq's critics. Anderson also reported happily that 'the more extreme promises of Fazlul Huq's original programme have been modified'. No reduction in ministers' salaries, no abolition of *zamindari*, no release of all political prisoners but only when 'consistent with public safety', no expansion of education without taxation (only 'an ambiguous phrase … without taxation of the poor').[3] This 'toning down' was approved by the Governor—possibly he had a hand in it. Of course, no one knew of these secret letters between Governor and Viceroy at that time, but a general perception developed that Huq had made too many compromises.

The Bengal Muslim League, we saw earlier, was rejuvenated by Jinnah's clarion call in 1936 and by the merger of the United Muslim Party (UMP) and Ispahani's Majlis with the League. Huq's intransigence had prevented the annexation of KPP. Huq had defeated in the 1936 election Khwaja Nazimuddin in Barisal district in an area that had been the Dhaka nawab family's special preserve for decades. This was not forgotten. Moreover, the ministerial aspirations of Muslim Leaguers could be satisfied if Huq could be removed. Finally, Jinnah was not happy with Huq's tendency to act like an independent satrap in Bengal. A series of no-confidence motions and demonstrations against Huq were engineered by his own minister, the ambitious young H.S. Suhrawardy; eventually resignation by all his League-wallah ministers forced Huq out of office in December 1941. Huq must have been at the end of his tether about that time due to the Leaguers' harassment: there is a very curious letter he wrote in confidence to the Viceroy in September 1941 asking for employment in the service of the Indian government, preferably "to represent the Government of India in Foreign Political Service in Arabia"! The Viceroy naturally sent a polite 'no' to Huq.[4]

The dislodgement of his first ministry forced Huq to look for new allies. He engineered a coalition of (*a*) some legislators he won over from the League, (*b*) some members of the old KPP who remained loyal to him, though the party had been split in the meanwhile by radicals dissatisfied with Huq, (*c*) some legislators who had left the Congress, and (*d*) even the Hindu Mahasabha, represented in the ministry by Syama Prasad Mookerjee himself. That such a medley could form a ministry at all was due to Huq's reputation as a senior leader and his ability to keep many happy with promises. The birth of this Progressive Coalition Party is significant not so much because it was progressive, nor because it was a lasting coalition—it was neither—but it was significant in revealing that the Muslim League, even in 1941, was not too strong. This emerges from M. Ispahani's reminiscences: 'Fazlul Huq betrayed the Muslim League.... It was then that we found that the hard core of the Muslim League in Bengal consisted of only 35 members'.[5] Eighty-eight Muslim Assembly members initially supported the coalition party. The other interesting point was that Hindu leaders were more than willing to join Huq's ministry. Syama Prasad's diary records his thoughts about this time:

> Bengal has suffered under the Communal Award.... The only way to fight this is to organise the Hindus and to establish cooperation with those Muslims who feel that Bengal's hope lies in joint work between the two communities.... Huq had discovered towards the latter half of 1941 how dangerous his position had become ... as soon as he discovered that he was going to be stabbed in the back by his colleagues and some co-workers, he wanted to get out of the ministry, but in a way which would again reinstall him as chief minister.... There was immense relief in the public mind at the termination of the League ministry [that is, de facto League, but nominally under Huq] which had caused immense injury to them between 1937 and 1941....[6]

Thus Syama Prasad defended his alliance with Huq. As for Sarat Bose, according to Syama Prasad, he was keen to join as home minister but was arrested shortly before the swearing-in ceremony; his followers, including two ministers he named, supported Huq, of course. Altogether 127 legislators notified their support in writing to the Governor—one Lt.-Col. Sir John Herbert, a rather undistinguished sort of person, except for the fact that he had married the daughter of the Sixth Earl of Ilchester. He seems to have planned a coup to bring the League hard core into power by delaying Huq's ministry formation (his hands were forced by the Viceroy who wanted to clear the decks, for World War II had just broken out). Herbert allowed Huq to form his ministry, put Sarat Bose in prison, and bided his time. Within fifteen months, Herbert struck and this he did in a manner that caused embarrassment to the British Government. In March 1943, he summoned Huq, who commanded a majority in the Assembly, and handed over to him a draft letter of resignation to sign. In this, the Governor was suspected to be in league with the European bloc in the Assembly (they opposed Huq's coalition ministry throughout its tenure) and the Muslim League. Viceroy Linlithgow was furious: in his confidential letters to London he said 'in this most important and difficult province' we need 'a Governor of very different calibre from Herbert', one of the 'backbenchers [of the ruling party in England] of no particular quality'.[7] However, nothing could be done about the unconstitutional act that had already been committed by the Governor. These were the circumstances in which Huq's second ministry fell in March 1943.

As soon as the Governor asked Khwaja Nazimuddin of the League to form a ministry, he could gather favour-seekers around him and the strength of the party in the Assembly increased to 79. With the help of the European and Anglo-Indian groups, and of Scheduled Caste members, a League Ministry was thus formed. To purchase support he had to offer many people ministerships—the sympathetic Governor allowed thirty ministers, whereas Huq had been allowed only eight. The shift of members to the ruling party was expected: Mansur Ahmed, an eminent journalist of those times, writes that 'everyone had formed the impression that the political character of the Muslim legislators was such that whoever formed a ministry the majority would join him'.[8] This could be said of many Hindu members as well. Moreover, Huq had become a *ghaddar* (traitor) in the eyes of the hard core League supporters while this brought him little support from the Hindus outside the Assembly. It cannot also be denied that in the initial months of the Famine of 1943 his ministry fumbled inexcusably.

Nazimuddin's League Ministry lasted for barely two years (March 1943 to March 1945)—unremarkable for anything other than the disastrous failure of governance in respect of the Famine. He had in his cabinet a rival, H.S. Suhrawardy—the Secretary of the League from 1937 to 1943, enjoying high-level business contacts as a Civil Supplies Minister under Nazimuddin, and a highly visible member of the 'Calcutta clique' in the League as opposed to the 'Dhaka clique' led by Nazimuddin. Abul Hashim, the new Secretary of the League (1943–7) wrote in his memoirs that at every session of the Assembly under the Nazimuddin ministry, conspiratorial moves to bring it down took place, the rumour mill was set in motion to create distrust, and bribery in cash was a part of routine floor management.[9] Economically, the situation was gloomy: the famine, which began before Nazimuddin took over, wrought havoc, while his minister for Civil Supplies, Suhrawardy, did little to alleviate it and possibly aggravated it by favouring his crony, Ispahani, as a government agent for procurement of food grains. There was also a 'cloth famine' for it was 'in the hiding in the hands of the Marwaris', according to Governor Casey, and 'black marketing was rampant' with the possible connivance of a minister.[10] The Governor suspected that Suhrawardy was using his business contacts to procure money to bribe legislators. Be that as it may, in March 1945 twenty-one legislators defected from Nazimuddin's side and, in a snap vote on 28 March 1945, his government lost by a margin of nine votes. Even some months earlier Viceroy Wavell had sent a secret telegram to Amery:

> Casey is shocked at the administrative weakness of Bengal and corruption of provincial politics. He says [legislature] members are being bought at Rs. 5,000 to Rs. 10,000 a time, and that the faint-hearted were kept in confinement by their party leaders during the last session. The opposition recently offered Suhrawardy the chief ministership and are hawking government appointments round Calcutta in hope of further disintegrating Nazimuddin's government.[11]

This disintegration eventually came to pass in March 1945. The Governor decided to avoid ministry formation till a general election.

The general election in early 1946 brought into the Assembly the Muslim League as the largest single party with 114 seats. This was inevitable due to the failure of the Congress in Bengal to intervene effectively in the chaos that prevailed and the success of the League in presenting itself as the party, under Jinnah's flag, to be the sole spokesmen of Muslims and a viable government. In terms of party politics, the League certainly gained an immense advantage in the elections of 1946. Ispahani was not far wrong when he wrote: the League 'literally crushed the opposition and totally annihilated the floating element in the legislature which had made it a normal practice to sell its votes to the highest bidder'.[12] The signal to the Hindu *bhadralok* was clear: *ardhanga tyajati panditah*, that is, the wise will give up half. It was put very succinctly by the wily old politician, Burrows, who became Governor of Bengal in the last days of British rule: 'There was a definite attempt, because of the feeling of frustration among the Hindus in Bengal, to get command of at least a part of the province'.[13] The point that the Hindus in Bengal wanted a partition—leave aside the compulsions—was important for the Governor of Bengal: 'We should as soon as possible put the responsibility for settling the problem of partition squarely on Indian shoulders'.[14] All this was predictable already by early 1946 when the general elections took place.

Being a little short of majority, Suhrawardy toyed with the idea of a coalition (Nazimuddin had, in disgust, retired and gone away to Hyderabad). Kiran Shankar Roy, leader of the Congress Assembly Party, had talks with him but these predictably failed. In the event, one Scheduled Caste minister was taken into his cabinet by Suhrawardy and the rest were Leaguers from his faction. This ministry is remembered chiefly because of the communal carnage on 16 August 1946 to observe the Direct Action Day prescribed by Jinnah. The other claim of this ministry to the historians' attention is that Suhrawardy was deeply involved in the abortive scheme that he and Sarat Bose and K.S. Roy pursued to set up 'United Independent Bengal'. We shall look at those events later.

This succession of ministries in Bengal, Huq's first ministry (1937–41) and second (1941–3), followed by the Nazimuddin (1943–5) and Suhrawardy (1946–7) ministries, are sometimes perceived as a period when 'Muslim ministries' ruled Bengal. That will be an error—an error typical of a communal outlook. It was the right-hand man of Jinnah, Ispahani, who wrote that in 1937 'Muslims regained political power in the Bengal which their forbears had once ruled'.[15] The significant fact about the period is not so much the community the ministers belonged to—in fact, among them there were a number of Hindus as well—but their policies, insofar as they had policies, and, above all, the political climate of which they were the creatures. The ruling characteristic of this period 1937–47 was the politics of mutual exclusion. Governor R.G. Casey confided to his private diary his impression, a totally correct one: 'Orthodox Congress vs. Bose group, Khadi group vs. others; Hindu Mahasabha vs. Congress; Fazlul Huq Muslims vs. Muslims'.[16] These were only some of the polarities and rivalries manifesting themselves. Each player in the game tried to exclude the rivals from power. This tendency could, of course, appear in any context but in Bengal this reached an extreme degree in 1937–47. It came to the surface when power, though limited, came within reach at the provincial level and at the same time the access to power was conditioned by a distribution of seats which made a comfortable majority in the Assembly unattainable for any party (and hence the importance of the role of the European bloc, crucial in terms of the arithmetic of Assembly votes). The problem of governance was compounded by internal divisions within both the Congress and the League, as well as tussles between regional chieftains like Sarat Bose or Fazlul Huq and the Congress High Command and Jinnah. The result, a politics of mutual exclusion, was preconditioned by the climate of communalism that infused all spheres of life in Bengal from the late 1930s, paving the way for the Partition of 1947. Let us now turn from the story of ministry formation to the inner working of politics.

Prajas, Landlords: Class and Community

To understand the increasingly pronounced communal rift in Bengal, it is vital to ask the question, how was the greater part of the Bengal peasantry, the Muslim part, alienated by the Congress? Abul Mansur Ahmed in his memoirs of political life reports Congress leader J.M. Sengupta's remark in 1929: Congress has not only lost the trust of Muslim Bengal, but also the trust of the peasantry.[17] Ahmed goes on to say that this is exactly what happened. How did that come about?

In an earlier chapter, it was suggested that an explanation cast wholly in terms of activities in the public sphere, the actions of political leaders and parties and propaganda, is incomplete. It was argued that no adequate answer could exclude the personal and social experiences of the Muslim individual in Bengali society in the early twentieth century. Now we turn to the public sphere. The situation there will be inevitably slotted in academic argot as 'communal politics in pre-Partition Bengal'. Does not this academic practice already prejudge what will be said about the complex processes that led to the Partition? In the nationalist narrative 'communalism' is a necessary construct for the explication of the failure of nationalism to bind together the Bengali people in the twentieth century. It certainly had its uses. But the retrospective attribution of communalism to mentalities, events, and processes one observes in Bengal in the decades preceding the Partition demands caution. This particularly applies to the struggle of the Bengal peasantry in a context where community and class boundaries were sometimes coterminous, or were commonly perceived as coterminous (for example, that the peasants' struggle against *zamindars* could coincide with conflict with high-caste Hindus).

The complexity of the interface between agrarian relations, communalism, and nationalist politics in Bengal in the 1930s may be illustrated if we look at the plethora of explanations offered by historians regarding one single incident in Bengal in 1930, the Kishorganj riots.

To a contemporary observer, Nirad C. Chaudhuri, the Kishorganj incidents were indicative of the fact that Muslims 'constituted a society of their own ... and would never be absorbed in a unified India'.[18] He remembered how

> the Muslim peasants of the western part of Kishorganj subdivision of Mymensingh, which was my subdivision as well as my district, rose in a body, attacked Hindu houses and property owned by Hindu landlords and moneylenders, killed people and massacred one family known to us.... The economic argument was, of course, trotted out after these riots were over. But there were landlords and moneylenders among the Muslims as well and they were in no way less extortionate than the Hindus. But in these riots their properties were never touched.

Historians looking back upon the incident have underlined different aspects. To Sugata Bose the important factor was that the Depression dried up rural credit, thus snapping the ties between moneylenders, predominantly Hindu, and Muslim peasants; the patron–client relationship between them was transformed into an inimical relationship when the *ulema* became new patrons;[19] their preaching, justifying refusal of debt repayment, influenced the Muslim peasantry.

The question, however, remains: why was a relative immunity (not total immunity, contrary to Chaudhuri's observation) enjoyed by Muslims practising moneylending? Is the 'gullibility' of the peasants, exposed to communal propaganda, the explanation, as another historian, Sarkar, has suggested?[20] Partha Chatterjee's work on land relations and politics in this period is outstanding. Were these riots 'fundamentally religious' disturbances, as Chatterjee has put it?[21] Were they directed against the Hindu *bhadralok* due to external intervention, chiefly the communal leadership and the government conniving with them? Taj ul-Islam Hashmi, critical of these views, suggests that focus on the peasants' 'gullibility' or on the external leaders' intervention from the top tends to deny the peasants' agency, that is, their ability to think or act on their own. No doubt there was such external intervention, and peasants did believe in rumours and the propaganda of the *ulema* and the top leadership. But 'one should not ignore the inner matrix of rural and peasant politics. Besides the so-called outsiders, *ulema* and peasant leaders coming from the lower middle and poor peasant families belonging to political parties ... or even locally organized Krishak Samitis, Anjuman-i-Islamias, or other quasi-political groups were also quite important in mobilizing anti-landlord, anti-moneylender sentiment among the lower peasantry'.[22] Hashmi also points out that, contrary to the received version, many Muslim moneylenders were attacked; he cites the view of the Magistrate of Mymensingh that 'Hindus have not been threatened or looted as Hindus but as moneylenders and many Muhammadan moneylenders have been equally threatened or looted'.[23]

The evaluation of this sort of evidence would involve assessment of the trustworthiness of the source itself, for example, the degree of objectivity of the civil servants who reported to the English officer. The weight to be attached to incidents of attack on Muslim moneylenders would depend on their frequency and distribution, which involves calculation of the proportion of Muslims among moneylenders as compared to Hindu moneylenders; this has not been attempted yet. Again, the degree of autonomy enjoyed by the village-level opinion leaders is open to question. After all, it is difficult to make out how autonomous those village-level opinion makers are so long as they are part of the chorus orchestrated by the top leaders; only when they play an adversarial role, contesting the higher-level leaders, can one establish the proposition put forward by Hashmi.

On the whole, debates of this kind reveal the inadequacies of the evidence hitherto collected towards the validation of alternative schemes of interpretation. Moreover, an eclectic assembly of the different elements of explication offered by Chaudhuri (1987), Chatterjee (1982), Sarkar (1987), Bose (1982), and Hashmi (1994) would not quite suffice for that would suffer from various internal inconsistencies. Evidently, if the interpretation of a single event like the Kishorganj disturbances can be so problematic, larger generalizations on agrarian relations interacting with communal and nationalist politics in rural Bengal would be subject to severe limitations.

In his well-documented research on the subject, Hashmi (1994), has suggested that the essence of the story was the progressive communalization of class politics of Bengal from the 1920s to the creation of Pakistan. The chief merit of this approach is that it avoids both simplistic cant about 'natural' or 'elemental' militancy, and pays great attention to stratification within the peasantry avoiding the common error of attributing a transcendental 'peasanthood' to all residing outside municipal limits, a failing of some *bhadralok* historians.

As regards the 1920s, it emerges from his study that in the days of the Non-Cooperation and Khilafat Movements, the Muslim '*ashraf*, their allies in the upper echelon of the *jotedars* ... and the aristocratic clergy or the *Pir Sahibs* ... supported the movement half-heartedly', while the real backbone of the movement were 'the *mofussil mullahs* [who] had nothing to lose by boycotting the government' and the lower peasantry. Hashmi uses Engels' term, 'the plebeian clergy' to describe the *mofussil mullahs*: 'Having lower class connections and origins, in spite of their status as clergy, they sympathized with the socio-economic problems of the lower peasantry'.[24] Under their leadership, lower and middle peasant strata took an active part in the Non-cooperation Movement in the form of boycotting imported cloth and joining *hartals* (strikes) called by the Calcutta leaders (for example, on 1 August 1920 when rural participation was remarkable), boycott of the elections to the Legislative Council (November 1920), boycott of revenue settlement operations, and refusal to cultivate jute (in 1920–1 the output of jute fell by 30 per cent compared to 1919–20 and jute acreage again fell in 1921–2).[25] The intensity of the common peasants' feelings against the government was illustrated by an incident reported by Maulana Abdur Rashid Tarkabagish interviewed by Hashmi: a peasant, fatally wounded in police firing at Salanga, on the Pabna–Rajshahi border, refused to take water from the hands of a policeman before breathing his last.[26]

This we might see as a symbolic act of contempt cast in terms of his culture, this peasant's refusal to take water. But it was also a political act invested with a passion which was not derived 'from above', from the political leadership. Nor, likewise, was the pattern of violent mob action on the occasion, nor the ire directed against the *zamindar–mahajan* and his minions. It was the quotidian life experience that identified to the peasant his enemy—the policeman, the moneylender, the landlord, and his agents—while the British were a distant entity. It was not even within his power to strike against the Raj by non-payment of taxes to the government for he paid none (except indirect tax, such as that on salt)—he could only withhold rent. Thus, the peasant course of action diverged from the pattern set for him in the Civil Disobedience movement, and class issues and nationalist leaders' prescriptions mingled inextricably.

One outcome of the combination of Khilafat with the Non-cooperation Movement was possibly retrogressive. Commonly this combination is looked upon as a master stroke in politics, promoting communal unity. The evidence in Hashmi's work suggests otherwise: it meant "the revival of Islamic solidarity and the re-appearance of the *ulema* on the political scene after a lapse of about half a century".[27] The *ulema*'s role as political spokesmen thus acquired legitimacy; even if they later moved away from the Congress umbrella to some other, their role from now on was crucial in rural politics.

Moreover, the sudden withdrawal of the movement by Gandhi, after Chauri Chaura, created a vacuum in which '*ashraf* and *jotedar* leaders, with their pro-government attitude, emerged as influential *praja* or peasant leaders'.[28] There developed by the late 1920s a notion of unity of Muslim *jotedars* and Muslim under-*ryots* against the Hindu *zamindars*. Unlike the Hindu landed classes, the Muslim *jotedars* had access to the predominantly Muslim under-*ryots* and *bargadars* (share-croppers), as 'their coreligionists and patrons'. Hashmi's analysis of the agrarian disturbances from the end of the Non-cooperation Movement till the Depression year of 1929, suggests two trends. First, prior to that, in 1921–2, the East Bengal Muslim peasants' anger and action were directed against *zamindars* who were predominantly Hindus; now, particularly in the communal riots in 1926–8 in the districts, 'high-caste Hindus (sometimes lower caste as well) became the targets of attack, irrespective of their socio-economic background'.[29] Second, there developed by the late 1920s a sentiment that united Muslim *jotedars* and Muslim under-*ryots* against Hindus. This emerged from a perception that was common, that is, 'the notion prevalent among the Muslims that they were the have-nots of Bengali society', belonging to an amorphous *praja* community vis-á-vis the Hindu landlords. Increasingly, 'class consciousness' merged with 'communalism' and hence 'the formation of a joint front of the rich, middle, and poor peasants under the *ashraf–ulema–jotedar* triumvirate against the Hindu *zamindar–mahajan–bhadralok* classes'.[30]

These two trends were consolidated and strengthened in the 1930s. A third and new trend was the co-optation of the peasant into legislative and electoral politics in the local district union boards and finally, in 1936, the elections to the legislature under the Government of India Act of 1935. The earlier pattern of dispersed, discontinuous peasant agitation of a localized kind was replaced, or, overlaid, with a new pattern of directed movements under the leadership of the new Muslim gentry of the *mofussil* towns and the *ashraf* and rich peasants. This growth of the KPP as the champion of the Muslim peasantry might have also served to minimize the threat to the status quo from the lower orders (except for targets selected with deliberation by those leaders). The representation of the Muslim 'community interests' as identical with the *prajas*' interests in East Bengal drew strength from this process of co-optation and, in turn, added strength to it.

Another new feature of the scene in the 1930s was, of course, the impact of the World Depression that began in 1929 and intensified the lower peasants' distress.

1. Dietmar Rothermund has shown that the price of rice did not fall till July 1931; but when it did, it was a decline of about 50 per cent in the Calcutta and Rangoon markets.[31] For the first time, rice in July 1931 was cheaper than wheat, whereas normally rice used to be 30 per cent dearer.
2. The World Depression had another consequence. The fall in jute exports and raw jute price meant that the farmers' strategy of shifting from jute to rice was no longer viable; the Indian Jute Mills Association, an organization of mill owners, contributed to the decline in jute price by their collective decision to reduce production of jute goods in the mills.
3. It is well-known that the British Indian government's deflationary policy created a regime that exacerbated the Depression. On the whole, in the rice and jute belt of Gangetic Bengal the Depression lowered the purchasing power of the cultivators and heightened distress and discontent among the rural poor from the second half of 1930. This dovetailed very neatly with the Civil Disobedience Movement and might have provided power to it. The collection of both government revenue and rent paid to landlords declined. The Report on Land Revenue Administration in Bengal for 1932–3 recorded that only 40.11 per cent of rent was collected from cultivators on the government's estates; we do not have corresponding estimates of rent paid to *zamindars*, but it was likely that it

declined substantially because non-payment of revenue by *zamindars* to the government increased, and there are numerous complaints from *zamindars* about defaulting tenants. Given the low price they obtained for their produce, the cultivators' inability to pay rent is understandable; added to that were the ripple effects of Civil Disobedience. This was a cause of the worsening peasant–landlord relations, particularly when the refusal to pay taxes extended to refusal to pay rent.[32]

4. Finally, during the Depression of the early 1930s, the poor among the occupancy *ryots* were forced to become *bargadars* or sharecroppers and tenants without occupancy rights, since they were unable to realize, under Depression conditions, the value they expected from their produce to repay the loans taken on mortgage. The overall scene was, therefore, one of intensification of peasant distress and hence agrarian disturbances. These took the form of peasant participation in Civil Disobedience and related agitations in some parts of East Bengal, *but* at the same time communal violence was endemic through 1929 to 1936. 'Due to the predominance of the *ulema*, rural *ashrafs* and the *jotedar* leaders', Taj ul-Islam Hashmi observes, 'the short-lived anti-British attitude of the peasants in certain districts which could develop into peasant nationalism, was transformed into an anti-high-caste-Hindu movement'.[33] This pattern was not substantially changed by isolated attempts by the Left to mobilize peasants on non-communal lines in East Bengal in the 1930s.

'We, the Muslim Congressmen', writes Abul Mansur Ahmed of the year 1929,

> left the Congress and formed the All-Bengal Praja Samiti under the leadership of Maulana Akram Khan.... The outcome was that irrespective of political beliefs and affiliation, all Bengali Hindu leaders allied themselves with the pro-*zamindar* Congress Party, and all Muslim leaders united in the pro-peasant *Praja Samiti*. J.M. Sengupta said sorrowfully: From now on Congress has lost the support not only of Muslim Bengal but also that of the common tenantry. Mr. Sengupta's judgement turned out to be absolutely right.[34]

Then a middle-level Muslim leader and an advocate in Mymensingh Zillah Court, Hashim saw that no Hindu Congressman joined the tenants' agitations, though he concedes that Benoy Sarkar, Naresh Sengupta, Atul Gupta, J.L. Banerjee, and others sympathized with the tenants.

> Hindu Congressmen who were against zamindari joined not the Praja Samiti, but other organizations like Kisan Sabha, etc. Many of them criticised the Praja Party as a movement of the *jotedars*. In a literal sense there was some truth in this. But this was, in my opinion, their ultra-leftism.... To the best of my knowledge and belief, the *Praja* movement was the form of mass movement appropriate at that juncture.[35]

That the Praja Samiti, later renamed Krishak Praja Party (1931), was a catalytic agent in precipitating a communal divide, coterminous with pro-*zamindar* and anti-*zamindar* positions, is by and large true. That was partly the outcome of the agrarian conflicts sketched above, as well as the political history of tenancy legislation in the 1920s which has been perspicaciously analysed by Partha Chatterjee.[36] The Swarajist–Congress legislators persistently opposed legislation to alleviate the condition of the lower tenantry.[37] The debates in the Legislative Council were not of course, read by the peasantry but they would hear of the broad alignments from the village *mullahs* as well as political leaders and patrons in occasional meetings. As for the superior tenantry, the *jotedar* and petty landlords among Muslims, the impact of the annulment of the Hindu–Muslim Bengal Pact of 1924 was great; as we have seen in a previous chapter, after the death of its progenitor C.R. Das in 1925, when the Congress reneged on the Pact it dashed to the ground expectations in the Muslim community. Thus, perhaps, the Congress lost much more than it had gained when C.R. Das devised the Pact.

Was the Praja Samiti, later KPP, a *jotedar* party? This was the issue that Abul Mansoor Ahmed raises. In very broad terms, some prominent historians of Bangladesh today have endorsed this view. A.R. Mallick and Syed Anwar Husain have underlined the fact that the legislative measures taken by the KPP 'benefitted mainly the rich peasants'; they approvingly quote John Broomfield's assertion that men like Fazlul Huq of the KPP were 'from that class of small town notables' interested in 'a strengthening of the position of the rural middle rung'.[38]

Actually the KPP seemed to consist of two rather disparate groups. One was led by leaders like Maulana Bhasani, Shamsuddin Ahmed, Shah Abdul Hamid, and others. They carried resolutions in the Praja Samiti

Conferences (for example, in Rangpur 1931 and Dhaka 1936) in favour of sharecroppers and small peasants and lower tenants; the renaming of the party as KPP was at their initiative to explicitly include the lowest rung. The other group in the Party consisted of educated town-dwellers, *jotedars*, and the richer farmers who stood against a radical stance; for example, they defeated and outvoted the opposite faction in 1934 when the latter proposed a resolution recommending that the government confer occupancy rights on sharecroppers. The leaders of this 'moderate' section were Maulana Akram Khan, Khan Bahadur Abdul Momin, H.S. Suhrawardy, and others. On balance one may agree with Adrienne Cooper's judgement that the KPP was 'primarily a party of the richer sections of rural society'; her detailed study of the sharecroppers' movements shows that the KPP did precious little to help classes below the well-off tenantry.[39]

Hashmi's opinion is similar: 'With tacit government support, rich peasants, along with petty landlords and upper-middle peasants, allocated a diminutive and subservient role to the lower peasantry.... Muzaffar Ahmed of the Communist Party was probably near the truth that the change of name of Praja Party was done to befool the militant lower peasantry...'.[40] If the radical section of the KPP had the active support of Left elements matters might have taken a different turn in the party. When the Praja Samitis first started their activities in a scattered manner in some districts, men like Muzaffar Ahmed and Nazrul Islam were associated. This eventually led to the foundation of the Workers' and Peasants' Party (1925) by the Left leaders but the latter did not make much headway; some top leaders were arrested and the Meerut Conspiracy Trials removed them from the scene at a crucial time just when the Praja Samiti took formal shape. The upshot was that 'the economic bondage of the lower peasantry to jotedars and mahajans, communal propaganda, and Hindu Congress Leaders' opposition to major tenancy reforms led the lower peasants [in East Bengal] en masse to join the Praja Camp by late 1936'.[41]

In the meanwhile, preparations were on for the elections to the legislature. On 17 August 1936, M.A. Jinnah came to Calcutta at the invitation of Bengali Muslim parties, including Krishak Praja. The cooptation of peasants in the greater part of Bengal east of the Padma River to communal political machinery and manoeuvres entered a new phase. Theirs was not a communal movement to begin with, but the course of development outlined above brought the Muslims, Krishak and Praja within the vortex of communal politics.

Landowner versus Peasant Interests: Legislation

To understand the growing alienation of the peasantry, of whom the vast majority were Muslim, we need to go back a little. The total insensitivity of the land-owning *bhadralok* to peasant grievances was revealed in the 1920s, particularly in the attitude and activities of the leaders of the Bengal Congress and the rump of the Swaraj Party after the death of C.R. Das. In December 1925, when a Tenancy Act Amendment was being discussed in the Bengal Legislative Council, a mild proposal to institute an enquiry into the proprietary and usufructuary rights in land was shot down by the right-wing majority of the Swaraj Party on the ground that such an enquiry 'questions the sanctity of the Permanent Settlement' and smacks of 'Bolshevism'.[42] In August 1928, the debate on the Bengal Tenancy (Amendment) Bill further revealed the *zamindars*' hegemony in the legislature and the unity of the representations of that class regardless of religious community or party affiliation. The Bill was intended to strengthen the hands of the *zamindars* vis-á-vis tenants, and *zamindari* interests were supported by Sir Abdul Karim Ghaznavi and Nalini Ranjan Sarkar with equal enthusiasm. The latter emphasizes the unwisdom of allowing 'tenants to insist … on anything like a complete upsetting of the acquired powers and rights and interests which the landlords have been enjoying from generation to generation'.[43] The Swarajist and Bengal Congress leaders and spokesman of *zamindar* interests spoke on those lines together and voted for legislation towards the same end throughout the debates: Kiran Sankar Roy, J.M. Sengupta, and Sarat Chandra Bose as well as big *zamindars* like Sirish Chander Nandy of Cossimbazar, Bhupendra Sinha of Mymensingh, Nawab Musharaf Husain of Murshidabad.[44] There was only a minuscule minority in the Legislative Council who challenged the *zamindars*' point of view: Professor Jitendra Lal Banerji, A.K. Fazlul Huq, Nausher Ali, and Azizul Huq. This minority point of view was reflected in amendments moved by them, which were invariably rejected by the majority in the Council. Banerji underlined the unquestionable fact that the Tenancy (Amendment) Bill 'is a Landlords' Protection Bill' and Fazlul Huq said he did not have even 'the forlorn hope that this [his anti-*zamindar* position] will have many supporters in the Council'. They were in a desperate minority pitted against the strongly represented landlord interests in the Legislative Council.[45] As regards the ministries elected from 1937 onwards, just one made some attempt to address peasants' grievances—the Fazlul Huq ministry in 1938–40, in the form of a new Tenancy (Amendment) Act. That gave some relief to the tenant farmer in respect of enhancement of rent within the first ten years of tenancy as well as abolition of *salami*, that is, a lump sum exacted by the land-holder for transfer of tenancy. While this benefited tenants and middle peasants, the grievances of the sharecroppers and landless agricultural labourers remained unaddressed.[46]

Peasant Movements and the Left

In Bengal, peasant participation in the Civil Disobedience Movement, as well as dispersed agrarian disturbances in the Depression years, prepared the basis for a new stage of peasant struggle. Although the All-India Kisan Sabha founded in 1936 had in its leadership men like N.G. Ranga, Sahajananda Saraswati, and some Congress Socialist Party leaders, the Kisan Sabha in Bengal, which met at its founding session a year later in 1937, was led mainly by Communists like Muzaffar Ahmed and Bankim Mukherjee and the district-level leaders were more often than not radicals from the *biplabi* or revolutionary nationalist ranks, for example, Benoy Chowdhury and Hare Krishna Konar in Burdwan, Moni Singh in Mymensingh, or Bhupal Panda in Medinipur. Thus, in Bengal, the Kisan Sabha was somewhat radical and, with the rise of the KPP from after the election of 1937, radicalism was reinforced for the KPP had many Leftist sympathizers among its leaders. Although Fazlul Huq kept them out of power in his ministry, expectations of governmental support began to arise. These were strengthened by the appointment of the Land Revenue Commission and its report, recommending, among other things, enhancement of *bargadars*' share in the crop. The Bengal Provincial Kisan Sabha's (BPKS) membership increased to about 50,000 by 1938–9. In 1939, the BPKS launched in Burdwan district a major movement, the Damodar Canal Tax Satyagraha. The aim was to reduce the canal tax of Rs 5.5 per cent per annum, on the ground that the crop yield did not justify that high a rate. The movement was successful in persuading the government to reduce the tax to Rs 2.6 per acre per annum.[47] In 1939, there was another BPKS movement in support of Adhiars (that is, *bargadars* or share-croppers) in north Bengal—an unsuccessful predecessor of the Tebhaga Movement. With the lifting of the ban on the CPI in July 1942, there was an opportunity for the BPKS to launch peasant movements but the CPI's notion of 'People's War' did not encourage militant action at that time. Such action picks up in 1945, hampered though it was by the communal strife all over Bengal. In September 1946, the Kisan Sabha issued a call to launch the Tebhaga Movement, demanding that the share of sharecroppers, who were subjected to many exactions by the landholder-cum-moneylender, should be half and not one-third.

The tactics adopted by sharecroppers in the Tebhaga Movement were to collect the paddy right after harvest in the sharecroppers' own homestead or threshing floor and yield to the landholder only a third of the crop. We have the account of Sunil Sen, an observer-participant who recalls that many grievances other than that of sharecroppers became part of the struggle, for example, the Hajong tribals' grievance (against the *tanka* tax levied in kind) or the tenants' grievances against *jotedars* (rich peasants who had tenants and sharecroppers under them).[48] By the end of 1946, altogether nineteen districts were affected by the Tebhaga Movement, the strongest centres being in Mymensingh, Dinajpur, and Jalpaiguri in the north and Medinipur and the 24 Parganas in the south. There were instances of landholders fighting the peasants and police firing; eventually in December 1946 about a thousand BPKS workers were arrested and, in March 1947, three thousand more. The League ministry then in power used massive repression, at the same time as it went through the motions of preparing legislation—the Bengal Bargadar Bill and the State Acquisition and Tenancy Bill. These were to be shelved repeatedly until Partition brought the shameful episode to an end.

The Muslim Community and the Politics of the Middle-Class

We may now turn to the political force Mr Jinnah represented, that is, the avowedly communal politics of the Muslims. That takes us back to 1936 when elections were held to form the ministries we have discussed earlier in this chapter. There were two Muslim parties, the old Muslim League and the new UMP; the KPP also was now a candidate for recognition as a Muslim party. Of the situation in 1936, M.A.H. Ispahani, a hard-core Leaguer and right-hand man of Jinnah, writes in his memoirs:

> The Provincial Muslim League did not exist, except in name. It had died years before through indifference and neglect.... At this time feverish activity was on particularly in Calcutta amongst the then Muslim Party of Bengal to set up its candidates at the General Elections.... There was a younger and leftist [*sic*] element at the time which was searching for a leader of stature. It comprised of Nausher Ali, a strong pro-Hindu Congressite, Shamsuddin Ahmed, Humayun Kabir (an individual more pro-Hindu than a Hindu himself) ... and Nawabzada Hasan Ali of Bogra. For them there could be no better person than the veteran A.K. Fazlul Haq. The party ... bore the name Nikil Banga Krishak Praja Samity.[49]

Ispahani himself did not yet belong to the League but to a small caucus of upper-class Muslim residents of Calcutta known as the New Muslim Majlis. In June 1936, Jinnah summoned a meeting of the All-India Muslim League Parliamentary Board at Lahore to discuss strategies for the elections to be held in November 1936 to constitute provincial legislatures under the new Government of India Act of 1935. Of forty people invited from Bengal only two attended, including Ispahani; others declined because, Ispahani says, the Bengali Muslim leaders 'wanted to rule in accordance with their own wishes and not involve themselves with a party [League] which operated on an all-India basis'.[50] Moreover, at that time, the All-India Muslim League had not even 'fifty coppers in its coffers. The President and the Secretary, both honorary, carried their offices in their respective portmanteaux'.[51] To sum it up, the leading role was that of the UMP, the KPP came next, and the Muslim League was a poor third.

In this forlorn state of the Muslim League, Ispahani and a few friends of his caucus, enthusiastic members of the League after the Lahore conference, played a clever trick. They persuaded Fazlul Huq to disrupt a crucial meeting called by the UMP at the Calcutta Town Hall and planted their own supporters in the hall to cause further disruption. Huq was told 'pandemonium is bound to result' and thus spoil the conference of his rival party. Huq was *not* told of the other part of the Ispahani group's plan: when Huq played his role as a disrupter and pandemonium ensued, Ispahani 'stood up and shouted that we be given a brief hearing'. He proposed that 'an open conflict between Muslims on the eve of elections' was unfortunate and Jinnah be invited to resolve the conflict. Huq, on behalf of the Praja Samiti, and the UMP leaders were forced to accept this mediation proposal, or else 'they would have lost prestige among the Muslims in the province and elsewhere'.[52] Such was the beginning of Jinnah's conquest of Bengal.

In the event, mediation by Jinnah failed. As expected, the *ashraf* party—that is, the UMP led by the Nawab of Dacca, H.S. Suhrawardy, Khwaja Nazimuddin, and others—merged with the Muslim League, and the KPP did not. Jinnah's mediation was extraordinary: he first tried to bring the UMP and KPP under the common League banner, and then to win over one of the two parties; 'each Party's yield of ground gave Mr. Jinnah added strength and courage to strike a harder bargain' with the other. 'He conducted the negotiations with such brilliance and skill that after some days the leaders of Muslim Bengal were in a state of daze and stupor. They had been reduced to a stage where they did not know whether they were going or coming!'[53]

These anecdotes from Ispahani are reproduced to give a flavour of the times when the born-again League entered the scene. Very soon it triumphed over all others until, to quote the quotable Ispahani, 'Muslims regained political power in the Bengal which their forbears once ruled'.[54] Not all who joined the Muslim League were, however, replicas of Ispahani, contrary to a widespread impression in West Bengal today. Consider for example Abul Hashim who rose to the position of General Secretary of the League. Hashim's father was a member of the Congress Party until he left it to join Sir Surendranath Banerjea's moderate party; his uncle was a Congressman, indeed a leading member of the Burdwan District Congress Committee; Hashim's nephew was in the Communist Party, and his brother-in-law H.S. Suhrawardy was a League leader. Hashim founded the Muslim Youth organization (1928) when he was twenty-three and, at thirty-one, was elected to the legislature (1936) as an Independent candidate with Muslim support, but not League backing. In 1937, he met Jinnah at Ispahani's house on Camac Street and wrote later: 'My meeting with Jinnah formed an impression that he wanted to make the League a progressive and fully democratic party, but I was deceived, for none except the Nawabs and big businessmen were of any value to him'.[55] Abul Hashim served the League, but he did not serve Jinnah. Moreover, in his view the proposal for Pakistan, later to be moved by Fazlul Huq (at the Lahore conference of the League, 1940), had no communal intent—it was a proposal to federalize India and create autonomous units. Soon after he became General Secretary, the draft manifesto he prepared (with the help of Nikhil Chakravartty, a young Communist) contained an anti-communal stance—it was, of course, rejected by the League's reactionary faction. The same year he was labelled an un-Islamic Communist in the daily *Azad* and an effort was made to dislodge him from secretaryship. On the eve of the annual League conference, he was summoned to Suhrawardy's residence and while he waited in the sitting room, in the bedroom his host consulted Khwaja Nazimuddin and other leaders about the modalities of Hashim's removal. At 2.30 in the morning of 16 November 1944, Hashim was asked to resign in the 'interest of party unity', though in the event, Hashim's willingness to resign was set aside by an overwhelming majority of the younger Council members and he was reinstated on 17 November.[56] This is one of many such instances of manoeuvres within the League reflecting conflict within. The tussles were not only due to ideological differences but also intergenerational differences of approach, differences between the urban elite and the *mofussil* cadre and middle-level leadership, regional factionalism with associated patron–client networks, and the aristocratic Urdu-speaking top layer and the Bengali-speaking middle and lower stratum of Leaguers.

M. Ispahani and Abul Hashim represented two poles—uncompromising Jinnahites and liberals—within the parameters of over-all party policies. Those in the middle are probably represented by Abul Mansur Ahmed who, while a student of Dhaka University, was attracted to the Khilafat and Non-cooperation Movements, and then taught in a National School, that is, a non-government institution started during the Non-cooperation Movement. He was associated with the Bengal Muslim Literary Society which included the great scholar Muhammad Shahidullah, the Communist leader Muzaffar Ahmed, and the radical poet Nazrul Islam. Abdul Mansur Ahmed began his career as a journalist by joining *Soltan*, which supported Swaraj Party and C.R. Das. He attended the Congress conference at Sirajgunj at which C.R. Das's proposal on the Hindu–Muslim Bengal Pact was accepted. Thereafter, Ahmed gradually drifted out of the Congress Party, disappointed with its reneging on the Pact. He was present at the talks between League and Congress leaders when both parties held their annual session in Calcutta in 1928. The talks failed to settle party conflicts.

> Responding to the Muslim leaders' demands, Dr. Bidhan Roy said in his acerbic language: 'So you Muslims are saying, give us a share of jobs but we will have no share in freedom struggle'. Sir Abdur Rahim's masterly retort was 'So, you Hindus are saying, "Take share in the freedom struggle but you will have no share of jobs."' Everyone laughed.[57]

That laughter was perhaps mirthless, but laughter in such a political gathering was still possible in 1928. Tension gathered in the 1930s when men like Ahmed moved into the KPP in large numbers. Many of them retained their Congress connections simultaneously. However, this was no longer necessarily an indication of faith in the Congress. Ahmed formally decided to leave Congress but the Secretary of the KPP, later a prominent League leader, Maulana Akram Khan, had a 'confidential circular issued to the effect that Congress Committees in the Muslim-majority districts in East Bengal should be captured by Muslims';[58] hence, no resignation from Congress. Prime Minister MacDonald's 'Communal Award' in 1932, enlarging Muslim representation in the legislature, as well as the post–Civil Disobedience eclipse of the Congress for the time being, encouraged a final exodus from the Congress to the KPP and the League. Ahmed was in 1935 both in the KPP and the League—in fact, the district president of the League and the de facto head of the district KPP in Mymensingh.[59] He was part of the group led by Ispahani who invited Jinnah to Calcutta in 1936. But, as we have seen, Jinnah settled with the League and excluded KPP. To Ahmed personally Jinnah's message was: 'I quite realise your anxiety for the welfare of peasants.... Don't argue with me. I know more than you do. Please go to every home and carry the message of Muslim unity to each and every Muslim. That will serve the peasants more than your Praja Party'.[60] Eventually, the rejection of KPP by Jinnah was decisive. Now it dawned on Ahmed that 'it was politically dishonest to be simultaneously in a communal party like the Muslim League and a non-communal party like the Krishak Praja Samiti' and he left the League.[61]

To sum it up, until 1936–7 and elections to the legislature under the Act of 1935, party boundaries were porous and this reflected the reality—an absence of clear-cut 'communal' and 'anti-communal' positions. This fact is disregarded in the depiction of the 1930s under the rubric, 'Rise of Communalism', in many works of history. Men like Mansur Ahmed served several parties at the same time or moved quickly from one to another: within the League there were fractions pulling in different directions, led by men like Abul Hashim, on the one hand, and M. Ispahani, on the other; and, of course, the leading 'political families' counted among their members people who belonged to altogether different and sometimes antagonistic political parties. At the same time, parties not avowedly communal acted on the basis of community interests, for example, the Krishak Praja group vis-á-vis high-caste Hindu landholders or the Congress, and the Swaraj Party in relation to the issue of tenancy reforms or reservation of government jobs for Muslims. Given this political flux till at least 1937, one should be cautious in attributing 'communalism' to the actors on the political stage, even if one sets aside the intractable problem of establishing intentionality in political behaviour.

The Rhetoric of Communal Politics: The Media

An analysis of the content of two leading newspapers, the *Ananda Bazar Patrika* and the *Star of India* of Calcutta is instructive. The latter newspaper, now forgotten, needs an introduction. It was directed by M.A.H. Ispahani and funded by the Ispahani business house, aided occasionally by the business leader Sir Adamjee Dawood, as an organ of the Muslim League. Ispahani, in his memoirs published from Karachi later, recalls: 'The English press was preponderantly owned by Hindus and only three or four papers were either wholly owned or directed and edited by Britishers.... Thus not only wealth but the power of the press was largely concentrated in Hindu hands'.[62] The only Muslim English language newspaper, other than the *Star of India*, was Khwaja Nooruddin's *Morning News*, and there were some vernacular newspapers like *Asre Jadid* and *Azad Bengali* in Calcutta. As late as 1942, Jinnah made a move to run a daily in Delhi and wrote to Ispahani of transferring the *Star of India* to Delhi 'not only for the benefit of Bengal but all India'.[63] Eventually, this led to the publication of the daily *Dawn* in Delhi.

A content analysis of the *Star of India*, selecting numbers at random, shows of course a heavy emphasis on communal questions. We shall focus on a period of normalcy, relatively free of communal riots, 1933–40. What were the major issues in the League mouthpiece? First, the Muslim share of jobs. This ranged from specific issues like how many Muslim excise sub-inspectors would be appointed by the government, or the demand for 33.3 per cent reservation of Calcutta Corporation appointments, to the bigger questions of principles of job reservation.[64] 'There is no denying the fact that qualified Muslims for posts are readily available nowadays in large numbers but the manner in which the legitimate claims of the Muslims are being intentionally ignored in filling up of vacancies in some government offices, is open to serious objection'.[65] It is reported that in 1935 Muslim members of the Calcutta Corporation boycotted its meeting in protest against 'Hindu communalism in the Corporation'.[66] Further, A.K. Fazlul Huq presided over a meeting at Mohammad Ali Park protesting 'Hindu preference in the Corporation'.[67] In 1937, when the Calcutta Corporation did concede 25 per cent reservation of jobs for Muslims, the *Star* editorialized that it was an 'eyewash.... There is no magnanimity in conceding what will eventually have to be given ... and this we feel will be the Muslim opinion on the "generosity" of the Calcutta Corporation after half a century or more of Hindu monopoly...'.[68] A few days later, the daily wrote in a huff, 'Muslim Bengal wants no concessions from the Corporation of Calcutta.... The politically outcasted [*sic*] Muslims who have lost all claims to speak in the name of their community [that is, the *Star* refers to the moderate Muslim leaders who negotiated the reservation] have been very useful to the communalist Hindus'.[69] After the Huq ministry was formed in 1937 there was less space for the job question in the *Star*.

The second major theme was discrimination against Muslims in the field of education. As a means of getting jobs, education mattered. In 1934, a Muslim Education Advisory Committee appointed by the Bengal government made some recommendations including, introduction of Islamic culture and history, choice of textbooks, languages, and so on.[70] The *Star* refuted the 'exhibition of communalism' on the part of 'our Hindu contemporaries', *Advance* and *Amrita Bazar Patrika* in particular.[71] The League daily said editorially: 'Why cannot our Hindu contemporaries be honest and say in public what their spokesmen say in private, namely, that the Muslims deserve very special consideration in both education and politics? … But instead of sympathy the Muslims are given abuse'.[72] When Fazlul Huq's ministry introduced the Secondary Education Bill which promised expansion of school education to benefit Muslims among others, objection was raised by Professor Sir P.C. Ray to the separation of the Secondary Education Board from Calcutta University. In the latter body, Muslims were poorly represented and the separation was supported by the League. Sir P.C. Ray, the *Star* said in an editorial entitled 'Knight-errant of Ram Raj', was one of the 'grossly communal caste-Hindu leaders'.[73] In this period, Huq received the support of the *Star*, though within a year he was accused of conspiring with Sarat Bose to sabotage the League ministry.[74]

The emphasis on jobs and education reflects the interests of the middle-class readership of the *Star*. Its attitude to the KPP was hostile. For example, the editorial on the eve of 1936 election, 'Let Not Islam Be Betrayed', says: 'Vote must be cast with only one aim in view—to put into power the Muslims in this province where they have every justification to hold the predominant position. Every honest Muslim will cast his vote for the League and against the Proja candidates'.[75] However, differences among the Muslims were overshadowed when the threat to the community as a whole was perceived or projected. Occasionally, highly emotive editorials were written, like the following: 'Political Lepers: In the name of truth and honesty and in the name of the motherland we denounce the infamy of the wretched and cowardly scribes of communal Hinduism who have spread and are spreading the most perfidious lies against innocent Muslims who assembled for prayer at Deshbandhu Park on the Id-ul-fitr day'.[76] This was in 1935 when Congress held a meeting with music, at the time of prayer. Again, the 'Day of Deliverance' declared by Jinnah to celebrate the resignation of Congress ministries in 1939 was a cause 'for jubilation of the entire Muslim community' and even Fazlul Huq got a friendly nod on such a day.[77]

The interesting thing in the political rhetoric of this kind was that 'communalism' was not only a pejorative word but specifically attacked and reviled repeatedly, but this communalism was characterized as a part of Hindu behaviour and mindset. On occasions the relevant distinction is made between the communal and the national, for example: 'The Congress is unable to satisfy the Hindu communalists. Where it has failed, the Hindu Mahasabha seeks to succeed.... Words and words strung together cannot make the Hindu Mahasabha a National organisation...'.[78] But, without any apparent consciousness of inconsistency, the exhortation issued from the same *Star of India* was, 'Muslims, Unite!'

The *Ananda Bazar Patrika*, which claimed the highest circulation among Bengali dailies in the late 1930s, was known for its close association with the Congress at this time. This probably qualified the daily's views on communal questions.[79] In the *Patrika*, unlike the *Star*, the job question does not figure prominently—the Hindus in any case held a disproportionately high share of jobs. Education, however, was a terrain of contestation, though the difference again was that there was no perception of threat. Among the issues which really exercised the political mind of the *Patrika* was the Communal Award, that is, the decision of Ramsay MacDonald on distribution of seats in legislatures, even after its modification by the Poona Pact (1932) at the instance of Gandhi. There were numerous editorials on the Communal Award making two points: (*a*) Bengali Hindus should not criticize Gandhi for the Poona Pact, for it was a by-product of MacDonald's decision; Gandhi had partly alleviated the problem by eliminating the provisions in MacDonald's formula dividing 'Caste Hindus' from the rest,[80] and (*b*) MacDonald's award was, of course, lambasted—'No Room for Hindus', that is to say statistics showed that Hindus were underrepresented in the legislature, under the Communal Award.[81]

The impact of MacDonald's Communal Award on public opinion fomented a sort of Hindu revivalism. In a rush, various grievances and problems came to the surface: the abduction of Hindu women allegedly by Muslim criminal elements,[82] 'pernicious' textbooks for Muslim schoolboys, interests of tax-payers of Calcutta Corporation at stake due to reservation of corporation jobs on communal bases, legitimate demands of peasants exploited by opportunist Muslim co-religionists, and so on.[83] The *Patrika* despaired of re-establishing communal amity in the face of aggressive communal demands from Muslim leaders.[84] In 1934, there was regular agitation worked up by the *Patrika*, among others. A conference opposing the MacDonald Communal Award was chaired by Ramananda Chatterjee, the eminent editor of *Modern Review*.[85] The decision of the Congress High Command 'neither to accept nor to reject the Communal Award' was criticized and, in a particularly severe editorial at the end of 1934, the *Patrika* raised the question, never posed before: Was there a place for Bengal in the Congress?[86] Early in 1935, the Bengal Hindu Conference proposed the Anti-Communal Award protest day, with the support of the Congress Nationalist Party led by M.M. Malaviya.[87] This was infructuous and the Congress in Bengal was, the daily said, ineffective due to factional struggles, fully revealed in the annual conference held after a gap of four years.[88] In the meanwhile, a new political organization stepped on to the stage, the Bengal Anunnata Jati Sammelan or Depressed Caste Conference, which met in Jessore in May 1935;[89] the *Patrika* apprehended that casteism in politics would divide Hindus as well as strengthen communalism by allying with it; the Namasudra movement, discussed in an earlier chapter, was cited as an example.

The battle against the Communal Award was lost. In Bengal it meant that 48.4 per cent of seats in the legislature would go to Muslims, 39.2 per cent to Hindus, and about 10 per cent to Europeans.[90] The Hindu grievance was directed against the fact that their representation was percentage-wise substantially lower than their proportion in the population. But their ire should have been directed more against the 10 per cent representation given to Europeans in various commercial, industrial, and ethnic lobbies. The European representation later proved to be a crucial factor in allowing the European lobby to hold to ransom any government formed in Bengal, for none of them had a substantial majority. While in their campaign against the Communal Award the Bengal leaders of the Congress failed—thanks to the obdurate line taken by the All-India Congress Committee (AICC) to neither accept nor reject the Award—they also lost the support of the Muslim segment among Congress sympathizers in the province. As regards the Muslim League, needless to say, the Award giving out of a total of 250 seats 119 to Muslims, 30 to 'depressed caste' Hindus, and 25 to Europeans (potential allies) was very satisfactory. The Communal Award of Ramsay MacDonald was a landmark in the course of events in twentieth-century Bengal. It not only framed the rules of the game in electoral politics for the decisive decade leading to 1947, but also made the outcome, the Partition, virtually inevitable, insofar as one can talk of inevitability in history. In reconfiguring the political system in Bengal, the Communal Award also changed the way the *bhadralok* thought about politics when the new communal representation regime and electoral politics got going after the elections in 1937.

This is reflected for instance in the *Ananda Bazar Patrika*. For one thing, the Bengal Hindu Mahasabha and the like got, in reporting and in political commentary, coverage as never before. *Patrika* reflected the opinions of Hindu *bhadralok*. It was by no means a Hindu Mahasabha mouthpiece, but the tone from 1937 was sympathetic and it also published grievances articulated by Hindu spokesmen without political party affiliations. The issues were trivial as well as serious: Why should both students' hostels of Rajshahi College go to Muslims? (21 September 1937); the head of a slaughtered cow has been thrown into a temple in a village in Sirajgunge (23 September 1937); Rashbehari Bose, the revolutionary leader, has approached the Hindu Mahasabha with a plea to unite the community (26 May 1938), and so on. The Huq ministry is seen as a 'puppet of communalists' (20 April 1937); B.C. Chatterjee, presiding over the Hindu Sabha is reported to have condemned Congress inaction on the communal question (11 January 1938); Bengali Muslims are criticized for their failure to respond to Nehru's 'Muslim mass contact programme' (9 May 1938); the Huq ministry's efforts to give jobs to Muslims is resented (26 August 1938; 17 May 1939); laudatory references are made to the Hindu Mahasabha's conference in Calcutta against the 'threat' to Hindus in Bengal (10 August 1939)—these are the political issues focused upon. An idea of the pitch of communal sentiments can be gauged from one incident in the middle of 1940: *Star of India* referred to the Hindu deity Krishna as 'the gay Lothario of Vrindaban'; the *Patrika* editorially commented on it (5 June 1940) demanding apologies; on June 8 a public meeting was organized by the Hindu Mahasabha to condemn this 'assault on Hinduism'; other Hindu newspapers also followed *Patrika* in protesting against the *Star* (15 June 1940); N.C. Chatterjee of the Mahasabha proposed in the Calcutta Corporation withdrawal of advertisements from the *Star* as a penal measure (20 June 1940). Thus a single literary flourish of someone who was proud of his knowledge of 'Eng. Lit.' produced a crisis of sorts.

One outcome of the sharper consciousness of community loyalties was that the upper-caste, literate, and urban Hindus began to pay attention to the problems of the Hindu depressed or backward castes who now enjoyed substantial representation in the legislature formed since 1937. Along with this came a new awareness of 'social evils' within the Hindu community. Prafulla Kumar Sarkar's series of essays in 1939–40 addressed the problem of 'the Hindus in decline'—essays which were also commented upon editorially in the *Patrika*.[91] Sarkar wrote:

> The Bengali Hindu is facing life and death questions.... That the 27 crores of Hindu in India do not constitute an organized community, what explains that? ... How has the proportion of Hindu population in Bengal been reduced to just 44 per cent? Is not the decline really due to evils of Hindu society, the oppressive caste system, the outcasting of Hindus, the pressure of superstitions, etc.?[92]

It was forcefully argued that the success of the British government's policy of building up the 'scheduled class' as a political entity separate from the rest of the Hindus was really due to 'the fruit of the sin of discriminatory policy of the upper castes'.[93] Sarkar praised the democratic spirit in Islam;[94] the spirit of Hindu social practices is the opposite. Drawing upon the research of Ruchiram Sahni on the demographic pattern in Punjab and the Bengal census data of 1901–31, Sarkar showed that there was a decline of the percentage of Hindu population (plus Sikh population in Punjab) in both these provinces. Broadly his argument was that the decline of Hindu percentage in Bengal population (from 48.8 in 1881, to 43.7 in 1921 and 43.5 in 1931) was due to Hindu social practices such as child marriage, sanctions against remarriage of widows, and the low social and health status of Hindu women.

Whether such views found widespread acceptance is difficult to say. Take for example the above perception regarding backward castes. There was resentment among the upper-caste *bhadralok* against the rising identity consciousness of the backward castes and at the same time an awareness of the abominable injustice they suffered under caste-Hindu domination. The *Patrika* wrote on the occasion of the first Bengal Scheduled Caste Conference in May 1935:

> We are unhappy that the organisers of the Conference have, to begin with, accepted the artificial divide between ... caste-Hindus and backward castes which does not augur well for the unity of the Hindu community or its future well-being.... This will divide the high and low castes and reduce the Hindu community to a nonentity in the political arena. We note with great anxiety that this is what the backward caste leaders are doing.

And, at the same time, 'In order to expiate the sin of spurning and ignoring the backward castes for so long, the upper castes must stand by their side and help them in political, economic and social fields.... If the upper caste Hindus cast off their *Sanatani* (traditional) goals and organize in unison with the backward castes, then alone can Hindu society be saved'. If not a guilty conscience, enlightened self-interest prodded the *bhadralok* towards a new outlook.[95]

Ambivalences in Bengali Muslim Identity

If we have underlined till now the limitations of the stereotypical and retrospective construal of Bengali Muslim politics solely in terms of communalism (which actually became a dominant discourse only in the late 1930s) it was out of regard for the ambivalence and variations that characterized their identity formation process. Two polar extremes were typified in the following statements: 'Having forgotten that Islam is a Religion not a Nation, the Bengali Muslims are loudly proclaiming that they are a Muslim Nation.... Thus today the Muslim community is alienated in that Bengal which nurtured them for a thousand years'. In contrast: 'Muslims, you are in a slumber! Now is the time to beware, to save yourself and to save the Nation. Do not be taken in by Congress deceptions and join the agitation against law, deceived by the mirage of independence. All this agitation is nothing but a scheme to establish independence for Hindus and suppression of the Muslims'. The extracts are, respectively, from the Bengali Muslim journals *Saugat* (1928) and the *Shariat-e-Islam* (1929), the former considered 'liberal' and the latter 'conservative'.[96] Side by side, and simultaneously, these two lines of thinking coexisted for years until the 1930s. Tazeen M. Murshid in her recent study of Bengali Muslim discourse makes the insightful observation that the concept of a 'monolithic Muslim mind' cannot be sustained in the face of evidence. Her analysis of 'the constructedness of identity formation' suggests that a Muslim identity in Bengal was being constantly rearticulated against an 'other' giving rise to 'conflicting nationalism'.[97]

Apart from the ideological level addressed by Tazeen Murshid, at the level of quotidian politics there are internal tensions in the Muslim League which come to light when one studies the private correspondence of the political leaders. The Muslim League might appear to be united compared to the Congress. But the internal tensions were great between Central and Bengal leadership, particularly in the late 1930s when the 'sole spokesman' began to assert his monopoly of ultimate decision-making. In his private correspondence published later, one can see that Fazlul Huq was given to speaking his mind and made many enemies, including Jinnah. Just before the elections of 1937 they fell out openly. 'You have had the impertinence to ask for an explanation from me.... I call upon you to explain your conduct', Huq wrote to Jinnah in October 1936.[98] Or again, Huq wrote to Liaquat Ali Khan protesting the League high-command's habit of taking Bengal for granted in expectation of obedience: 'I will never allow the interest of thirty-three millions of the Muslims of Bengal to be put under the domination of any outside authority...'.[99] H.S. Suhrawardy was more circumspect than the plain-speaking Huq, but he too was assertive on occasion, for example, his letter to Jinnah in July 1937 asking bluntly for more freedom from central control: 'If you want to run the League here, we are prepared to assist but if you are really lukewarm about it and not very much care ... please let me know so that we can start our own separate organization'.[100] In his letters a decade later, Suhrawardy was, of course, reverentially addressing 'Quaid-i-Azam', but his object then was to obtain from the centre freedom of action to discipline his rival, Fazlul Huq.[101] Apart from the tensions between the Bengal leaders and the central leadership, there was also factionalism within the League, for example, between the Calcutta and Dhaka cliques, as we have seen in an earlier chapter. However, on the whole, the authority of the 'Sole Spokesman', Jinnah, gave the League a semblance of unity even in faction-ridden Bengal.

In the recently published Jinnah correspondence, there is an interesting letter from Suhrawardy to Jinnah where Fazlul Huq is shown to be 'again at his nefarious business' of 'undermining the solidarity of Muslims'.[102] This was in 1947 when the communal divide was complete. By then Jinnah's hold in Bengal was so complete that the slightest concession to a non-Muslim category was tantamount to betrayal of Muslim solidarity. Even when Fazlul Huq spoke of Bengali interests, it was unacceptable: 'What is the meaning of your suggestion', Jinnah writes to Huq, 'that I should not impose any decision on the steps that you may take in Bengal?'[103] This is the climax of a long process of communalization but this was not how it always was. The point is that communalization was not a process that was free from contestation.

It will be a grave error to dismiss all those who were in the Bengal Muslim League as communally minded persons. Fazlul Huq might have appeared to some Bengali Hindus as communal, but there is much evidence to the contrary. Syama Prasad Mookerjee—who cannot be accused of being soft on Muslim communalists—held Huq's unimpeachable credentials in such high regard that, when Khwaja Nazimuddin invited Mookerjee to join his ministry, the latter laid down the condition that Huq's party must also be invited and that, of course, was unacceptable to Nazimuddin.[104] Mookerjee knew that occasionally Huq gave in under pressure from communal politicians, but he never charged Huq with being communal in his outlook. It is no exaggeration to say that Huq and the KPP were pushed into the arms of the communalist Muslim leaders by the Congress policy of not entering into a coalition ministry. Abul Hashim, Secretary to the Bengal Muslim League, is another exemplar of a non-communal approach. The Draft Manifesto he drew up in March 1945 for the forthcoming elections is an apposite instance. His aim was to outline the future constitution of East Pakistan:

> Such an outline will be effective not only in inspiring the entire Muslim humanity of East Pakistan but will be equally helpful in instilling confidence and understanding among the millions of non-Muslims, steeped in prejudices and misgivings against the Muslim national movement.... The Muslim League leadership in Eastern Pakistan enjoins upon it the solemn responsibility of acting as the custodian of the interests of non-Muslims, including the Depressed Classes and backward peoples, to whom it guarantees not only common rights but also provision for their betterment in accordance with their own respective traditions and culture.[105]

A co-author of the Draft Manifesto, Hashim wrote later, was the young communist intellectual, Nikhil Chakravartty.[106] Hashim was aware 'that the Working Committee of the BPML [Bengal Provincial Muslim League] would never put their thumb impression on the draft Manifesto I prepared'. He was denounced by his opponents dominating the party, Khwaja Nazimuddin and Liaquat Ali Khan, and although their attempt to throw him out failed in 1945 he was slowly marginalized; we have noted elsewhere in this book his political role till he migrated to East Pakistan in 1950. Men like Huq or Hashim represent a section of opinion which cannot be labelled communal.[107] From the 1920s to the 1940s, from the Buddhir Mukti Andolan to the East Pakistan Renaissance Society founded in 1942, there was a continuity in the pursuit of a non-communal culture within Muslim society. In fact, the Renaissance Society, led by Mujibur Rahman Khan and Abul Mansur Ahmad—unlike the purely intellectual movements earlier—acquired a political role of some importance in the turbulent pre-Independence days. Moreover, the presence of a secular Muslim intelligentsia is also in evidence in the Nationalist Muslim Parliamentary Board. In September 1945, the KPP joined the all-India conference of all the non-League nationalist Muslim organizations in Delhi initiated by the Jamiat-ul-Ulema-e-Hind which expressly rejected the two-nation theory of M.A. Jinnah; the KPP was also represented in the Nationalist Muslim Parliamentary Board set up in October 1945. In the elections which followed, the nationalist intellectual Humayun Kabir commented that 'the electors lost their freedom of judgement on account of interference by their religious teachers and threats of divine displeasure'.[108] However, the KPP and the Nationalist Muslims obtained only 2.7 per cent of Muslim votes in urban and 7.1 per cent in rural constituencies, whereas the Muslim League obtained 95 and 89.6 per cent respectively.[109] Thus, it must be conceded that they constituted a small minority compared to the mainstream opinion in the community in the 1940s when Jinnah swept all before him everywhere in India except Badshah Khan's 'Pakhtunistan'.

The terms in which the contestation was cast altered over time according to the political context. Contestation of Muslim nationalism striving for a Pakistan could be in terms of (*a*) 'Bengaliness' or (*b*) in terms of secularism. With the exception of a few individuals like Humayun Kabir, the latter course of thinking was limited to a negligible Left on the margins. An incipient debate on this question among historians in Bangladesh is on the other track. Professor Harun-or-Rashid argues that in colonial Bengal the moving spirit in Muslim politics was a Bengali sub-nationalism, not so much the Pakistan movement.[110] On the other hand, Professor A.R. Mallick and Syed Anwar Hussein argue that Bengali sub-nationalism was only a post-1947 phenomenon, and that it was really a non-religious and material objective, their own uplift, which motivated the Bengali Muslims. In Mallick's opinion the assertion of Bengali Muslim identity 'was essentially a reaction of a marginalized community in quest of its due share in the political and economic milieu'; but 'tactical use of religion by the elite leadership for mobilization purposes' gave it a religious turn.[111] Harun-or-Rashid's focus is not on the material aspirations of Muslim rich peasants, *jotedars*, and the urban elite, but on 'Bengali loyalties'. He goes so far as to say: 'Never in history India was a single state or a nation' and at the same time maintains that in 'the maze of differences Bengal stood out most pre-eminently from the rest of India, and, allowed uninterrupted development, it had the brightest prospect of growing into a nation state'. But that was aborted since political leaders planted 'the two-nation theory based on religion and sectarianism'.[112] This approach may have an appeal to a segment of Bengali sentiment, but it underestimates the integrative forces linking the political movements in Bengal with the subcontinental mainstream of the Congress, the Muslim League, and the Left parties. Even at its most insular moments, casting off those links was on no political party's agenda till 1947. It was only in 1947 that a few leaders momentarily experimented with the idea of 'united independent Bengal', and there was a long interval till 1971 when finally there was the movement that led to the triumphant entry of Bangladesh into the world.

These interpretations of Bengali Muslim politics have one point in common: that the 'religious turn' was imparted to Muslim politics from above by the leadership as a means of mobilization, while the *real* motive force was 'Bengali nationalism' or the aspirations of a 'marginalized' community. However, the rhetoric of Muslim politics, through the campaign rallies, the writings in Muslim news organs, the symbolic value attached to special places or edifices, and so on—whatever the originative or inner motive force might have been—increasingly gave a centrality to religious identity. Contestation against it, at least in the public sphere, became progressively weaker in the late 1930s and the early 1940s. The rhetoric of 'nationalism of religion' was not necessarily the *cause* of the political actions that ensued, but it was a pervasive perceptual *context* which inscribed new meanings on events, practices, words. Hence a political culture of communalism. The same process was at work across the fence in the Hindu community.

Changing Fortunes of the Hindu Mahasabha

We may take the diary of Syama Prasad Mookerjee as a text to explore the mindset that went into Bengali *bhadralok* participation in the Hindu

Mahasabha and the communally oriented activities that distinguished the party from the Indian National Congress. The diary was probably not written with a view to publication; it is quite poorly organized and much of it is Mookerjee reminiscing about earlier days. However, it is highly interesting as a personal document of the only leading Bengali politician who joined the Hindu Mahasabha.

It appears from the diary that Syama Prasad Mookerjee's activities in the Mahasabha began as late as 1939 when he was thirty-eight years of age and it was personal acquaintance with V. Savarkar in August 1939 which initiated him.[113] Mookerjee was then in a perturbed state of mind due to his feeling that there was 'Hindu oppression [that is, oppression of the Hindus] at the hands of a communal ministry with Fazlul Huq at its head'.[114] Among the political issues he mentions are: 'ratio of communal representation in the [government] services', 'preferential treatment of Muslims in educational and technical spheres', 'encouragement of riots, and so on, and the Calcutta Municipal and the Secondary Education bills which were likely to diminish the space for Hindus in running the Corporation and school education. The second factor that turned Mookerjee towards the Mahasabha was his disappointment with the Congress in Bengal. 'The party which evoked my sympathy and support was the Congress. The Congress however lamentably betrayed the interests of the Hindus'.[115] It failed in respect of the Communal Award, it did not make any effort to get together a coalition to form a ministry in Bengal, and it 'hesitated to fight openly for Hindu rights as it would then be dubbed as a communal organization'.[116] Even the dissidents within the Congress like Sarat Chandra Bose and Subhas Bose were, to Mookerjee, disappointing in this regard.

> I asked them to take up the Hindu cause in Bengal so as to render it unnecessary for us to organize a separate political body. They expressed their inability to do so—first because they thought it might still further rouse Muslims, and, secondly, because they themselves being 'non-communal Congressites' could not openly do what I asked them to do.[117]

Thus Mookerjee felt the need for a political organization; as a member of the legislature he was already speaking his mind, but 'I belonged to no political party whose platform I could utilise'[118] It was at such a juncture that he met Savarkar who had come to preside over the

Provincial Mahasabha conference at Khulna (1939). Mookerjee threw himself into the act. First, he merged the two Hindu Sabhas that existed into one and soon after, in December 1939, the All-India Hindu Mahasabha's conference was held in Calcutta. Next, he plunged into the elections to the Calcutta Corporation in March 1940; this was when he had a conversation with the Bose brothers and met with their refusal. Mookerjee managed to win about fifty per cent of the seats: 'We had defeated Subhas whom Gandhi's followers in Bengal feared to challenge'.[119] It seems that Mookerjee started negotiations with Subhas to form a coalition but after 'breaking away from us he came to terms with the Muslim League'. Mookerjee felt 'admiration' for Subhas but 'his trouble however was too much of first person singular'. From then on, the Mahasabha gained an increasing following, and 'the Dacca riots brought the Sabha into great prominence'.[120] This was followed by riots in Narayanganj, Tripura, and other places. Clearly this aided the Mahasabha: 'These riots and disturbances opened the eyes of the Hindus considerably and the work of the Sabha received a great impetus'.[121] Obviously, the Mahasabha and, more than the party, Mookerjee, had reached a position of strength when Huq offered him a position in the Progressive Coalition Party Ministry, which he accepted despite all his reservations about Huq. In fact, the ministry came to be known popularly as the Syama–Huq ministry. (Mookerjee submitted his resignation in August 1942—it was accepted in November 1942—on the issue of government measures during the 1942 movement.) But neither his performance as a Finance Minister nor the work of this second Huq ministry as a whole created much impact. Mookerjee's main achievement as a minister was what he did for famine relief by mobilizing funds from Marwari businessmen and the Hindu public. Here too there was a communal divide: he served the Hindu famine victims, Suhrawardy the Muslims.

The Mahasabha came into its own in the 1942–7 period. In the first phase, Mookerjee's view was 'No Partition', and in the second 'Nothing but Partition'. Till 1946 he said many times that 'India's vivisection' was unacceptable.[122] He also thought that it was demonstrated during his ministership in the Huq ministry that 'working together as colleagues' was possible for Hindu and Muslim leaders. 'Leaders must be in a position to assure their communities that their interests are being well looked after' and 'if the leaders of both communities played the game there could be no communalism in the province at all'.[123] Mookerjee's letters as President of the Mahasabha, elected in place of Savarkar in December 1944, among the papers of the Akhil Bharat Hindu Mahasabha, now open to researchers, are marked by a consistent aversion to the idea of Partition.[124] At this time organizationally the party was doing well in Bengal according to the reports of Asutosh Lahiri on the Eastern Zone.[125]

In 1946, Mookerjee's opinion changed entirely. He came to realize, he writes in his Bengali diary on 3 January 1946, that 'howsoever much I disliked the League ... it must be admitted that within a short time the League had miraculously infused the Muslim masses with a new spirit.... But alas the Hindus never thought or worked on those lines'.[126] This disappointment was exacerbated by the refusal of the Hindu Mahasabha Committee to endorse his proposal that the impending elections in 1945 should be opposed since they were on the basis of the MacDonald Communal Award. Thirdly, it seems that the results of the elections in December 1945 deeply disappointed Mookerjee. He was the only winner among the thirty-one candidates put up by the Mahasabha. The results were quite risible in some cases. For instance, the Mahasabha candidate against Sarat Chandra Bose got 88 out of 7,400 votes. Syama Prasad confided to his diary: 'It is no use being angry with my countrymen for rejecting the services that I or my organization offered.... So, it was proved once for all that the Hindus wanted the Congress and the Muslims were all for the League'.[127] Hereafter, it seems, Mookerjee began to rethink the Partition question. He did make the usual anti-Partition and anti-Pakistan gestures in April 1946 at his meeting with the Cabinet Mission.[128] But one surmises that the psychological impact of the Calcutta Riot of August 1946 and the arrival of Mountbatten with his quick-cooking recipes altered the scene substantially. The demand for a separate homeland for the Bengali Hindus became the new war cry, that is, the Partition of Bengal. Mookerjee presided over the conference convened by the Provincial Mahasabha on 15 March 1947 which endorsed this new programme. The Congress was no longer criticized all that much, the idea was to influence it. We have, in S.P. Mookerjee's unpublished private papers in the Nehru Museum in Delhi, an interesting 'confidential' letter of October 1945 from M.R. Jayakar proposing 'an understanding with the Congress in connection with the next elections' on the ground that 'vital differences between the Congress and Hindu Mahasabha have diminished'.[129] This understanding never came about. But from early 1946 the diminution of differences mentioned by Jayakar was more marked. On 4 April 1947, a largely attended meeting, calling itself the Bengal Partition Convention, as well as the executive committee of the Bengal Provincial Congress met on the same day. They both resolved that Partition of Bengal was desirable. We shall see in a later chapter how the few dissidents were marginalized and the Partition became almost an all-party agenda among the Hindu leaders, except for the proponents of a scheme for a so-called United Independent Bengal.

We have looked at the course of activities of Syama Prasad Mookerjee because he *was* virtually the Mahasabha in Bengal from 1939 to 1947. Though the Mahasabha did succeed in pushing forward the idea of Partition in 1947, it was not an agenda exclusively its own and it was the Congress support at the central level that would prove to be decisive. Though there was a communal consciousness in the culture of the Hindu *bhadralok*, as we have seen in an earlier chapter, its political translation in the hands of the Hindu Mahasabha did not find popular acceptance, as Mookerjee acknowledged to himself in his diary. The 1946 general elections were decisive—thirty out of thirty-one Sabha candidates were defeated. Though the Hindu Mahasabha was able to put forward a clear-cut position and strategy, it lost out to the Congress which accommodated a wide range of positions and opinions with an ease that came of a long history of compromise with the incompatible. Finally, although the Mahasabha presented a picture of a Hindu community in a reactive response to the League, *was* there one Hindu community? Mookerjee reflected on this question in his diary: 'Islam had a singular spirit of unity and equality that Hinduism lacked. Differences along lines of caste, creed, or religion kept one Hindu from empathizing with another. On the other hand, one Muslim invariably felt a bond with another…'.[130] This was at an abstract level; at the practical level Mookerjee experienced the difficulty of keeping the scheduled castes within the fold that he wanted to encompass as one community; having secured a number of seats in legislature they 'were being made to demand separate political entity antagonistic to Hindus'. For all these reasons, the Mahasabha, unlike the Congress and the League, never became a serious contender for power in Bengal.

Politics of Exclusion in the Congress

As a residuary legatee of C.R. Das, the Congress in Bengal in the 1930s behaved like a spendthrift *zamindar* squandering the patrimony. We have seen in an earlier chapter that John Gallagher was not far wrong when he talked of the Congress in decline in those years. To understand how the politics of exclusion worked in the Congress we have to go back to that for a while.

After C.R. Das's death, his lieutenants fought over party control. Chiefly, it was between J.M. Sengupta and Subhas Bose. The All-India Congress Committee Papers, now in the Nehru Museum, are full of these fights. Minor things like Provincial Congress's Flood and Famine Relief Committee set off a spate of letters from both factions to the AICC and Working Committee: Subhas made an issue of the fact that Gandhi had endorsed Sir Prafulla Chandra Ray's relief efforts, though Ray was in the wrong camp, that is, Sengupta's Relief Committee and not Bose's Committee.[131] (Bose was then in the 'official Congress'.) The same factionalism extended to more important matters like the Civil Disobedience Committee—there were two of them in 1930–1. Even Motilal Nehru, when asked to settle the dispute in 1929, had failed; the Central Working Committee then decided that newly elected members of Bengal to AICC should not be allowed to join because their election was suspect due to procedural flaws pointed out by J.M. Sengupta. Bose resigned his working committee membership to protest this 'unconstitutional procedure ... influenced by representations from Mr. J.M. Sengupta'.[132]

In 1931, M.S. Aney was sent by the High Command to enquire into the Bose–Sengupta disputes. Bose wrote to Aney of Sengupta's record of 'indiscipline' and how he 'shattered the solidarity of the Congress party'.[133] Sengupta, on the other hand, claims that Bose's complaints 'contain half-truths and untruths'.[134] Aney's report in September 1931 contained a detailed history of disputes and 53 charges and counter-charges. The bottom line was:

> Misunderstandings. among leading members of the Bengal Congress Committee have arisen since last three or four years with the result that the entire Congress organization has been divided into two rival parties, one led by Mr. Subhas Chandra Bose and the other by Mr. J.M. Sengupta.... Congress organization reached a very high degree

> of efficiency and strength, particularly after 1920, under the dynamic leadership of the late Deshbandhu C.R. Das. It was impossible for the Working Committee to remain indifferent when the strength and prestige of this most powerful organization was being undermined by internecine quarrels and petty rivalries.... The two parties have been fighting against each other for getting a dominant position in the BPCC, AICC and the Corporation of Calcutta.[135]

If you look into the papers of the AICC, now preserved in the Nehru Museum and Library at New Delhi, you will find numerous letters, representations, allegations, and sometimes enquiry committees related to factional divisions in Bengal Congress in the 1930s. The Governor of Bengal, Anderson, seemed to be quite well informed about it: Congress, he wrote in 1936 from Calcutta in a confidential report to Viceroy Linlithgow, 'has a long history of internal faction.... Formerly the quarrel was between Subhas Bose, corresponding to the Jugantar group among the revolutionaries, and J.M. Sengupta, whose affinities were more with the Anushilan revolutionaries...'.[136] He went on to say that the Sengupta faction had receded by 1936 (Sengupta died in 1933) and the 'important group opposed to Subhas and his brother Sarat is now that of Dr. Bidhan Chandra Roy: their differences are more personal than of principle'. Anderson expected these differences to show up at the time of elections in 1936 and this is what did happen in the choice of candidates. Among various views on the Subhas Bose versus J.M. Sengupta factional struggle it is interesting to note that Sugata Bose is quite critical of Sengupta: 'Sengupta had been appointed to his posts [in Bengal Congress] by Gandhi after C.R. Das's death, and was generally inclined to obey the dictates of the Congress high command, Bose represented the rebellious tendency in Bengal, not just against the British but against the all-India leadership of the Congress as well'.[137]

Sarat Chandra Bose and B.C. Roy fell out, as predicted by Anderson, on election nominations. (Subhas Bose was first in Austria and then, upon returning to India, in jail; J.B. Kripalani, by the way, subjected him to petty harassment by denying him primary membership on the ground that the last date had expired.)[138] From the private papers of B.C. Roy it appears that a settlement, worked out by Jawaharlal Nehru, brought Bose and Roy together. In July 1936, an agreement of 'all the groups of Congressmen in Bengal' decided that Roy would be President of the Parliamentary Committee in Bengal, while Subhas Bose would be President of the BPCC and that during his absence Sarat Bose would act in his place.[139] But the latter and Dr Roy could not agree on several nominations; the majority in the Parliamentary Committee supported Roy and thereafter Bose offered to resign. Roy then approached Govind Ballabh Pant of the Central Parliamentary Committee for a decision. The Central Committee decided to vet all nominations to appease Bose who then withdrew his resignation. Now it was Roy's turn to resign. This he did on the ground that he 'tried to work harmoniously' with Bose but failed; 'unitary direction and control are essential' and either Roy or Bose should be given such control, not both of them. Eventually he was persuaded to withdraw his resignation. But the whole episode was illustrative of the kind of faction struggle that went on in the Bengal Congress, even on the eve of the general election of 1936.

As a result, the Congress was far from being an instrument of effective political action in the crucial decade 1937–47. Ironically, there was quite another side to it: Subhas Bose represented a new, spirited effort to bring the youth into the Congress, to build bridgeheads into the ranks of the socialists in or near the Congress, to assert, when necessary, views that were not acceptable to the Congress Establishment. The only Bengal leader of his times to whom the term charismatic could be applied, Subhas was destined, however, to get repeatedly embroiled in conflicts both in Bengal and in the Central Congress decision-making bodies.

The last of these clashes is well-known: his presidentship at the Haripura Congress in 1938, his re-election as President of Tripuri Congress in 1939 in the teeth of Mahatma Gandhi's disapprobation, the persistent non-cooperation of senior Congressmen loyal to Gandhi, his consequent failure to form the Working Committee, and the resignation of presidentship forced upon him in April 1939. From then till he jumped his home-internment to make his way to Germany, he was in a sort of political wilderness, an exile from the party he had served since 1921. Sulking in defeat, Subhas alienated many friends, or at least colleagues, like Nehru. Nirad C. Chaudhuri, who was a secretary to Sarat Bose, reminisced later: 'Subhas Bose accused Nehru of being the principal instigator of his persecution. Nothing could be more lacking in dignity and moderation in the Boses than their way of taking defeat'.[140]

The entire correspondence published recently does show that Subhas was 'unfair in his criticism'.[141]

In any event, what mattered was not so much the incidents—that series of events showed that the Boses were no match for Gandhi in politics—but the issues involved. First, Bose underlined the importance of 'the existence of multiple parties and the democratic basis of the Congress', for example, his Haripura Congress Address in 1938.[142] This was not acceptable to those who hegemonized the party, through informal means; this fact may be acknowledged without necessarily accepting the rightness of either of the factions that clashed. Second, Subhas was keen on a coalition ministry in Bengal with Congress participation while Gandhi and Nehru stoutly opposed it. Bose's strategy would have been, he wrote to Gandhi, to form coalition ministries in Bengal, Punjab, and Sindh to enhance Congress's claim to represent all of India; he suspected that G.D. Birla, M.K. Azad and Nalini Ranjan Sarkar had dissuaded Gandhi from supporting this strategy.[143] Thirdly, there might have been differences, which never quite came into the open, between the idea of socialistic planning promoted by Bose and the conservative elements in the ranks of the Gandhians. To the National Planning Committee that he appointed as President, he expressed his awareness of 'apprehensions in certain quarters' regarding consistency between planned modern industrialization and promotion of Khadi and cottage industries.[144] While Nehru or J.B. Kripalani would agree with Bose, there were many Congressmen who suspected his approach. According to Sugata Bose, '[t]he socialist agenda of the [Congress] National Planning Committee incensed leaders of the right wing of the Congress'.[145] Among these opponents, he says, were G.D. Birla 'a powerful backer of the Gandhian Congress' and K.M. Munshi, 'a close friend of Patel'.

The degree of mutual hatred revealed in the private correspondence, now available, is astonishing. Patel complains to Rajendra Prasad that Subhas 'is making a mess of Congress politics',[146] Azad reported to Patel of Subhasists' propaganda against Patel the 'anti-socialist',[147] Prafulla Chandra Ghosh complains to Prasad of Subhasist persecution of loyal Congressmen like B.C. Roy and himself,[148] Kiran Shankar Ray complains to Kripalani of the 'partisanship' of Subhas,[149] B.C. Roy carries tales from Bengal to Patel,[150] and, of course, Sarat Bose complains bitterly to Gandhi of 'mean, malicious and vindictive' treatment of Subhas at the Tripuri Congress.[151] It was an unedifying spectacle, displaying the trend of 'politics of exclusion' prevailing in Bengal.

In Bengal the showdown came in August 1939 when disciplinary proceedings against Subhas were discussed in the Provincial Congress Committeee. While P.C. Ghosh, B.C. Roy, Abdus Sattar, and K.S. Roy led 138 against Subhas, the majority of 213, including Somnath Lahiri, A.M.A. Zaman, and Bankim Mukherjee supported Subhas.[152] Nevertheless, the central Congress's decision to expel Subhas stood and was enforced. This naturally deepened the rift in the Bengal Congress. Subhas Bose's Forward Bloc gave the dissidents a political nucleus outside the Congress. Incidentally, factional struggle also encouraged corruption. As early as 1931, the AICC received complaints of false enrolment of party members and rejection of nomination to party elections on arbitrary grounds.[153] Abul Mansur Ahmed records the routine method of bogus enrolment as a means of controlling district congress committees in the early 1930s.[154]

The year 1942 constituted an exceptional episode in the history of the Bengal Congress. The murky atmosphere in the Congress Party contrasts sharply with the spirit of the individuals who took part in the Quit India movement—individuals like Matangini Hazra, a widowed peasant woman of seventy-three who died in police firing holding on to the Tricolour she carried. The Quit India movement appears to have, judging by recent well-documented studies, the following distinguishing features. First, while the Congress leadership was weakened by faction fights, the common Congress workers and people unconnected with that party, or any other party, spontaneously joined the movement. In Medinipur, where the movement was the strongest, the Congress had become particularly weak. The membership had declined in 1939–41 from 31,000 to 19,000; but during the Quit India movement membership increased to 59,000.[155] The Congress did not have a large mass following to deploy in the movement; on the contrary, the movement brought to the Congress a following that numbered thrice that of the previous year. Secondly, the articulation between local and provincial Congress leadership was weak during the movement and at the peak of activities the Congress had no control over local actions. The attack on government establishments, post offices, police stations, and so on, was followed by underground activities carried out and materially supported by peasants. The Congress was a flag to rally around, not an instrument of control and guidance. Thirdly, in Medinipur, like the Marathi 'pratisarkar' in Satara, a parallel government developed, instituting systems of taxation, justice, and a sort of participatory administration by the people. Militant action was not unusual in many parts of India in 1942, but to build a system countervailing the colonial state in this manner was an exceptional achievement, however short-lived the 'Jatiya Sarkar' in Medinipur might have been.

The 1942 movement divided the 'moderates' from those who wanted to push the movement into a militant trajectory. Forms of militant action adopted by the Jatiya Sarkar turned *zamindars*, *jotedars*, traders, and professional people from sympathizers to hostile elements that the Sarkar had to tackle. Its news bulletins defended paddy-looting and condemned those who were 'amassing fortunes by depriving millions of men'.[156] When Mahatma Gandhi visited Medinipur in 1945 he said: 'What you have done is heroic and glorious. However, you have deviated from the path of non-violence'.[157] Finally, we must also note that the politics of exclusion we have focused upon in this chapter affected the Quit India movement as well. Mohammad Khairul Anam, in a recent work of research, points out that 'Muslim participation in the Quit India movement is minimal'; in the district of Murshidabad which had a large Muslim population there were a few Muslim participants, but even in that district out of over a hundred persons arrested by the police only two were Muslim.[158] The Quit India movement was an isolated episode and Bengal Congress reverted to its usual faction fighting as soon as the impetus of the movement was exhausted.

Distant Drums: Subhas Bose and the INA

It was Bengal's misfortune that the man who, despite all the foibles we have noticed earlier in these pages, had the calibre to take Bengal Congress out of this morass, Subhas Chandra Bose, ceased to be one of the players in politics. We have examined the circumstances in which he was denied the position to which he had been duly elected and the rationale for his eventual expulsion from the party, and the conclusion is unavoidable that whatever might have been the circumstances and reasons, the Congress inflicted on itself an immense loss. And he launched into a course of action outside India that he hoped would have a political impact in India; but his expectations of a civil uprising in response to the entry of his Indian National Army (INA) into India were not to be fulfilled. The distant drums of the Burma front were scarcely heard in India, though in later times that story became the stuff of heroic legends.

It is interesting to speculate what might have happened had Subhas Bose remained in his own country. The course of history might have been different, but probably that is idle speculation. He was left with no option. On the one hand, he had been expelled from his party by former colleagues, on the other, he was imprisoned in his own residence by the British Indian government. Politically incapacitated by the Congress Party and the British Indian government, he either had to accept being a political non-entity and sink into the dust of history, or break away from it all and take to the adventurous path he did choose. That path was the only one acceptable to a man of his ideas and temperament. In hindsight it seems that his chief achievement was to look for an alternative to the trajectory the Congress had plotted for itself after the outbreak of the Second World War. In a sense it was not unlike the Swarajist and the *biplabi* and the Leftist search for alternatives to the Gandhian Congress in Bengal (Chapter 5). It seems that the essence of his strategy was the *internationalization* of the Indian freedom struggle, taking advantage of the global situation during the World War. This interpretation appears to be justifiable if we look at three major lines of actions he followed after his famous exit from India in disguise.

First, he tried to assert independence outside of home territory by setting up a provisional government in exile—an effort analogous to those of Charles De Gaulle and Josip Broz Tito.[159] Since they were on the winning side, De Gaulle and Tito were successful; Bose was with the Axis Powers on the losing side—but in terms of international law their positions were the same. Second, Subhas Bose's strategy of internationalization included an effort to take advantage of the Indian diaspora in southeast Asia by drawing upon the support of Tamil merchants and bankers in Burma, or the descendants of Telugu and Tamil immigrant labourers in Malaya and Singapore, or the Indian businessmen and professionals in Shanghai or Manila or other parts of southeast Asia. The idea was not only to mobilize manpower and resources, but also to make them citizens of a state yet without territory—a diasporic citizenship of an incipient state. The Proclamation of the Provisional Government of

Azad Hind on 21 October 1943 declared: 'The Provisional Government is entitled to and hereby claims the allegiance of every Indian'.[160] His provisional government was, of course, manned entirely by diasporic Indians. Thirdly, Subhas Bose's aim was to draw upon the assistance of the Axis Powers but he maintained the freedom and integrity of the Azad Hind Government as a sovereign entity. Even before the creation of that Provisional Government he asserted a degree of freedom that was irreconcilable with the hegemony Adolf Hitler desired and hence Subhas's break with Nazi Germany. Although Benito Mussolini and his foreign minister Galeazzo Ciano were quite responsive, Hitler was unresponsive to Bose's overtures seeking material assistance. Bose wrote very frankly to a personal friend in the Deutsche Akademie that he saw Hitler's outlook as 'not only narrow and selfish but arrogant' in its racialism; and that conflicted with Bose's view that any understanding with Germany 'must be consistent with our national self-respect'.[161] As regards his alliance with Japan, Bose's assertions of independence sometimes caused conflicts with authorities at the lower levels of the Japanese Army, but Prime Minister Hideki Tojo and foreign minister Hajime Sugiyama, as well as nine other nations, gave full diplomatic recognition to Bose and his Provisional Government as a sovereign entity.

The flag raised by Bose in the Andamans in December 1943 was the Indian National Congress Tricolour, the National Anthem chosen by Bose was the future National Anthem 'Jana-gana-mana', brigades of the INA were named after Gandhi, Nehru, and Maulana Azad—and in these and many other ways Bose signalized a symbolic unity with a Congress that scarcely acknowledged his struggle outside India. It is interesting to reflect on the fact that while Bose's endeavour ended in military failure, in the brief span of time he spent in building the Azad Hind Fauj, in respect of some matters he succeeded where the Congress had failed. While a resolution of the communal problem and separatism eluded the Congress in India, Bose's Azad Hind Fauj and Sarkar conspicuously displayed national unity and inter-communal harmony. Moreover, the Indian Congress failed to come up with an adequate response to the World War. Was a simple withdrawal and resignation of the Congress ministries enough? What did it mean except self-exile from governance in a large number of provinces where Congress had a majority and had formed the ministry? How did that advance the freedom struggle? Bose was one among other Asian leaders who tried to utilize the opportunity created by the war—Burmese (Myanmarese) nationalist Aung San collaborated first with the Japanese and then with the British; Indonesian national leader Achmed Sukarno collaborated with the Japanese who replaced the Dutch rulers, and the right-wing Chinese nationalist Chiang Kai-shek also advanced his own ends vis-á-vis the Communists and the Japanese whom he fought. Likewise, Bose too tried to use Japanese arms and resources against the British. The war was a complex situation demanding flexible responses and, the Indian Congress, perched on what it took to be high moral ground and wedded to the idea that resignation was politically adequate, failed in that respect till 1942.

Unfortunately, the above-mentioned rationale behind Subhas Bose's line of action has received little attention, the story of the heroic fight of the INA on the outskirts of Imphal gets all the attention. It was beyond doubt a heroic story but, judging by contemporary accounts, defeat on the battlefield was almost inevitable.[162] First, in the battle on the Imphal front the Allied forces—British, British Indian, US, and West African troops—numbered 155,000, and thus they vastly outnumbered the 84,000 Japanese and 12,000 INA soldiers on the other side. Second, the supply line for the Japanese and INA forces to Rangoon and beyond was too long, and hence armaments and even rations were in short supply. On the other side, the troops were entrenched in Imphal adequately armed and the US Air Force continuously brought in fresh supplies. Towards the end of the field struggle, the INA and the Japanese were reduced to living on jungle fruits and roots and reportedly on fish they caught with mosquito nets. Apart from the supply deficiency, there was a third problem—the superior air power of the Allied forces; their aircraft outnumbered tenfold those available to the Japanese. Consequently, the INA soldiers did not get the air cover they needed when they emerged from the forest areas out into the open plains. Finally, the greatest disappointment was that although some local Nagas and Manipuris were supportive, there was no reaction to the advance of INA troops into Indian territory. In Assam or Bengal the people in general never got to know that the Tricolour had been raised on Indian territory a few miles from Imphal at Moirang (this is today a small town, a centre of smuggling across the Myanmar border), or that the INA had commanded the mountain heights around Kohima (north of Imphal and near the sole railway head, Dimapur). In any event, during the war extraordinarily repressive laws like the Defence of the Realm Act in British colonial possessions everywhere put a lid on popular movements.[163] When Bose realized how the INA campaign had failed, he gave a touching speech on the eve of retreat: he looked to the future and quoted Lord Byron's famous words, 'Freedom's battle once begun, bequeathed from bleeding sire to son, tho' baffled oft, is ever won'.[164]

Strict censorship of the Press in India suppressed all news about Subhas Bose and the INA. There were broadcasts by the Azad Hind Radio but listening to those was illegal and, after all, there were only 120,000 receiving sets in the whole of India, and these only in the homes of relatively well-to-do people. Only after the end of the war did the heroic deeds of the INA begin to seep into people's minds and ironically it was the British government that aided this process when they put on trial three INA officers, formerly of the British Indian army. The event was rich in symbolism. The accused three were Hindu, Muslim, and Sikh respectively, as if highlighting the unity of the communities in the INA. Poignantly, the venue was the Red Fort, which Bose had declared to be the INA's destination. The defence of the accused was conducted by nationalist Congressmen. It was, in a way, the vindication of the position Subhas Bose had taken.

If further vindication was needed, none could have been more complete than the massive popular reaction to the trial of the INA officers, in their defence and in memory of the new icon 'Netaji'. On 21 November 1945 there began a student protest in Calcutta that snowballed into a city-wide general strike with the participation of industrial and transport workers, as well as an unprecedented joint participation of the Congress, the Muslim League and the Communist Party of India. 'Conditions are the worst the city has experienced during the past twenty years', the Intelligence Department of the police reported; military vehicles were burnt, barricades were erected on the streets, many meetings were held 'in favour of the INA'.[165] There was another outburst in February 1946 to protest the trial of Capt. Rashid Ali of the INA. Once again, students and youths took the lead, particularly the communist Students' Federation and the Muslim Students' League supported by the Congress. Troops of the Lancashire and Yorkshire Regiments, as well as the Gurkha Rifles, were deployed on the streets of Calcutta and, according to official estimates, eighty-four people were killed in firing.[166] A notable feature was that in sympathy with the general strike in Calcutta, twenty-two towns in West and East Bengal observed a general strike. The massive demonstrations of solidarity with INA in Bengal and elsewhere in India—and, of course, the Naval Mutiny in Bombay—had two important consequences. First, despite Wavell's obduracy in insisting on the trial of the INA officers, the Government of India conceded defeat in that the Commander-in-Chief was compelled to negate the punishment awarded by the military court. Second, the Government of India began to doubt whether the loyalty of the Indians in the British Indian army could be depended on any longer. Thus the INA, which failed on the battlefield, succeeded in causing huge damage to the morale of the British Indian army.

Throughout the period we have surveyed in this chapter, we have seen that the fault lines in the polity, the communal divide and the caste barriers, were exploited by the politicians. But those fault lines were not their creation, their roots—as we have argued in the previous chapters—lay in the social and cultural spheres of life in Bengal. With the exception of a few far-sighted individuals, none of the public figures took an effective stand against the politics of exclusion. They seemed to have failed to read the warning signals of an impending unmaking of Bengal. That is the theme of the next chapter.

Notes

1. Abul Mansur Ahmed, *Amar dekha rajnitir panchas bacchar* (Dhaka, 1995), p. 104. Sir P.C. Mitter's Private Papers, file no. 35, Nehru Memorial Museum and Library (NMML), show that he had a difficult time due to pressures from Hindu members of the legislature, the Marwari Association, and others in Bengal in 1931; Mitter was criticized for having 'failed to represent Bengal Hindus' at the Round Table Conference. It also appears from his papers (file no. 22, Second Report by J. Ramsay MacDonald, 18 November 1931) that MacDonald 'offered to act, and give a decision of *temporary* validity if he were requested to do so' (emphasis mine: S.B.).
2. Governor J. Anderson to Viceroy Linlithgow, 7 April 1937, National Archives of India (NAI), microfilm no. 3169. I have found the following works useful in respect of this chapter: Muhammad Shah, 'Social and Cultural Basis of Bengali Nationalism' in *History of Bangladesh, 1704–1971*, vol. III, ed. S. Islam (Dhaka, 1992), ch. 20; Harun-or-Rashid, 'A Move for

Independent Bengal', in *History of Bangladesh*, vol. I, ed. Islam, ch. 25, pp. 368–99; Kamala Sarkar, *Bengal Politics, 1937–47* (Calcutta, 1990); Sugata Bose, *Agrarian Bengal: 1919–47* (New Delhi, 1987); Gautam Chattopadhyay, *Bengal Electoral Politics and Freedom Struggle, 1862–1947* (Delhi, 1984); Joya Chatterjee, *Bengal Divided: Hindu Communalism and Partition, 1932–47* (Cambridge, 1994); Suranjan Das, *Communal Riots in Bengal, 1905–47* (Delhi, 1991); Harun-or-Rashid, *The Foreshadowing of Bangladesh: Bengal Muslim League and Muslim Politics* (Dhaka, 1987); Shila Sen, *Muslim Politics in Bengal, 1937–47* (Delhi, 1976); Bidyut Chakrabarty, *Subhas Chandra Bose and Middle-Class Radicalism* (London, 1990).

3. Anderson to Linlithgow, 9 March 1937, NAI, microfilm no. 3169.
4. A.K. Fazlul Huq to Viceroy Linlithgow, 27 September 1941; Linlithgow to Huq, 5 October 1941, Office of Secretary to Government of Bengal, file no. 15, 1941–42, NAI, microfilm no. 3169.
5. M.A.H. Ispahani, *Quaid-e-Azam Jinnah as I Knew Him* (Karachi, 1976), p. 29.
6. Syama Prasad Mookerjee, *Leaves From a Diary* (Calcutta, 1993), pp. 38, 46, 51.
7. Linlithgow to Amery, 4 April 1943, cited in N. Mansergh (ed.), *The Transfer of Power, 1942–1947* (hereafter *TOP*) (12 vols, London, 1970–83), vol. IV, 152.
8. Ahmed, *Amar dekha rajnitir panchas bacchar*, p. 174.
9. Abul Hashim, *In Retrospection* (Dhaka, 1974), p. 49.
10. R.G. Casey, *An Australian in India* (1947), cited in Kamala Sarkar, *Bengal Politics, 1937–47* (Calcutta, 1990), p. 86.
11. Wavell to Amery, Secret Cable, 29 June 1944, *TOP*, IV, 1055.
12. Ispahani, *Quaid-e-Azam Jinnah as I Knew Him*, p. 29.
13. Burrows in Viceroy's meeting with governors, Minutes of 1 May 1947, *TOP*, X, 507.
14. Note by Governor Burrows (n.d., c. 24 April 1947), *TOP*, X, 508. Dr Joya Chatterji's argument in *Bengal Divided: Hindu Communalism and Partition, 1932–1947* (Cambridge, 1994) is anticipated here in essence.
15. Ispahani, *Quaid-e-Azam Jinnah as I Knew Him*, p. 29.
16. R.G. Casey's diary, Eur. F. 48/3, cited in K. Sarkar, *Bengal Politics*, p. 85.
17. Ahmed, *Amar dekha rajnitir panchas bacchar*, pp. 45–6.
18. Nirad C. Chaudhuri, *Thy Hand, Great Anarch! India, 1921–1952* (London, 1987), pp. 329–30.
19. Sugata Bose, 'The Roots of Communal Violence in Rural Bengal: A Study of the Kishorganj Riots, 1930' in *Modern Asian Studies* 16, no. 3 (1982).
20. Tanika Sarkar, *Bengal, 1928–34: The Politics of Protest* (New Delhi, 1987).

21. Partha Chatterjee, 'Agrarian Relations and Communalism in Bengal, 1926–35' in *Subaltern Studies*, ed. R. Guha (New Delhi, 1982).
22. Taj ul-Islam Hashmi, *Peasant Utopia: The Communalization of Class Politics in East Bengal, 1920–47* (Dhaka, 1994), p. 156.
23. DM to Chief Secretary, Govt. of Bengal, 17, 18 July 1930, cited in Hashmi, *Peasant Utopia*, p. 170, fn. 131.
24. Hashmi, *Peasant Utopia*, pp. 54–5.
25. Hashmi, *Peasant Utopia*, pp. 55–61; on this basis he rejects Rajat K. Ray's view that the jute-boycott ended in failure, Ray, 'Masses in Politics: The NCO Movement in Bengal, 1920–22', *Indian Economic and Social History Review* XI, no. 4 (1974).
26. Hashmi, *Peasant Utopia*, p. 70.
27. Hashmi, *Peasant Utopia*, p. 78.
28. Hashmi, *Peasant Utopia*, p. 71.
29. Hashmi, *Peasant Utopia*, p. 107.
30. Hashmi, *Peasant Utopia*, pp. 117–18.
31. D. Rothermund, *India in the Great Depression, 1929–39* (Delhi, 1992) and *Global Impact of the Great Depression 1929–39* (London, 1996), ch. 9; I am equally indebted to oral communications from Saugata P. Mukherjee.
32. Report on Land Revenue Admn. 1932–3, 1933–4, cited in Hashmi, *Peasant Utopia*, p. 169, fn. 9.
33. Hashmi, *Peasant Utopia*, p. 124.
34. Ahmed, *Amar dekha rajnitir panchas bacchar*, pp. 45–6.
35. Ahmed, *Amar dekha rajnitir panchas bacchar*, p. 48.
36. Partha Chatterjee,
37. Possibly the last straw was the Swaraj Party's rejection of Nurul Haq's motion to increase *bargadars'* share of crops. Shila Sen, *Muslim Politics in Bengal, 1937–47* (Delhi, 1976), pp. 68–9.
38. A.R. Mallick, Syed A. Husain, 'Bengali Nationalism', in *History of Bangladesh, 1704–1971*, ed. Islam, p. 556.
39. Adrienne Cooper, *Sharecropping and Sharecroppers' Struggles in Bengal, 1930–50* (Calcutta, 1988), p. 126.
40. Hashmi, *Peasant Utopia*, p. 166; Muzaffar Ahmed, *Krishak Samasya* (Calcutta, 1947), pp. 44–6, cited in Hashmi, Peasant Utopia.
41. Hashmi, *Peasant Utopia*, p. 166.
42. Debate on Hemanta Sarkar's resolution in the *Proceedings of the Bengal Legislative Council*, 10 December 1925, pp. 331–2.
43. Nalini Ranjan Sarkar's speech in *Proceedings of the Bengal Legislative Council*, 7 August 1928, p. 398.
44. *Proceedings of the Bengal Legislative Council*, 7, 13, 14 August 1928 and 3, 4 September 1928.

45. *Proceedings of the Bengal Legislative Council*, 7 August 1928, p. 391, 3 September 1928, p. 823.
46. A. Rasul, *Krishak sabhar itihas* (Calcutta, 1969).
47. A.R. Desai (ed.), *The Peasant Struggle in India* (Bombay, 1979), pp. 404–7.
48. Sunil Sen, *Agrarian Struggle in Bengal, 1946–47* (Calcutta, 1982); after retirement from political activism, Sen acquired a Ph.D. and taught history.
49. Ispahani, *Quaid-e-Azam Jinnah as I Knew Him*, pp. 14–15.
50. Ispahani, *Quaid-e-Azam Jinnah as I Knew Him*, pp. 15–17.
51. Ispahani, *Quaid-e-Azam Jinnah as I Knew Him*, p. 21.
52. Ispahani, *Quaid-e-Azam Jinnah as I Knew Him*, pp. 22–4, gives a full account of the incident, apparently in expectation of credit for this manoeuvre.
53. Ispahani, *Quaid-e-Azam Jinnah as I Knew Him*, p. 25.
54. Ispahani, *Quaid-e-Azam Jinnah as I Knew Him*, p. 29.
55. Hashim, *In Retrospection*, pp. 20–31 contains memories of these times.
56. Hashim, *In Retrospection*, pp. 78–9.
57. Ahmed, *Amar dekha rajnitir panchas bacchar*, p. 45.
58. Ahmed, *Amar dekha rajnitir panchas bacchar*, p. 53.
59. Ahmed, *Amar dekha rajnitir panchas bacchar*, reminiscences in ch. 7.
60. Ahmed, *Amar dekha rajnitir panchas bacchar*, p. 95.
61. Ahmed, *Amar dekha rajnitir panchas bacchar*, p. 96.
62. Ispahani, *Quaid-e-Azam Jinnah as I Knew Him*, p. 67.
63. Jinnah to Ispahani, 13 May 1942, Ispahani, *Quaid-e-Azam Jinnah as I Knew Him*, pp. 68–70.
64. *Star of India* [hereafter cited as *SI*], 17 December 1934, 4 December 1933.
65. *SI*, 28 December 1934.
66. *SI*, 14 December 1934.
67. *SI*, 16 December 1935.
68. *SI*, 18 December 1937.
69. *SI*, 23 December 1937.
70. *SI*, 17 December 1934.
71. *SI*, 19 December 1934.
72. *SI*, 21 December 1934.
73. *SI*, 26 December 1940, 30 December 1940.
74. *SI*, 1 December 1941.
75. *SI*, 23 December 1936.
76. *SI*, 30 December 1935.
77. *SI*, 12, 21, 23 December 1939.
78. *SI*, 28 December 1939.
79. *Ananda Bazar Patrika* [hereafter cited as *ABP*], 17 April 1934, claims circulation of 36,000, said to be the 'highest in India'. This was the first daily in Bengali Linotype, vide *ABP*, 9 February 1934.

80. *ABP*, 6 January 1933, 13 January 1933.
81. *ABP*, 17 March 1933.
82. *ABP*, 12 April 1933.
83. *ABP*, Editorials: 'Protection of Women', 1 September 1933; 'Molestation of Women in Bengal', 6 August 1933; 'Communalism in Education', 2 December 1933; 'Communalism in the Corporation', 19 December 1933; 'Proja Movement in Bengal', 18 March 1933.
84. *ABP*, Editorial, 'Communal Disunity', 30 December 1933.
85. *ABP*, 26 October 1933.
86. *ABP*, Editorial, 'Bengal's Problems', 3 November 1934.
87. *ABP*, Editorial, 'Struggle against Communal Award', 10 February 1935.
88. *ABP*, 20 April 1935.
89. *ABP*, 'Depressed Caste Conference', 8 May 1935.
90. Chattopadhyay, *Bengal Electoral Politics and Freedom Struggle*, p. 129.
91. Prafulla Kumar Sarkar, *Khoishnu hindu* (Calcutta, 1940), published first in *Desh* serially 1939–40; *Rachana sangraha* (Calcutta, 1394 BS).
92. P.K. Sarkar, *Khoishnu hindu*, pp. 643–5.
93. P.K. Sarkar, *Khoishnu hindu*, p. 653.
94. P.K. Sarkar, *Khoishnu hindu*, pp. 659–60.
95. *ABP*, Editorial, 8 May 1935.
96. Sadat Ali Akhand, 'Bengali', in *Saugat* VI, no. 5 (1335 BS); Editorial, *Shariat-e-Islam* V, no. 3 (1336 BS); extract from the collection of reprints in Mustafa Nurul Islam (ed.), *Samayik patre jiban o janamat, 1901–1930* (Dhaka, 1977), cited hereafter as *SPJJ*. For the views of liberal Muslim intellectuals I found the following reprint collection illuminating: Muhammad Nasiruddin, *Bangla sahitye saugat jug* (Dhaka, 1985).
97. Tazeen M. Murshid, *The Sacred and the Secular: Bengal Muslim Discourses, 1871–1977* (Calcutta, 1995), chs 2–3; Mustafa Nurul Islam, *Bengali Muslim Public Opinion as Reflected in the Bengali Press, 1901–1930* (Dhaka, 1973); Husainur Rahman, *Hindu–Muslim Relations in Bengal, 1905–47* (Bombay, 1974).
98. Fazlul Huq to M.A. Jinnah, 30 October 1936; Z.H. Zaidi (ed.), *Jinnah–Ispahani Correspondence, 1936–48* (Karachi, Forward Publication Trust, 1976), p. 639.
99. Huq to Liaquat Ali Khan, 8 September 1941, Zaidi (ed.), *Jinnah–Ispahani Correspondence*, p. 641.
100. H.S. Suhrawardy to M.A. Jinnah, 5 July 1937, Quaid-i-Azam Papers, F-458, 9–10, in document collection edited by Harun-or-Rashid, *Inside Bengal Politics, 1936–47: Unpublished Correspondence of Partition Leaders* (Dhaka, 2003), pp. 61–2.

101. H.S. Suhrawardy to Jinnah, 20 February 1947, Quaid-i-Azam Papers, F. 458, 54–Harun-or-Rashid, *Inside Bengal Politics*, pp. 71–2.
102. Zaidi (ed.), *Quaid-i-Azam M.A. Jinnah Papers*, vol. I, part I, QA Project, National Archives of Pakistan (Islamabad, 1993); this officially sponsored edition can be supplemented with S.M. Grewal (ed.), *Jinnah–Wavell Correspondence* (Lahore, 1986); R. Ahmed (ed.), *Quaid-i-Azam Papers, 1941–42* (Lahore, 1976), and M. Rafique Afzal, *Selected Speeches and Documents of Quaid-i-Azam, 1911–1934* (Lahore, 1986). However, in these selections from the Jinnah papers I found little of significance so far as Bengal is concerned.
103. Jinnah to A.K. Fazlul Huq, 10 February 1944, in Syed Sharifuddin Pirzada (ed.), *Quaid-i-Azam Jinnah Correspondence* (Karachi, 1971); this is the best collection, barring Zaidi's.
104. S.P. Mookerjee, *Selected Speeches in the Bengal Legislative Assembly, 1937–1947*, Asutosh Mookerjee Memorial Institute, Calcutta, 2002, p. x.
105. Draft Manifesto of the BPML by Abul Hashim, *Star of India*, 23 March 1945, cited in Harun-or-Rashid, *Inside Bengal Politics*, pp. 177–8.
106. Hashim, *In Retrospection*, p. 79.
107. In Bangladeshi historiography, Hashim has a special place as one of the progenitors of the concept of the Muslim Bengali national movement leading to the foundation of Bangladesh. Harun-or-Rashid, *Inside Bengal Politics*, pp. 176, 235, 281, and so on.
108. Humayun Kabir's statement, *Amrita Bazar Patrika*, 14 April 1946, cited in Rakesh Batabyal, *Communalism in Bengal* (Delhi, 2005), p. 262.
109. Batabyal, *Communalism in Bengal*, p. 218.
110. Harun-or-Rashid, 'A Move for United Bengal' in *History of Bangladesh*, ed. Islam, vol. I, ch. 15, p. 400; also Harun-or-Rashid, *The Foreshadowing of the Bangladesh*.
111. A.R. Mallick and S.A. Husein, 'Political Basis of Bengali Nationalism' in *History of Bangladesh*, ed. Islam, ch. 20.
112. Harun-or-Rashid, 'A Move for Independent Bengal', in *History of Bangladesh*, vol. I, ed. Islam, p. 400.
113. Syama Prasad Mookerjee, *Leaves from a Diary* (Calcutta, 1993), p. 29.
114. Mookerjee, *Leaves from a Diary*, p. 27.
115. Mookerjee, *Leaves from a Diary*, pp. 27–8.
116. Mookerjee, *Leaves from a Diary*, p. 30.
117. Mookerjee, *Leaves from a Diary*, p. 32.
118. Mookerjee, *Leaves from a Diary*, p. 28.
119. Mookerjee, *Leaves from a Diary*, p. 33.
120. Mookerjee, *Leaves from a Diary*, p. 35.

121. Mookerjee, *Leaves from a Diary*, p. 40.
122. K. Sarkar, *Bengal Politics*, p. 135; Mookerjee, *Leaves from a Diary*, p. 64.
123. Mookerjee, *Leaves from a Diary*, p. 65.
124. File no. C-51-1944, S.P. Mookerjee's letters as president, in Hindu Mahasabha Papers, NMML.
125. File no. P-32-1945, A. Lahiri's Report, Hindu Mahasabha Papers, NMML.
126. Mookerjee, 'Bengali Diary', *Leaves from a Diary*, p. 106.
127. Mookerjee, 'Bengali Diary', *Leaves from a Diary*, pp. 109, 146.
128. Note on meeting between Cabinet Mission and Dr S.P. Mookerjee, *TOP*, VII, no. 111.
129. S.P. Mookerjee Private Papers, II–IV Instalment, NMML, Sub File no. 85, Correspondence Regarding Hindu Mahasabha, M.A. Jinnah to Mookerjee, 8 October 1945.
130. Mookerjee, 'Bengali Diary', *Leaves from a Diary*, p. 129.
131. Mookerjee, 'Bengali Diary', *Leaves from a Diary*, p. 32.
132. Subhas Bose to President, AICC, 27 December 1929, AICC Papers, File no. G-115-1929, NMML.
133. Subhas Bose to M.S. Aney, 17 October 1931, in AICC Papers, File no. P-15-1931, NMML.
134. J.M. Sengupta to Patel, 6 September 1931, AICC Papers, File no. P-15-1931, NMML.
135. Report by M.S. Aney, 25 September 1931, AICC, File no. P-15-1931, NMML.
136. J. Anderson to Linlithgow, 3 December 1936, Bengal Governor's Reports, NAI, microfilm no. 3169.
137. Sugata Bose, *His Majesty's Opponent: Subhas Chandra Bose and India's Struggle against Empire* (Harvard, 2011), pp. 79–80.
138. J.B. Kripalani to Secretary, South Calcutta DCC, 16 November 1935, AICC Papers, File no. P-6-1935, NMML.
139. Private Papers of Dr Bidhan Chandra Roy, File no.37, NMML.
140. Chaudhuri, *Thy Hand, Great Anarch!* p. 517.
141. S.K. Bose and Sugata Bose (eds), *Netaji Collected Works*, vol. IX (Delhi, 1995), p. xxiv.
142. S.K. Bose and S. Bose (eds), *Netaji Collected Works*, vol. IX, pp. 3–30.
143. Subhas Bose to Gandhi, 21 December 1938, S.K. Bose and S. Bose (eds), *Netaji Collected Works*, vol. IX, pp. 124–6.
144. Subhas Bose, Inaugural Speech at Planning Committee (of Congress), 17 December 1938, S.K. Bose and S. Bose (eds), *Netaji Collected Works*, vol. IX, pp. 62–4.
145. Sugata Bose, *His Majesty's Opponent*, p. 154.

146. V. Patel to Rajendra Prasad, 19 November 1938, *Rajendra Prasad Correspondence and Select Documents*, edited by Valmiki Choudhary, vol. II (New Delhi, 1984) [hereafter cited as *RPC*, followed by volume number].
147. Patel to Prasad, 2 November 1938, *RPC*, II.
148. Prafulla Chandra Ghosh to Prasad, 20 July 1939, *RPC*, III.
149. Kiran Shankar Roy to J.B. Kripalani, 6 July 1939, *RPC*, III.
150. B.C. Roy to Patel, 17 July 193, *RPC*, III.
151. Sarat C. Bose to Gandhi, 21 March 1939, *RPC*, III.
152. P. Basu to Prasad, 2 September 1939; Prafulla C. Ghosh was particularly vocal against Subhas in his letter of 11 August 1939 to Prasad; in the same letter he displayed his usual perspicacity in saying that 'I feel there will be no war', that is, World War II, *RPC*, III.
153. AICC File no. P-15-1931, NMML, New Delhi.
154. Ahmad, *Amar dekha rajnitir panchas bachhar*, p. 111.
155. Bidyut Chakrabarty, *Local Politics and Indian Nationalism: Midnapur, 1919–1944* (New Delhi, 1997), p. 135.
156. H. R. Sanyal, 'Anti-Union Board Movement in Medinipur', in *Congress and Indian Nationalism: The Pre-Independence Phase*, eds R. Sisson and Stanley Wolpert (Berkeley, 1988), p. 363.
157. Chakrabarty, *Local Politics and Indian Nationalism*, p. 137.
158. Md. Khairul Anam, *Indian Freedom Movement and Murshidabad District, 1905–1947* (Calcutta, 2008), pp. 130–9.
159. Charles De Gaulle, *War Memoirs: Call of Honour, 1940–1942*, tr. J. Griffin (London, 1955), contains De Gaulle's defence of his battle against the government of France under German occupation, a battle that could be interpreted as treason; De Gaulle was twice tried and convicted of treason, just as the Indian National Army personnel were tried by the British Indian government.
160. Proclamation of the Azad Hind Sarkar, in Sugata Bose, *His Majesty's Opponent*, p. 253; I have elaborated on this theme in Sabyasachi Bhattacharya, *The Endgame of the Raj and Subhas Bose's Political Strategy, 1943–1945*, Netaji Memorial Lecture, Netaji Subhas Open University, Calcutta, 2013.
161. S.C. Bose to Dr M. Thierfelder, 25 March 1936, document in the archives of the Netaji Research Bureau, obtained by courtesy of Mr Subrata Bose, Member of Parliament.
162. The contemporary accounts have been ably marshalled in the following works: Peter Ward Fay, *The Forgotten Army: India's Armed Struggle for Independence* (Ann Arbor, 1993); Joyce Lebra, *Jungle Alliance: Japan and the Indian National Army* (Singapore, 1971); and the well-documented survey in Sugata Bose, *His Majesty's Opponent*, ch. 8.

163. Sugata Bose, 2011, pp. 273–4.
164. Bose's speech in Rangoon, 11 July 1944, in Sugata Bose, *His Majesty's Opponent*, p. 279.
165. Home (Pol.) F. 21/16/1945, NAI, cited in Chattopadhyay, *Bengal Electoral Politics and Freedom Struggle* (ICHR, Delhi, 1984), p. 199.
166. Home (Pol.) F. 13/2/46, 5/22/46, NAI, p. 201.

7

THE WARNING SIGNALS
The Crises of the 1940s

In historical hindsight sometimes one can discern trends which were not visible to the contemporaries. Nevertheless, one cannot but reflect on the failure of the leaders in Bengal's civil and political life in the late 1930s and 1940s to read the warning signals of the crisis the province faced. Some of the constituent elements of this crisis we have touched upon earlier. Here we shall focus upon the rise in the scale of corruption in public life, the economic impact of the Second World War, the degradation of civic life in the city of Calcutta and its municipal administration, the social consequences of wartime price inflation, the Famine of 1943 which killed more persons of the civil population in Bengal than the total number of military personnel of Britain and the USA killed during the entire World War, and, finally, the catastrophic communal riots in Calcutta in August 1946.

Corruption in Public Life

In the recently published private papers of Muhammad Ali Jinnah there is a letter written to him by the poet Sir Muhammad Iqbal in 1937. Since 1935, Iqbal said, the 'higher posts go to sons of upper classes, the smaller ones to the friends or relatives of the Ministers', and, therefore, the 'Muslim masses' are indifferent to politics.[1] Mahatma Gandhi writes in the *Harijan* in 1938: 'Rich and unscrupulous persons are controlling the affairs of the Congress organization, keeping skillfully the genuine and devoted workers out of the way'.[2] He went on to say that 'untruth and corruption have made inroads enough in Congress to warrant drastic measures...'. 'Corruption', M.A. Jinnah wrote privately to a follower a few years later, 'is a curse in India and amongst Muslims, especially the so-called educated and intelligentsia. Unfortunately, it is this class that is selfish and morally and intellectually corrupt.... All this is due to the demoralised and degenerated state to which we are reduced and for want of character'.[3] These observations, each from a person totally above corruption, reflect a general perception of Indian politicians already prevalent in the last ten or fifteen years before Independence. The British officials, in their confidential correspondence, had much worse things to say but we leave those aside for their criticism was not always free of malicious pleasure that the natives were proving to be unfit for responsible political roles. What was the basis of the anxiety that Gandhi or Iqbal or Jinnah voiced? It is a question that is relevant in India today.

It is useful here to distinguish between the influence of interest groups publicly operating through constitutionally correct means of pressure, and so on, on the one hand, and clandestine corruption through misuse of public office held by persons in or out of government, on the other. The first kind of phenomenon is part of political systems where money, business or landed interests, or even bodies like trade unions may legitimately pursue their interests by exercising pressure or influence. The second kind is corruption in the true sense of the term, working in non-transparent subterranean channels; occasionally the term 'corruption' is extended to cover the first kind of behaviour as well but the difference lies in transparency. In the period we are considering, corruption was perceived chiefly as the second of these two types of phenomena. No doubt 'corruption' is a subjective term and what is corrupt to one man is quite legitimate to another. Thus an action that was viewed as moral corruption by some contemporaries, could be, and was, defended in terms of real politik. That notwithstanding, a belief appeared to be growing in the 1930s that corruption in political life was increasing. Even if we dismiss allegations in newspapers, pamphlets, and the like, in course of partisan and factional struggle we do find in the private correspondence of political leaders and parties evidence that cannot be easily dismissed.

Gandhi, with characteristic clarity, pointed to, as we have seen, the growing power of people with money to manipulate Congress party decisions. This was a consequence of electoral politics. Consider, for example, the case of Professor Nripendra Chandra Banerji who failed to get selected as a Congress candidate in the election of 1937. His own version is independently supported by documents in the files of the All-India Congress Committee and the private papers of Rajendra Prasad. Banerji's own account of the elections to the Bengal Legislative Assembly in 1936 in his district, Hooghly, has it that

> there was a vacancy and X [name omitted by me—S.B.], an old pupil, who had influence over the District Committee, was keen on filling the seat. I was persuaded by my friends to seek Congress nomination for this seat but the District Committee, financed by my pupil, was persuaded to vote for him and I had to withdraw.... In fact the running of the party machine is apt to blunt the edge of moral susceptibilities and those who boss and control elections, either to the organizational committees or to the legislatures, are inclined to be hard and even unscrupulous. Tammany Hall methods are not peculiar to America alone.[4]

Mr X, who was preferred over Banerji, was a rich businessman giving 'monetary doles' to the district Congress; Banerji was a Congress leader of middle rank since he joined the Civil Disobedience Movement, having resigned his professorship in Calcutta's Presidency College in 1921. How was Banerji's claim ignored? We have part of the answer in the private correspondence of Rajendra Prasad; the Gandhian P.C. Ghosh, later chief minister of West Bengal, wrote to Prasad to lobby in favour of the other candidate on the ground that he was not only a prosperous businessman who funded the election of the previous incumbent but, what is more, was 'a habitual wearer of Khadi'.[5] Prasad was on the Parliamentary Committee which did eventually follow P.C. Ghosh's advice. Banerji's indignation was such that he complained to the All-India Congress Committee. In the All-India Congress Committee (AICC) correspondence we can now see Jawaharlal Nehru's response: he had no powers to intercede in respect of such grievances, and 'as I cannot interfere, I do not take interest in them'.[6] This answer scarcely met the grievances put before him and it elicited the rueful observation that 'in selecting candidates for the Bengal Council, Congress principles and Congress allegiance were at a heavy discount and the power of the purse, the landed interests and caucuses came uppermost'.[7]

I have allowed a lot of space to this case because it typified a pattern. There were other complaints similarly dealt with by Nehru.

For example, Dr Nalinaksha Sanyal said in 1937 that 'monetary contributions towards the election fund' were taken from 'reactionary and non-Congress candidates' for legislature seats. Nehru's response: these 'commitments you refer to were made by Dr. [B.C.] Roy at an early stage of the election'.[8] More and more money was being spent on elections and hence it was convenient to get candidates who paid for themselves. Dr Bidhan Chandra Roy wrote to Bhulabhai Desai, of the Congress Parliamentary Board in 1934 that 'a better type of Congressmen' as candidates meant more expenditure amounting to Rs 10,000 to Rs 20,000, which in those days was a lot of money.[9] The logic is clear: it is convenient to get as a candidate a less desirable Congressman who pays for his election campaign than a better candidate who cannot pay for his election. In the same source, B.C. Roy's private papers, we find Bhulabhai's lament that except 'merchants … there is no other class from which there is any chance of getting any substantial sum'; then followed the sage advice, 'after ascertaining what financial assistance can be secured, then candidates would be finally fixed up'.[10]

Was it possible for those thus elected to recover the investments in their own election? This is difficult to answer. However, allegations were made against legislators who became ministers. For example, Rajendra Prasad, at the head of the Congress in Bihar was already being charged with failure to check ministerial corruption; there were allegations of 'nepotism' in giving jobs, 'rumours of gratification' connected with 'repeated visitings [*sic*] to magnates of the big estates', that is, *zamindaris*, excessive travel allowance drawn by ministers, and so on.[11]

In Bengal, worse allegations were occasionally made in respect of purchase of votes in the Legislature, particularly in periods when a coalition ministry ruled by a thin majority—as happened several times in 1937–47. Abul Hashim, who succeeded H.S. Suhrawardy as General Secretary of the Bengal Muslim League in 1941, writes in his memoirs that almost at each session of the Legislative Assembly efforts were made to dislodge the ministry in power and this made it imperative for 'the government party' to pay out bribes in cash and also to allow patronage. In particular, he says, Chief Minister Khwaja Nazimuddin made it a method of retaining power; the responsibility to keep happy members who might stray from the parliamentary party by payment of necessary gratification was that of Khwaja Shahabuddin and Fazlur Rahman. The Congress legislators, Hashim adds, kept watch on these goings-on and awaited their opportunity.[12] The Governor of Bengal, Anderson, in private and confidential reports in 1939 to Viceroy Linlithgow, said: 'I am reliably informed that he [I omit the name—S.B.] and others of his kidney in the previous Council used to be paid by the Congress on important divisions by means of cut currency notes—one half in advance and the other half after they had gone into the appropriate lobby', when Division was called on a resolution.[13] When Sir Khwaja Nazimuddin's ministry fell, M. Ispahani wrote to Jinnah privately: 'Money had passed from the Marwaries to certain purchasable commodities through the leaders of the opposition groups'; due to a thin majority the defection of eighteen members brought down the ministry.[14] This was the occasion when Jinnah made the remarks cited earlier about the lack of character of the Muslim middle classes.

It is impossible to prove or disprove these allegations now. Responsible men made them and that was done privately, not to gain propaganda mileage. For propaganda purposes a lot was said which we can ignore for the present. Access to power in provincial governments certainly opened up possibilities of patronage, and of raising money. The desire to award jobs to political followers was pervasive. In the Calcutta Corporation under C.R. Das and Subhas Bose a number of Congress political sufferers were accommodated. Nirad C. Chaudhuri had direct personal knowledge of developments in the Calcutta Corporation as a secretary to Sarat Bose. In his memoirs he writes in detail of the corrupt practices of the elected councillors of the corporation: concocted electoral rolls, bribery for securing jobs, bargains and deals over appointments to be given to those favoured by Congress leaders, manipulation in award of contracts, and so on. 'Corruption in Calcutta Corporation, so tragic in certain cases, became such a low farce ... that one could not work up indignation over it' and Sarat Bose, himself above corruption, 'took it as if it was all in the day's work'.[15] Chaudhuri was occasionally prejudiced in his judgement about 'Indian character', though the details he provides tally with other evidence. The regime of corruption in the Calcutta Corporation seemed to be accepted by public men as a permanent evil. For example, Bidhan Chandra Roy, in a private letter to Vallabhbhai Patel, writes in 1931 that J.M. Sengupta in his 'fight for purity' complains of corruption in the Calcutta Corporation but 'I know, now being in the midst of it all, what purity there was during the few years that Mr. Sengupta was the Mayor'. At this time Roy was, of course, in a faction opposing Sengupta.[16]

If not jobs, ministers could provide protection. Consider for example, the letter from H.S. Suhrawardy to Bijoy Prasad Sinha Roy which has survived among the private papers of Sinha Roy. Suhrawardy writes on 1 May 1939 to protect a person who ran a 'combined drug shop' selling *ganja*, *bhang*, and opium; upon discovering adulteration, the government Chemical Examiner cancelled that man's licence but could something be done about it, for Suhrawardy had found him a useful fellow, 'extremely valuable, particularly in dealing with the Red Flag menace in Barrackpore'.[17] We do not know what happened to this worthy fellow but such an attempt to extend protection even to the criminal fringe of society provides an insight into another aspect of corruption. In Sinha Roy's private correspondence one can see favours being sought from that end to the highest stratum—the chief Bengal *zamindars* requesting small favours along with small talk about lunch at Peleti's, a fashionable restaurant, and the merits of the new Daimler model.

Nepotism in the award of government jobs was difficult but changes in principles of appointment were being introduced in the 1930s. In Bengal in that decade a drive to increase the proportion of Muslim appointees in government employment was a public policy and cannot be called by any means a corrupt practice, though Hindus took a dim view of it. Likewise, after the 1937 elections, many provincial governments adopted bias as policy: Rajendra Prasad, for instance, argued in favour of 'the provincial government's right to recommending in a general way provincials for appointments' because 'hardly any native of the Province is in any of the higher grades'.[18]

In any event, the number of jobs the government could offer was limited. Within the civil service the complaint that was voiced was not so much about jobs being given but political influence. The Indian Statutory Commission Report (1930) carried a memorandum of the Bengal Governor which complained that 'political influence ... have affected the control of the services by Ministers'; 'appointments have been given and transfers have been made for political purposes'.[19] So far as the government was concerned the really important source of patronage was award of contracts. On this we have little evidence. Businessmen like M.A.H. Ispahani and Adamji at the helm of the Muslim Chamber of Commerce of Calcutta were known as fundraisers for the League, and likewise G.D. Birla or Nalini Ranjan Sarkar were fundraisers for Congress.[20] What transpired between the fund-givers and fund-receivers is a matter of speculation. The Congress was not in power in Bengal and had little patronage to dispense to businessmen. Moreover, political funding by an Adamji or a Nalini Ranjan Sarkar did not necessarily mean clandestine deals. Secret deals can be established in rare cases. One such was the award of the sole agency to Ispahani to purchase food grains on behalf of the government just before the Famine of 1943. Syama Prasad Mookerjee was in the Fazlul Huq ministry when this happened and he wrote in his personal diary: 'The firm of Ispahani's acting through a *benamdar* was selected for handling so-called surplus rice and paddy. The whole transaction was made behind the back of the ministers'.[21] 'I was then in Delhi, and on my return we took up the matter. We made some alterations, changing the scheme for giving monopoly to Ispahani's, put the details in the shape of an agreement, but even then sufficient mischief had been done'. The minister concerned was the Nawab of Dacca, soon to be succeeded by H.S. Suhrawardy as civil supplies minister. On the eve of the Famine, Mookerjee noted 'various kinds of corruption and bribery' and even purchase by government of rice 'at rates higher than what were fixed by the government itself'. Another glaring case of corruption was exposed by Mookerjee. One Barada Prasanna Pain was a junior minister with him in Huq's ministry and then he joined the ministry of Sir Khwaja Nazimuddin, a token concession to caste Hindus. Mookerjee, in a widely reported speech, on a motion by him against Pain, exposes how 'Pain has been carrying on business in *benami* [under an assumed name or an agent's name] through favoured contractors of his' while being minister in charge of the Department of Works. The unedifying details of the case need not be reproduced here but they were made on the floor of the House in Syama Prasad's speech in the Legislative Assembly and the facts were never challenged or refuted by the Nazimuddin Ministry.[22] The Famine and the World War created a whole new culture of business and a new phrase—'black market'—entered the Bengali lexicon. We shall return to this subject later.

The Famine of 1943

With Burma falling under the Japanese onslaught, the frontline of the World War moved closer to eastern India. Calcutta, the focal centre of this region, began to play a vital role as a base.

> It is reasonable to assume that any large-scale military operation to dislodge the Japanese from South East Asia and China will require a sizable land base. India alone, at present, provides a favourable operating base from which a large-scale offensive can be launched against the enemy. However, India will continue to be only a potential source of supply until definite steps are taken to help solve the domestic food crisis.[23]

Such was the report of the US Board of Economic Warfare in July 1943. India was, of course, already an important supply base for the Allied war effort. Kirby mentions, in the official history of the War, the diversion of India's railway equipment (10 per cent of existing resources) and men to meet Allied railway requirements in 1939–40.[24] This contributed to transport shortage for food grains movements in India. Further, from August 1941, the British Indian Government began to procure food grains in India for export to the West Asian battlefront (this reached the figure of 3,000 tons monthly export in April 1942 and amounted to 40,000 tons in the preceding nine months).[25] In July 1943, Winston Churchill decided to reduce sailings to the Indian Ocean region by 60 per cent in order to improve the supply position in the UK; this made the Allied military personnel in that region heavily dependent on local supplies and thus reduced supplies available for local civilian populations.[26]

At the same time in 1942, the eastern part of India was being prepared for war operations. 'The outstanding feature of the situation', the official Famine Commission Report said in its report, 'was the rapid approach of the enemy to the border of the province (Bengal), and the universal expectation of an invasion of the province itself. The danger of a Japanese invasion compelled the military authorities to put into operation early in 1942, a Denial Policy…'.[27] The 'Denial' involved: (*a*) the removal from the coastal districts, on the Bay of Bengal, of the rice that was judged by officials to be 'in excess of local requirements' and (*b*) the destruction or removal of all boats in areas considered vulnerable to invasion.

The amount of rice requisitioned under the Denial Policy was not very large—40,000 tons.[28] But it created a panic in the market leading to hoarding and added to price escalation; and, of course, it left the districts subjected to government requisition bereft of stocks so that the failure of the rains the next year hit them hard. The policy of denial of boats to the enemy forces hit the system of transportation of food grains in eastern Bengal where commercial traffic was almost entirely riverine.[29] According to government estimates, about 26,000 boats were destroyed or seized and 20,000 more were removed from the coastal region; this 'had a considerable restricting effect on the movement of food grains from the denial areas'.[30] The fall of Burma stopped the supply of her rice into neighbouring Bengal in 1942 even as export from Bengal increased, partly due to purchases made for military personnel.

The result was a net export of 185,000 tons from Bengal in the first half of 1942 (compared to net import of 296,000 tons for the same period in 1941). In July 1942, food grains export from Bengal was prohibited by the Government, but a drastic depletion of the stocks in Bengal had already taken place. Denial Policy in respect of boats, net export of food grains, removal of stocks from some districts, again under the Denial Policy suggested by military authorities, the cessation of rice supplies from Burma, and the reduction of shipping services in the Indian Ocean under Churchill's instructions—these were the factors that prepared the way for the Famine of 1943, the first in the twentieth century in Bengal.

Against this background, we have to assess the strategy in respect of the city of Calcutta. The first Japanese air raids in December 1942 (although short-lived and militarily ineffective) created a panic in government circles, leading to drastic measures. These were: (*a*) the diversion towards Calcutta of the food grains seized in rural areas under the Denial Policy; (*b*) procurement of stocks of grains traders in Calcutta, on payment of a compensation at a price lower than that prevailing in the market, and (*c*) a policy of supplying the needs of labour forces in selected industries through government channels instead of the usual free trade machinery.

These policies of the Government of British India signalized a reversal of a century-old laissez faire policy.[31] The government machinery was scarcely ready to take on such responsibility, bypassing the normal channels of trade. The civil servants were unaccustomed to the new tasks. A leading citizen of Calcutta said in his deposition before the Famine Inquiry Commission: 'A Clive Street [that is, the business centre of Calcutta] friend told me that the Indian Civil Service and Bengal Civil Service could not distinguish a tramway ticket from a bill of lading'.[32] This might have been equally true of the civil service in most other countries in the 1940s; what the bureaucracy did not know, they could learn on the job. The real problem in this regard lay elsewhere. Here one must note the basic difference between the Asian colonial and metropolitan European scenes of action on the supplies front. In a country such as Britain, the switch to governmental intervention was no doubt a departure from tradition. But the polity in such a country did not allow government to be insensitive and unresponsive to the needs and demands of the citizens. In the colonial context, such sensitivity was rare, slow to mature into action, and powerless against superior British interests and pressure groups.

The overall strategic considerations regarding the supply position, as perceived by the British authorities, was clearly enunciated by the chief of the Civil Supplies Department: 'It had become a fight for survival, for the collapse of Calcutta—not only headquarters of government, but with its port, railways, its industrial area—would have been a disaster for the successful prosecution of the war'.[33] It was a question of a strategic choice between starving rural people to feed Calcutta, on the one hand, or, on the other, allowing food to remain in the countryside and risk hampered war effort and depleted services and production in ports and railways and factories in Calcutta.

> There was a choice between permitting the essential services in Calcutta to get enough, or to allow stocks to remain with the people. For these reasons large stocks were allowed to accumulate in the city. It meant death of a large number of people in the rural areas, or chaos in the city. There was danger either way. If the services were not served [supplied] adequately, there was danger of chaos and rioting and Government war efforts would be affected. Otherwise slow death of a percentage of population. The first choice was taken.[34]

The consequence of the supply strategy outlined above was, on the one hand, a severe subsistence crisis in the hinterland of Calcutta causing about three million deaths and, on the other, the migration of about

200,000 famine-affected destitutes into Calcutta in search of food. The latter estimate is a conjecture. The Famine Inquiry Commission of the government put it down at 100,000 while Dr M.U. Ahmed, a medical practitioner and a representative of the Calcutta Municipal Corporation, estimated the number of immigrants at 200,000.[35] How many of them died in Calcutta? Officially registered deaths started to exceed the previous year's average in June 1943; between October 1943 and March 1944 the officially registered deaths numbered 52,000 as compared to the average of the previous five years, 24,000.[36] This suggests that in six months, the peak food scarcity period, the number of famine immigrants who died *in Calcutta* was a minimum of 28,000. These mortality figures are likely to be underestimates; as late as 1965 a demographer found that under-registration of deaths in urban areas was at least 28.2 per cent (male) and 30.2 per cent (female).[37] Under wartime conditions, such under-registration was likely to be higher than in normal conditions in the 1960s.

As for total mortality in Bengal, the official estimate by the Famine Inquiry Commission was that in 1943–4 'about 1.5 million deaths occurred as a direct result of the famine and the epidemics which followed in its train'; the most-often cited unofficial estimate was the one made by Professor K.P. Chattopadhyaya of the Department of Anthropology, Calcutta University, and the figure he arrived at was 3.5 million to 3.8 million famine deaths in 1943; the latest estimate of 'excess deaths' is 2.8 million made in 1991 by the demographer Arup Maharatna.[38] One might compare that with the mortality figure of US Forces in Europe—150,000—announced by the Secretary of War on 10 May 1945, two days after Victory in Europe Day.

Among the documents on the Famine of 1943, one which merits attention was the speech of Syama Prasad Mookerjee from the Opposition benches in the Legislative Assembly in July 1943. A few months earlier, Mookerjee was in the government as Fazlul Huq's finance minister—he resigned in November 1942 to protest the policies of the Bengal government and the ICS bureaucracy against the Quit India movement—and thus Mookerjee had first-hand knowledge of the inner machinery of governance. His speech in the Legislative Assembly debate on the famine situation is therefore an informed insider's view. In plain words, his opinion was that a major cause of the Famine of 1943 was the fact that H.S. Suhrawardy, Minister of

Civil Supplies from April 1943, was involved in corrupt dealings with contractors engaged in rice hoarding, profiteering, and exploitation of the political protection they enjoyed under the Nazimuddin ministry. Other factors were that in early 1943 the government had started: (*a*) Seizure of rice stocks as part of the Denial Policy in expectation of a Japanese invasion in coastal areas. (*b*) The purchase of rice for export to the theatre of war to feed the army. (*c*) The encouragement of rice acquisition by factory managements to feed the industrial labour force. When Suhrawardy took over as Civil Supplies Minister, he appointed a businessman and a Muslim League patron, Hasan Ispahani, 'as the sole purchaser [of rice] on behalf of the government of Bengal.... It was nothing short of a scandal that the Ministry should have appointed a particular firm as the sole agent, and, what is more, advanced about two crores of rupees to that firm.... No tenders were invited. The terms have not been offered to others'.[39] (*d*) in the distribution of rice thus collected, as ration to the needy, the government rejected the open market system in favour of government shops allotted to a favoured few. (*e*) When the Famine was knocking at the door in the shape of refugees from the starving villages, the hospitals refused to admit the famine stricken because beds were reserved and kept vacant for the Air Raid Protection service. In September 1943, Mookerjee revealed more facts regarding corrupt government dealings involving the sole agent, the firm of Ispahani:

> The prices at which the Ispahanis are supposed to have sold rice to the Bengal government are in many instances much higher than the prices prevailing in the market.... It is not Nature's hand alone that has given Bengal a death blow. Political maladministration lies at the root of the present economic catastrophe and no lasting solution can come until India is politically and economically free. (Cries of 'Ah, Ah', from the European Benches).[40]

As the statement of an observer who had recently had, as finance minister, first-hand knowledge of the affairs of the government, Mookerjee's statement provides weighty evidence, even if we evaluate it as a partisan Opposition critique. There is no evidence in the government's Famine Enquiry Commission that refutes the factual basis of Mookerjee's statement, nor was it challenged on the floor of the Legislative Assembly.

The Moral Economy and the Famine

Perhaps the most important aspect of the Famine of 1943 is the one most invisible in the archival records and reports—the moral impact of the famine. On the one hand, the famine experience raised the consciousness of the intellectual elements in the middle classes in respect of the exploitation and immiserization the rural poor were subjected to, and on the other, the famine impacted the moral economy of Bengal, the mores and values which were supposed to reside in the social order.

The first of these two trends is a well-known part of the history of literature and the arts in Bengal. The middle class efforts to provide famine relief was in the hands of politicians and it was not a great success for predictable reasons: the Congress had a Relief Committee split down the middle due to the rivalry between the Gandhians and Subhas Bose's followers; relief work was hampered by the meagreness of resources they could raise; and the efforts made by the Communists through the People's Relief Committee were likewise hampered. In contrast to the politician's endeavours, the reaction of the artists and writers was truly remarkable.[41] The response to the challenge of the catastrophic famine came in 1943–4 in many artistic and literary works. We can only mention some without crowding these pages with too many names of personalities who were part of that trend. There were many innovations distinguishing that trend from ones before or since. Leftist intellectuals focused on dramatic performances and songs to reach out to the masses. Their cultural organization, the Indian People's Theatre Association (IPTA) was set up while the famine was at its peak in May 1943; this was a sister organization in collaboration with the All-India Progressive Writers' Association founded in 1940. Artists of the stature of Uday Shankar and Shambhu Mitra took part in such performances. Some of the innovations popularized by them were open-air theatre without the proscenium, the genre of *gana-sangit*, or people's songs, often a fusion of Indian folk and modern music, and the IPTA also took theatre from Calcutta to district towns and villages to reach out to the public. The most memorable of the IPTA productions was the playwright Bijan Bhattacharya's *Nabanna*, an iconic representation of Bengal between 1942 and 1944. About the same time, the 'Calcutta Group' of painters and sculptors came into existence—it included Gopal Ghosh, Paritosh Sen, and Nirod Mazumdar, who drew upon the famine theme in 1943. They as well as artists like Jainal Abedin and Chitta Prasad in their depiction of the famine-stricken made for the first time famine and starvation a respectable subject of art; this helped to break the barrier between academic 'Art' that stood on a pedestal and the art representing reality in the streets of the city. Sculptor Somnath Hore's series entitled 'Wounds' began to take shape in his mind at this time. Abedin and Chitta Prasad became a part of an innovative trend of those times in producing prints of their etchings to sell in various cities in India to raise relief funds. In literary writings, the innovations were perhaps less obvious—basically what was new in this phase in response to the famine experience was a realism that broke away from the traditional literary conventions, and a centrality accorded to political consciousness in creative work. The litterateurs belonged to different groups, each nucleating around a journal. There was a core group of writers commonly identified as Leftist, for example, Gopal Haldar, Subhas Mukhopadhyay, Sukanta Bhattacharya, Bishnu Dey, Samar Sen, and Manik Bandyopadhyay, many of whom were associated with the Anti-Fascist Writers' and Artists' Association. And there were others, not avowedly Communist, but generally regarded as 'fellow travellers' at that time. Tarashankar Bandyopadhyay's *Manwantar*, Bhabani Bhattacharya's *So Many Hungers*, and Bibhuti Bhushan Bandyopadhyay's *Asani sanket* were some memorable writings on the Famine.

Parallel to this intellectual response to the Famine one has to consider its other aspect, the impact on the moral economy. Where was the *zamindar*, the landlord, the *ma-bap* of the *praja*s in their domain in this crisis? Did the sympathy of some members of the *bhadralok* stratum make any difference in terms of the material existential condition of the famine-affected rural poor? What remained of the carefully constructed image of the *bhadralok*s as the leaders of Bengali society? The notion of that social order under the guardianship of the *bhadralok* became obviously questionable in the crisis of 1943. The classic depiction of that social order and its break-down was *Asani sanket* (Distant thunder) by Bibhuti Bhushan Bandyopadhyay, later filmed by Satyajit Ray in 1973. The central protagonist is Gangacharan, an upper-caste *bhadralok* among the peasants to whom he is teacher and self-taught physician. With his spectacles and umbrella and his learning he is a respectable figure in the village and that secures him not only a living but reverence from the peasant inhabitants. He is adept at the compromises a middle-class man has to live with—for instance, when his wife questions him about the efficacy of the spells he uses to ward off cholera in the village, he says that they might help along with the scientific health care measures he also recommends. Like all *bhadraloks* he thinks that if his wife starts working for money outside the home that would be unacceptably *infra dig*. Such a man and such a tranquil life would be exposed to breakdown and chaos very soon, and the first sign of that is the sight of an aircraft in the sky, a cause of much speculation in the village. That metaphor for the external world foreshadows what the World War would bring in its wake: rising prices, hoarding by merchants, disappearance of food grains from the village market, villagers searching for substitutes for rice in the form of wild fruits and roots, and eventually the first starvation death in the village. As the villagers, afflicted with silence at the sight, look at the dead wife of the cobbler, it dawns on them that they have to leave their hearth and home in search of food. This exodus of hungry people brings the narrative to a closure. Woven into that narrative is the voice of the *bhadralok* Gangacharan, his slow awakening to the realities beyond social norms and mores he had accepted all his life, his realization that the old relationships of trust and the entire civil order were breaking down. Thus Bibhuti Bhushan Bandyopadhyay and Satyajit Ray show in the microcosm of Gangacharan's village the impact of the War and the onset of famine on the moral economy of rural Bengal.

Finally, a question that arises is: What of the critics of the old social order? What was the role of the Left in this crisis in rural Bengal? Did it lead peasants to expropriate merchants and landholders who had hoarded rice while peasants were starving to death? Abani Lahiri was a middle-rank CPI leader at the time, given charge of four north Bengal districts by the Provincial Committee of the party. His memories are revealing:

> It was not on the agenda of the peasant organization to loot hoarded rice.... To the best of my knowledge there was no looting.... The reason was that neither the Krishak Samiti nor the Communist Party called [upon peasants] to resort to loot [of hoarded rice].... The call to commence loot never came from any organized peasants' organization—that is why the peasants never took that action even during the famine.[42]

The fact that there was no looting of hoarded rice was commented upon by many contemporary observers. One of them was the Communist leader Bhowani Sen who writes of the peasants' 'uncomplaining surrender to death'.[43] It is useful to bear in mind the fact that by some strange logic the 'People's War' to protect the land of socialism was prioritized in India over class struggle so that agrarian disturbance was as unwelcome as industrial strikes that would hamper the Allied war effort. As a sincere party leader, active in 1943 and the next few years, Abani Lahiri, assessed that period in hindsight many years later:

> Admittedly, there was [in 1943] clearly an inclination of Communist leadership to bring into an anti-Fascist front the *jotedars* and the *zamindars*.... When the famine was imminent while the *jotedar*, moneylender, wholesale merchant had hoarded rice in their possession, and exported it, the Krishak Samiti or the Communist Party might have issued a call to capture the hoarded rice and to distribute the rice, and that would have changed the rural scenario.... The biggest crisis peasants faced might have been an opportunity to bring about a revolutionary transformation. That was an opportunity we lost.[44]

In short, the Communists, due to their international commitments, failed the famine-stricken peasantry of Bengal. They were unable to put on their political agenda a peasants' movement against hoarding and profiteering, although the intellectuals in the party and the 'fellow travellers' admirably displayed in their creative work their identification with the cause of the victims of the Famine of 1943.

The Impact of the War on Urban Society

One of the major consequences of the creation of a large 'black market' sector in the economy and price inflation during the World War was the sharp increase in cost of living. Table 7.1 indicates the middle-class cost of living indices (base August 1939 = 100) in the city of Calcutta.

The rise in cost of living meant a decline in the living standards of salaried fixed-income earners. Their salaries were not upgraded unlike the wages of workers in organized industries with increasing demand for both skilled and unskilled manual labour due to war-related construction and manufacturing activities. The salary-earning, educated, professional stratum (often of a high caste and designated as *bhadralok*

Table 7.1 Middle-Class Cost of Living Index, 1940–5, Calcutta

	Food	Fuel, Lighting	Clothing	Combined Index
January 1940	107	106	125	107
July 1940	106	106	119	106
January 1941	110	108	124	109
July 1941	117	117	179	120
January 1942	118	148	192	125
July 1942	133	166	215	138
January 1943	208	328	361	206
July 1943	302	231	410	261
January 1944	256	194	322	226
July 1944	305	194	300	250
January 1945	301	202	273	244
July 1945	315	185	328	259

Source: Bengal Chamber of Commerce; *Capital*, a trade journal, cited in *Census of India*, 1951, vol. VI, Part I-A, pp. 125ff.
Note: The last column includes items not listed here; the weightage wage constant, being 53.6, 4.4, and 12.4 for the items in the first three columns above and 29.6 for other items not listed here.

or gentlemen) underwent a traumatic demotion in the social hierarchy. A new class of people began to enjoy social prestige and prosperity of a kind that was not theirs till now: this class consisted of contractors supplying labour and material to the army and war-related constructions, retail and wholesale dealers in food grains and scarce items like kerosene or drugs, speculators and hoarders whose mainstay was the 'black market' and business in areas verging on criminal activities. Vis-á-vis this class of people, the position of the traditional middle-class gentry, that is, the *bhadralok*, drastically changed for the worse.

The social costs of such a reshuffling in status hierarchy would have been acceptable had the nouveau riche constituted the spearhead of genuine innovative entrepreneurship leading towards productive development, for example, in the industrial sphere. But it is doubtful whether gains in business pursued that path of development; instead, the heritage of the war years on the business scene was the black market, systematic corruption of the bureaucracy in so far as it attempted to control and ration commodities, and the accumulation of unaccounted profits in 'black money' which could not be invested in the open market.

The Census Superintendent and Development Commissioner of West Bengal remarked at the end of the decade in 1951:

> The first three years of the Second World War (1939–41), fortified by the Defence of India Act and the remoteness of the theatre of war were almost uneventful ... but things started humming as soon as the war knocked on the eastern frontier. Commerce and trade sprang into fierce life, and aided by hoarding and the black market, drew more and more persons into their orbit.... Apart from big business and wholesale trade which raised a really big class of the *new rich*, anybody (of business class) who had ever so little to spare went into trade.[45]

Windfall profits in merchandizing, speculation, and military contracts attracted much more capital than in industrial investments. For example, in the leading industry of Calcutta, jute textiles, there was neither any marked increase in production (there was actually a fall in 1941 and 1943) nor any fresh investment in machinery throughout the 1940s.[46]

There can be no doubt that the quality of life for the Calcutta citizens deteriorated drastically in the war years and immediately thereafter. This can be judged from indices like the number of dwellers per house, the number of inhabitants in municipally unauthorized slums, decline in per capita filtered water supply and in sewage disposal, and other falling indices like literacy (due partly to immigration caused by demand for unskilled labour). We have to depend on statistics which do not fully convey the quality of life, nor were statistics collected very vigorously and comprehensively in the war years.

The population of Calcutta increased in 1941–51 by 20.9 per cent. In the 1940s, Calcutta was on the way to earning its present unenviable reputation. The congestion in urban dwellings with municipal conveniences increased. It is not possible to isolate the war years, but the general trend is evident in Table 7.2 from Census returns.

Table 7.2 Number of Persons per Municipal Premises in Calcutta

1931	16.8
1941	27.5
1951	31.0

Source: Census of India, 1951, vol. VI, Part I-A, p. 243.

At the same time, the municipal services deteriorated. We take the simplest measure, the supply of filtered water per capita, which is the most relevant in terms of civic health (see Table 7.3).

In the same period the municipal disposal of sewage declined from an average daily per capita of 164.8 gallons in 1931–2, to 91.2 in 1941–2, and 82.8 in 1950–1.

The immigration of famine-stricken people from the countryside into Calcutta worsened the health and conservancy situation. 'Removal of corpses from the streets' became one of the major duties of the Health Officer of the Calcutta Municipal Corporation.[47] Calcutta hospitals reported a high death rate from 'dysentery and diarrhoea' which was in fact a starvation-related disease. 'Many patients showed famine oedema or dropsy.... Dropsy invariably makes its appearance under famine conditions; for example, it was widely prevalent in the underfed population of Central Europe during and just after the last war. In the Bengal Famine victims it was often associated with anaemia'.[48] We have already noted the high famine mortality in Calcutta in 1943–4.

The congestion we have mentioned earlier was exacerbated by jerry-built slums brought on by rapid growth of population and labour immigration. Shortly after the war, the Government of India conducted a survey (1946). It revealed that 50 per cent of one-room houses in Calcutta were inhabited by families of six to seven persons.[49] Another survey in 1948 of slums (called *bustees* in Calcutta) showed that of these one-room tenements only about one-third had any water supply arrangement. It was recorded that of 820,000 people living in such *bustees* 55 per cent had no access to water other than from street hydrants or polluted ponds. Further, a separate kitchen space was provided only in 15.5 per cent of huts in the *bustees*.[50] These figures are, however, possibly subject to sampling error and are not comparable in terms of accuracy with the census estimates we have cited earlier.

Table 7.3 Calcutta Municipality Water Supply, 1931–51, Per Capita Daily Average in Gallons

	1931–2	1941–2	1950–2
Filtered Water	52.3	34.5	26.5
Unfiltered Water	44.1	32.2	38.6

Source: Census of India, 1951 VI, Part I-A, p. 246.

Table 7.4 Percentage of Literates in Population of Calcutta

	Persons	Male	Female
1901	24.82	31.58	11.49
1911	32.13	39.57	16.45
1921	41.88	50.15	24.30
1931	39.57	44.49	29.07
1941	53.86	58.12	44.44
1951	53.12	58.69	43.35

Source: Census of India, 1951, vol. VI, Part I-C, Statement VI.3.

Finally, we may note that the years immediately following the war witnessed a decline in the level of literacy in Calcutta. The district of Calcutta had the highest literacy rate in the whole of eastern India and consistently showed an upward trend from the last decades of the nineteeth century. During 1941–51, for the first time, this trend was reversed. The proportion of literates in the population of Calcutta was 53.86 per cent in 1941 (58.12 per cent male and 44.44 per cent female) as compared to 53.12 per cent in 1951 (58.68 per cent male and 43.55 per cent female) (see Table 7.4).

To sum it up, the war years and those immediately succeeding it were characterized by a striking decline in the quality of civic life. *Health* and access to *education* are regarded today as basic indices of quality of life; in both respects, statistics of decline in literacy and of living space, supply of water, and so on, indicate a worsening situation in Calcutta in the 1940s.

How the civic and political institutions responded to this crisis and the demands of the war situation is the question to be addressed next.

Community, City, Nation, and the War

The highly diversified mosaic of the Calcutta population, with immigrants from all linguistic regions of India, each with its specific caste stratification, and the co-existence of religious communities subject to political mobilization, presents an exceedingly complex picture. During the period we are concerned with, it was the Hindu–Muslim communal conflict that was in the forefront in city politics and we shall address ourselves to this aspect.

On the eve of the war, in 1939, the communal question was revived by an amendment to the constitution of the Calcutta Municipal Corporation.[51] The Calcutta Municipal Act of 1923 was amended in 1939 to introduce communal electorates; likewise four members of the corporation were to be elected by 'lower castes' (scheduled castes) and one by Anglo-Indians (that is, people of mixed English and Indian blood). The dominant role of the Hindu gentry of Calcutta was threatened by this restructuration of the corporation. Apart from that, the communal electorate was also criticized widely on the ground that it was inconsistent with nationalist principles. But the communal divide was already clear, and the restructured corporation reflected that reality.

The controversy over the communal electorates and the general atmosphere of communal tension hampered efficiency in handling the problem created by the war situation. The Corporation of Calcutta, it must be acknowledged, was no better in the pre-war days, when it was dominated by the Indian National Congress and the Hindu *bhadralok* class. The electorates were small in size—only about 4 to 8 per cent of the population in different wards of the city had voting rights. Corporation employees themselves being electoral officers, polls for membership of that body were subject to manipulation. Upon being elected, councillors (77 in number under the Act of 1923 and 85 under the Act of 1939) were able to participate in a system of corruption in the award of contracts and employment.[52] Nirad C. Chaudhuri has recorded in his autobiography a graphic description of the corruption he witnessed in municipal corporation affairs while serving as secretary to one of the prominent city politicians.[53] This was the chief problem, not the creation of communal electorates, in the efficient discharge of the civic duties of the Calcutta Corporation in respect of the short-term problems brought about by the war, namely, immigration of large numbers at a time when house construction material was in short supply, increased demands on municipal services, particularly water supply, need for roads and other infrastructure to serve the port and industrial and army installations, and critical pressures on health and conservancy services during the Famine and the ensuing epidemics in 1943–4. The long-run problems of the decline in the quality of life indices mentioned earlier were also exacerbated by the ineffectiveness of the Calcutta Municipal Corporation.

It was not merely the failure of an institution, the city corporation. The civic community itself was split down the middle during the war and the following years. The first Muslim Mayor of Calcutta was elected to office in 1933 and allowances were made for Muslim demands for special representation in the Corporation in 1939. But these developments did not abate the ambient communal tensions and the provincial government of Bengal did not act, as might have been expected, as a corrective and stabilizing force making up for the failings of the Calcutta Corporation.[54] Except for short-lived cooperation between S.P. Mookerjee and Fazlul Huq between December 1941 and February 1943, the leaders of the two religious communities were almost perpetually in conflict, even in the midst of the war crisis. This situation allowed the British officials and business leaders to intervene in and influence decisions. The Hindu communal leaders as well as the Bengal Congress leaders complained that the British consistently backed the Muslim leaders. Be that as it may, the political squabbles on communal lines did hamper the government's response to crises caused by the war, including the Famine. The Famine Inquiry Commission later observed:

> In a situation such as that arose in Bengal in 1942 and 1943, endangering the food supply and the very life of the people, it was already necessary that the measures taken by the government should receive the full support of public opinion. This was difficult when counsels were divided.... We are convinced that political strife in Bengal was a serious obstacle to an effective attack on the problems created by high prices and food shortage.[55]

While the force of these remarks applies to the Famine situation, it must be observed that in relation to the War effort as a whole this explanation of lack of public support for the government does not hold. And this takes us into the issue of popular sentiments in Calcutta and Bengal regarding the War. In so far as backing the provincial government meant backing the British India regime and the Allied powers, popular attitudes were ambivalent, and very often negative. There was a strong popular sentiment that the war was 'their war, not our war', that India had been dragged into it bound to the chariot wheels of imperial Britain. Further, there was also a fairly widespread tendency to look upon Japan with admiration since the battle of Tsushima.

Thirdly, the ties forged by Subhas Chandra Bose between the Indian National Army and Japan during the World War appealed to nationalist sentiments, though not much was yet known of the actual history of that relationship. Finally, to Bengal's national sentiments the brutal suppression of the 'Quit India' Movement in 1942 (particularly in Medinipur, close to Calcutta) was a fresh reminder of the essentially coercive nature of British rule behind the facade of an electoral system allowing representation and limited Indian participation in government.

The outcome of all the above historical factors was translated into Calcutta's quotidian life and attitudes. Nirad C. Chaudhuri observed that upon every British defeat in the war 'exultation among the Bengalees of Calcutta was great'.[56] In contemporary literature, penned mainly by Bengali Hindu citizens of Calcutta, one can see this attitude to the British along with unfavourable portrayals of British and American soldiers, seen in the streets of Calcutta for the first time in large numbers. Likewise, one can also see in contemporary Bengali fictional literature (not subjected to censorship, unlike news) an intense hatred for what was perceived as the British government's apathy to the victims of the Bengal Famine in 1943–4.

At the same time, the Bengal intelligentsia and their capital city, Calcutta, appear to have failed to respond adequately to the challenge of the Famine and the War. There was a failure of social leadership. The comment of the Famine Inquiry Commission was not unfair: '*Society, together with its organs, failed to protect its weaker members. Indeed there was a moral and social breakdown, as well as an administrative breakdown*'.[57] The absence of vigorous non-governmental relief and social work was a marked feature of Calcutta's social organization. The bulk of the relief administered during the Famine was through the Chambers of Commerce, chiefly in the form of food supplies to keep their workers alive; relief work by missionary and sectarian organizations was more widespread among the actually famine-stricken, but available resources were woefully inadequate.[58]

The Last Warning Signal: The Communal Riot in Calcutta, 1946

We have seen that the Famine Inquiry Commission perceived in the impact of the Famine of 1943 a 'moral and social breakdown'.[59]

The communal riot in Calcutta in August 1946 was another event that signalized the same kind of breakdown and many contemporaries also regarded it as a defining moment that precipitated the decision to accept the partition of Bengal. The riot is to this day etched in the darkest colour in the memory of those who witnessed it. Such are the memories recounted in their autobiographies by two eye-witnesses, the sociologist Andre Beteille and the historian Tapan Raychaudhuri. Beteille, then a school-going teenager, saw some parts of the city where Muslims were in the majority, and Raychaudhuri was a resident in the Scottish Church College in a Hindu-majority area. It was an experience that, judging by their accounts, changed the image of Calcutta in their minds forever.[60] Shaista Ikramulla, the author of the only dependable biography of Suhrawardy, recounts how she saw men being chased and beheaded like animals.[61]

There are a few things of general significance in the history of the riot of 1946 that merit attention more than the details of events. Those events are too well known to need recounting: M.A. Jinnah issues a call to observe 16 August 1946 as Direct Action Day; Chief Minister of Bengal H.S. Suhrawardy declares it a day of *hartal*; Muslim efforts to enforce the *hartal* and Hindu efforts to resist it lead to clashes; on 17 August dispersed clashes get organized and communalist slogans and processions exacerbate hostility; in Hindu and Muslim neighbourhoods butchery of isolated members of the other community begins; rumours of atrocities add fuel to communal propaganda; the police are overwhelmed by the magnitude of clashes; the government calls in the army when it is too late; peace begins to be restored on the fourth day, 19 August; thousands of corpses are removed from the streets by the army and the municipal corporation; political leaders take out peace processions; Viceroy Wavell tours a peaceful Calcutta on 26 August. Beyond these events, some points of general significance emerge in the contemporary accounts.

1. For the first time the *bhadralok*, the upper-caste, educated, middle-class Hindus, participate in butchering members of the other community in their neighbourhood. Tapan Raychaudhuri says that this experience was 'very humbling. I had a certain pride in the non-communal outlook of educated Bengali Hindus. What I witnessed during those days [16 to 19 August 1946] destroyed that

self-regard forever'.[62] He saw in the vicinity of the Scottish Church College where he resided neighbouring *bhadraloks* as well as his own fellow-students engaging in arson and murder of defenceless isolated Muslims in that Hindu-dominated neighbourhood. Till then, the rich *bhadralok* and the Marwari businessmen employed servants and security guards in their employ to do the dirty work. In 1946, the gentry did not shrink from the grisly task, their notions of cultural and moral superiority notwithstanding. The 'educated Bengali Hindu' Raychaudhuri is speaking of, the *bhadralok*, liked to think of themselves as the inheritors of the Bengal Renaissance tradition that ushered in new humanist values.

2. A fact to which historians have paid no attention is that the riot brought about a demographic change in Calcutta. It emerges from contemporary accounts that the multi-ethnic neighbourhoods where Muslims and Hindus lived together side by side received a death blow. During and immediately after the riot, there was a massive but publicly unacknowledged relocation or exchange of population on a communal basis, the Hindus moving away from areas with Muslim majority, and likewise Muslims from Hindu-dominated areas. There are reliable statistics provided by the military authorities who provided transport for rescue and relocation: a total of 24,100 people were evacuated by military vehicles, and there were many others who moved out on their own.[63] This population movement meant, of course, further social distance between the two communities, and lesser possibility of interaction in quotidian life. As we have argued earlier, historians have neglected the fact that interactions in the private space mattered as much if not more than the attitudes and policies adopted by the communities in the public sphere.
3. Another interesting fact was that the elected government and the Chief Minister did not command the confidence of the Hindu community, the British army did. For example, the press statement of a leader of that community, Sarat Chandra Bose, on 20 August 1946 said: 'Strong military pickets should be posted all over Calcutta and the suburbs under the command of a high military officer who may be expected to hold the scale even'.[64] Viceroy Wavell knew of this and when he visited Calcutta on 26 August 1946 the army officers confided to him their impression of the 'communal attitude' of the Chief Minister. Wily Wavell used this as an argument with

Gandhi: this was the reason, he said, why the continued presence of the British army in India was a necessity, even if an Interim Government of India took over. Gandhi vehemently rejected this view in a letter to Wavell: the Congress must not 'impose its will on warring elements in India through the use of British arms'.[65] Gandhi also wrote that though the riot was a terrible event that was no reason why 'the Congress should bend itself and adopt what it considers a wrong cause'.

4. Finally, although Gandhi boldly wrote thus, there can be little doubt that—as we shall see in the last two chapters—the catastrophic carnage in Calcutta deeply influenced Jawaharlal Nehru and the Congress High Command who feared a repetition of that carnage, and that facilitated the acceptance of partition. In the next few months, this apprehension was enhanced: Nehru wrote that the situation was 'tense and volcanic' in Punjab and Bengal; reportedly arms were being made or smuggled in to prepare for a civil war, and so forth.[66] In early 1947, Nehru often recalled the suffering caused by the Calcutta Riot and the threat of a situation approximating a civil war to argue that partition was the only alternative. One may surmise that this was the trend of thinking in Bengal as well, although we have no means of documenting it.

While these aspects of the communal riot of Calcutta in 1946 spring to the eye on account of their general significance, many particularities and details remain obscure and hidden for two reasons: there is conflicting evidence on most matters because there are two different narratives, Hindu and Muslim, and, secondly, the duly appointed Calcutta Disturbances Inquiry Committee was not allowed, by an order passed by Viceroy Mountbatten, to report their findings.[67] We shall probably never arrive at firm answers to many questions. How many lives were lost? The official statistics put it down at 3,000; the unofficial estimates go up to 5,000. What is known is that there were many corpses that were gathered from the streets by army units and disposed of, unidentified, especially corpses of the urban poor who were the main victims. Why was the riot allowed to fester for three days and the army not called in till it was too late? We do not know the role of the Chief Minister in this matter, but we have dependable evidence from Sir Francis Tuker, the GOC of the Eastern Command.

Years later, after retirement, he recalled that the Calcutta Police had indeed requested military assistance on the first day of the riot, and 'as a result of the request, the Governor, Sir Frederick Burrows, made a tour of the city ... and decided that the time had not yet come for military aid.... From August 19 the situation was under control and all that was left for the army to do was to carry out the terrible task of clearing the streets of the bodies of the victims of the killing'.[68]

Was Chief Minister Suhrawardy part of a conspiracy to provoke and prolong the riot? We have no decisive evidence on either side, though the spokesmen of the Hindu community claimed that there was evidence of his complicity in the sequence of events: Did he not call for a *hartal* [general strike or suspension of work] on Direct Action Day, August 16, and were not the Muslim attempts to enforce a *hartal* the immediate cause of disturbances? Did he not appoint to the controlling position in the police force men of his choice just before the Riot? Was he not present in the police control room for long hours while it was in progress? Why did he not insist on the intervention of the army at an early stage? On the other hand, it has been argued, it would have been foolhardy of Suhrawardy to start a battle when his community was a small minority of the city's population; he did issue statements calling upon all citizens to maintain peace; army intervention depended ultimately on the decision of Governor Burrows and not Suhrawardy, and he might not have foreseen the pattern of resistance and reprisal in both the communities.

Harun-or-Rashid, an eminent Bangladeshi historian, has argued in a recent work that the main aim of Suhrawardy was to ensure a complete *hartal* and secure maximum attendance at the Muslim League's meeting on Direct Action day: 'It seems unfair to say that by declaring a public holiday he deliberately incited people to violence'.[69] 'The riot in Calcutta in 1946, according to Ayesha Jalal, was against the grain of Jinnah's objective, for he was 'a man of orderly constitutional advance' and he was the last person to allow an 'unthinking mob' to take over.[70] Be that as it may, the sparseness of evidence does not allow us to form any firm conclusion about Suhrawardy's responsibility. Perhaps the question is of little importance. The huge catastrophe of August 1946 cannot be adequately explained in terms of the role of any single individual like Suhrawardy. Without prior preparation on both sides, the battle, the aggression, defensive resistance, and vengeful reprisals, would have been impossible, and vicious psychological warfare involving the whole community was part of that preparation on either side. Consider, for example, the statement issued by secretary of the Calcutta District Muslim League, on 10 August. 'I appeal to the Muslims of Calcutta ... to rise to the occasion. We are in the midst of the month of Ramzan fasting. But this is a month of real *Jehad*'. And the statement went on to recall that 'the Battle of Badr, the first open conflict between Islam and Heathenism, was fought and won' during Ramzan. And the Hindu Mahasabha did not fail to perform its usual role: 'Beware!... The Bengali Hindus and every non-Muslim is opposed to Pakistan. Under these circumstances to observe *hartal* on the 16th as proclaimed by the League ... would mean supporting their demand.... The Hindus will have to give a clear reply to this high-handedness of the Muslim League'.[71] Both of these statements convey to us the flavour of the inflammatory rhetoric of those days.

About a week after the Riot, Mahatma Gandhi, in a letter to Viceroy Wavell, wrote in frank anger of 'the brutal exhibition recently witnessed in Bengal'.[72] The Mahatma wrote in anger but he was not wrong. The Great Calcutta Killings, as the media called them, were a climactic moment in the long history of fission along the fault lines in society and in the politics of exclusion. They were not just a political event of great magnitude but also a moment of moral significance, marking a break from the humanist values which some of the makers of modern Bengal hoped to instal at the core of the 'Bengal Renaissance'.

To sum up, in our survey of the impact of the Second World War on the life and institutions of Bengal and Calcutta, we have seen that in economic terms the immediate consequence of the war, as it escalated in the eastern theatre, was acute scarcity of food grains leading to the Famine that took 1.5 million (official estimate) to 3 million lives (unofficial Indian estimates).[73] As we have already mentioned, according to the US Secretary of State the total number of US armed forces killed in the European War was 150,000; the corresponding figure for British and Commonwealth Forces, according to Churchill, was 307,000. Compared to the number of combatants who died on the Allied side, the non-combatant fatalities in Bengal were enormous. And what was the response from the civic and political leadership in Bengal? We shall simply reproduce an extract from a report by the Governor of Bengal. The Famine, he wrote, 'does not constitute grave menace to peace or tranquility of Bengal or any part thereof, for sufferers are entirely submissive and the emergency threatens, not maintenance of law and order, but preservation of public health and economic stability'.[74] Given the presence of the Allied Forces and the supply strategies, the Famine was almost inevitable and it brought to Calcutta thousands of famine-stricken people; the sight of their dying in the streets was a daily experience, and yet the passive sufferers had very few of the civic community or the political leadership standing by them, ready to intervene. We have also seen how the social scene changed rapidly during the War—most notably the increased cost of living under inflationary conditions, the decline in the real income of the salary-earning urban middle-classes, the rise of a *nouveau riche* class that made money in war-related contracts and black market operations. There was a drastic decline in the quality of urban life in Calcutta, increase in population density and congestion, decline in municipal services like water supply and sewage disposal, proliferation of slums to accommodate immigrants for whom there was no housing due to scarcity of construction material during the War. These problems were unresolved not only due to short-run factors arising out of the War situation, but also due to certain long-run characteristics of the polity of Bengal and Calcutta, for instance, the decline in the efficiency of the Calcutta Municipal Corporation, the lack of social leadership to address the city's problems, either short-term and war-related, or long-term and arising out of the colonial pattern of urbanization on a weak industrial base. Finally, the general state of political instability due to intensifying communal conflict led ultimately to the Calcutta Riot on the Muslim League's Direct Action Day in August 1946. Thus the years from the beginning of the war to the Riot of August 1946 constituted in a sense a watershed in the history of Calcutta. The city was never the same again.

Notes

1. Dr Sir M. Iqbal to M.A. Jinnah, 28 May 1937, in Syed Sharifuddin Pirzada (ed.), *Quaid-i Azam Jinnah's Correspondence* (Karachi, 1977), p. 138.
2. M.K. Gandhi in *Harijan*, 25 September 1938.
3. Jinnah to M.A.H. Ispahani, 6 May 1945, in M.A.H. Ispahani, *Quaid-e-Azam Jinnah as I Knew Him* (Karachi, 1976), p. 198.
4. Nripendra Chandra Banerji, *At the Crossroads: An Autobiography* (Calcutta, 1974), pp. 226–7.

5. P.C. Ghosh to Rajendra Prasad, 12 June 1937, *Rajendra Prasad Correspondence and Select Documents*, edited by Valmiki Choudhary, vol. III (New Delhi, 1984) [hereafter cited as *RPC*, followed by volume number].
6. Jawaharlal Nehru to B. Banerji (son of N.C. Banerji) at Baidyabati, 28 June 1937, AICC Papers, F. no. E-5-Pt. I/1936.
7. B. Banerji, Baidyabati, to J. Nehru, 25 June 1937, AICC Papers, F. no. E-5-Pt. I/1936.
8. Nalinaksha Sanyal to J. Nehru, 20 February 1937; Nehru to Sanyal, 24 February 1937, AICC Papers, F. no. E-5-Pt. I/1936.
9. Dr Bidhan Chandra Roy to Bhulabhai Desai, INC Parliamentary Board, 14 October 1934, B.C. Roy Private Papers, File no. 34 (II), Nehru Memorial Museum and Library (NMML).
10. B. Desai to B.C. Roy, 17 August 1934, B.C. Roy Private Papers, File no. 34 (II), (NMML).
11. S. Banamali to Rajendra Prasad, 9 December 1938, *RPC*, III.
12. Abul Hashim, *In Retrospection* (Dhaka, 1974), p. 49.
13. J. Anderson, Governor of Bengal to Linlithgow, Viceroy, 3 December 1936, National Archives of India (NAI) microfilm no. 3169.
14. M.A.H. Ispahani to M.A. Jinnah, 24 April 1945, in Ispahani, *Quaid-e-Azam Jinnah as I Knew Him*, p. 197.
15. Nirad C. Chaudhuri, *Thy Hand, Great Anarch! India, 1921–1952* (London, 1987), pp. 491, 487–99.
16. B.C. Roy to V. Patel, 7 September 1931, AICC Papers, F. no. P-15-1931, NMML.
17. H.S. Suhrawardy to B.P. Sinha Roy, 1 May 1939, Private Papers of B.P. Sinha Roy, file no. 3, Pt. I, Correspondence as Minister-in-charge, Revenue Dept., Govt. of Bengal; NMML.
18. Rajendra Prasad to J.B. Kripalani, 31 December 1938, *RPC*, II.
19. Report of Indian Statutory Commission (Simon Commission), vol. VIII, Memo. by Government of Bengal.
20. Hashim, *In Retrospection*, p. 54.
21. Syama Prasad Mookerjee, *Leaves From a Diary* (Calcutta, 1993), pp. 67–9.
22. S.P. Mookerjee's speech on 'No-Confidence Motion against B.P. Pain', *Proceedings of Bengal Legislative Assembly*, vol. 67, no. 6, 31 May 1944, 21 June 1944.
23. 'Report on Indian Agriculture and Food Supply Problems', July 1943, Board of Economic Warfare, Technical Branch, USA, cited in M.S. Venkataramani, *The Bengal Famine of 1943: The American Response* (Delhi, 1973), p. 36. I have drawn upon, other than documentary sources, some noteworthy studies of the Famine of 1943 by A.K. Sen, 'Starvation and Exchange Entitlements: A General Approach and its Application to the

Great Bengal Famine', *Cambridge Journal of Economics* no. 1 (1977): 33–59, and *Poverty and Famines* (Oxford, 1981); Paul R. Greenough, *Prosperity and Misery in Modern Bengal: The Famine of 1943–44* (New York, 1982); Arup Maharatna, *The Demography of Famines: An Indian Historical Perspective* (Delhi, 1996); Madhushree Mukherjee, *Churchill's Secret War: The British Empire and the Ravaging of India during World War II* (Delhi, 2010).

24. S.W. Kirby, *History of the Second World War: The War against Japan* (London, 1958), pp. 188–9.
25. M.S. Venkataramani, *The Bengal Famine of 1943*, p. 7.
26. C.B.A. Behrens, *History of the Second World War, U.K. Civil Series: Merchant Shipping and Demands of the War* (London, 1955).
27. *Famine Inquiry Commission: Report on Bengal* (Govt. of India, Delhi, 1945), p. 25; the Commission was also known as the Sir John Woodhead Commission; hereafter this report is cited hereafter as *FIC*. On British strategies, see L. Wigmore, *The Japanese Thrusts* (Canberra, 1957), pp. 449–52.
28. *FIC*, p. 26.
29. S. Bhattacharya, chapter 3, in *Cambridge Economic History of India*, eds D. Kumar and M. Desai, vol. II (Cambridge, 1982).
30. *FIC*, pp. 26–7.
31. S. Bhattacharya, 'Laissez-faire in India', *Indian Economic and Social History Review* (*IESHR*) I, no. 2 (1965).
32. Statement by J.K. Biswas, Justice of Peace, 14 September 1944, *FIC*, vol. II, p. 920.
33. Statement 'Off the record' by Mr Pinnell, ICS, Head of Civil Supplies Department, in private papers of M.L. Nanavati, Member, Famine Inquiry Commission, file no. 6 (NAI, New Delhi).
34. Statement 'Off the record' by Mr Pinnell in private papers of M.L. Nanavati, Member, Famine Inquiry Commission, file no. 6 (NAI, New Delhi).
35. *FIC*, vol. IV, pp. 1242ff.
36. *FIC*, vol. IV, p. 1245.
37. K.E. Vaidyanathan, 'Testing Deficiencies in Death Registration Statistics and Mortality Estimates in India', *Studies in Mortality in India* (Gandhigram, 1972).
38. Greenough, *Prosperity and Misery in Modern Bengal*, pp. 305–9; Maharatna, *The Demography of Famines*, ch. 4; and T. Dyson and A. Maharatna, 'Excess Mortality during the Bengal Famine: A Re-Evaluation', *IESHR* 28, no. 3 (1991): 281–97, offer an estimate of 2.8 million 'excess deaths' in the Famine of 1943.
39. Syama Prasad Mookerjee, *Speech on Food Situation in Bengal in Proceedings of Bengal Legislative Assembly*, vol. 56, no. 1, 14 July 1943.

40. S.P. Mookerjee's speech, in *Proceedings of Bengal Legislative Assembly*, vol. 66, no. 1, 17 September 1943.
41. I have drawn upon the latest study of this trend in this period in Amit Kumar Gupta, *Crises and Creativities: Middle-Class Bhadralok in Bengal, 1939–1952* (Kolkata, 2009), pp. 146–65; equally useful is Amit Kumar Gupta, *The Agrarian Drama: The Leftists and the Rural Poor in India, 1934–1951* (Delhi, 1996).
42. Abani Lahiri, *Tirish challisher bangla* (Calcutta, 1999), pp. 69–71.
43. Bhowani Sen, *Rural Bengal in Ruins* (Bombay, 1945), p. 17, cited in Gupta, *Crises and Creativities*, p. 142, who contests Sen's statement; according to Gupta, although there are extremely few instances of looting of hoarded rice, the statistics of incidents of dacoity show a marked increase in the first half of 1943 and 'these dacoities were virtually cases of grain looting'. Since the crime statistics compound various crimes in the category 'dacoity', it is difficult to form a firm conclusion about the frequency of grain looting; further the frequency of 'dacoity' may be connected with the aftermath of the Quit India movement.
44. Lahiri, *Tirish challisher bangla*, pp. 68–70.
45. Asok Mitra, ICS, *Census of India, 1951*, vol. VI, Part I-A, p. 119.
46. Mitra, *Census of India, 1951*, vol. VI, Part I-A, p. 126.
47. *Famine Inquiry Commission*, Evidences, vol. IV, p. 1274.
48. *FIC*, Report, pp. 116–18.
49. Mitra, *Census of India, 1951*, vol. VI, Part I-A, p. 145.
50. Mitra, *Census of India, 1951*, vol. VI, Part I-A, p. 147.
51. Keshab Chaudhuri, *Calcutta: Story of Its Government* (Calcutta, 1972), pp. 250ff.
52. K. Chaudhuri, *Calcutta*, pp. 266–73.
53. N.C. Chaudhuri, *Thy Hand, Great Anarch!* pp. 376–83, 487–99 on the Calcutta Corporation.
54. J.H. Broomfield, *Elite Conflict in a Plural Society: Twentieth-Century Bengal* (Berkeley, 1968), pp. 284–7.
55. *FIC*, p. 84, para 24.
56. N.C. Chaudhuri, *Thy Hand, Great Anarch!* p. 567.
57. *FIC*, p. 107.
58. *FIC*, pp. 30–1.
59. See note 51.
60. Andre Beteille, *Sunlight on the Garden: A Story of Childhood and Youth* (New Delhi, 2012), ch. 6; Tapan Raychaudhuri, *The World in Our Time: A Memoir* (Delhi, 2011).
61. Shaista Ikramullah, *Husseyn Shaheed Suhrawardy: A Biography* (Karachi, 1991).

62. Raychaudhuri, *The World in Our Time*, p. 172.
63. The statistics provided by the army authorities are in the papers on Rescue Organization, Calcutta Disturbances Enquiry Committee, F. No. 351/46, B-II, cited in Rakesh Batabyal, *Communalism in Bengal* (Delhi, 2005), p. 249.
64. Sarat Chandra Bose, *I Warned My Countrymen, Being the Collected Works, 1945–50* (Netaji Research Bureau, Calcutta, 1968), p. 155.
65. Gandhi to Wavell, 28 August 1946, in Penderel Moon (ed.), *Wavell: The Viceroy's Journal* (London, 1973), p. 342.
66. J. Nehru to Asaf Ali, 23 May 1947, in Sucheta Mahajan (ed.), *Towards Freedom, 1947*, part 1 (New Delhi, 2013), ch. 12, doc. no. 7.
67. The Calcutta Disturbances Enquiry Committee did gather a lot of evidence from eyewitnesses and officials though they were not allowed to write a report; some of the data have been used by in his excellent study Suranjan Das, *Communal Riots in Bengal, 1905–1947* (Delhi, 1990).
68. Sir Francis Tuker, in C. H. Philips and M Wainwright (eds), *The Partition of India* (London, 1970), p. 133.
69. Harun-or-Rashid, *The Foreshadowing of Bangladesh: The Bengal Muslim League and Muslim Politics, 1906–1947* (Dhaka, 2003), p. 242.
70. Ayesha Jalal, *The Sole Spokesman: Jinnah, the Muslim League and the Demand for Pakistan* (Cambridge, 1985), pp. 216–17.
71. These documents were produced in *Legislative Assembly Debates*, 20 September 1946.
72. Gandhi to Wavell, 28 August 1928, in Moon (ed.), *Wavell*, p. 342.
73. Royal Institute of International Affairs, *Chronology and Index of the Second World War* (London, 1975), p. 351; Churchill stated on 29 May1945 that the total number of deaths of British Commonwealth and Empire Armed Forces personnel till 28 February 1945 was 307, 210; Royal Institute of International Affairs, *Chronology and Index of the Second World War*, p. 354.
74. M. Mukherjee, *Churchill's Secret War*, p. 396; this work by Mukherjee sheds new light on policy-making in London and the role of Churchill which I have tried not to cover in this book for it will take us on a tangent into party politics in the UK in those times.

8

'THE EDGE OF A VOLCANO' 1946–7

The rush of events leading to the Partition of Bengal was vertiginous. A very perceptive contemporary journalist, Abul Mansur Ahmed, writes: 'One could not understand at all for what reasons how and what happened.... It was as if it was all magical'.[1] The sequence of events and the decision-making processes at the level of the Viceroy and the clients and contestants among the Congress and Muslim League leaders need to be narrated in some detail with the help of documents now available. Unlike the other chapters in this book, this and the following chapter aim to give a narrative closely following the sequence of events. This may answer some questions: What was the role of Mountbatten in Delhi and Governor Burrows in Calcutta in determining the fate of Bengal? Why was Calcutta proposed to be constituted as an international 'free' city outside of both West and East Bengal? How was the idea of setting up an independent State of Bengal as a sovereign entity born and how did it meet its end? What was the attitude of the much-maligned central leadership of the Congress and the Muslim League? Knowledge of some of these developments was always limited because a great deal that happened in the corridors of power in Delhi and Simla did not become public until the publication of the Transfer of Power documents. Memory of what was known is fading and, to begin with, a bias enters into what we would like to remember—each community will cast blame on the other by means of a selective public memory and excision from it. Finally, a sense of guilt afflicts the elite on both sides of the divide, giving rise to a marked tendency to transfer the guilt to some agency of history beyond the borders of Bengal, chiefly the central leadership. All this makes a narration and examination of what happened difficult and yet necessary.

'Plan Balkan'

On 22 March 1947, Kiran Shankar Roy, the leader of the Opposition and a member of the Legislative Assembly since 1933, met the Governor of Bengal, Sir Frederick Burrows. The Governor was new to his job but had had vast political experience as the President of the National Union of Railwaymen in England. He was supposed to have said—or this was said of him maliciously by the upper crust—that he was unlike his predecessors who were in the 'hunting-and-shooting set' in that he was better at 'shunting and hooting' like a railway-man. Whatever his social background might have been, he proved to be a good watchdog of imperial interests. In their long conversation, K.S. Roy, by way of testing the waters, raised the question whether Bengal should 'stand by itself as an independent state'.[2] Burrows tried to persuade Roy that 'to enable a peaceful transfer to be made' in Bengal a coalition ministry, including the Congress and the League, was needed—'irrespective of what happened in the rest of India'. The latter point is interesting in that it sought to delink the emergent status of Bengal from the Indian Union. Roy apparently agreed with the Governor that a coalition was desirable.

What were the chances of a coalition ministry? A quick glance at major news items in *Ananda Bazar Patrika* will convey the state of communal relations in late 1946 and early 1947. Chief Minister Suhrawardy was suspected by the Hindu community of complicity in the Calcutta Riot of August 1946 on Direct Action Day called by Jinnah.[3] Grievances were exacerbated by the rejection of a Congress demand in the Legislative Assembly for an enquiry—by 29 votes to 17.[4] On top of this came a government circular in September 1946 threatening a ban on newspapers that reported communal incidents in a 'provocative way'. The *Ananda Bazar*, in defiance of this, wrote a strong editorial.[5] Soon there was another circular controlling the type and size of headlines.[6] The incidents of communal violence in Noakhali in East Bengal attracted national attention; J.B. Kripalani and Sarat Bose visited Noakhali in October and Gandhi himself came to Calcutta to discuss the problem with the Governor.[7] On 4 November 1946,

Nehru, Patel, and Maulana Azad came to Calcutta and heard Mahatma Gandhi's reports and views on communal violence in Noakhali.[8] Gandhi began his historic tour through that district on 3 January 1947.[9] Thus the climate of opinion could not be favourable to the idea of coalition when, in the beginning of 1947, Governor Burrows and Chief Minister Suhrawardy began to push the idea of a coalition ministry. On 11 April 1947, Burrows sent a secret report to Mountbatten that the 'partitionists mean business'; at the Tarakeshwar Conference, the Hindu Mahasabha authorized SyamaPrasad Mookerjee to form a council of action and a volunteer force to secure a 'homeland for Hindus of Bengal'.[10] The Bengal Provincial Congress urged the formation of two regional ministries to enable smooth transfer of power to the portion of Bengal that would join the Indian Union.[11]

It was well known that Governor Burrows in Calcutta was strongly in favour of an 'Independent United Bengal'. So was Chief Minister Suhrawardy. The latter called on Sir Thomas Showe, in the middle of April and 'expressed his utmost distaste for a divided Bengal'.[12] He 'wanted foreign capital and the assistance of British enterprise to develop Bengal', and desired 'close connexion with Great Britain'—indeed he could 'offer Bengal to England on a platter'.[13] The report of this conversation was, of course, transmitted to the Viceroy as was no doubt intended by the Chief Minister. Suhrawardy's prediction was that India would 'split into a considerable number of separate portions'. This fitted into what was known at that time as 'Plan Balkan' in Mountbatten's inner circle. He expounded the idea at a staff meeting on 12 April; no Indian was present. If the Cabinet Mission plan or some modified form of it, was not acceptable to the Indian leaders, the 'Top Secret' memo of proceedings of the staff meeting says, the alternative would be 'Plan Balkan… leaving to each Province the choice of its own future' leading to the 'eventual abolition of Centre'.[14]

'Edge of a Volcano'

On 15 April, at Mountbatten's first Provincial Governors' Conference, Burrows was absent due to illness. His representative, J.D. Tyson, ICS, his Secretary, announced that in their opinion 'Eastern Bengal alone was not a going concern', no more than 'a rural slum', and thus to 'sell East Bengal as a feasible proposition' to the Muslims was impossible. Tyson reported the Governor's view that Suhrawardy 'wanted to run Bengal as an independent province with a Muslim majority'.[15] Mountbatten was convinced that Suhrawardy would not agree to a partition of Bengal while Jinnah might react against an independent status for Bengal; the Congress would also be against it for it went 'against everything that Congress stood for'. Both difficulties, Mountbatten thought, could be removed 'if the majority of both communities in Bengal opt for independence and unity of Bengal'.[16] He reported to the Secretary of State, the Earl of Listowel, his opinion that 'we are sitting on the edge of a volcano' and Bengal was one of the craters where an explosion might take place—this was by way of incidentally highlighting what a great job he (Mountbatten) was doing.[17] While aware of the need for caution, Mountbatten was at the same time, like Governor Burrows, supportive of the idea of an independent and united Bengal. The next day, 8 April, Burrows sent a secret cable to the Viceroy that he had 'made it clear to Suhrawardy' that acceptance of the Cabinet Mission plan or 'a very strong coalition government ... immediately in Bengal'[18] were the only options, coalition being evidently a means towards unity and independence.

In the meantime, the pro-Partition group made an effort to catch the attention of the Viceroy. Dr S.P. Mookerjee met him on 23 April to urge 'the necessity for partitioning Bengal if the Cabinet Mission plan were to fail'. Mountbatten gave him little time—they met at 12.30 p.m. shortly before lunch—and asked him to talk to his Chief of Staff, Lord Ismay, making no comment on Mookerjee's plea.[19] Later in the afternoon that day, Mountbatten and his aides met Jinnah. The latter is reported, in the official minutes, to have said that he would be 'prepared to consider any plan which Congress might let him have for the partition of Bengal and the Punjab'.[20] At the same time, he said that 'he had not accepted the partition of Bengal and the Punjab, as reported in certain Hindu newspapers, but had not considered it worthwhile to issue denials'. This ambiguity remained a feature of Jinnah's pronouncements on the partitioning of Bengal.

Special Dispensation for Calcutta

The next day, 24 April, the Governor of Bengal wrote an important memo to the Viceroy, once again marked 'Top Secret':

> The Hindus at the General Election (1946) may be said to have voted for Congress ideals and against Pakistan. The present Partition agitation

> is in fact an anti-Pakistan movement—those who support it would rather face the division of Bengal, in order to retain a connection with a Hindu-controlled Central Government, than remain in an independent Bengal (whether Muslim-controlled or under joint Hindu–Muslim control) or a Bengal linked with some form of Pakistan. On the other hand, more than 90% of the Muslim voters of Bengal at the General Election supported the Muslim League's Pakistan programme.... This means that in existing circumstances the only safeguard is to assume that all Muslims favour some form of Pakistan and most Hindus (there are no other significant non-Muslim communities in Bengal) oppose coming into any form of Pakistan and would prefer a partitioned Bengal with the Hindu part linked with a Central Government at New Delhi.[21]

Burrows maintained that contiguity of Hindu areas made partition possible. But he made two other vital points:

1. He said he had given his views only in response to a query despatched from Delhi to all Governors regarding contingency plans for partition, and was putting up a scheme of partition because he had been asked to do so and not because he believed in it. Burrows also held forth on 'a revolt in East Bengal and furious rioting in Calcutta' in the event of Partition.
2. For Calcutta, he proposed a special provision:

   > If a means could be found, within the formula of partition, to preserve for the future province of East Bengal an equal right with West Bengal to facilities in, to revenues accruing from, and to unrestricted access to, the city and suburbs of Calcutta, it would be unquestionably for the benefit both of Calcutta and of the two Provinces and would really be a fair solution. The constitution of Calcutta as a sort of condominium might go a long way in the last resort to reconcile the Muslim League to the partitioning of Bengal.[22]

The next day, 25 April, Mountbatten at his staff meeting raised the issue of a special dispensation for Calcutta since it was 'the second largest city of the Empire and it was bound to be a major issue'.[23] Should the Government of India agree to a plebiscite in Calcutta? The consensus of senior ICS officers was against it, because it was tantamount to 'inviting a bloodbath', and because the same logic could apply to other cities like Lahore. However, Mountbatten did not, as we shall see later, give up this line. Calcutta was a useful bargaining counter in negotiations to dissuade the pro-partitionists.

The very next day, 26 April, the Governor of Bengal cabled to the Viceroy that 'Jinnah's attitude is likely to be strongly influenced by arrangement contemplated for Calcutta'.[24] It was suggested to the Viceroy that the draft of HMG's ('His Majesty's Government' in bureaucratic acronym) announcement in London of transfer of power modalities be revised to include a special arrangement for Calcutta; this was said to be—and this is rather extraordinary from a subordinate government—'mandatory in announcement'. The arrangement now proposed by Burrows was that the city of Calcutta would not be included, in the event of a partition, in either of the two Bengals and would be separately administered by a Council with an equal number of members from both sides.

A group of Mountbatten's aides led by Lord Ismay considered this plan impracticable; they thought that since the draft had already been circulated to the Indian leaders, changes suggested by the Governor of Bengal could not be inserted without reopening troublesome negotiations with them, risking delay in action.[25] However, the plan given by Governor Burrows had many lives and reappeared in later negotiations over and again. It is probable that not only Muslim leaders' assertion of a claim to a share of Calcutta in some form, but also British business interests there desired a special status for the city outside the proposed 'Hindu' and 'Muslim' provinces or states of West and East Bengal.

Opinions Harden

As the political forces began to line up on either side of the battlefront, for and against Partition, the Bengal government began to find the 'Hindu' newspapers troublesome. The *Ananda Bazar Patrika*, along with *Amrita Bazar*, took the lead in pushing forward the partition proposal. The former editorialized on 7 April on the desirability of 'A Separate Province of Bengal';[26] this was followed on 12 April by a memorandum by many members of the central legislature proposing separation.[27] It may not be a coincidence that by the end of the month *Ananda Bazar* forfeited the deposit with the government, Rs 7,000, for objectionable reports on the Noakhali riots; a fresh deposit of Rs 17,000 was demanded by the government.[28]

In fact, since the August 1946 Riot, this newspaper had been very outspoken in criticizing the League Ministry in Bengal under Suhrawardy. Editorials entitled 'They Should Go', 'Crisis of Hindu Community', 'A Government Hiding from Light', 'Demand of the *Akhand* (Indivisible) Hindu Community', in late 1946 and early 1947 had raised the pitch of the dissenting voice in League-ruled Bengal.[29] On 15 January 1947, the *Ananda Bazar* editorialized on 'Bengal's Demand' to put forward a plea for an end to 'communalist' rule and to demand the protection that membership of the Indian Union would ensure.[30] In March 1947, many of the Bengali members of the central legislature met Nehru and Patel to convince them that a separate state of West Bengal was a desideratum in the political context prevailing.[31] A Hindu Mahasabha Conference chaired by S.P. Mookerjee endorsed the same demand.[32] Hindu sentiment was so strong that it was proposed that until Partition took place, as an interim measure separate ministries be set up in West and East Bengal; this was the suggestion of the Bengal Provincial Congress Committee on 22 April 1947. This was also the proposal, with the full-throated support of newspapers like the *Ananda Bazar*, in the resolution passed by the Council of the Calcutta Corporation three weeks later.[33]

On 26 April, at 3 p.m., Suhrawardy met Mountbatten at the Viceregal Palace, to be followed by Jinnah at 5 p.m. Mountbatten told Suhrawardy: 'Although I was against splitting India up into many units, I considered it far better to keep Bengal as one economic unit than to have it partitioned'. Suhrawardy thought that the Bengal partition was avoidable and 'given enough time he was confident that he could get Bengal to remain as a complete entity'.[34] Earlier, Suhrawardy had been given a briefing by Chief of Staff, Ismay, to convey to him 'an idea of the general way our minds were working'. And what Suhrawardy said to Mountbatten was in perfect accord with the Viceregal plans. The next day, on 27 April, Suhrawardy issued a celebrated statement from Delhi, proposing the establishment of a United Independent Bengal. In the meanwhile, within an hour of Suhrawardy's leaving the room, Mountbatten checked with Jinnah: the Viceroy asked 'straight out what his views were about keeping Bengal united at the price of its remaining out of Pakistan'. Jinnah said, according to Mountbatten's notes, he would be 'delighted' and 'what is the use of Bengal [that is, East Bengal] without Calcutta; they had much better remain united and independent; I am sure that they would be on friendly terms with us'.[35]

This is the background to Suhrawardy's statement on 27 April 1947 on a united and independent Bengal. Starry-eyed idealists who retrospectively pine for a United Bengal might pay attention to these circumstances. In this statement Suhrawardy very correctly described the pro-partition sentiment as a consequence of the frustration of Bengali Hindus with their exclusion from the Bengal Ministry, 1937–47. He underlined, again quite appropriately, the desirability of keeping Bengal united in the interest of economic integration and the needs of a strong workable state. Suhrawardy indulged in harsh criticism of non-Bengalis who had no roots in Bengal, a rather risky political line in view of their presence among Muslim League bigwigs and particularly businessmen. He also claimed for a sort of greater Bengal some adjoining districts in Assam and Bihar. Suhrawardy's statement included a noble appeal to the goodwill of the Hindu community. Such an appeal from someone like Fazlul Huq might have worked, and it might have worked at some other time when communalism did not taint the mind of Bengal. As it happened, the day Suhrawardy issued the statement communal conflicts took place in the streets of Calcutta; on 28 April *Ananda Bazar* reported six deaths and curfew orders; incidentally, this newspaper's deposit was forfeited to the government three days later.[36]

There was a section in both communities that sincerely believed in an undivided Bengal. Among them was Abul Hashim of the Muslim League who received, on the day Suhrawardy made his statement, a deputation from Sarat Bose's camp. On 29 April, Hashim issued a statement against defeatist and reactionary pro-partition sentiments that tended to surrender to a leadership alien to Bengal, in disregard of her great traditions.[37] We shall come to Sarat Bose's role later, but what was remarkable was that Hashim's proposal for *joint* electorates and *equal share* of both communities in administration was immediately attacked by many Muslim leaders although they had issued statements in support of Suhrawardy's position; to demand a united Bengal and to fail to translate what that meant in terms of future electorates and power and jobs was not, however, a sustainable position and failed to create confidence on the other side of the communal divide.[38] The fact that veteran leaders like former chief minister Nazimuddin and Bengal Muslim League President Maulana Akram Khan and some Muslim newspapers attacked Abul Hashim, casts some doubt on their sincerity in advocating a united Bengal with the two communities.

To get back to the 'central' forum of transfer of power in Delhi, there was little doubt about the position of Patel and much confusion about the stance of Jinnah. Patel's position coincided with the latest position of the Hindu Mahasabha. Early in April, he told Mountbatten that 'the mistake all the British had permanently [*sic*] made with Mr. Jinnah was always to give way to him'. Patel believed it would be best for the Viceroy to announce straightaway that Bengal would be partitioned and that would compel the League to climb down.[39] He reported to Mountbatten his belief that 'the feeling in Bengal among non-Muslims was that, whether there was partition or not, they could not remain united unless joint electorates were introduced'.[40] Patel tried, according to Mountbatten, to manipulate public opinion in favour of his position by leaking transfer of power plans and discussions to the Press. Actually, these two men could not get on with each other right from the beginning when Mountbatten threatened to resign rather than put up with his 'impudence': 'I was flying home to resign my appointment unless Patel left the Interim government', he said.[41] The latter backed down under this pressure but they did not become the best of friends. And Patel's consistent opposition to anything except partition for Bengal irritated Mountbatten. While the Hindu Mahasabha campaign in 1947, led by Dr S.P. Mookerjee and N.C. Chatterjee, went ahead on its own steam, Patel encouraged it from a distance; from a distance, because Patel worked through the Congress, the Mahasabha having been shown up as a rather weak force with only one win in thirty-one seats contested in the Bengal general elections in 1946. Patel's correspondence indicates contact with Dr Mookerjee in the early part of 1947.[42]

M.A. Jinnah managed to thoroughly confuse the British aides of the Viceroy on the Bengal question during the secret negotiations in Delhi in April and May 1947. By the end of April, the Viceroy's Chief of Staff, Lord Ismay, told Governor Burrows that Jinnah was ready to accept Partition in Bengal. When Mountbatten, by way of testing out a possible scenario, told Jinnah that if he insisted on Pakistan partition of Bengal and Punjab would follow, 'Jinnah made astonishingly little protest and our strong impression is that he is so keen to get the principle of Pakistan settled once for all, that he will acquiesce' that is, accept 'what has come to be known as truncated Pakistan, which excludes Calcutta'.[43] This impression was shared with Ismay by Mountbatten who told the Governors' Conference on 15 April that the idea of partition of Bengal was 'virtually accepted' by Jinnah.[44] On 23 April, Jinnah, at a meeting with the Viceroy 'said that he would be prepared to consider' partition of Bengal.[45] His sister, Fatima, told Lady Mountbatten the next day that exchange of population was on the cards in Bengal and Punjab.[46] Thus it would be inaccurate to say that Jinnah never accepted the partitioning of Bengal.

However, once the principle of Pakistan was settled, Jinnah altered his approach a little. On 26 and 30 April—possibly after being briefed by Suhrawardy, who visited Delhi, on the strong support, almost amounting to an initiative, of Governor Burrows on 'United Bengal'—Jinnah began to speak of the need to ascertain the 'will of the people'.[47] He specially harped on the point that the Scheduled Castes might not line up with the high-caste Congress leadership. Whatever his real views might have been, it is probable that he saw merit in the idea of a united, independent Bengal, and of Calcutta as an 'international city', as bargaining points in his negotiations on larger issues.

Lobbies and Pressures

'There was a definite attempt, because of the feeling of frustration among the Hindus in Bengal, to get command of at least a part of the province'.[48] Thus summed up the Governor of Bengal, on 1 May1947, anticipating many a future Ph. D. theses.

Based on this characterization of the 'Hindu' attitude to the Partition question, there was a strategy developed by Governor Burrows. He bounced back into action, after a spell of illness, and secured an important concession from the Viceroy at the Governors' Conference on 1 May. To prepare ground for a 'united and independent Bengal', which Suhrawardy had already publicly announced on 26 April, a coalition government would be useful and Burrows had been pressing this advice on Suhrawardy for a long time; now the Viceroy endorsed the idea and asked Burrows to renew his effort. Secondly, the Viceroy instructed him 'to persuade Mr. Suhrawardy to make a promise of joint electorates in the future if a decision on a unified independent Bengal was reached'. Some other proposals of Burrows were not accepted, at least for the moment. For example, Burrows wanted to keep Calcutta outside the administration of the two Bengals in the event of Partition: Calcutta 'should if possible be given the chance to serve both halves of Bengal, if the province was partitioned'; it would slightly alleviate the economic condition of East Bengal, although Burrrows maintained that Partition would be a disaster for East Bengal for 'economically it could not survive'. Suhrawardy, he reported, was 'prepared to accept Calcutta as an international city' administered by, as Burrows proposed, a council of five Hindus and five Muslims elected from each half of Bengal.[49] At the Governors' Conference this idea was considered dubious by some of those present on the grounds that 'Hindus represented 76% of the population of the city and owned 90% of investments', and that 'a degree of goodwill between communities was surely being assumed that was not likely to exist'.[50]

Burrows had expressed his opposition to the partition of Bengal earlier and he had said that 'we should as soon as possible put the responsibility for settling the problem of partition squarely on Indian shoulders'.[51] Now that such surrogates did indeed materialize, in the form of pro-partitionists among Congress and Hindu leaders, he was far from being pleased. 'Dr. Mukherjee [*sic*] was a clever and unscrupulous politician. The Hindu Mahasabha had failed completely to gain representation in the Legislative Assembly, except for Dr. Mukherji's own seat. They were, however, good propagandists'.[52]

Mookerjee, perhaps acting on a shrewd guess about Burrows' advice to the Viceroy, shot off a long letter to Mountbatten on 2 May and K.S. Roy went to meet him the next day. Roy, the leader of the Opposition in the Bengal Legislature, was allowed by Mountbatten only half an hour. He came with the signature of seventy-four non-Muslim legislators demanding partition. When Mountbatten underlined the desirability of a unified Bengal, Roy's reply was that he was 'driven to recommending partition by the intransigence of the Muslim League and pressure from Congress'. Roy was persuaded, somewhat too easily, by Mountbatten to go back to Suhrawardy and Burrows and try a coalition government. Thus Roy came to demand one thing and was sent back to Bengal with a totally different plan of action.

> Mr. Roy got more and more excited as the meeting progressed … he now wanted to have my advice as to what he ought to do. I advised

> him strongly to go straight back to Calcutta and see Mr. Suhrawardy and then go on to Darjeeling and see the Governor. 'You have not a moment to lose', I told him; upon which he got up dramatically, shook me warmly by the hand, and left the room.

Mountbatten's account makes the encounter rather laughable.[53]

The letter that S.P. Mookerjee wrote to Mountbatten on 2 May was basically premised upon Jinnah's argument. It is curious how enemies end up mimicking each other. 'Mr. Jinnah's claim for Pakistan is based on the theory that Hindus and Muslims are two separate nations.... The same logic and argument applicable to Pakistan apply also to the partition of Bengal'.[54] Mookerjee added for good measure that, if 24 per cent of India's Muslim population had a legitimate claim to a separate homeland, 45 per cent of Bengal's population, being Hindu, had an equal claim. He went on to say, rather glibly, how population exchange was possible; however, he added elsewhere in his letter that protection of minority communities was bound to be implemented as a matter of mutual interest by both the governments. Finally, Mookerjee ended with a denunciation of the 'loose talk of sovereign undivided Bengal ... sovereign undivided Bengal will be virtual Pakistan'.[55] Here again he echoes Jinnah who said that if such a Bengal emerged, it would be 'on friendly terms with us', that is, Pakistan.[56] Mookerjee asked: 'Who will frame the constitution of sovereign Bengal? Obviously that will be left in the hands of the majority of the Muslim Leaguers who will be guided by fanatical notions of separate nationhood.... Further, we do not in any case want to be cut off from the rest of India'.[57] Thus, he says, there must be 'a territory assigned to us wherein we can live without fear and enjoy the fruits of peace and freedom, without depriving the other major community of the rightful interests in the area in which it predominates'.

Thus the battle lines were drawn. If he dithered—most unusually for him—and dither he did till now, he dithered no longer. He supported partition of Bengal with the same vehemence as that displayed by pro-partitionists; so did Jinnah till it became clear that the Viceroy and the Government in England had decided irrevocably in favour of Partition in India, and at that point Jinnah reverted to his earlier ambivalent position and eventually accepted the *fait accompli*.

Huffing Calcutta

Neither the Viceroy nor the Governor of Bengal gave up their project. The day Mountbatten received Mookerjee's memorandum, 2 May, he wrote to Burrows:

> You pointed out to me that Eastern Bengal would be in a bad way after Partition because all the jute factories were located in Calcutta in Western Bengal. It has since occurred to me that Calcutta could be completely huffed by Eastern Bengal if approaches were made at once to the various jute factories (most of which are in British hands and, I believe controlled from Dundee) to transfer their machinery to a suitable location in Eastern Bengal so that the jute and the factories would be in the same half of the province. This would be such a serious matter for Calcutta that if it could be converted into a live threat by preliminary negotiations being started and the news being allowed to 'leak' I feel it might influence the Hindus to accept independent unity rather than partition. This is only one of the many things that could be thought out to frighten off those who wish Partition.[58]

This Viceregal brainwave proved to be useless. No more useful was his further suggestion to 'frighten off' the pro-partitionists by threatening 'to insist on a general election on the electoral roll' of 1946. As regards huffing Calcutta by transferring the jute mills, Burrows pointed to the facts Mountbatten was unaware of. Of about a hundred jute mills in Bengal, all were located in the Calcutta industrial area; a dozen were completely Indian-owned and 'it is estimated that probably 75% of capital of the rest is in Indian hands, with Hindus vastly predominating. Only four or five are sterling companies'.[59] Not only would the threat of shifting the industry be incredible under these circumstances, but there was no power supply and infrastructure in East Bengal.

As regards the threat of general elections, Burrows was compelled to junk that idea as well. His Ministry would not like another election within a year of being elected and an election would need preparation for at least four months.[60] This last point must have been decisive against election or referendum so far as Mountbatten was concerned for he was, as is well-known, a man in a hurry. He could fall back on an alternative scheme which he privately confided to Listowel, the Secretary of State for India.[61] This was to make a special provision for a vote by the Bengal legislators, first to decide on independence *or* Pakistan *or* Hindustan, and a second vote on Partition. 'Burrows' great point is that his Chief Minister, Suhrawardy, is almost certain to be able to fix the first voting in favour of independence', and, therefore, the demand for Partition would fail. In the event, as we shall see, this scheme also failed.

Apart from half a dozen sterling companies in the jute industry, and at least 25 per cent interest in eighty other jute mills, the British had substantial trading and banking interests in Calcutta. That apart, it was such a focal point of the Empire that it is understandable that the fate of Calcutta exercised the Viceroy's and the British bureaucracy's mind. Whether Rear-Admiral Mountbatten, as an oceanic strategist, also appreciated the utility of hanging on to Port Calcutta, as a 'free city', is difficult to say. In any case, the lengths to which he was prepared to go at this point of time—contemplating deliberate 'leakage' of negotiations or 'fixing' votes—appears extraordinary. Sympathy for the League played no role in this; it was common knowledge that he had begun to dislike Jinnah intensely—'psychopath' was a term he often applied to him—and, as for Burrows, he seemed to look upon Suhrawardy merely as a not-too-difficult instrument that he had to live with.

Burrows, Suhrawardy, Bose

Burrows continued his efforts behind the scenes with Suhrawardy. On May 3, they met, and after having 'put him in good humour' with a compliment—that he had 'made a hit with the Viceroy' at the April 26 tête-à-tête which has been described—Burrows broached the issue of a coalition government.[62] In his report to Mountbatten, he said: 'It is evident that he had taken no active step whatever on my previous suggestion.... For the formation of a coalition he must make terms with the Hindus in Bengal'. Suhrawardy 'undertook to initiate steps immediately on these lines and informed me that he was seeing Sarat Bose on the matter that afternoon'.[63] Thus primed by the Governor of Bengal and explicitly encouraged by the Viceroy, the Chief Minister of Bengal met Sarat Chandra Bose to frame the well-known Suhrawardy–Bose Plan.

Bose was being brought in at a rather late stage. Nor did he have, as far as our evidence goes, any knowledge of the discussions between

Suhrawardy, Mountbatten, and Burrows over the past several weeks. He was embittered by his experience in the Congress; not only did his brother, Subhas Chandra, nurse a grievance against the Congress establishment, but Sarat Bose himself was pushed out unceremoniously from the central Interim Government within a very short time of his inclusion. As early as October 1946, Sarat Bose had confided to Abul Hashim, the General Secretary of the Bengal Muslim League, his disillusionment with the central Congress leaders, particularly Patel. According to Hashim, it was he who converted Bose into a supporter of the idea of a united independent Bengal.[64] Be that as it may, when Suhrawardy met Bose he found the latter enthusiastically in favour of the concept of Bengal put forward in Suhrawardy's April 27 statement.

It will be clear later in this narrative that action on the lines of Suhrawardy's scheme needed, on his part, two separate but connected manoeuvres vis-á-vis the 'Hindu' leadership: (*a*) creation of an atmosphere for exchange of views on Bengal's future, probable political structure of a unified Bengal, the features of a constitution for independent Bengal, and so on, and (*b*) forming, or gestures towards forming, a coalition government that would include Hindu leaders so as to facilitate transfer of power to a united Bengal. Creating a good impression in the first manoeuvre was necessary to attain the second objective. In the first of these two lines to be pursued, Sarat Bose was a man who mattered due to his undoubted integrity, his track record and that of his brother, and his predisposition to support the idea of an independent Bengal. In the pursuit of the second objective, a coalition or an impression that this was in the offing, the cooperation of Kiran Shankar Roy was needed for he was the Leader of the Opposition.

There began talks between Suhrawardy (aided by League representatives Khwaja Nazimuddin, Fazlur Rahman, Abul Hashim, and two others) and Sarat Bose (aided by K.S. Roy, N.R. Sarkar, and S.R. Bakshi—all Hindus). The outcome was a joint statement on 20 May signed by both groups at Sarat Bose's house. Let us anticipate that development for the sake of completing this episode: the agreement propounded a 'Free State of Bengal' as the objective. It was assumed that its constitution would provide joint electorates with seat reservations proportionate to the population of the two communities. It was also declared that upon transfer of power from HMG a new Ministry of the State of Bengal would be formed with a Muslim chief minister and a Hindu home minister. Pending the formation of a legislature under the constitution to be framed, for the time being Hindus and Muslims would have equal share in state services thereafter. Finally, it was declared that a Constituent Assembly of 16 Muslims and 14 Hindus would draw up the constitution of the future state.

This was too little and too late. Had there been an attempt to draw up a constitution and a political framework of the projected unified independent Bengal earlier in the day, it might have had a slight chance of success. May 20 was only two weeks away from the scheduled day of the announcement by His Majesty's Government of the modalities of transfer of power; Mountbatten was already in London ironing out details with the Prime Minister and the Cabinet. For the administrators in India, the Partition plans were no longer on the drawing board open to amendment. Moreover, among politicians, opinions had hardened and irrevocable positions been taken. However, let us revert to the chronological sequence of events.

The Fear of Balkanization

In the early part of May, while negotiations between Suhrawardy and Bose were going on, news of the scheme for a United Independent Bengal began to spread. One unfortunate thing was that most of the statements highlighted in both Muslim and Hindu newspapers were those from Muslim League leaders against partition of Bengal: Maulana Akram Ali, the President of the Bengal League, on 19 April, Khwaja Nazimuddin on 23 April, Suhrawardy on 27 April and again 7 May. Although many of these leaders, described by Harun-or-Rashid as *akhand* Pakistanis, were dissembling or confused for a while, their public statements created an impression.[65] Thus the scheme was identified with the Muslim League in many people's perception while Sarat Bose was busy explaining the finer points of the scheme talking with Gandhi. The latter did not approve the scheme, as we shall see later.

In the meanwhile, opponents of the scheme began to gather forces. Vallabhbhai Patel's letters to Syama Prasad Mookerjee, K.C. Neogy, Binoy Roy, and others in the second and third week of May indicate that. Moreover, Patel was not alone in thinking it was a 'trap' set by the League; men like V.P. Menon doubted whether Jinnah could agree to the demands of the Hindu half of the alliance proposed and thus, without attributing any motivation to the Bengal leaders, cast doubts on the eventual outcome.[66] Curiously, Nehru, at the regular meetings with the Viceroy and his aides, refrained from making any remark till May 11. He only referred to Suhrawardy's statement of May 7; the statement, Nehru said, was 'in the main sweet and reasonable containing as it did an appeal not to split Bengal' but it contained an implied threat to Calcutta.[67] Actually, Suhrawardy had simply said that the move to partition Bengal was 'merely an attempt to get the rich prize of Calcutta and thus to deprive Muslims of trade and commerce', and if Calcutta thus became a bone of contention, 'what will remain of it?'[68]

Later, Mountbatten asked Burrows about the warning or threat Nehru read in Suhrawardy's statement. Burrows stoutly defended Suhrawardy—'sound and conciliatory', 'statesmanlike'—and refuted the view that a threat was implied. He said, at the same time, that realistically speaking it was probable that Calcutta would 'become a battleground'.[69]

At a routine meeting with the Viceroy and his aides, Nehru made on 11 May his first statement on the question in that forum.

> Congress had been forced to recommend Partition. He personally hoped that the conception of partition would recede. He would be willing to consider any special arrangements with Bengal and the Punjab but the feeling of the people in Western Bengal was an important factor. The situation in Bengal had become intolerable for them. There was not likely to be more than one per cent of non-Muslims who would agree to independence; Calcutta had been half-ruined in the last six months.[70]

His chief argument was that 'the division of Bengal was harmful from many points of view', he was willing to consider 'special arrangements' for Bengal. Now we come to the factor that really spoilt all chances the 'united independent Bengal' scheme might have had with Nehru and the Congress. What Nehru said above on 11 May at the meeting was insignificant compared to what he wrote to Mountbatten the same day; this was a personally addressed letter along with an official sort of memorandum. These were written in the morning of 11 May after Nehru had spent the night poring over the draft of the Transfer of Power plans, given to him by Mountbatten the previous evening with the request to Nehru, a house-guest of the Mountbattens at that time, to comment on the plans 'as an act of friendship'.[71] The contents of these papers were to have been discussed with Nehru by Lord Ismay; but since Ismay had, Mountbatten says, the Delhi belly, Mieville stood in for him. Perhaps there was some failure of communication there. Moreover, the plans were redrafted in London by the Cabinet Committee.[72] At any rate, the draft given now by Mountbatten was quite unacceptable to Nehru. To Mountbatten, Nehru's letters conveying this feeling were 'bombshells'.

What was Nehru's objection and how did it affect Bengal? Nehru's impression, upon reading the draft by the HMG, was that it presented 'an entirely new picture'; it was a picture of 'fragmentation and conflict and disorder' in post-1947 India, which produced 'a devastating effect upon me'.[73] Nehru formed the impression that the modalities and format of transfer of power now proposed by HMG would promote Balkanization and fragmentation of India: 'The proposals start with the rejection of an Indian Union as the successor to power and invite the claims of large numbers of succession states who are permitted to unite if they so wish in two or more states'.[74]

Nehru had in mind a crucial passage in the HMG draft of the Transfer of Power announcement.

> HMG are satisfied that the best procedure in time available is to enable different parts of India [this included all the Provinces of British India, as clarified in two succeeding paragraphs] to decide through representatives chosen for this purpose whether their constitution shall be framed (a) in collaboration with existing constituent assembly, (b) or jointly with other parts of India, (c) separately.[75]

This, translated into the action contemplated, was a choice to be exercised by every province whether it would (*a*) join the Indian Union, (*b*) join Pakistan, or (*c*) opt for Independent Status separate from both India and Pakistan. It will be recalled that Mountbatten had contemplated for Bengal precisely this set of options; to propose that as a special arrangement for Bengal was, however, one thing and to extend that by the logic of parity to all provinces of British India was quite another. Nehru said that the HMG had now proposed a procedure that would (*a*) 'invite Balkanization of India', (*b*) promote a further 'breakdown of central authority which alone can prevent the chaos that is growing', and (*c*) 'create many Ulsters in India'.[76] In conclusion, Nehru wrote:

> Whatever the views of my colleagues might be to various details of the proposals, I have no doubt that their main reaction will be as I have

> indicated above. That is that they cannot accept these proposals and they are not prepared to acquiesce in the throwing overboard of the basic all-India Union or to accept the theory of Provinces being initially independent successor states.[77]

It is probable that if the case of Bengal had been unique in the HMG proposals, that is, if for Bengal alone a choice between India or Pakistan or independence had been proposed as an exceptional measure in the interest of preserving its unity, the chances of acceptance would have been better. But under the transfer of power proposal drafted by the Cabinet Committee in London, as it stood on 11 May, when Nehru saw it, each province of British India could develop into an independent state. From this moment, the fear of Balkanization seemed to dominate the mind of Nehru and his colleagues and this moulded their attitude to the Suhrawardy–Bose scheme.

A Fateful Day: 12 May

On receiving Nehru's letter and memorandum—which Mountbatten described as a 'bombshell'—he shot off a secret telegramme to Prime Minister Attlee. He told the latter that further proceedings of the Indian Government on the transfer of power question were on hold; he also cabled Nehru's memo of 11 May to London for circulation to the Cabinet Committee for India.[78] He telegraphed Ismay in London instructions to prepare ground for revision of the draft proposals on transfer of power.[79] Sir E. Mieville cabled Lord Ismay: 'We are naturally a bit rattled by Nehru's volte-face'.[80]

On 12 May at his staff meeting in the morning, Mountbatten declared that he had 'decided that the plan should be redrafted on the basis of no option for independence being given to Bengal or any other province. It would, he pointed out, always be possible to reconsider this decision at any time if there was a united request for independence'.[81]

While Mountbatten was conducting his staff meeting, exactly at the same time, 11.30 a.m. on 12 May, there began a Chiefs of Staff meeting in London, as yet unaware of the dramatic developments in Delhi. The Chiefs of Staff discussed a query from the Prime Minister regarding the strategic military implications of accepting, inter alia, Bengal as a member of the Commonwealth when the rest of India goes out. The possession of a seaboard by a Commonwealth country was considered important by the PM.[82] The Chiefs of Staff, including Admiral Cunningham, Field-Marshall Montgomery, and Lord Tedder of the Royal Air Force (RAF), decided that it would be useful to have Bengal as well as any other territory as parts of the Commonwealth—especially Pakistan, said Montgomery of Alamein.[83]

The same day, 12 May, General Smuts of South Africa took it upon himself to give the Prime Minister an interesting suggestion. If the choice of independence was being given to the provinces of British India, surely the choice of remaining under British rule should also be offered to them? Smuts wrote,

> Britain on her part again may well pause before voluntarily quitting India with a prospect before it of partition, chaos, and possibly civil war.... Britain still has a duty to India's dumb millions.... All I can suggest under these circumstances is that the dissenting communities should have the choice, not only of independence and partition, but also of remaining, if they wish, under the British Raj. It is possible that Indian States [that is, Princely States] and minorities, even perhaps the Muslims themselves, exposed to the threat of Hindu domination may opt for continuance of the British connection.... Britain may thus retain a solid footing in India....[84]

However bizarre this may seem today after decades of decolonization, and however out of touch with India of 12 May 1947 General Smuts might appear to be, his letter to Prime Minister Attlee illustrated a line of thinking so well that it seemed to be devised to exemplify some of Nehru's apprehensions.

In the meanwhile, on the same day, Lord Ismay sadly reconciled himself, sitting in his temporary office in India House, to the task of redrafting the transfer of power proposals. He cabled indignantly to Mountbatten at 11.55 p.m. that the Cabinet members had been told of Nehru's 'general agreement with plan I brought here' and, therefore, 'Ministers will not understand Nehru's reference to entirely new picture'. To be fair to Ismay and Mieville, they had worked on Nehru and many details were agreed on part by part, but the overall picture that emerged from the HMG draft with all parts put together and the option given to all provinces to opt for independence outside of the Indian Union turned the scale.

Thus 12 May 1947 was a day when the cables hummed in the British Empire and the fate of 'independent Bengal' was decided.

Bengal Partition Restored?

As we have seen, on 12 May 1947, the Viceroy decided that the option of independence could not be given to all the provinces. A special arrangement for Bengal could be possible and there was strong pressure from Governor Burrows and the Ministry in Bengal in its favour as well as the support of leaders like Sarat Bose and Kiran Shankar Roy. Mountbatten was unwilling to delay the process of transfer of power and thus was unable to allow the Suhrawardy–Bose scheme to mature, nor was he keen to introduce other parties into the tripartite negotiations between himself, Nehru, and Jinnah. He had, therefore, a very tricky job ahead of him.

Mountbatten immediately revised the draft of the HMG on transfer of power and sent it to Ismay at London to convey it to the Cabinet. (In the event Ismay threw up his hands, cabled Mountbatten that 'Ministers here feel much in the dark.... I am unable to enlighten their darkness', and flew to Delhi. Mountbatten had to visit London to take up the task of explaining to the Cabinet the problem and his solution). Mountbatten's revision was as follows:

> I have omitted choice to Provinces for standing out independently. In principle, if choice is given to one province we cannot deny it to others. If it is desire of all parties in a particular province to stand alone we shall not be able to prevent them, but I do not now like the idea of HMG giving them that choice.[85]

Mountbatten mentioned that Nehru's main reaction was a criticism of the government encouraging Balkanization. As for Suhrawardy, the Viceroy planned to 'tell him that I cannot make provision in the plan for Bengal remaining independent; but that there is nothing in the plan to prevent the Bengal Legislative Assembly passing a resolution for independence which I would treat on its merit'.[86] There were some other changes that did not concern Bengal, but so far as that province was concerned this change was a vital one.

The next day, 13 May, Mountbatten summoned Suhrawardy, an appointment arranged by Burrows. Mountbatten possibly found it impolitic to reveal the fact that he had himself deleted the option for independence for British Indian provinces, including Bengal. He put it as follows: 'In the most recent correspondence with HMG the suggestion was that provinces or parts of provinces... were going to be given the option of voting for Hindustan or Pakistan and not the option for remaining independent'.[87] Secondly, on the idea of a coalition government, of which Mountbatten was very supportive earlier, he said that if it could be formed before 2 June, the date of HMG's announcement of transfer of power modalities, he would try to persuade the leaders to agree to the exclusion of any announcement of a partition in Bengal. But this left little chance for such a coalition, given that the scheduled announcement was only two weeks away. Before Mountbatten made those points, he softened up Suhrawardy's resistance by talking to him sternly on quite a secondary matter. When the latter reported to Mountbatten the discussions between him and Sarat Bose and K.S. Roy, Mountbatten struck quickly to score a point. '[Suhrawardy] did not tell me, however, that the document which Bose and Roy had handed to him, but of which I fortunately had already procured a copy myself, contained in its opening clause the words that "Bengal was to be a Socialist Republic". I tackled him about this...'.[88] Mountbatten's triumphant account goes on to describe how he heckled the Chief Minister, that it was 'silly' to have that clause, that the place for such a state would be not the Commonwealth—which Suhrawardy was keen to join—but the USSR, and so on. Suhrawardy asked if cutting out that bit about the socialist republic would improve Bengal's chances of getting into the Commonwealth; he was told sternly it would not, unless the rest of India would also make a similar request. And it was Mountbatten who suggested the phrase 'Free State of Bengal', which later actually appears in the Suhrawardy–Bose agreement, in place of 'Socialist Republic'. On the whole, one gets an impression that it was all a charade. Incidentally, at this meeting, Mountbatten let drop a warning that Nehru was against 'an independent Bengal, unless closely linked to Hindustan' and that Nehru believed that in the event of a partition a few years would 'bring East Bengal into Hindustan'. This revelation was not calculated to improve Hindu–Muslim ties.

The next day, 15 May, Mountbatten met Liaquat Ali Khan, commonly regarded as the second-in-command in the League, and put to him the crucial question, 'whether the Muslim League was going to accept partition of Punjab and Bengal, to which he replied, "we shall never agree to it, but you may make us bow to the inevitable"'.[89] This was a significant admission.

Suhrawardy may have got wind of it, for he was camping in Delhi, and he wrote to Sir E. Mieville the same day, 15 May, requesting a clarification. If the government was preparing for partition of Bengal there was 'no point in my carrying the independence resolution'.[90] As regards the fuss Mountbatten had made about the phrase 'Socialist Republic', Suhrawardy explained: 'Hindus want to browbeat me to accept a Socialist Republic.... If I reject this, as indeed I must, Mr. Sarat Bose walks out, and Mr. Kiran Shankar Roy is too weak to fight the Hindu Mahasabha which has captured the imagination of the Hindus on the score of partition'. At the end, Suhrawardy raised the question of Calcutta, that 'it will be criminally unfair if Calcutta is taken out of Muslim zone'; should that happen, it should not be placed in the Hindu zone either, but it should be a 'free international zone'. In talking of these zones he seems already to be reconciled to the idea of Partition.

In the meantime, Jinnah was moving towards a position that he maintained in public to the end; he was opposed to partition of Bengal and also to an independent Bengal. On the question of Independence as an option to be offered to British India provinces, Jinnah was in agreement with Nehru, a rare but not unexpected occurrence. Jinnah's note to the Viceroy on the draft for the HMG prepared by him said that he contemplated two Constituent Assemblies for Pakistan and Hindustan and that 'all powers and authority should be transferred to the Pakistan and Hindustan Constituent Assemblies'.[91] On the partition of Bengal and Punjab, Jinnah's arguments now were the same as in his press statement published in the *Dawn* on 1 May. The unjustified demand for those partitions was to 'create more difficulties in the way of the British government and the Viceroy'; there should be no partition in Punjab or Bengal or else 'the Muslims will get a truncated or moth-eaten Pakistan', a famous phrase.[92] In this note of 7 May, having said that he could not agree to partition of Bengal, Jinnah goes on to discuss what would happen in case there was a partition; thus he gives an impression that he agreed with what Liaquat Ali said to the Viceroy, that without agreeing to partition of Bengal, they would accept it as inevitable. In the event of a partition, Jinnah said, Calcutta should not go to West Bengal; 'if worst comes to the worst, Calcutta should be made a free port'.[93] He also desired that the wishes of the people be ascertained by referendum, particularly those of the Scheduled Castes. This note was circulated, along with Nehru's, to the Cabinet

Committee in London. The conclusion drawn by the Secretary of State for India, Listowel, was: 'In the later paragraphs of his letter Mr. Jinnah appears to accept the fact that partition in these provinces (that is, Bengal and Punjab) will take place and I have no doubt that the Viceroy is right that the Muslim League will, in fact, acquiesce in and operate the scheme'.[94] Thus Jinnah's public statements against partition in Bengal were dismissed as mere eyewash. Prime Minister Attlee's notings on the matter were on the same lines: 'Mr. Jinnah acquiesced in them [HMG proposals] in private conversation although in a subsequent public statement he has protested against any proposal to partition Bengal and the Punjab'.[95]

Thus, by the middle of May 1947, the Partition of Bengal appeared certain, but this we know from historians' hindsight and from documents and conversations recorded at that time, very little of which was made public till recently. Some proponents of a 'united Independent Bengal' soldiered on. In the next chapter, we shall see what the outcome of their effort was and what the mindset was of the chief protagonists in the drama enacted in the last days of undivided Bengal.

Notes

1. Abul Mansur Ahmed, *Amar dekha rajnitir panchas bachchar* (Dhaka, 1995), p. 223.
2. Record of Interview: Sir F. Burrows and K.S. Roy, 22 March 1947, in N. Mansergh (ed.), *The Transfer of Power, 1942–1947* (12 vols, London, 1970–83), vol. X, p. 6 (hereafter *TOP*, followed by volume number and page number).
3. *Ananda Bazar Patrika* [hereafter cited as *ABP*], editorial, 'Hindu samajer sankat', 16 September 1946.
4. *ABP*, 1 October 1946.
5. *ABP*, 1 October 1946.
6. *ABP*, 3 November 1946.
7. *ABP*, 21, 31 October 1946.
8. *ABP*, 4 November 1946.
9. *ABP*, 4 January 1947.
10. F. Burrows to Mountbatten, 11 April 1947, *TOP*, X, 203.
11. F. Burrows to Mountbatten, 11 April 1947, *TOP*, X, 203.
12. Note by Sir T. Showe, 17 April 1947, *TOP*, X, 292–4.
13. Note by Sir T. Showe, 17 April 1947, *TOP*, X, 292–4.
14. Viceroy's Staff Meeting, record of discussion, 12 April 1947, *TOP*, X, 207.

15. Minutes of First Governors' Conference, 15 April 1947, *TOP*, X, pp. 242–255.
16. Minutes of First Governors' Conference, 16 April 1947, *TOP*, X, 269–74.
17. Viceroy's Personal Report no. 3, n.d. (April 1947), *TOP*, X, 302.
18. F. Burrows, Governor of Bengal to Mountbatten, Secret Cable, 18 April 1947, *TOP*, X, 324.
19. Record of Interview between Viceroy and Dr S.P. Mukherji, 23 April 1947, 12.30–1.20 p.m., *TOP*, X, 374.
20. Minutes of Viceroy's meetings, 23 April 1947, *TOP*, X, 380.
21. Note by Burrows, n.d. (24 April 1947?), with covering letter by Tyson, 24 April 1947, *TOP*, XI, 391, 393.
22. Note by Burrows, n.d. (24 April 1947?), with covering letter by Tyson, 24 April 1947, *TOP*, XI, 391, 393.
23. Minutes of Viceroy's Staff Meeting, 25 April 1947, *TOP*, X, 416.
24. Christie to Abel, 26 April 1947, secret cable, *TOP*, X, 455.
25. Lord Ismay to Sir F. Burrows, 28 April 1947, by Secraphone, *TOP*, X, 472.
26. *ABP*, Editorial, 7 April 1947.
27. *ABP*, 13 April 1947.
28. *ABP*, 30 April 1947.
29. *ABP*, 'Apasarita hauk', 21 August 1946; 'Hindu samajer sankat', 16 September 1946; 'Sarkeri pechakbritti', 3 November 1946; 'Akhanda hindu samajer dabi', 29 May 1947.
30. *ABP*, 'Banglar dabi', 15 January 1947; 'Nutan bangla pradesh', 7 April 1947.
31. *ABP*, 12 March 1947.
32. *ABP*, 18 March 1947.
33. *ABP*, 14 May 1947.
34. Record of Interview between Viceroy and Suhrawardy, 26 April 1947, *TOP*, X, 452.
35. Record of Interview between Viceroy and Jinnah, 26 April 1947, *TOP*, X, 452.
36. *ABP*, 28 April and 1 May 1947.
37. Abul Haṣhim, *Amar jiban o bibhagpurva bangladesher rajniti* (Calcutta, 1988, and Dhaka, 1978), pp. 122–6.
38. Hashim, *Amar jiban*, pp. 126–8.
39. Record of Interview between Viceroy and Sardar Patel, 12 April 1947, *TOP*, X, 214.
40. Minutes of Viceroy's Meeting, 25 April 1947, *TOP*, X, 424.
41. Mountbatten surmised that Patel was responsible for the leak, Minutes of Staff Meeting, 3 May 1947, *TOP*, X, 579; the Viceroy threatened resignation at interview with Patel on 24 April 1947, *TOP*, X, 394.

42. Patel to S.P. Mookerjee, 17 May; to K.C. Neogy 13 May; B. Roy, 23 May; Durgadas (ed.), *Sardar Patel's Correspondence*, vol. IV (Ahmedabad, 1972).
43. Ismay to Burrows, 28 April 1947, *TOP*, X, 472.
44. Minutes of Governors' Conference, 15 April 1947, *TOP*, X, 254.
45. Minutes of Viceroy's Meeting, 23 April 1947, *TOP*, X, 380.
46. Viscountess Mountbatten to Mountbatten (Interviews), 24 April 1947, *TOP*, X, 388.
47. E. Mieville to Mountbatten, 30 April 1947, *TOP*, X, 487.
48. Minutes of Viceroy's Meeting, 1 May 1947, *TOP*, X, 407–13.
49. Minutes of Viceroy's Meeting, 1 May 1947, *TOP*, X, 407–13.
50. Minutes of Viceroy's Meeting, 1 May 1947, *TOP*, X, 407–13.
51. Note by Burrows, n.d. (24 April 1947), *TOP*, X, 392.
52. Minutes of Viceroy's Meeting, 1 May 1947, *TOP*, X, 508.
53. Record of Interview between Viceroy and K.S. Roy, 3 May 1947, *TOP*, X, 585.
54. S.P. Mookerjee to Mountbatten (extract), 2 May 1947, *TOP*, X, 556–8.
55. S.P. Mookerjee to Mountbatten (extract), 2 May 1947, *TOP*, X, 556–8.
56. Record of Interview between Viceroy and Jinnah, 26 April 1947, *TOP*, X, 452.
57. S.P. Mookerjee to Mountbatten, 2 May 1947, *TOP*, X, 558.
58. Mountbatten to Burrows, 2 May 1947, *TOP*, X, 554.
59. Burrows to Mountbatten, 4 May 1947, *TOP*, X, 614.
60. Burrows to Mountbatten, 4 May 1947, *TOP*, X, 614.
61. Viceroy's Personal Report, no. 5, 1 May 1947, *TOP*, X, 539.
62. Burrows to Mountbatten, 7 May 1947, *TOP*, X, 651.
63. Burrows to Mountbatten, 7 May 1947, *TOP*, X, 651.
64. Hashim, *Amar jiban*, pp. 118–19.
65. Harun-or-Rashid, 'A Move for Independent Bengal', in *History of Bangladesh, 1704–1971*, vol. I, ed. S. Islam, (Dhaka, 1992), p. 408.
66. Viceroy's Meeting, Minutes, 7 May 1947, *TOP*, X, 657.
67. Minutes of Viceroy's Meeting, 10 May 1947, *TOP*, X, 737.
68. Minutes of Viceroy's Meeting, 10 May 1947, *TOP*, X, 737, extract.
69. Burrows to Mountbatten, 11 May 1947, *TOP*, X, 772.
70. Minutes of Viceroy's Meeting, 11 May 1947 (Simla), *TOP*, X, 764.
71. Mountbatten to Ismay, Cable: Immediate and Secret, 11 May 1947, 9.30 p.m., *TOP*, X, 776.
72. E. Mieville to Mountbatten, 30 April 1947, *TOP*, X, 488.
73. Nehru to Mountbatten (Simla), 11 May 1947, *TOP*, X, 756.
74. Note by Pandit Nehru (Simla), 11 May 1947, *TOP*, X, 767.
75. Text of HMG announcement, as revised by Cabinet Committee, in Ismay to Viceroy, 9 May 1947, *TOP*, X, 724.

76. Note by Nehru (to Viceroy), 11 May 1947, *TOP*, X, 768–72.
77. Note by Nehru (to Viceroy) 11 May 1947, *TOP*, X 768–72.
78. Mountbatten to Ismay, 11 May 1947, *TOP*, X, 776.
79. Mountbatten to Ismay, 11 May 1947, Top Secret Cable, 11 May 1947, 11.40 p.m.
80. Mieville to Ismay, 12 May 1947, *TOP*, X, 780.
81. Minutes of Viceroy's Staff Meeting, 12 May 1947, *TOP*, X, 781.
82. Chiefs of Staff Committee, meeting on 12 May 1947, *TOP*, X, 786–92.
83. Chiefs of Staff Committee, meeting on 12 May 1947, *TOP*, X, 786–92.
84. Message from General Smuts to Prime Minister of UK, 12 May 1947, conveyed by High Commissioner for the Union of South Africa in London, *TOP*, X, 797.
85. Mountbatten to Ismay, 13 May 1947, *TOP*, X, 807.
86. Mountbatten to Ismay, 13 May 1947, *TOP*, X, 807.
87. Mountbatten to Burrows, 16 May 1947, *TOP*, X, 849–50.
88. Mountbatten to Burrows, 16 May 1947, *TOP*, X, 849–50.
89. Record of Interview between Viceroy and Liaquat Ali Khan, 15 May 1947, *TOP*, X, 825.
90. Suhrawardy to Mieville, 15 May 1947, *TOP*, X, 830.
91. Note from Jinnah, n.d. (17 May 1947?) in Viceroy's Conference Papers, *TOP*, X, 851.
92. Jinnah's statement on Partition in *Dawn*, 1 May 1947, appended to Viceroy's Personal Report, 1 May 1947, *TOP*, X, 543.
93. Jinnah's note, n.d. (17 May 1947?) in Viceroy's Conference Papers, *TOP*, X, 853.
94. Memorandum by Secretary of State for India, 21 May 1947, *TOP*, X, 934.
95. Noting by Attlee, 22 May 1947, *TOP*, X, 934.

9

'DIVISION OF HEARTS'
The Last Days of United Bengal

The birth and the death of the concept of 'United Independent Bengal' is a complex story that has a significance beyond the domain of constitutional history and the history of the negotiations on transfer of power modalities. Bangladeshi historians have found in the concept the roots of a Bengali subnationalism, while others see in this history the continuation of the *bhadralok* Hindu's endeavour to preserve their hegemony in the non-Muslim part of Bengal, and yet others consider it the subordination of Bengal's interest to those of the putative centres of the Indian Union and Pakistan as perceived by the central leadership in the Congress and the Muslim League.[1] That is why it is worthwhile to examine the records and writings of the chief participants in the process with great care. The Partition was an event that altered the course of Bengal's history and more than any other single event in the twentieth century, the Partition story merits our attention.

The *mise en scene* in Bengal in 1947 was a trifle depressing. It is true that there were among the provincial leaders in Bengal sincere believers in the indivisible unity of Bengal but then these were indeed *provincial* leaders, without access to the decision-making processes in Delhi. In the Muslim League in Bengal there were some leaders, unlike the central leaders given to prevarication in their negotiations with the Viceroy, truly committed to the idea of a united Bengal. One of them was Abul Hashim, of a distinguished family of Burdwan and educated in Burdwan town and Calcutta University (which he preferred, having abandoned Aligarh within a few days of his admission there); within the League, as provincial General Secretary for years, he consistently championed oneness of Bengal. H.S. Suhrawardy, the son of a prominent Calcutta barrister and an alumnus of St Xavier's College, sometime the Deputy Mayor of Calcutta, a member the Calcutta Bar, was firmly rooted in West Bengal. He may have dithered when pressured by the League establishment, but he was probably sincere in trying to avert a partition. Men like him had a great deal to lose in the event of a partition. On the other side of the communal divide, the same applied to persons such as Kiran Shankar Roy who had almost all his estates in East Bengal. Suhrawardy stayed on in the West Bengal and Roy in the East Bengal Assembly for a year or two even after Partition. While provincial leaders like them were genuinely opposed to Partition, at least for a while, they were marginal to the game that was under way. To Mountbatten, the best way to work out a quick solution—and he was a man in a hurry to get on to higher things back home—was to limit the number of participants in the negotiation process. Basically, his strategy was to reduce it to a neat three-person game—between the Viceroy, Nehru, and Jinnah—or else the process would be messy and time consuming. As we have seen, both the proponents and the opponents of the partition of Bengal were treated with scant attention by the Viceroy and his aides. This was true even of Syama Prasad Mookerjee, a prominent member of the Bengali elite; but he happened to be, as a pro-partitionist, on what proved to be the winning side. Among the opponents of Partition the only leader in Bengal whose name approximated a nationally recognized stature was Sarat Chandra Bose. He was known not only as the elder brother of Subhas Chandra, but also for his past role at the head of the Bengal Provincial Congress and the Congress Assembly Party. His success as a barrister, and his hospitality to Congress leaders, have been described graphically by his secretary Nirad C. Chaudhuri, but in 1947 Sarat Bose was marginalized. He nursed a grievance against Patel and the central leaders for his recent ouster from the Interim Government, proudly stayed away from the Delhi *durbar* where the fate of the country was being decided, and might have been rather unaware of the inner ploys behind Burrows and Suhrawardy's initiative towards independent Bengal. On the whole, the leadership of the province was noticeably ineffective.

Another feature of Bengal politics at the time was the lack of unity both in the Congress and the League. Not that these parties were short of leaders; they had too many. Coordination of action between Khwaja Nazimuddin, H.S. Suhrawardy, Maulana Akram Khan, and Abul Hashim, was conspicuously lacking. It seems that there was a division between the Dhaka and the Calcutta cliques, hampering united moves by the provincial Muslim League; for years, Nazimuddin and Suhrawardy had been rivals for chief ministership, and Akram Khan and Hashim, president and general secretary respectively, were poles apart in their views on the question of a united Bengal.[2] Abul Hashim recalled later that 'reactionary' elements in the Bengal League were lukewarm to the idea of an independent, united Bengal, although they publicly made statements against Partition—which was the official publicity line of the central League leadership.[3] The then editor of *Ittahad*, A. Mansur Ahmed, records how *Azad* and the *Star of India* adopted positions dictated by the central leadership and 'our leaders were mere supplicants for posts, looking to central leaders, especially Quaid-i-Azam for favours'.[4] The group in the League led by Nazimuddin were in favour of joining Pakistan, rather than setting up a united Bengal which would require compromise and accommodation with the Hindu population. There is a debate among Bangladeshi historians: on the one hand, Harun-or-Rashid holds the view that 'there was existing a sense of nationality among a section of Bengali Muslims' at this time; on the other, A.R. Mallick and S.A. Husain consider this debatable and hold the contrary opinion that neither any sort of subnationalism nor any 'identity other than that of a marginalised community ... propelled the Bengali Muslims towards the Pakistan movement'.[5] Be that as it may, it is curious that the project of an independent Bengal was not on the agenda of the Muslim leaders of Bengal until 1947, that is till the time it was felt that Partition might be averted. Undoubtedly, in the pronouncements of that far-sighted leader, Fazlul Huq, for example, in his Lahore speech of 1940, there were anticipations of a nebulous idea resembling the hastily put together Suhrawardy–Bose plan. But the pursuit of immediate political gains, often of a personal kind, and perhaps the allegiance to an all-India movement, did not allow the League to formulate, not to speak of acting upon, the scheme that emerged in 1947. But it was too late, and too little effort went into it.

The provincial Congress Party was in complete disarray in 1947, divided between the majority who stoutly defended the partitioning of Bengal and incorporation of the western part into the Indian union, and a small minority who made a futile gesture towards a vague notion of a united Bengal.[6] Most Congressmen had doubts about the scheme of an independent Bengal because an assurance from the League regarding joint electorates and equitable distribution of positions in government and the services was, as we have noted, very long in coming—20 May, barely a dozen days before the scheduled announcement of the transfer of power plans on 2 June. This was too late for, by then, the entire basis of Mountbatten's original plan had been changed, the option for independence was withdrawn. What was signed on 22 May by Sarat Bose and Abul Hashim was only an ad hoc agreement and it contained some loopholes which Gandhi pointed out. Nevertheless, it might have had a chance of success had it come a little earlier. Blame for this cannot be laid at the door of the League alone. The Congress had been enormously successful in the General Election in 1946, winning 87 of the 90 seats it contested—including 24 of the 25 Scheduled Caste seats—whereas in 1937 it had won only 54. But the Bengal Congress failed to cash in on its success and dithered at the moments when opportunity came its way. In April 1946, Suhrawardy was inclined to negotiate terms with K.S. Roy, and so also in September 1946.[7] The latter occasion was, however, unpropitious—soon after the Calcutta Riot in which Suhrawardy was suspected by the Congress of complicity—but in April certainly an opportunity was missed. The reluctance of the Congress High Command to allow an alliance with the League was one factor, and another was the Bengal Congress's lack of trust in Suhrawardy. The first of these factors has often been emphasized to the exclusion of all others. The question is whether there was any truth in Governor Burrows' judgement: 'Bengal will be sacrificed on the altar of Nehru's all-India outlook'.[8] Evidently, this ignores the ambivalent part played by Jinnah, which has been described earlier. As far as the Congress attitude is concerned, how true is this judgement?

The Congress High Command

From our narrative it may be inferred that Jinnah was ambivalent as regards the concept of 'united independent Bengal' till about the latter part of May and thereafter decided against giving Bengal the option for independence; however, he remained aware of the bargaining point provided by the issues of Bengal and of the status of Calcutta. In the Congress, the central leadership was not entirely unanimous on the question till the very end. That leadership was known as the High Command, a phrase reminiscent of Fascist Germany. In fact, Tagore's comment on the Congress in 1939 was that 'the higher command who are at its helm' might have fallen victims to the 'pride of power' as a party, and also to the 'intoxication of personal power'.[9] This was written at a time when Subhas Bose's conflict with the party establishment had created much bitterness in Bengal, admittedly an unusual time. However, some of that bitterness persisted through the 1940s. At the same time sections of Bengal leadership cottoned on to one or the other of the central leaders to consolidate their own positions.

Gandhi's position was well above the High Command. And it is possible that the latter had ceased to pay attention to him. He gradually veered towards a despairing denunciation of the idea of Partition, tempered by the suspension of his intervention—which in effect allowed the course of events to move towards Partition unimpeded by his personal views. In any case, he claimed that none of the so-called High Command wanted his advice, as we shall see later. Mountbatten, with his usual acuteness in sizing up people, pointed this out. In May 1947, he met Churchill who happened to be in bed and mulling over in his mind the Indian problem. Churchill 'asked me if I foresaw any difficulties, particularly with Mr. Gandhi. I told him that I doubted whether he would create any difficulty which would not be dealt with by Patel and Nehru'.[10] It is evident from the Mountbatten Papers and Patel's personal correspondence, now published, that Patel's stance was unambiguous: it closely resembled that of Dr S.P. Mookerjee with whom he was in touch.[11] Nehru's position changed as the negotiations progressed.

It fell to Nehru to be the official spokesman of the Congress at the transfer of power negotiations. One of his earliest conversations with Mountbatten is interesting. Nehru, at the beginning of April 1947, 'had not yet had an opportunity of discussing with Mr. Gandhi his [Gandhi's] reasons for opposing the Congress resolution on partition; but he realised that Mr. Gandhi was immensely keen on a unified India, at any immediate cost, for the benefit of the long-term future. I told Pandit Nehru', Mountbatten writes, 'that I recognised that there were long-term and short-term considerations ... and that although the long-term ones should theoretically predominate, I hoped he would agree that I could not base any decision solely on them if the consequences were to be greatly increased chance of heavy bloodshed in the immediate future. He said that no reasonable man could argue with these premises'.[12] This philosophical, almost donnish conversation on 1 April 1947, creates an impression—which may not have been unintended by Nehru—that he was being reluctantly persuaded to disagree with Gandhi. Two weeks later, Nehru adopted Mountbatten's argument as his own and linked it with the bloodbath in Calcutta on Direct Action Day in August 1946. He wrote to the Viceroy:

> It does little good to blame others for misdeeds of large numbers of people of all groups and communities. Nevertheless, I think it is perfectly true to say that what we have seen in India during the last eight months are the resultants of the deliberate policy of the Muslim League called Direct Action. The violence had bred violence in others also.[13]

He went on to say that a negative policy of repression would not answer; they needed a positive policy. 'That positive policy must be to create a feeling that no group will be dominated over by another. It was with this object in view that we [that is, the Congress] suggested division of the Punjab and Bengal, much as we dislike it'.[14]

At his meeting with the Viceroy on 10 May Nehru reverted to the theme of the Calcutta Riot once again: he felt, perhaps unreasonably, an implied threat when Suhrawardy talked about 'what will remain of Calcutta' if it became 'a bone of contention'.[15] The next day, Nehru said that he 'personally hoped that the conception of Pakistan would recede'; with reference to Mountbatten's question about Bengal being 'given chance of remaining united and independent', Nehru said that he was 'willing to consider special arrangements for Bengal'.[16] Nehru received from Bengal alarming reports about possible riots; one such, from a Muslim friend, unnamed, led him to ask the Viceroy to contemplate the use of the army.[17] This fear of riots in Calcutta, on the scale of August 1946, seems to have weighed heavily with Nehru. Secondly, as we have seen in the previous chapter, there was a fear of Balkanization when the option for independence was contemplated as a part of the package deal for every province, not only Bengal. Eventually, he took a position close to Patel's: 'The independence of Bengal really means in present circumstances the dominance of the Muslim League in Bengal. It means practically the whole of Bengal going into Pakistan area, although those interested may not say so'.[18] That was Nehru's statement to the *News Chronicle* on 27 May. If this was sacrificing Bengal on 'the altar of Nehru's all-India outlook', as Sir George Burrows wrote the next day, that did not seem to worry Nehru unduly.[19]

A Coalition and a Constitution for Bengal

Opinion in the Congress thus seemed to harden. But Governor Burrows in Bengal did not give up easily. He took it upon himself to hustle Suhrawardy and K.S. Roy's parties into a marriage of convenience. It will be recalled that Suhrawardy had acted upon the Viceroy's advice: since the Viceroy objected to the bit about 'Socialist Republic of Bengal' it was being dropped by Bose and Roy who had proposed it. Further, Burrows urged Suhrawardy and Kiran Shankar to first form a coalition ministry, and to talk about the future constitution later, so as to be "untrammelled by conditions" such as those set out in Sarat Bose's list of points.[20] Burrows also sent with this report to the Viceroy a copy of the agreement to be signed that evening, on 10 May, by Bose and the League representatives. It was actually signed on 20 May by Bose and Abul Hashim.

The agreement provided for: (*a*) Joint electorates with reservation of seats proportionate to population among Hindus and Muslims, while ensuring among the Hindu quota the 'existing proportion' of Scheduled Caste seats. (*b*) A Constituent Assembly was to be elected by the Legislature, formed by election as above; these constitution makers would comprise 16 Muslims and 14 Hindus, the latter including Scheduled Castes. (*c*) Muslims and Hindus would have equal share in state services, *pending* the formation of legislature and the new constitution. (*d*) In the *interim* a coalition ministry would function consisting of a Muslim chief minister and ministers who would be in equal number from both communities; the Home Minister would be a Hindu.[21] This agreement, destined to be infructuous, was signed and celebrated at a dinner meeting in Sarat Bose's house in Woodburn Park on 20 May.[22]

Here we must go back a little to understand Sarat Bose's role in this event. According to Abul Hashim, who called on him in October 1946 soon after Bose returned from Delhi to Calcutta, he was supportive of the idea of a federal structure in post-Independence India, allowing autonomy to its units.[23] As the transfer of power negotiations gathered pace, some of the League members became vocal against the partitioning of Bengal and Hashim's contact with Bose was revived; along with the growth of a rhetoric of Bengali patriotism, there were appeals to the memory of C.R. Das's Bengal Pact, and Fazlul Huq's Lahore resolution which could be read as a plea for a federal or even multi-state structure, and a very admirable attempt to bridge the communal gulf. Soon after Suhrawardy's and Hashim's statements on united Bengal on 27 and 29 April respectively, a meeting was held at the former's residence on Theatre Road, Calcutta, which led to the appointment of a committee, including Sarat Bose, Suhrawardy, K.S. Roy, Hashim and a few others to prepare an agreement.[24] Governor Burrows encouraged this development from behind the scenes.

Sarat Bose, a veteran, knew what he was up against even if he may not have had full knowledge of the role of Burrows and Mountbatten in the initiative by Suhrawardy. Bose sought the blessings of Gandhi, the one Indian leader standing out against Partition. Pyarelal has described in detail the visit of Bose and Hashim to Gandhi at Sodpur on 10 May. Gandhi was sceptical. He asked whether Bengali Muslims would decline if Pakistan invited them to join a federation based on Islamic culture and principles? If cultural distinctiveness was an argument for separation of Bengal, did not the culture that Tagore ideally represented include the Upanishadic tradition which was common to many other cultures of India? The next day, 11 May, when Suhrawardy and Hashim visited Gandhi they got into quite a wrangle. Was the bloodshed daily happening in Bengal a good augury for united Bengal?[25] Although Sarat Bose was brought into the picture at a later stage by Suhrawardy, Bose's crucial value was his acceptability as an elder statesman. It fell to him to sell the idea of a 'united independent Bengal' to the all-India leadership. Gandhi was the likeliest buyer, given his dissent from the Congress decision on the partition of India. In this task Bose did not succeed.

Bose followed up his visit to Gandhi with a letter on 23 May enclosing the agreement he had already signed, describing it as a *pro tem* arrangement subject to amendment when it was to be approved by the Bengal Congress and the League.[26] Gandhi's comment was, first, that the agreement failed to mention the fact that Bengal shared a common culture and mother tongue. The point of this enigmatic remark was probably that the agreement read like a contract born of political expediency. Secondly, Gandhi was surprised that under the proposed structure, all decisions could be made by simple majority by the executive and the legislature. To protect the Hindu minority Gandhi proposed that on major constitutional issues a two-thirds majority should be required in place of simple majority.[27] Although Bose informed Gandhi that the first point was acceptable and the second was to be discussed, Gandhi was apparently unconvinced of the feasibility of his plans.[28]

Meanwhile, in the Corridors of Power

At the Governor's House in Calcutta, Burrows continued his lobbying with the Viceroy. He reported on 21 May that both Suhrawardy and K.S. Roy were preparing to talk to their party bosses, and on 28 May that they were doing so in Delhi.[29] He pressed the Viceroy to 'impress on the All-India leaders of *both* sides the danger' of a communal conflagration in the event of a partition[30] and briefed Mountbatten on two sets of negotiations in progress: one between Bose, Suhrawardy, and Roy on the future 'Free State of Bengal' and another between the last two on the formation of a coalition government. The latter process of negotiations was 'inaugurated at my suggestion', he said, because 'the three of us', that is, Burrows, Suhrawardy, and Roy, agreed that it was needed immediately to avoid partition.[31]

As far as appearances go, Mountbatten continued to encourage Burrows' efforts. However, he had already told Burrows that the Congress was of the view that Bengal had 'no future except in Hindustan'.[32] London was, as was often the case, one step behind the latest position of the hyperactive Viceroy. Thus the somewhat laid-back fifth Earl of Listowel, the Secretary of State, was unaware that the provinces' 'independence', that is, separation from both India and Pakistan, was no longer on the agenda, that it had been dropped after Nehru's tumultuous protests and revisions made at Simla on 12 May. So Listowel wrote a memo saying that independence could be offered to Bengal.[33] Likewise, the Board of Trade in England took it for granted in a note to the Cabinet Committee that steps were needed to be taken when Bengal 'decides to hive off as an independent state'.[34]

The Secretary of State was a little out of touch with the latest situation in India, but what he wrote may be significant as it bears the stamp of senior civil servants' thinking in the India Office on the Bengal question. The Secretary of State thought that Bengal could be allowed to be independent because (*a*) the 'Cripps offer' clearly included such a right for any province of British India and (*b*) for Bengal there were 'strong practical arguments' in favour of allowing independence, for example, that Bengal was 'large enough' and that it was undesirable to separate Calcutta from its hinterland.[35] This suggests that apart from Burrows, Tyson, and other, in Calcutta, in India Office too there was a strong British interest in setting up an independent state in Bengal and keeping Calcutta out of the Indian Union.

At any rate, the views of the India Office or the Secretary of State for India were pushed aside by the rush of events. Mountbatten flew to London to brief the Cabinet Committee on India at a meeting on 19 May. Prime Minister Attlee was in the chair and among those present were: Sir Stafford Cripps, President of Board of Trade; A.V. Alexander, Minister for Defence; Viscount Addison, Secretary of State for Dominion Affairs; and Earl Listowel. The Viceroy stated, inter alia, the latest position on the question of independence as an option to be given to the province. 'Neither Congress nor the Muslim League favoured the grant to provinces, or part of provinces, of the option to remain independent, since this suggested that India might be Balkanized and might also encourage the Princes to adopt a separatist policy'.[36] That decidedly put to an end the prospects of an independent Bengal. Mountbatten gave an appreciation of the situation in Bengal: Governor Burrows was 'anxious' to avoid a partition, Chief Minister Suhrawardy 'thought that it might be kept united', Jinnah expected that 'an independent Bengal would be a sort of subsidiary Pakistan'. The Congress would accept independent status for Bengal only if 'special arrangements, which were unlikely to be acceptable to the Muslims, were made with the Central Government of Hindustan. They were opposed to Mr. Jinnah's proposal that Calcutta should become a free city as they believed that, without Calcutta, Eastern Bengal might, within two or three years, rejoin the western part of the province'.[37]

The day Mountbatten thus addressed the Cabinet Committee, 19 May, Burrows cabled him and the Secretary of State an advance copy of the agreement to be signed by Bose and the League.[38] The next day Mountbatten told the Cabinet Committee of this development and that if the agreement worked out before 2 June, His Majesty's Government (HMG in bureaucratic acronym) might make a special provision for Bengal.[39] He was later authorized by the Committee to make such a last-minute special provision in the event of an agreement by 2 June. Mountbatten also persuaded the Committee to reject Jinnah's proposal of a referendum on the ground that it would take too much time and probably cause a communal conflict.[40]

The Ultimate Problem: 'Division of Hearts'

It is doubtful if Mountbatten still expected a generally agreed-upon decision from Bengal. Not only had Nehru issued an intemperate statement, equating united Bengal with Muslim domination, but other factors also cumulatively seemed to block the prospects of averting Bengal's partition.[41] So much so that by 28 May the Prime Minister and the Cabinet Committee had come to the conclusion that 'there was no prospect that agreement would be reached for the grant of independence to Bengal as a separate Dominion'.[42] These factors were as follows: (*a*) As Burrows pointed out, the talks between the League leaders and Sarat Bose had been going on for a very long time but 'I cannot say that finality has been reached even among the principals'.[43] This was as of 28 May. (*b*) As regards the coalition government, 'the formula has not been put to or accepted by either party's Working Committee in Bengal'. (*c*) Burrows reported, his optimism beginning to falter at last, that there was an atmosphere of latent communal conflict. 'In the Press generally there was a feeling of pessimism and almost resignation to the prospect of communal strife.... Wild rumours were circulating...', Calcutta was 'particularly jittery', and Burrows had information that both sides were 'preparing for trouble' with bombs and firearms. (*e*) An essential element was missing: mutual confidence. Suhrawardy was not 'prepared to burn his boats' unless he could be assured that K.S. Roy would be 'able and willing to bring the Congress in'.[44] On the Congress side, Gandhi confided to Abul Hashim, no one trusted Suhrawardy.[45] Even when Roy promised to resign if the High Command did not listen to him, Burrows and Suhrawardy doubted whether, if Roy did that, it would have any effect; 'if Nehru and Patel prove adamant Roy is not the man to move them'.[46] Sarat Bose, the only one with some influence outside Bengal, had already failed with Gandhi. In desperation, Bose also wrote to Jinnah, requesting instructions to Muslim legislators to vote against Partition, and also against accession to Pakistan or India; Jinnah acceded to the first request happily, not to the second.[47]

All this helps to explain the circumstances in which Governor Burrows failed in a project for which he had lobbied for months with the Viceroy. Burrows saw failure ahead of him, but he continued to maintain that the project was a sound one.

> Hindus of Bengal are determined not to surrender their ideal of a link with a Hindu Centre (and the protection they think that would afford to a Hindu minority) unless they can be guaranteed that they will not be forced under a Pakistan Centre and, lacking that guarantee, they demand partition; the Muslims, on the other hand, while not so adamant about joining a North-Western Pakistan, are determined not to come under a Hindu-controlled centre. To be independent, for the time being, of either Hindustan or Pakistan is the only platform on which they can unite.[48]

Burrows puts this forward as a sound reason for giving Bengal independent status. But he failed to ask, if this was the moral basis of the projected 'free state of Bengal' in the opinion of each of its major proponents, what were the prospects of united Bengal as a viable entity?

Let us consider the apparently inconsequential fact reported in the *Forward* that there was a new commodity in the market: 'Hindu biri', that is, Hindu cheroots.[49] (I have myself seen in 1946 shops in Calcutta suddenly sprouting on their signboards an addition daubed in tar: 'Hindur dukan' or 'Musalmaner dukan', that is, Hindu's shop or Musalman's shop; these declarations of faith, depending on the locality, were made as an insurance against looting and arson in the next communal riot). The poison of communalism had eaten deep into the Bengali mind by 1947, affecting quotidian life. Leaders who tried to reverse a trend they had themselves helped forward, by design or by default, now faced an impossible task. Nehru cited the August 1946 Riot as a decisive event. He did not take into account the communalization of almost the entire public space and every public issue over the past years. The community-wise distribution of jobs, the disbursement of famine relief, the problem of rural credit, the enumeration of population in the Census, the Urduization of the Bengali language, admission to school and college education, and so on, were only some of the issues infused with communalism. Gandhi, with his canny instincts for politics, had sized up the situation when he wrote to Sarat Bose in June 1947 that there had taken place an irrevocable division of hearts: it was best, he wrote sadly, to agree to 'a frank partition, it being a recognition of the established *division of hearts*...'[50]

The Gandhian Approach

That last statement of Gandhi's may surprise those who have an unqualified belief that he was opposed to Partition. He was, and he was not. That calls for an explanation, or, more accurately, an attempt at explanation, for Gandhi was enigmatic on the question. Till May 1947 he held the view that the Partition was abominable in principle, and avoidable from the pragmatic point of view. He continued to denounce the principle of it, but by the beginning of June he seemed to lose hope that it would be avoidable. A change was marked by his most important pronouncement on the question at the Congress Working Committee meeting in Delhi on 2 June; curiously the text of this speech is not available, though tens of thousands of his utterances have been recorded in nearly one hundred volumes of his *Collected Works*. This was the day when the HMG announcement on Transfer of Power was made; the same day, when Mountbatten called on Gandhi, he was told that Gandhi could not speak to him since it was Monday, a day of silence for him. However, at the Working Committee meeting Gandhi did express his opinion and the substance of that was reported in the records as follows: 'Though he did not agree with the decision of the Working Committee regarding the division of India, he did not want to take any step which would stand in the way of the Working Committee in implementing its previous decision'.[51] Then he addressed himself to some details of the HMG statement, such as lack of clarity regarding right of secession and absence of any assurance from the League that it accepted the statement as a final settlement. Accordingly, Nehru's letter on behalf of the Congress was redrafted. Gandhi made his differences with Nehru's and Patel's view abundantly clear to both of them. The most trenchant of his statements on this was a personal letter to Nehru. 'The oftener we meet the more convinced I am becoming that the gulf between us in the thought-world is deeper than I feared'.[52]

The letter from Nehru to the Viceroy, revised after Gandhi's intervention at the Working Committee meeting, included two significant passages. One was paragraph 3 which reiterated that Congress had always upheld the unity of India, the other was paragraph 9 which asserted: 'We believe as fully as ever in a united India.... We earnestly trust that when present passions have subsided our problems will be viewed in their proper perspective and a willing union of all parts of India will result therefrom'.[53] This was an assertion of a faith, functionally irrelevant as it was.

In the evening the same day, June 2, Gandhi talked more specifically about Bengal at his prayer meeting. He did not like the partition of Bengal, but 'a large number of Hindus desire partition, for how long can one put up with turbulence? ... Division of Bengal is certain under the new proposal'. Sarat Bose, Gandhi said, was against Partition, but 'Sarat Babu has his views, I have mine'.[54] At another prayer meeting a few days later, Gandhi said that although Congress was 'forced to accept' Partition, he was hopeful that if Hindus do not forget how to live with Muslims in future the two countries would not remain separate and 'the artificial partition would become meaningless'.[55] Gandhi wanted, even after Partition, to keep the Bengal Provincial Congress Committee unified, that is, the same committee for both Bengals, for the party was outside government laws and government's decision to divide Bengal.[56] In a letter, he reminded Bose of 'the unfortunate experience of Hindus'—which might have been a reference to what he himself observed in Noakhali and Calcutta in 1946 and 1947. And, finally: 'Unless you get the written assurance of the local Muslim League, supported by the Centre, you should give up the struggle for the unity of Bengal and cease to disturb the atmosphere that has been created for the partition of Bengal'.[57] At the same time, when Gandhi met a group of East Bengal Hindus who expressed their apprehension about their fate in post-Partition East Pakistan, Gandhi veered back to his earlier position and denounced the 'madness of dividing Bengal'. Under moral stress, compelled to accept a situation he hated, not all of Gandhi's statements at this time are consistent in the literal sense. But basically he allowed the course of events to proceed towards what seemed to be inevitable, for his reason began to accept what his heart rejected.

About this time, Sarat Bose and Suhrawardy became embroiled in a needless controversy with Gandhi. In response to Bose's plea for support for his 'united independent Bengal' project, Gandhi had written that he had reports from the opposite faction in the Bengal Congress that 'money was being lavishly expended in order to secure Scheduled Caste votes'.[58] Gandhi also mentioned at his prayer meeting on 8 July that money was being 'squandered to stall the partition of Bengal'.[59] Bose retaliated with a furious telegram and Suhrawardy wrote to Gandhi on 10 June to protest 'the irreparable mischief' thus caused by Gandhi. The latter answered the 'long and angry letter': 'You should be thankful to me that I have dispelled all suspicions, if there was no ground for any'.[60] And he added a mildly sarcastic word to Suhrawardy: '[The Partition] can still be undone by you if you have the Muslim opinion behind you'. This was a challenge that Suhrawardy could not answer for the Partition was an irreversible process by then. And what of Muslim opinion?

Cards on the Table

Muslim opinion was put to its final test in June 1947 in an atmosphere of intense internal conflict and indeed bloodshed in the presence of Jinnah and all the leaders at a crucial meeting of the All-India Muslim League in Delhi. Abul Hashim provides a detailed account as an eyewitness and as the General Secretary of the Bengal Muslim League. It seems that latent differences became manifest at this climactic moment.

Bengal's Muslim League delegates to the impending All-India Conference in Delhi, scheduled for 3 June, met at Suhrawardy's house in Calcutta prior to the meeting. The decision was to reject the Mountbatten scheme for Partition. Suhrawardy arrived in Delhi, by air, before the other delegates. When the latter turned up, by train, they found Suhrawardy converted into a staunch supporter of the position that Jinnah took, that is, acceptance of the Mountbatten scheme while demurring on some details. Suhrawardy lobbied the Bengal delegates to vote against the consensus arrived at in the Calcutta meeting. Outside the venue of the meeting, the Imperial Hotel on what was then called the Queen's Way (Janpath), thousands of Muslim youths assembled—pleading with the delegates to bear in mind the fate of the Muslim minorities in many provinces in the event of a Partition.

Just before the meeting began Suhrawardy, questioned by Hashim, declared his intention to speak in favour of Jinnah's proposal and the acceptance of the Mountbatten scheme. When Jinnah began speaking *khaksars* armed with *belchas* (swords of a sort) emerged from the kitchen to disrupt the meeting and a fight ensued between them and volunteers of the League. Hashim, puffing at a cigar, looked on along with the other leaders present. The Imperial Hotel carpets were stained with blood. The *khaksars* were driven out and discussions began. Hashim wanted to place before the meeting his point of view, that is, rejection of the Mountbatten schemes for Partition and, of course, his defence of the concept of a united, independent Bengal. Jinnah refused to allow Hashim an opportunity, although there was a demand from the floor of the house to let Hashim speak. Jinnah said it would be a waste of time for, along with Hashim, his opponents also may demand time; therefore, Jinnah said, the house must decide by vote simply whether the Mountbatten scheme was to be accepted or not. Suhrawardy counted the votes and declared that the Quaid-i-Azam's proposal had been passed; only eleven votes were against the Mountbatten scheme. Soon after, Suhrawardy made a press statement: 'Dhaka is now in Pakistan'.[61]

In the above account, there may be other perceptions as to the details. For example, Abul Mansur Ahmed presents a less unflattering picture of Suhrawardy. But the main trend of events given by Abul Hashim above appears to be beyond dispute. After the conference, in a press statement, Hashim exposed these incidents and said that many delegates had voted in favour of Jinnah's proposal out of fear, greed for positions in the future government of Pakistan, and apprehension about an uncertain future. *The Dawn* editorialized against him in an article entitled 'Snake in the grass'.

Thus a 'moth-eaten Pakistan' was gratefully accepted and dissenting opinion, admittedly a small minority in that forum, suppressed. When the moment of truth arrived, the rhetorical fervour about territorial unity was shed in favour of communal unity.

On the other side of the communal divide, the picture was much the same. The March 1947 resolution, sponsored by N.C. Chatterjee of the Hindu Mahasabha, putting forward the Bengali Hindu Central Legislators' demand for Partition in Bengal, was vigorously followed up not only by Dr S.P. Mookerjee, as discussed earlier, but also by others provincial and local level leaders. The lawyers of the Calcutta Bar as well as the local bars in small towns were particularly vocal. The Bengal Provincial Hindu Mahasabha conference in Calcutta on 15 March 1947, the Bengal Partition Convention at Tarakeswar on 4 April, and the Bengal Provincial Congress Committee's meeting on 4 April demanding immediate formation of separate governments for West and East Bengal, and so on, were backed up by a deluge of resolutions from *mofussil* Hindu organizations or ad hoc organizations set up to advocate Partition.[62]

The gravity of decision-making on the Partition issue was sized up quite well by H.S. Suhrawardy in a private letter to Liaquat Ali Khan in May 1947: It was 'impossible to arouse Hindu public opinion against' Partition, he wrote. 'The Hindu leaders Mr. S.C. Bose and Mr. K.S. Roy are indeed taking a great risk in setting their face against partition. They do not hope to be able to convince their community.... Even the Hindus of East Bengal, who do not count in the voting, are supporting the partition with death staring them in the face'.[63] In the years that followed, this observation proved to be truly far-sighted.

The proponents of united Bengal failed to swing public opinion in the Hindu section of their audience for a number of reasons. Suhrawardy had said less than a year ago in his deposition to the Cabinet Commission of 1946 that there was no alternative to Pakistan; his sudden conversion to the cause of 'united and independent Bengal' did not inspire confidence, and indeed, as has been discussed earlier, he abandoned that cause equally suddenly at the All-India Muslim League Conference on 3 June 1947 in Delhi. Moreover, he was delightfully vague about the basis of the unity he talked about—the basis in terms of share of power and jobs. Abul Hashim did offer a basis in concrete assurances on equal division of political and administrative positions.[64] That immediately provoked a protest from the President of the Bengal League, Maulana Akram Khan who completely rejected the 50:50 division.[65] Again, despite all the fine words about coalition ministry to be formed—the subject of so many letters, cited earlier here, between the Governor, the Chief Minister and the Leader of the Opposition—the non-Muslims remained rather sceptical; the reason was that Suhrawardy had talked of a 5:7 Hindu:Muslim ratio in the ministry in April 1946 during his talks with the Congress (these proved infructuous), and the ministry he formed had a ratio of 3:8.[66] Abul Hashim also points out that another cause of an atmosphere of distrust was that the few Hindus who were included in the ministries formed by Muslim chief ministers from

1936 to 1947 excluded the 'accredited' Hindu leaders and the exercise was generally regarded as an eyewash;[67] perhaps this statement needs an amendment that Fazlul Huq did try to break away from this pattern. Finally, it appears that the image of Suhrawardy was not very helpful in creating trust on the other side. Many discreditable acts were attributed to him, on the basis of little or no evidence, and in this he was more unfortunate than even the more rigid Leaguers like Nazimuddin. The responsibility of not stemming the tide of violence during the August 1946 Riots of Calcutta is laid at his door although it has been said in extenuation that he was poorly served by the police, and that he did call in the army, although a bit late, to stop the riot. He was believed to have bribed the Muslim League legislators to bring down the Nazimuddin Ministry so as to clear his route to chief ministership. It is alleged that Suhrawardy built up good relations with businessmen while he was civil supplies minister under Nazimuddin so as to have access to slush funds to corrupt politicians.[68] Strangely enough, the fact that he was distrusted by Jinnah did not secure for him the confidence of the Hindus. What we are concerned with here is a question of perception, and not the validity of these and other allegations. In so far as the leaders of the Hindu community perceived Suhrawardy in this light, the chances of any political understanding were reduced because he was an unpredictable quantity in the predictable equation desired by them. If we may anticipate a later development, ironically Suhrawardy did not command the confidence of his colleagues in the League at the crucial moment when he expected to be elected chief minister in East Pakistan. On 5 August 1947, he was soundly defeated by Nazimuddin in the contest for leadership of the Muslim League Parliamentary Party; within a few minutes the West Bengal Parliamentary leader of the League was to be elected and Suhrawardy, one of his political colleagues recounts, rushed to that meeting to secure his own election. Thus, Hashim remarks, the man who minutes ago had decided to go to East Pakistan to be chief minister, pushed himself into the West Bengal parliamentary party's leadership.[69]

Acting Out the Scenario

On the second and third day of June, the fate of Bengal and of Calcutta was decided by the announcement of His Majesty's Government regarding the modalities of transfer of power and the acceptance of those terms by the Working Committee of the Congress and by the Muslim League at their meetings in Delhi. The scenario thus decided upon was enacted in the days between then and 15 August. The Governor of Bengal sent a telegram to Mountbatten at 3.15 p.m. on 20 June 1947. 'Legislative Assembly this afternoon decided upon paragraph seven of HMG's statement by 126 votes to 90 votes to join a *new* Constituent Assembly'. At 5 p.m. he cabled again: 'West repeat West Bengal L.A. this afternoon decided upon para six of HMG's statement by 58 votes to 21 votes that province should be partitioned; and ... that West Bengal should join the *existing* Constituent Assembly...'.[70] The East Bengal legislators voted by 106 to 35 against Partition, and by 107 to 34 to join a new Constituent Assembly. Behind the legalese what the Governor said was that (*a*) *first* the joint meeting of the Legislative Assembly, inclusive of members of East and West Bengal, by majority voted in favour of joining Pakistan; (*b*) *thereafter*, the Legislators of West Bengal, at a separate meeting, voted in favour of Partition and joining the Indian Union; and (*c*) legislators of East Bengal voted against Partition—which is to be viewed in the light of the first resolution on joining Pakistan—and, in the event of Partition, resolved to join Pakistan. The sequence of voting (as decided by the HMG statement) on the different issues was important in structuring the decision-making: if there was no Partition, Bengal as a whole would be in Pakistan. Voting on Partition, under (*b*) above, took place in full knowledge of the decision under (*a*) on joining Pakistan if Bengal remained undivided.

The decision of the legislators on 20 June leading to the Partition of Bengal was momentous but not unpredictable. In anticipation of it moves were being made in Delhi. In order to ensure a peaceful atmosphere at the time when such a decision was made, the Viceroy had requested the leaders to issue 'peace appeals'. Jinnah, in a broadcast on 3 June, after having invoked the names of the Viceroy and God in that order, talked about the duty to make the Viceroy's task 'less difficult' by maintaining peace.[71] Nehru's broadcast was longer and rambling. The crucial passage was typically Nehruvian: 'It is with no joy in my heart that I commend these proposals [of HMG regarding Partition] to you' for the secession of some parts of India was 'painful to contemplate', but the 'India of our minds and hearts cannot change' and under the conditions prevailing he was convinced that the decision for Partition of India was right.[72] The Viceroy was very pleased with the effect of Jinnah's speech in Bengal. 'Calcutta is remarkably quiet.... Likewise Bengal as a whole was quiet', he reported to the Secretary of State for India.[73] In fact, at the moment of partition in August, Bengal was to remain quiet, while Punjab burned and bled. It might have been the quiet of surrender to the inevitable, or of satisfaction with the security of communal homelands, or simply one of incomprehension of the enormity of the event.

In the meanwhile, a minor hiccup in the process, smoothly pushed forward till now by the Viceroy with unexpected cooperation from Nehru and Jinnah, was a question raised by Jinnah. It proved to be a red herring which distracted the government for a while. Suhrawardy wrote to Mieville:

> Jinnah asked me if I had seen H.E. [that is, the Viceroy, whom he had seen] and may the Lord forgive me, I told him 'no' as I did not want him to think HE had seen me. He told me that if HE were to see me tomorrow, I should impress upon him the necessity of ascertaining the views of the people.... He insists Calcutta should be a free city, otherwise it will always remain a bone of contention.[74]

As suggested by Jinnah and Suhrawardy, Mountbatten, even at this late stage, suggested that Calcutta be allowed to be 'a free city or at any rate under joint control' at least for the time being.[75] But at this late stage to introduce such a provision in the announced modalities was considered dangerous by the Bengal Governor.[76] Moreover, Mountbatten had sent as his intermediary V.P. Menon to Patel to propose joint control for at least six months; 'Patel's reply was very firm, "not even for six hours"'.[77] So Mountbatten had to say 'no' at his next meeting with Nehru, Patel, Jinnah, and Liaquat Ali; and he mentioned the fact that London had rejected this plan for Calcutta already and a renewed demand for free city status or a referendum could not be entertained at this late hour, in fact a few hours before the announcement of the HMG on the Transfer of Power.[78] That was the end of the matter. This was a bit of shadow-boxing on both sides by now, for the die had been cast.

With Partition decided upon, one or two minor matters were being sorted out in June. On 5 June, Suhrawardy met the Viceroy to tell him that the negotiations regarding coalition ministry in Bengal—ridiculously prolonged by Suhrawardy and K.S. Roy—were being dropped. It seemed that Roy did not want it any more since it was useless now; another reason might have been what Mountbatten reports, 'Jinnah's absolute refusal to allow Suhrawardy' to form a coalition.[79]

Mountbatten, for reasons which are not clear from the records, was keen to stop further inquiries into the Calcutta Riot of 1946; possibly he reasoned that after Partition it would be pointless to go on with the enquiries. The Chief Justice of the Calcutta High Court said that in any case witnesses were 'too frightened to give evidence'. The party leaders in Delhi agreed with the Viceroy that the inquiries should be terminated.[80] It was only Gandhi who was still keen on them. But, by then, Gandhi was marginal to the processes afoot. Even his views on the unity of India were being ignored. His favourite disciple, Patel, as reported by V.P. Menon in confidence at the Viceroy's staff meeting, said that "not too much account should be taken of the recent utterances of Mr. Gandhi in favour of a united India."[81] The leaders and future ministers and prime ministers of the emerging states of India and Pakistan were anxious to get on with the business of Partition.

In the undergrowth of footnotes in scholarly writings a debate has been going on in response to scholars who have looked at the causality of Partition. In 1985, Ayesha Jalal was virtually the sole spokesperson for the brilliantly argued thesis that Jinnah was forced to accept the partition of India because of the recalcitrance of an Indian National Congress desirous of bifurcation.[82] In 1987, Anita Inder Singh's work questioned that view and she attributed to Jinnah the agenda of creating a sovereign Pakistan, an objective that Jinnah is usually credited with in the conventional historiography in Pakistan.[83] The next year, R.J. Moore published his research which attributed the responsibility to Nehru's Congress that agreed to the quick deal proposed by Mountbatten.[84] Sucheta Mahajan argued that the Congress accepted Partition because there were no options left—given the fact that Jinnah's obduracy brought matters to a dead end—and that is exactly what Nehru had said in the All-India Congress Committee (AICC) a week before 15 August, the fateful day.[85] Bimal Prasad, in his study of the birth of Pakistan in three volumes, the latest in 2009, saw in the Partition the inevitable denouement of the existence of a 'nation within a nation'.[86] While these different readings of the great events at the power centre are interesting in themselves, the impression is unavoidable that although ultimately the deal arrived at in Delhi inevitably determined the final outcome, politics in Bengal had acquired an autonomy of their own in those days. Mahatma Gandhi, who spent a good deal of time in Bengal at that time, steadily distanced himself from Congressmen in Delhi who were busy with the process of transfer of power. Congress leadership in Bengal, such as it was, had scarcely any presence in the command centre of the party. The papers of the All-India Congress Committee and the private correspondence of Bengali politicians show little evidence of decisive interaction. The Bengal Provincial Muslim League was a house divided, and on the main issue of Suhrawardy and Sarat Bose's 'United Bengal', confusion prevailed due to the oft-changing position taken by the sole decision-maker in distant Delhi, M.A. Jinnah. The salience of the notion of united Bengal, in a sovereign or provincial status in the Bengali discourse of Partition in 1947, epitomized the disconnect between the all-India leadership and the provincial leadership in Bengal. In hindsight, one can see two trends emerging in the days preceding Independence—the provincialization of the Bengal Congress and the foreshadowing of Bangladesh.

A 'Sticky Business' for Cyril Radcliffe

The final business on the agenda was dividing up the territories. The Congress and the League received on 13 June Mountbatten's proposals on the Boundary Commission: 'an independent chairman', two nominees of the Congress, two of the League, all men of high judicial standing.[87] (This was the only time when I have noticed in the records that Jinnah allowed himself a joke: that 'there was always trouble when two or more lawyers get together'). This meeting on 13 June was followed by nominations of members of the Bengal Boundary Commission by Nehru (C.C. Biswas and B.K. Mukherjee, each a senior Calcutta High Court judge) and by Jinnah (A.S.M. Akram and S.A. Rahman, of the Calcutta and Punjab high courts respectively).[88] Others were nominated to the Punjab Commission. The important appointment was that of the Chairman, Radcliffe.

Sir Cyril Radcliffe had been the Vice-Chairman of the General Council of the Bar in England since 1946; Mountbatten knew him when he was the Director General of Ministry of Information in 1941–5.

He could be said to have an open mind on Indian questions: he had never been to India. Jinnah wanted a senior member of the Bar from England. Secretary of State Listowel managed to persuade Radcliffe who probably did not know what he was taking on. Later, Radcliffe told an interviewer that his only briefing was half an hour with an official at India Office over a large-scale map of India.[89] It was only when he met Mountbatten, Nehru, and Jinnah that the Viceroy told him that his was a job that had to be finished in five weeks.

On 8 July, Radcliffe arrived in Delhi, on 9 August he finished his work on Bengal and most of his work on Punjab, and left on 15 August. It was an appalling task and Radcliffe said later: 'They asked me to come in to do this sticky job for them, and when I had done it they hated it. But what could they expect in the circumstances?'[90] One cannot but agree with that. His terms of reference for Bengal were: 'to demarcate the boundaries of the two parts of Bengal on the basis of ascertaining the contiguous majority areas of Muslims and non-Muslims. In doing so it [the Commission] will also take into account other factors'. All this had to be done, along with the Punjab boundary determination, in five weeks. Possibly Radcliffe's attitude to what he was compelled to do is indicated by the fact that he formed a decision during his days in India 'formally to relinquish any claim to salary or remuneration' for his services as Chairman of the Boundary Commission.[91]

The years beyond the Partition of August 1947 are outside the purview of this volume but we might briefly look at some aspects of the impact of the partition on the part of Bengal that remained in the Indian Union. The political rationale for the bifurcation of Bengal was deliberated upon by the leaders *ad infinitum*, but the economic consequences were not seriously considered till after the event. West Bengal witnessed a steady flow of migration from East Pakistan in the following years. In the first five years after 1947 alone, the number of migrants totalled 3,105,000 in the period 1947–51. The Report on the Census in 1951 observed that the rise in population from 1946 to 1957 in West Bengal on account of the refugee influx amounted to about fifty years of population increase due to normal growth.[92] The result was increase in population density of West Bengal by 12 per cent and that of Calcutta by 20 per cent.[93] Later, in 1981, the West Bengal government estimated that the total number of East Pakistan refugees in West Bengal was about eight million, that is, one-sixth of the population of the state.[94] A common complaint in West Bengal at the time was the discrepancy between the central government expenditure on displaced persons from West Pakistan, Rs 237 crore, and the expenditure on East Pakistan refugees, Rs 109 crore, between 1947–8 and 1956–7, according to statistics published by the Rehabilitation Ministry of GOI.[95] In 1950, C.N. Vakil of Bombay University prepared an incisive evaluation of the economic consequences of the Partition of 1947, in particular the loss of a huge portion of the hinterland of Calcutta Port and the disconnection with the raw material supply area for the jute mills of Calcutta.[96] The economic consequences in terms of the migration of refugees was not fully explored by him but later research has thrown light on that to reveal not only the economic disaster the mass migration from East Pakistan brought about, but also the immense human tragedy in that episode.[97] The crises of the 1940s that we have discussed earlier (Chapter 7)—the inflation and commodity supply shortage caused by the World War, the Famine of 1943, the Great Calcutta Killings of 1946, and so on—had already deeply impacted the economy and society of Bengal; the Partition of 1947 exacerbated the critical situation West Bengal faced at the moment of its birth.

The machinery to bring into existence the state of West Bengal in the Indian Union, and East Pakistan, was inexorably in motion. The scenario chalked out in May and finalized on 2 and 3 June was enacted with the fullest cooperation of the leaders. The leaders on both sides of the communal divide displayed a spirit of cooperation in this business of dismembering India, a spirit of cooperation which was conspicuously lacking in the preservation of India's unity.

'The River of Blood'

The first Partition of Bengal in 1905 was made by alien rulers, the Partition of 1947 was not. That fracture in 'Bengali patriotism', its failure at a crucial moment of history, marked the future of the Bengali-speaking people in more ways than just a political division could bring about. In the long run, the Partition laid the basis of a reassertion of Bengali patriotism in East Bengal, first in the cultural domain and increasingly in a political form, eventually leading to the formation of Bangladesh. In West Bengal it took the form of retrospective irredentism, a continual effort to redeem in imagination the undivided Bengal, a loss never to be regained, ever to be mourned. It has been my argument in this survey of events that actually the Partition of Bengal was brought about by tacit agreement between the politicians of both communities, Muslim and Hindu. To apportion blame for it has been usually an exercise in self-deception on both sides. The romantic yearning in post-Partition Bengal for the Bengal that was before 1947, is perhaps the sublimation of a sense of guilt. The same sense of guilt for our complicity in dividing Bengal leads to a tendency to search for agencies outside Bengal, for example, in the central leadership, in the Congress High Command, M.A. Jinnah, and so on. Probably Gandhi was not far wrong when he asked Bengal to look inwards and to see that there was indeed a 'division of the hearts'.[98] And in saying so he recognized the Partition to be no longer avoidable at that point of time when decades of communal conflict had done their work. Nirad C. Chaudhuri, a perspicacious political observer and a secretary to Sarat Bose for some years, remarks: 'As soon as the Bengalis realised the mistake they had made [in acquiescing in Partition] they completely repudiated their responsibility and began to blame the British, the Congress, Gandhi and Nehru for their misfortunes. Like all weak people they would not take the blame on themselves'.[99]

What of the people who were the victims of a process in which they had no other part to play? One sees so often in older persons of both nationalities a love and nostalgia for the world which was once theirs on this or that side of the Padma. No one put it in better words than the poet Jibanananda Das who spent his childhood and youth and half his working life in Barisal, a place he had to flee when it fell in East Pakistan. Not only did he capture perfectly the nostalgia in many of his poems—'Some day I will return to the banks of Dhansiri, to this Bengal…' (1932)—but also the tragedy of 1947. His long poem '1946–1947' is memorable:

> 'I have killed men—man's blood has bathed my body
> If I call out, the river of blood will murmur intimately "I am Yasin, Hanif, Mohammad…."
> The river of blood will burble names, "Gagan, Bipin, Shashi…"
> Who knows where they lived; of the lower order
> Were they not, after all?[100]

On 15 August 1947 the exulting people of Calcutta, Hindu and Muslim, roamed the streets—one recalls truckloads of these revellers that, in one child's perception, appeared to be much like those that ferried goons during the riots—and the crowd entered the Governor's House and strolled through the Council Chamber.[101] Who remembered the martyrs who died to stop communal carnage, to stop the inexorable machine moving towards Partition? They were, to borrow Stephen Spender's words, 'aliens in their own land—history their domicile'.

Notes

1. Harun-or-Rashid, *The Foreshadowing of Bangladesh: Bengal Muslim League and Muslim Politics* (Dhaka, 1987), and 'United Independent Bengal' in *History of Bangladesh, 1704–1971*, vol. I, ed. S. Islam (Dhaka, 1992), ch. 15; Amalendu De, *Independent Bengal: The Design and Its Fate* (Calcutta, 1975); Joya Chatterji, *Bengal Divided: Hindu Communalism and Partition, 1932–1947*, Cambridge South Asian Studies (Book 57) (Cambridge University Press, 1994); A.R. Mallick and S.A. Husain, 'The Political Basis of Bengali Nationalism' in *History of Bangladesh*, ed. Islam, ch. 20.
2. Harun-or-Rashid, 'United Independent Bengal'.
3. Abul Hashim, *Amar jiban o bibhagpurva bangladesher rajniti* (Calcutta, 1988, and Dhaka, 1978), pp. 126ff.
4. Abul Mansur Ahmed, *Amar dekha rainitir panchas bachchar* (Dhaka, 1995), p. 227.
5. Mallick and Husain, 'The Political Basis of Bengali Nationalism', p. 557.
6. Kamala Sarkar, *Bengal Politics, 1937–1947* (Calcutta, 1990), ch. I.
7. Burrows to Wavell, 25 April 1947, 10 September 1947, in N. Mansergh (ed.), *The Transfer of Power, 1942–1947* (12 vols, London, 1970–83), vol. VII, p. 142, and vol. VIII, p. 303 (hereafter *TOP*, followed by volume number and page number).
8. Burrows to Mountbatten, 28 May 1947, *TOP*, X, 1025.
9. Rabindranath Tagore, 'The Congress', *Modern Review* (July, 1939); the original Bengali essay was collected in *Kalantar*.
10. Record of Interview between Mountbatten and Winston Churchill, 22 May 1947, *TOP*, X, 945.
11. Durgadas (ed.), *Sardar Patel's Correspondence*, vol. IV (Ahmedabad, 1972), pp. 39–43, 52.
12. Record of Interview between Viceroy and Nehru, 1 April 1947, *TOP*, X, 70.
13. Nehru to Mountbatten, 17 April 1947 (Secret and Personal), *TOP*, X, 304–7.
14. Nehru to Mountbatten, 17 April 1947 (Secret and Personal), *TOP*, X, 304–7.
15. Minutes of Viceroy's Meeting, 10 May 1947, *TOP*, X, 737.

16. Minutes of Viceroy's Meeting, 11 May 1947, *TOP*, X, 764.
17. Nehru to Sir John Colville, 23 May 1947, *TOP*, X, 96.
18. Selections from news, India Office, 30 May 1947; extract from *News Chronicle*, 27 May 1947; interview with Nehru, *TOP*, X, 1039.
19. Burrows to Mountbatten, 28 May 1947, *TOP*, X, 1025.
20. Burrows to Mountbatten and Listowel, 19 May 1947, *TOP*, X, 904.
21. Burrows to Mountbatten and Listowel, 19 May 1947, enclosing text of Memorandum re. talks between Suhrawardy, Roy and Bose, *TOP*, X, 905.
22. Hashim, *Amar jiban*, p. 133.
23. Hashim, *Amar jiban*, pp. 118–19, 122.
24. Hashim, *Amar jiban*, p. 129.
25. Pyarelal, *Mahatma Gandhi: The Last Phase*, vol. II (Ahmedabad, 1956), cited in Hashim, *Amar jiban*, pp. 130–1.
26. Hashim, *Amar jiban*, p. 134.
27. Gandhi to Sarat Chandra Bose, 24 May 1947, *Collected Works of Mahatma Gandhi* (hereafter cited as *CWMG*), vol. 87.
28. Sarat Bose to Gandhi, 26 May 1947, cited in Hashim, *Amar jiban*, p. 136; Hashim obtained from the Bose family copies of Bose's letters.
29. Burrows to Mountbatten and Listowel, 21 May 1947, and 28 May 1947, *TOP*, X, 926, 1023.
30. Burrows to Mountbatten, 28 May 1947, *TOP*, X, 1023.
31. Burrows to Mountbatten, 28 May 1947, *TOP*, X, 1023.
32. Mountbatten to Burrows, 18 May 1947, *TOP*, X, 889.
33. Cabinet, India and Burma Committee (United Kingdom), Memorandum by Secretary of State for India, 17 May 1947, *TOP*, X, 876.
34. Cabinet, India and Burma Committee, Memo. by President of Board of Trade, 27 May 1947, *TOP*, X, 998.
35. See note 33.
36. Cabinet, India and Burma Committee, 19 May 1947, *TOP*, X, 898–9.
37. Cabinet, India and Burma Committee, 19 May 1947, *TOP*, X, 898–9.
38. Burrows to Listowel and Mountbatten, 19 May 1947, *TOP*, X, 904.
39. Viceroy's Remarks (the right-hand column) as Congress and League Proposals, Cabinet Committee on India and Burma, 20 May 1948, *TOP*, X, 913.
40. Cabinet, India and Burma Committee, 20 May 1947, minute no. 4, *TOP*, X, 922.
41. See note 18, Nehru in *News Chronicle*, 27 May 1947.
42. Cabinet Committee on India and Burma, 20 May 1947, minute no. 5, *TOP*, X, 1018.
43. Burrows to Mountbatten, 28 May 1947, *TOP*, X, 1023.
44. Burrows to Mountbatten, 28 May 1947, *TOP*, X, 1023.

45. Hashim, *Amar jiban*, p. 131.
46. Burrows to Mountbatten, 28 May 1947, *TOP*, X, 1025.
47. Sarat Bose to Jinnah, 9 June 1947, reprinted in Hashim, *Amar jiban*, pp. 137–8.
48. Burrows to Mountbatten, 28 May 1947, *TOP*, X, 1025.
49. *Forward*, 21 September 1940, cited in Rupamanjari, 'The Second World War and Bengal: A Socio-Political Perspective', Ph.D. thesis, Delhi University, 1996.
50. Gandhi to Sarat Bose, 8 June 1947, *CWMG*, vol. 88, p. 103.
51. Speech at CWC meeting (summary) in AICC files, 2 June 1947, *CWMG*, vol. 88, p. 61.
52. Gandhi to J. Nehru, 7 June 1947, *CWMG*, vol. 88, p. 94.
53. Draft of letter from Nehru to the Viceroy, 2 June 1947, AICC file no. 1499-I, 1947, *CWMG*, vol. 88, pp. 478–81, Appendix.
54. Speech at Prayer Meeting, 2 June 1947, *CWMG*, vol. 88, p. 109.
55. Speech at Prayer Meeting, 10 June 1947, *CWMG*, vol. 88, p. 126.
56. Speech at Prayer Meeting, 15 July 1947, *CWMG*, vol. 88, p. 303.
57. Gandhi to Sarat C. Bose, 21 June 1947, 8 June 1947, *CWMG*, vol. 88, p. 186, 103; the next citation from Speech at Prayer Meeting, 15 July 1947, *CWMG*, vol. 88, p. 343.
58. Gandhi to Sarat Bose, 8 June 1947, *CWMG*, vol. 88, p. 183.
59. Speech at Prayer Meeting, 8 July 1947, *CWMG*, vol. 88, p. 110.
60. Gandhi to H.S. Suhrawardy, 12 June 1947, *CWMG*, vol. 88, p. 137; extracts from Suhrawardy to Gandhi, 10 June 1947, *CWMG*, vol. 88, p. 137.
61. Abul Hashim, *Amar jiban*, pp. 139–41.
62. Excellent accounts of these events are provided by Shila Sen, *Muslim Politics in Bengal, 1937–47* (Delhi, 1976); Sarkar, *Bengal Politics*; Chatterji, *Bengal Divided*.
63. H.S. Suhrawardy to Liaquat Ali Khan, 23 May 1947, Harun-or-Rashid, *Inside Bengal Politics, 1936–47: Unpublished Correspondence of Partition Leaders* (Dhaka, 2003), pp. 86–7.
64. Hashim, *Amar jiban*, pp. 122–6, Statement of 29 April 1947, an extremely valuable analysis.
65. *Azad*, 24 May 1947, cited in Sen, *Muslim Politics in Bengal*, p. 235.
66. F. Burrows to Viceroy, 25 April 1946, *TOP*, VII, p. 142.
67. Hashim, *Amar jiban*, p. 99.
68. Kamala Sarkar discusses these allegations about Suhrawardy in *Bengal Politics, 1937–47*, pp. 88, 95, 102ff.
69. Hashim, *Amar jiban*, p. 143.
70. F. Burrows to Viceroy Mountbatten, 20 June 1947 (cable. en clair), *TOP*, XI, 536.
71. Text of broadcast by Jinnah, 3 June 1947, *TOP*, XI, 97.

72. Text of broadcast by Pandit Nehru, 3 June 1947, *TOP*, XI, 93.
73. Viceroy's Personal Report, no. 9, 12 June 1947, *TOP*, XI, 301, 307.
74. Suhrawardy to Mieville, 31 May 1947, *TOP*, XI, 20.
75. Mountbatten to Burrows, 1 June 1947, *TOP*, XI, 36.
76. Burrows to Mountbatten, 2 June 1947, *TOP*, XI, 65.
77. Viceroy's Personal Report, no. 8, 5 June 1947, *TOP*, XI, 158.
78. Minutes of Viceroy's meeting with leaders, 2 June 1947, *TOP*, XI, 41.
79. Mountbatten to Burrows, 5 June 1947, *TOP*, XI, 145; Viceroy's Personal Report, no. 11, 4 July 1947, *TOP*, XI, 895.
80. Viceroy's Personal Report, no. 11, 4 July 1947, *TOP*, XI, 894.
81. Minutes of Viceroy's Staff Meeting, 31 May 1947, *TOP*, XI, 3.
82. Ayesha Jalal, *The Sole Spokesman: Jinnah, the Muslim League and the Demand for Pakistan* (Cambridge, 1985).
83. Anita Inder Singh, *Origins of the Partition of India, 1936–1947* (New Delhi, 1987).
84. R.J. Moore, *The Endgames of Empire: Studies of Britain's India Problem* (Delhi, 1988).
85. Sucheta Mahajan, *Independence and Partition: The Erosion of Colonial Power in India* (Delhi, 2000).
86. Bimal Prasad, *The March to Pakistan, 1937–1947* (New Delhi, 2009).
87. Minutes of Viceroy's Miscellaneous Meeting, 13 June 1947, *TOP*, XI, 328.
88. Mountbatten to Jinnah, 19 June 1947, *TOP*, XI, 507; Jinnah to Mountbatten, 24 June 1947, *TOP*, XI, 588.
89. L. Mosley, *The Last Days of the British Raj* (Bombay, 1965), p. 220; although not fully documented this work contains information from interviews.
90. Mosley, *The Last Days of the British Raj*, p. 228.
91. C. Radcliffe to Secretary of State for Commonwealth Relations, 21 August 1947, *TOP*, XI, 708. Since the research done by Wilhelm von Schendel, Joya Chatterji and Ranabir Samaddar, a whole new area, borderland studies, has developed; see Wilhelm van Schendel, *The Bengal Borderland* (London, 2005); Joya Chatterji, 'The Fashioning of a Frontier', *Modern Asian Studies* 33, no. 1 (1999): 185–242; Ranabir Samaddar, specialized on refugee studies, is more focused on the impact on West Bengal in *The Marginal Nation: Transborder Migration from Bangladesh to West Bengal* (New Delhi, 1999).
92. Asok Mitra, *Census of India (West Bengal)*, vol. 6, Part-1A (Calcutta 1953).
93. Tai Yong Tan and Gyanesh Kudaisya, *The Aftermath of Partition in South Asia* (London, 2000), pp. 172–5.
94. Tai and Kudaisya comment that this fact and the dissatisfaction of the immigrants with the aid given by the Congress government meant a 'reconfiguration of Calcutta's political world' and contributed to the rise of the Left in the period beyond the purview of this volume.

95. *Report of the Ministry of Rehabilitation for 1956–57*, Government of India, New Delhi, 1957, cited in Tai and Kudaisya, *The Aftermath of Partition in South Asia*, p. 276.
96. C.N. Vakil, *Economic Consequences of Dividing India* (Bombay, 1950).
97. Prafulla K. Chakrabarti, *The Marginal Men: The Refugees and the Left Political Syndrome in West Bengal* (Calcutta, 1990).
98. Gandhi to Sarat Bose, 8 June 1947, *CWMG*, vol. 88, p. 103.
99. Nirad C. Chaudhuri, *Thy Hand, Great Anarch!: India, 1921–52* (London, 1987), p. 835.
100. Jibanananda Das, '1946–1947', *Shreshtha kavita* (Calcutta, 1966), p. 135.
101. *Ananda Bazar Patrika*, 16 August 1947; on Independence Day in Dhaka, *Ananda Bazar Patrika*, 23 August 1947; the author of this book was among the eyewitnesses to these events as a child.

SELECT BIBLIOGRAPHY

Documentary Sources

Since the focus in this project was on the public intellectuals, opinion makers, and the political leadership, not on the government and its policies and actions in British India, a great many of my sources were outside the governmental archives. In the early chapters of this work where we looked at the interface between the political developments and social, cultural, and ideational elements, the documentation that was required took us to contemporary newspapers, speeches of public figures, literary journals, first-person accounts ranging from diaries to full-fledged autobiographies, and other published material. As we moved in the latter part of this work to the political story, we depended on conventional archived sources. Among these, the important governmental or public records I have used were: **Home Department (Political Branch)** Fortnightly Reports (National Archives of India, New Delhi); **Secret Fortnightly Reports, Home (Pol)** 1937–47 (West Bengal State Archives); *Proceedings of the Bengal Legislative Council*, 1920–1937 (National Library of India, Calcutta); *Proceedings of the Bengal Legislative Assembly*, 1937–1947 (National Library of India). For the period 1942–1947 all major official documents in England are available in Nicholas Mansergh (ed.), *Transfer of Power*, vols I–X (HMSO, London), and Indian government documents for the periods 1937–41 and 1943–46 are thoroughly covered in the *Towards Freedom*

(ICHR, New Delhi) series (general editor, S. Gopal, followed by Sabyasachi Bhattacharya, volume editors being P.S. Gupta, Basudev Chatterjee, Sumit Sarkar, Mushirul Hasan, K.N. Panikkar, Bimal Prasad, Arjun Dev, and A.K. Gupta). The major manuscript sources I have used are: the **AICC Papers**, that is, All-India Congress Committee files (Nehru Memorial Museum and Library, hereafter NMML); All-India Trade Union Congress, or **AITUC Papers** (NMML); private papers of Dr Bidhan Chandra Roy, or **B.C. Roy Papers** (NMML); private papers of Sir Bijay Prasad Singha Roy, Revenue Minister in Government of Bengal, cited as **Singha Roy Papers** (NMML); the **Nanavati Papers** (NAI), that is, the correspondence and other documents in the collection of M.L. Nanavati, member of the Famine Inquiry Commission (available in the National Archives of India); **Sir P. C. Mitter Papers** (NMML); **Meerut Conspiracy Case Papers** (P.C. Joshi Archives, JNU); **Viceroy Linlithgow's Papers** (NMML, microfilm); Governor of Bengal **J. Anderson's Letters to Viceroy** (microfilm no. '3169); **Hindu Mahasabha Papers** (NMML); **Syama Prasad Mookerjee's Private Papers**, up to Installment no. IV (NMML).

There is a great deal relevant to Bengal political history of the 1930s and 1940s in the correspondence of three national-level leaders: Sardar Vallabhbhai Patel, Rajendra Prasad, and, of course, Mahatma Gandhi—*Collected Works of Mahatma Gandhi*; Durgadas (ed.), *Sardar Patel's Correspondence*; and Valmiki Chaudhuri (ed.), *Rajendra Prasad:Correspondence and Selected Documents*. The fourth, M. A. Jinnah, has been poorly served by archivists and editors; only some parts of the Quaid-i-Azam M.A. Jinnah Papers are accessible in India in published form (S. Pirzada [ed.], *Quaid-i-Azam Jinnah's Correspondence*, Karachi, 1977; Z.H. Zaidi [ed.], *Jinnah–Ispahani Correspondence, 1936–48*, Karachi, 1976; Z.H. Zaidi [ed.], *Quaid-i-Azam M A. Jinnah Papers*, Islamabad, 1993–). The only Bengali leader of this period whose correspondence has been adequately edited and published is Subhas Chandra Bose (Sisir Kumar Bose [ed.], *Subhas Chandra Bose: Correspondence, 1924–1932*, New Delhi 1967; Sisir Kumar Bose et al. [eds], *Netaji: Collected Works*, 1980–2007). The letters and other documents of Muslim League leaders cited in this book are available in Harun-or-Rashid, *Inside Bengal Politics, 1936–47: Unpublished Correspondence of Partition Leaders*, Dhaka, University Press, 2003.

Works in English

Ahmad, Aijaz. 'Azad's Careers: Roads Taken and Not Taken'. In *Islam and Indian Nationalism: Reflections on Abul Kalam Azad*, ed. Mushirul Hasan. New Delhi, 1992.

Ahmad, Rafiuddin. *The Bengal Muslims, 1871–1906: A Quest for Identity*. Delhi, 1981.

Ahmad, S. 'Urbanization and Urban Classes'. In *History of Bangladesh*, ed. S. Islam, vol. III. Dhaka, 1992.

Ahmed, R. (ed.). *Quaid-i-Azam Papers, 1941–42*. Lahore, 1976.

Akos, Ostor. *The Play of the Gods*. Chicago, 1980.

Amin, Sonia Nishat, 'Women and Society'. In *History of Bangladesh*, ed. S. Islam, vol. II, ch. 19. Dhaka, 1992.

Anam, Md. Khairul. *Indian Freedom Movement and Murshidabad District, 1905–1947*. Calcutta, 2008.

Bandyopadhyay, Sekhar. 'A Peasant Caste in Protest'. In *Caste and Communal Politics in South Asia*, eds S. Bandyopadhyay and S. Das, pp. 145–90. Calcutta, 1993.

Bandyopadhyay, Sekhar. *Caste, Culture and Hegemony: Social Dominance in Colonial Bengal*. New Delhi, 2004.

———. *Caste, Politics and the Raj: Bengal, 1872–1937*. Calcutta, 1990.

———. 'Caste and Society in Colonial Bengal: Change and Continuity', *Journal of Social Studies* 28 (April 1985).

Banerjee, Sumanta, 'Marginalization of Women's Popular Culture in Nineteenth-Century Bengal'. In *Recasting Women: Essays in Indian Colonial History*, eds K. Sangari and S. Vaid. New Delhi, 1989.

Banerji, Nripendra Chandra. *At the Crossroads*. Calcutta, 1950, 1974.

Bannerji, Himani. 'The Mirror of Class: Class Subjectivity and Politics in 19th Century Bengal', *Economic and Political Weekly* 24, no. 19 (13 May 1989): 1041–51.

———. 'Fashioning a Self: Educational Proposals For and By Women in Popular Magazines in Colonial Bengal', *Economic and Political Weekly* 26 (October 1991).

———. *Inventing Subjects: Studies in Hegemony, Patriarchy and Colonialism* (New Delhi, 2001).

Batabyal, Rakesh. *Communalism in Bengal*. Delhi: Sage, 2005.

Berry, Kim. 'Lakshmi and the Scientific Housewife: A Transnational Account of Indian Women's Development and Production of an Indian Modernity', *Economic and Political Weekly* 38, no. 11 (15–21 March 2003): 1055–68.

Bhattacharya, Buddhadev et al. (eds). *Satyagrahas in Bengal, 1921–1939* (Calcutta, 1977).

Bhattacharya, Buddhadev (ed.). *The Freedom Struggle and the Anushilan Samiti* (Calcutta, 1979).

Bhattacharya, Ranjit K. *Moslems of Rural Bengal: Socio-cultural Boundary Maintenance*. Calcutta, 1991.

Bhattacharya, Sabyasachi. 'The Intelligentsia in Colonial India', *Studies in History* I (January 1979): 89–104.

———. 'Swaraj and the Kamgar: Indian National Congress and the Bombay Working Class, 1919–31'. In *Congress and Indian Nationalism: The Pre-Independence Phase*, eds Richard Sisson and Stanley Wolpert. Berkeley, 1988.

———. 'Tod in Kalkutta, 1943: Ein Abschnitt des Zweiten Weltkrieges'. In *Stadt in Zweiten Weltkrieg*, eds E. Jackel and J. Rohwer. Essen, 1997.

——— (ed.). *The Mahatma and the Poet: Letters and Debates between Gandhi and Tagore, 1915–1941*. Delhi, 1997.

———. 'Calcutta: Economic Life of the Common People During World War II', *Rekishigaku Kenkyu: Journal of Historical Studies*, Tokyo, no. 612 (1997): 54–61.

———. *Rabindranath Tagore: An Interpretation*. New Delhi, 2011.

———. *The Endgame of the Raj and Subhas Bose's Political Strategy, 1943–1945*, Netaji Memorial Lecture, Netaji Subhas Open University, Calcutta, 2013.

———. *Rabindranath Tagore: An Interpretation*. New Delhi, 2011.

———. *Talking Back: The Idea of Civilization in the Nationalist Discourse*. New Delhi, 2011.

Borthwick, Meredith. *The Changing Roles of Women in Bengal, 1844–1905*. Princeton, 1984.

Bose, Nirmal Kumar. *My Days with Gandhi*. Calcutta, 1972.

Bose, Pradip Kumar. *Classes in a Rural Society: A Sociological Study of Some Bengal Villages*. Delhi, 1984.

Bose, Sarat Chandra. *I Warned My Countrymen*. Calcutta, 1968.

Bose, Subhas Chandra. *The Indian Struggle, 1920–42*. Bombay, 1964.

Bose, Sugata. 'The Roots of Communal Violence in Rural Bengal: A Study of the Kishorganj Riots, 1930', *Modern Asian Studies* 16, no. 3 (1982).

———. *Agrarian Bengal: 1919–47*. New Delhi, 1987.

———. *His Majesty's Opponent: Subhas Chandra Bose and India's Struggle against Empire*. Harvard, 2011.

Broomfield, J.H. *Elite Conflict in a Plural Society: Twentieth-Century Bengal*. Berkeley, 1968.

Calcutta, University of. *Hundred Years of the University of Calcutta*. Calcutta, 1957.

Casey, R.G. *An Australian in India*. London, 1947.

Chakrabarti, Prafulla K. *The Marginal Men: The Refugees and the Left Political Syndrome in West Bengal*. Calcutta, 1990.

Chakrabarty, D. and C. Bhattacharya (eds). *Congress in Evolution: Congress Resolutions*. Calcutta, 1935.

Chakrabarty, Bidyut (ed.). *Biplabi: A Journal of Open Rebellion*. Calcutta, 2002.

———. *Local Politics and Indian Nationalism: Midnapur, 1919–1944*. New Delhi, 1997.

———. *Subhas Bose and Middle-Class Radicalism*. London, 1990.

Chakrabarty, Dipesh. 'Modernity and Ethnicity in India: A History for the Present', *Economic and Political Weekly* 30, no. 52 (30 December 1995): 3373–80.

———. 'The Difference–Deferral of a Colonial Modernity: Public Debates on Domesticity in British Bengal', *History Workshop* 36 (1993).

Chatterjee, D.K. *C.R. Das and Indian National Movement*. Calcutta, 1965.

Chatterji, Joya. *Bengal Divided: Hindu Communalism and Partition, 1932–1947*. Cambridge, 1994.

Chatterji, Joya. 'The Fashioning of a Frontier: The Radcliffe Line and Bengal's Border Landscape, 1947–1952', *Modern Asian Studies* 33, no. 1 (1999): 185–242.

Chatterjee, Partha. 'The Nationalist Resolution of the Women's Question'. In *Recasting Women: Essays in Indian Colonial History*, eds K. Sangari and S. Vaid. New Delhi, 1989.

———. 'Agrarian Relations and Communalism in Bengal, 1926–35'. In *Subaltern Studies*, ed. R. Guha. New Delhi, 1982.

———. *Bengal, 1920–47: The Land Question*. Calcutta, 1984.

Chatterji, Suniti Kumar. *The Origin and Development of the Bengali Language*. Calcutta, 1st edn 1926, reprint 1985.

Chattopadhyay, Gautam. *Bengal Electoral Politics and Freedom Struggle, 1862–1947*. ICHR, Delhi, 1984.

———. *Communism and Bengal's Freedom Movement, 1917–29*. New Delhi, 1974.

Chattopadhyay, Gouranga. *Ranjana: A Village in West Bengal*. Calcutta, 1964.

Chaudhuri, Nirad C. *Thy Hand, Great Anarch! India, 1921–1952*. London, 1987.

Chowdhury-Sengupta, Indira. 'Reconstructing Spiritual Heroism: The Evolution of the Swadeshi Sannyasi in Bengal'. In *Myth and Mythmaking*, ed. Julia Leslie, pp. 124–43. London, 1996.

Cooper, Adrienne. *Sharecropping and Sharecroppers' Struggles in Bengal, 1930–50*. Calcutta, 1988.

Das, Amal. *Urban Politics in an Industrial Area: Aspects of Municipal and Labour Politics in Howrah, 1850–1928*. Calcutta, 1994.

Das, Chitta Ranjan. *India for Indians: Speeches. October 1917–February 1921*. Madras, 1921.

Das, Chitta Ranjan *Deshbandhu Chitta Ranjan: Brief Survey of Life and Work, Provincial Conference Speeches etc.* (Calcutta, 1926).

Das, Suranjan. *Communal Riots in Bengal, 1905–1947*. New Delhi, 1991.

Dasgupta, Swapan. 'Adivasi Politics in Midnapur, 1760–1924'. In *Subaltern Studies*, IV, ed. Ranajit Guha. New Delhi, 1985.

De, Amalendu. 'Formation of the Communist Party in Faridpur'. In *National and Left Movements in India*, ed. K.N. Panikkar. Delhi, 1980.

———. *Independent Bengal: The Design and Its Fate*. Calcutta, 1975.

Desai, A.R. (ed.), *Peasant Struggles in India*. Bombay, 1979.

Durgadas (ed.). *Sardar Patel's Correspondence, 1945–50*, vols I–IV. Ahmedabad, 1972.

Dutt, Sachin. *Deshapriya J.M. Sengupta*. Delhi, 1983.

Dutta Gupta, Sarmishta. *Identities and Histories: Women's Writings and Politics in Bengal*. Kolkata, 2010.

Eaton, Richard M. *The Rise of Islam and the Bengal Frontier, 1204–1760*. University of California, 1993.

Elwin, Verrier. *Religious Banditry*. All-India Arya Dharma Seva Sangha, Delhi, 1947.

Gallagher, John. 'Congress in Decline in Bengal, 1937–39'. In *Locality, Province and Nation: Essays in Indian Politics, 1870–1940*, ed. Anil Seal. Cambridge, 1973.

Galanter, Marc. 'The Religious Aspects of Caste: A Legal View'. In *South Asian Politics and Religion*, ed. D. E. Smith. Princeton, 1966.

Gandhi, Mohandas Karamchand, *Collected Works of Mahatma Gandhi*. Publications Division, Government of India, New Delhi, 1994 edn.

Gaulle, Charles de. *War Memoirs: Call of Honour, 1940–1942*, tr. J. Griffin. London, 1955.

Ghosh, Srabashi, 'Birds in a Cage: Changes in Bengali Social Life', *Economic and Political Weekly* (25 October 1986).

Gordon, L.A. *Bengal: The Nationalist Movement, 1876–1940*. New Delhi, 1979.

Gourlay, S.N. 'Nationalists, Outsiders and the Labour Movement in Bengal during the Non-Cooperation Movement'. In *Congress and Classes*, ed. Kapil Kumar, pp. 34–57. New Delhi, 1988.

Government of India. *Report of the Central Committee* (Sir Sankaran Nair, Chairman). Calcutta, 1929.

———. *The Indian Labour Year Book*. Delhi, 1946.

Ghosh, Parimal. 'A History of a Colonial Working Class: India, 1850–1946'. In *Economic History of India*, ed. B.B. Chaudhuri, vol. VIII. Delhi, 2005.

Greenough, Paul. 'Death of an Uncrowned King', mimeo, Iowa University, 1984.

Grewal, S.M. (ed.). *Jinnah–Wavell Correspondence*. Lahore, 1986.

Guha, Ranajit (ed.). *Subaltern Studies*, III. Delhi, 1984.

Guha, Ranajit (ed.). *Dominance without Hegemony: History and Power in Colonial India*. Cambridge, Mass., 1997.

Gupta, Amit Kumar. *Crises and Creativities: Middle-Class Bhadralok in Bengal, 1939–1952*. Calcutta, 2009.

———. *The Agrarian Drama: The Leftists and the Rural Poor in India, 1934–1951*. Delhi, 1996.

Gupta, Bishan Kumar. *Political Movements in Murshidabad, 1920–47*. Calcutta, 1992.

de Haan, Arjan and Samita Sen (eds). *A Case for Labour History: The Jute Industry in Eastern India*. Calcutta, 1999.

Haq, Muhammad Enamul. *A History of Sufism in Bengal*. Asiatic Society, Dhaka, Bangladesh, 1973.

Harun-or-Rashid. *The Foreshadowing of Bangladesh: Bengal Muslim League and Muslim Politics*. Dhaka, 1987, revised edn 2003.

———. *Inside Bengal Politics, 1936–47: Unpublished Correspondence of Partition Leaders*. Dhaka, 2003.

———. 'A Move for Independent Bengal', in *History of Bangladesh*, ed. S. Islam, vol. I. Dhaka, 1992.

Hasan, Mushirul (ed.). *Islam and Indian Nationalism: Reflections on Abul Kalam Azad*. Delhi, 1992.

Hashim, Abul. *In Retrospection*. Dhaka, 1974.

Hashmi, Taj ul-Islam. *Peasant Utopia: The Communalization of Class Politics in East Bengal, 1920–47*. Dhaka, 1994.

Heehs, Peter. *The Bomb in Bengal: The Rise of Revolutionary Terrorism in India, 1900–10*. Delhi, 1993.

———. *Nationalism, Terrorism, Communalism*. Delhi, 1998.

Hore, Somnath. *Tebhaga: An Artist's Diary and Sketchbook*. Calcutta, 1989.

Inden, Ronald B. and R.W. Nicholas. *Kinship in Bengali Culture*. Chicago, 1977.

Islam, Mustafa N. *Bengali Muslim Public Opinion as Reflected in the Bengali Press, 1901–1930*. Dhaka, 1973.

Islam, Sirajul (ed.). *History of Bangladesh, 1704–1971*, vols I–III. Dhaka, 1992.

Islam, Sirajul. 'Life in the Mufassal Towns of 19th-Century Bengal'. In *The City in South Asia*, eds K. Ballhatchet and J.B. Harrison. London, 1980.

Ispahani, M.A.H. *Quaid-e-Azam Jinnah As I Knew Him*. Karachi, 1976.

Jalal, Ayesha. *The Sole Spokesman: Jinnah, the Muslim League and the Demand for Pakistan*. Cambridge, 1985.

Jayawardena, K. *The White Women's Other Burden: Western Women and South Asia during British Colonial Rule*. New York, 1995.

Jeffrey, Robin. 'Bengali: "Professional, Somewhat Conservative" and Calcuttan', *Economic and Political Weekly* 32, no. 4 (25–31 January 1997): 141–4.

Kabir, Humayun. *Muslim Politics, 1906–1947, and Other Essays*. Calcutta, 1969.

Kakar, Sudhir. *The Inner World*. New Delhi, 1981.

Karlekar, Malavika. *Voices From Within: Early Personal Narratives of Bengali Women*. Delhi, 1991.

McPherson, Kenneth. *The Muslim Microcosm: Calcutta, 1918–36*. Wiesbaden, 1974.

Mahajan, Sucheta. *Independence and Partition: The Erosion of Colonial Power in India*. Delhi, 2000.

Mallick, A. R. and S. A. Husain. 'The Political Basis of Bengali Nationalism'. In *History of Bangladesh*, ed. S. Islam. Dhaka, 1992.

Mansergh, N. (ed.), *The Transfer of Power, 1942–1947* (12 vols, London, 1970–83).

Marriott, McKim and Cohn, B.S. 'Networks and Centres in the Integration of Indian Civilization', *Journal of Social Research* I (1958): 1–9 reprinted in B.S. Cohn, *An Anthropologist among Historians and Other Essays* (Delhi, 1987).

Marriott, McKim, 'Little Communities in an Indigenous Civilization'. In *Village India*, ed. McKim Marriott. Chicago, 1955.

———. *Caste Ranking and Community Structure in Five Regions of India and Pakistan*. Deccan College, Pune, 1960.

Mitra, Asok. *Census of India (West Bengal)*, vol. 6, Part-1A. Calcutta, 1953.

Momen, Humaira. *Muslim Politics in Bengal: A Study of Krishak Praja Party and the Elections of 1937*. Dhaka, 1972.

Mondal, Swadesh Ranjan. *The Cracked Portait of a Patriot: Deshapran Birendranath Sasmal, 1881–1934*. Institute of Historical Studies, Calcutta, 2012.

Mookerjee, S. P. *Selected Speeches in the Bengal Legislative Assembly, 1937–1947*. Calcutta, 2005.

Mookerjee, Syama Prasad. *Leaves from a Diary*. Calcutta, 1993.

Moon, Penderel (ed.). *Wavell: The Viceroy's Journal*. London, 1973.

Moore, R. J. *Endgames of Empire: Studies of Britain's Indian Problem*. Delhi, 1988.

Mosley, Leonard. *The Last Days of the British Raj*. Bombay, 1965.

Mukherjee, Aditya. 'The Workers' and Peasants' Party, 1926–30', *Studies in History* III, nos 1–2 (1981): 1–44.

Mukherjee, Madhushree. *Churchill's Secret War: The British Empire and the Ravaging of India during World War II*. Delhi, 2010.

Mukherjee, Prithwindranath. *Bagha Jatin: Life and Times of Jatindranath Mukherjee*. New Delhi, 2010.

Mukhopadhyay, B. D. and S.P. Datta. *Indian Republic Army: Chattagram Biplab*. Calcutta, 1995.

Mallick, A.R. and Syed A. Husain. 'Bengali Nationalism'. In *History of Bangladesh, 1704–1971*, ed. S. Islam. Dhaka, 1992.

Murshed, Ghulam. *Reluctant Debutante: Response of Bengali Women to Modernization*. Rajshahi, 1983.

Murshid, Tazeen M. *The Sacred and the Secular: Bengal Muslim Discourses, 1871–1977*. Calcutta, 1995.

Nag, Dulali. 'Fashion, Gender and the Bengali Middle-Class', *Public Culture* III, no. 2 (1991).

Pandey, Gyanendra (ed.). *The Indian Nation in 1942*. Calcutta, 1988.

———. *Remembering Partition: Violence, Nationalism and History in India*. Cambridge, 2001.

Panigrahi, D. N. (ed.). *Economy, Society and Politics in Modern India*. New Delhi, 1985.

Porter, A.E., ICS. *Census of Bengal 1931*. Calcutta 1931.

Prasad, Bimal. *Pathway to India's Partition: The March to Pakistan, 1937–1947*, vol. III. Manohar, Delhi, 2009.

Rahman, Husainur. *Hindu–Muslim Relations in Bengal, 1905–47*. Bombay, 1974.

Ray, Asim. *The Islamic Syncretistic Tradition in Bengal*. Dhaka, 1983.

Ray, Prithwis Chandra. *Life and Times of C.R. Das*. London, 1927.

Ray, Rajat Kanta. *Urban Roots of Indian Nationalism: Pressure Groups and Conflict of Interests in Calcutta City Politics, 1875–1939*. New Delhi, 1979.

———. *Social Conflict and Political Unrest in Bengal, 1875–1927*. New Delhi, 1984.

———. 'Masses in Politics: The Non-Cooperation Movement in Bengal, 1920–22', *Indian Economic and Social History Review* XI, no. 4 (1974).

Ray, Samaren. *The Twice-Born Heretic: M.N. Roy and the Comintern*. Calcutta, 1986.

Redfield, Robert and Milton Singer. 'The Cultural Role of Cities', *Economic Development and Cultural Change* III (1954): 53–73.

Redfield, Robert. *Peasant Society and Culture*. Chicago, 1955.

Risley, H.H. *The Peoples of India*. Calcutta, 1915.

Rothermund, D. *India in the Great Depression, 1929–39*. Delhi, 1992.

Rothermund, D. *The Global Impact of the Great Depression, 1929–39*. London, 1996.

Roy, M. N. *The Future of Indian Politics*. London, 1926.

Roy, Moxham. 'Salt Starvation in British India: Consequences of High Salt Taxation in Bengal Presidency, 1765 to 1878', *Economic and Political Weekly* 36, no. 25 (23–29 June 2001): 2270–4.

Rupamanjari. 'The Second World War and Bengal: A Socio-Political Perspective', Ph.D. thesis, Delhi University, 1996.

Samanta, Amiya K. *Terrorism in Bengal: A Collection of Documents on Terrorist Activities from 1905 to 1939*, vols I–VI. Government of West Bengal, Calcutta, 1985.

Sangari, K. and S. Vaid. 'Recasting Women: An Introduction'. In *Recasting Women: Essays in Indian Colonial History*, eds K. Sangari and S. Vaid. New Delhi, 1989.

Sanyal, H. R. 'Congress in Southwestern Bengal: The Anti-Union Board Movement in Eastern Medinipur, 1921'. In *Congress and Indian Nationalism*, eds R. Sisson and S. Wolpert, pp. 352–76. Berkeley, 1988.

Sanyal, Hites Ranjan. 'Congress Movements in the Villages of Eastern Medinipur'. In *Asie du Sud: Traditions et Changements*, ICNRS, no. 582 (Paris, 1979).

Sarkar, Chandi Prasad. 'Bengal Muslim Politics, Society and Culture during the Khilafat and Non-Cooperation Movements', *Bengal: Past and Present*, 107 (January 1984).

Sarkar, Kamala. *Bengal Politics, 1937–47*. Calcutta, 1990.

Sarkar, Sumit. 'The Logic of Gandhian Nationalism: Civil Disobedience and the Gandhi–Irwin Pact, 1930–31', *Indian Historical Review* (July 1976).

Sarkar, Sumit. *The Swadeshi Movement in Bengal, 1903–1908*. Delhi, 1973.

Sarkar, Tanika. 'The Hindu Wife and the Hindu Nation: Domesticity and Nationalism in 19th-Century Bengal', *Studies in History* 8, no. 2 (1992).

———. *Bengal, 1928–1934: The Politics of Protest*. New Delhi, 1987.

———. 'Communal Riots in Bengal'. In *Communal and Pan-Islamic Trends in Colonial India*, ed. M. Hasan. Delhi, 1981.

Schendel, Wilhelm van. *The Bengal Borderland: Beyond State and Nation in South Asia*. London, 2005.

Sen, Amiya P. *Explorations in Modern Bengal, c. 1800–1900*. New Delhi, 2010.

Sen, B.K. and R. Sen (eds). *Deshbandhu Chitta Ranjan: Brief Survey of Life and Work. Provincial Conference Speeches, etc.* Calcutta, 1926.

Sen, Bhowani. *Rural Bengal in Ruins* Bombay, 1945.

Sen, Mrinal. *Always Being Born: A Memoir* Calcutta, 2005.

Sen, Prabodh Chandra. *Bengal: A Historiographical Quest*. Calcutta 1995; Bengali edn 1953.

Sen, Samita. *Women Labour in Late Colonial India: The Bengal Jute Industry*. Cambridge, 1999.

———. 'Gendering Class: Wives and Workers in the Jute Industrial Economy'. In *A Case for Labour History: The Jute Industry in Eastern India*, eds Arjan de Haan and Samita Sen. Calcutta, 1999.

Sen, Shila. *Muslim Politics in Bengal, 1937–47*. Delhi, 1976.

Sen, Sukumar. *History of Bengali Literature*. Delhi, 1979.

Sen, Sunil. *Agrarian Struggle in Bengal, 1946–47*. Calcutta, 1982.

Sengupta, Nitish. *Bengal Divided: The Unmaking of a Nation, 1905–1971*. Delhi, 2007.

Shah, Muhammad. 'Social and Cultural Basis of Bengali Nationalism'. In *History of Bangladesh*, ed. S. Islam, vol. III, ch. 20. Dhaka, 1992.

Singh, Anita Inder. *The Origins of the Partition of India, 1936–1947*. New Delhi, 1987.

Singh, Lata. *Popular Translations of Nationalism: Bihar, 1920–1922*. Delhi, 2012.

Sinha, Bhupendra Chandra, of Susanga. *Changing Times*. Anthropological Society, Calcutta, 1965.

Sinha, Soumitra. *The Quest for Modernity and the Bengali Muslim, 1921–47*. Calcutta, 1995.

Sinha, Surajit. 'The Bhumij Kshatriya Social Movement in South Manbhum', *Bulletin of the Department of Anthropology*, VIII, no. 2 (1959).

———. 'Coexistence of Multiple Scales and Networks of a Civilization: India'. In *Scale and Social Organization*, ed. F. Barth. Oslo, 1978.

———. 'Kali Temple at Kalighat'. In *Cultural Profiles of Calcutta*, ed. S. Sinha. Calcutta, 1972.

Sisson, R. and Stanley Wolpert (eds). *Congress and Indian Nationalism: The Pre-Independence Phase*. Berkeley, 1988.

Sitaramayya, Pattabhi. *The History of the Indian National Congress*. Indian National Congress, Madras, 1935.

Tagore, Rabindranath. 'Congress', *Modern Review*, July 1939; reprinted in S. Bhattacharya (ed.), *The Mahatma and the Poet* (New Delhi, 1997).

———. 'The Cult of the Charkha', *Modern Review*, September 1925; reprinted in S. Bhattacharya (ed.), *The Mahatma and the Poet* (1997).

———. 'The Call of Truth', tr. of 'Satyer Ahvan' in *Pravasee* (Kartik, 1326 BS or 1919 CE); reprinted in *Kalantar* (Calcutta, 1937).

———. *Letters from Russia*, tr. S. Sinha. Visva-Bharati, Calcutta, 1970).

Tan Tai Yong and Ganesh Kudaisya. *The Aftermath of Partition in South Asia*. London, 2000.

Vakil, C.N. *Economic Consequences of Divided India* Bombay, 1950.

Venkataramani, M.S. *The Bengal Famine of 1943: The American Response*. Delhi, 1973.

Walsh, J. 'What Women Learned When Men Gave Them Advice: Rewriting Patriarchy in Late-Nineteenth-Century Bengal', *The Journal of Asian Studies* 56, no. 3 (1993).

Zaidi, Z.H. (ed.). *M.A. Jinnah–Ispahani Correspondence, 1936–1948*. Karachi, 1976.

——— (ed.). *Quaid-i-Azam M.A. Jinnah Papers*; series published under Q. A. Project, National Archives of Pakistan. Islamabad, 1993.

Works in Bengali

Abdussalam, Mohammad. *Purdah-tattwa* (Theory of purdah). Calcutta (?), 1331 BS, 1926 CE.

Ahmad, Abul Mansur. *Amar dekha rajnitir panchas bachhar* (Fifty years of politics as I saw it). Dhaka, 1995.

Ahmed, Muzaffar. 'Urdu bhasha o bangiya musalman' (Urdu language and Bengali Muslims), *Al Islam* III, no. 4 (1324 BS, 1917 CE).

Ahmed, Muzaffar. *Amar jiban o bharater communist party* (My life and the Communist Party), vol. I (Calcutta, 1984), vol. II (Calcutta, 1988).

Ahmed, Muzaffar. *Krishak Samasya* (The peasant problem), (Calcutta, 1947).

Alam, Jafar. *Bangladesher smaraneeya baraneeya* (Respected and memorable personalities of Bangladesh). Indian edn, Calcutta, 1995.

Bandhyopadhyay, Upendra Nath. *Nirvasiter atmakatha* (Memoirs of an exile). Ninth edn, Calcutta, 1976.

Bandyopadhya, Bibhuti Bhushan. *Pather panchali* (Song of the road). Calcutta, 1985.

Bandyopadhyay, Manik. *Putul nacher itikatha* (The saga of the puppets). Nineteenth edn, Calcutta, 1987.

Bandyopadhyay, Suprasanna. *Itihasasrita Bangla Kavita 1751–1855* (Historical verses in Bengali). Calcutta, 1361 BS, 1954 CE).

Bhar, Haladhar (pseudonym of Mohit Ghosh). 'Urdoskrita pracharinee sabha', *Sanibarer Chithi* (1339 BS).

Bhattacharya, Nanilal. *Narir adhikar* (Rights of women). Calcutta, 1925.

Bhattacharya Sabyasachi. *Oupanibeshik bharater arthaniti* (The economy of colonial India). Calcutta, 1989.

Bhattacharya, Nirmal Chandra. *Bismrita bangla* (Of a forgotten Bengal). Calcutta, 1997.

Bhattasali, K. *Manabendranath rayer baktritabali* (Collected speeches of Manabendra Nath Roy). Calcutta, 1937.

Gupta, Nalini Kanta. *Bolsheviki* Calcutta, 1931.

Bose, Debkumar. *Kallol goshthir katha sahitya* (Literature of the Kallol group). Calcutta, 1387 BS, 1980 CE.

Bose, Nirmal Kumar. *Hindu samajer gadan* (The structure of Hindu society). Calcutta, 1949.

Bose, Priyanath. *Griha dharma* (Domestic dharma). Calcutta, 1934.

Bose, Subhas Chandra. *Taruner Swapna* (Dreams of the youth). Calcutta, 1928, reprint 1967.

Chakrabarty, Abanimohan. 'Narir katha' (About women), *Bharati* (1330 BS, 1923 CE): 752–7.

Chanda, R.P. *Gauda-raja mala* (The Gauda royal dynasty). First edn, Calcutta, 1912, reprint 1973).

Chandra, Amitabha. *Abibhakta banglaye communist andolan* (The Communist movement in undivided Bengal). Calcutta, 1992.

Chatterjee, Sarat Chandra. *Pather dabee* ('The call of the road', serialized in *Bangabani*, 1923); reprinted in *Collected Works* (Calcutta, 1977), vol. I.

Choudhury, Pramatha. 'Bangali patriotism', *Sabuj patra* (Agrahayan, 1327 BS).

Das, Jibananada. *Shreshtha kavita* (Best poems). Calcutta, 1966.

Das, Khudiram. *Kabikankan chandi*. Calcutta, 1987.

De, Amalendu. *Bangali buddhijibee o bicchinnatabad* (Bengali intellectuals and separatism). Calcutta, 1991.

De, Barun (ed.). *Mukti sangrame banglar chhatra samaj* (The students in freedom struggle in Bengal). Calcutta, 1992.

Deb, Chitra. *Antahpurer atmakatha* (Story of the women's quarters). Calcutta, 1984.

———. *Thakurbarir andar mahal* (Inner quarters of the Tagore family house). Ananda Publishers, Calcutta, 1391 BS, 1984 CE.

Devi, Jyotirmoyee. 'Narir pratibha' (Women's talent), *Bharati* (1331 BS, 1924 CE): 796–801.

Dey, Rakhal Chandra. *Bandir jiban smaranika* (Memories of prison life). Jalpaiguri, 1974.

Dey, Sunil Kanti. *Anjuman-e Ulema-e Bangala 1913–19*. Calcutta, 1992.

Dhar, Prafulla Kumar. *Strir sahit kathopakathan* (Conversation with a wife). Calcutta, 1332 BS, 1925 CE.

Dutta, Bhupendra Nath. *Bharater dwitiya swadhinata sangram* (India's second war of independence). Calcutta, 1949.

Ghosh, Naresh Chandra. *Chittajayee Chittaranjan* (Chittaranjan who has won our mind). Calcutta, 1378 BS, 1971 CE.

Guha, Sachindranath (ed.). *Chattogram biplaber bahnisikha* (The flame of the Chittagong insurrection). Calcutta, 1974.

Haldar, Gopal. *Rupnarayaner kule* (On the banks of the Rupnarayan), 2 vols. Calcutta, 1st edn 1969, reprint 1988, 1992.

Hashim, Abul. *Amar jiban o bibhag-purva bangladesher rajniti* (My life and the politics of pre-partition Bengal). First edn Dhaka 1978, reprint Calcutta, 1988).

Isalamabadi, M.M. *Bharate musalman sabhyata* (Islamic civilization in India). Calcutta, 1914.

Islam, M. Nurul. *Samayik patre jiban a janamat 1901–1930* (Life and public opinion in newspapers). Bangla Akademi, Dhaka, 1977.

Lahiri, Abani. *Tirish challisher bangla* (Bengal in the thirties and forties). Calcutta, 1999.

Lahiri, Subodh Kumar. *Biplaber pathe* (On the road to revolution). Calcutta, 1950.

Majumdar, R.C. *Bangla desher itihas* (History of Bengal), vol. IV. Calcutta, 1982.

Majumdar, Satyendra Nath. *Nirbachita rachana sangraha* (Selected writings). Calcutta, 1984.

Mandal, Panchanan. *Sahitya prabeshika* (Introduction to literature). Visva Bharati, 1960.

Mukhopadhya, Nandalal. *Swami-stree* (Husband and wife). Calcutta, 1340 BS, 1933 CE.

Mukhopadhyay, Jadugopal. *Biblabi jibaner smriti* (Memories of my life as a revolutionary). Calcutta, 1982.

Mukhopadhyay, Anima. *Satero sataker radh banglar samaj sahitya* (Society and Literature in 17th century western Bengal). Calcutta, 1990.

Mustafi, Sreemati Nagendra Bala. *Garhasthya dharma* (Domestic duties). Burdwan, 1904.

Nasiruddin, Muhammad. *Bangla sahitye saugat jug* (Saugat era in Bengali literature). Dhaka, 1985.

Pakrashi, Satish. *Agnijuger katha* (About the fiery era). Calcutta, 1971.

Rakshit Ray, Bhupendra Kumar. *Bharate shasastra biplab* (Armed insurrection in India). Calcutta, 1970.

Rauf, Mohammad Abdul. *Basorey: Swami strir kathopakathan* (Conversations between husband and wife on the nuptial night). Calcutta, 1923.

Roy, Jeebendra Sinha. *Kalloler kal* (The age of Kallol), Calcutta, 1973, 2nd edn 1987.

Sarkar, Benoy. *Naya banglar gorapattan*. Calcutta, 1924, 1932.

Sarkar, Sipra and Anamitra Das (eds). *Bangalir samyavad charcha*. Calcutta, 1998.

Sarkar, Sudhir Chandra. *Amar desh, amar kal* (My country, my times). Calcutta, 1994.

Sehanobis, Chinmohan. *Rabindranath o biplabi samaj* (Rabindranath and the revolutionary groups). Calcutta, 1985.

Sen, Samar. *Babu brittanta* (Chronicle of the babus). Calcutta, 1978.

Sengupta, Naresh Chandra. *Yuga parikrama* (A journey through an era), vol. I. Calcutta, 1961).

Sengupta, Subodh Chandra (ed.). *Sansad bangla charitabhidhan* (Sansad Bengal biographical dictionary). Calcutta, 1994.

Tagore, Rabindranath. 'Birodhmulak adarsha' (The principle of opposition), *Bangadarshan* (1308 BS, 1901 CE); reprinted in *Rabindra Rachanavalee*, vol. V.

———. 'Charka', *Sabujpatra* (1332 BS, 1925 CE), and *Kalantar* (Calcutta, 1969), English translation in S. Bhattacharya (ed.), *The Mahatma and the Poet* (1997), pp. 99–113.

———. 'Deshanayaka', written in c. January 1939, posthumously published in 1960, reprinted in *Kalantar* (Calcutta, 1969).

———. 'Maha jati sadan', *Pravasee* (1346 BS, 1939 CE), reprinted in *Kalantar*.

———. 'Nation ki?' (What is a nation?), 'Bangabasi' (1308 BS, 1901 CE), *Rabindra Rachanavalee*, vol. II.

———. 'Path o patheya' (Ends and means), *Bangadarshan* (1335 BS 1908 CE), *Rabindra Rachanavalee*, vol. X.

Tagore, Rabindranath. 'Shikshar milan' (Unity in education), *Pravasee* (1930) and *Kalantar* (Calcutta, 1969).

———. *Char adhyay* (Four episodes), Calcutta, 1934; reprinted in *Rabindra Rachanavalee*, vol. VII.

———. Presidential Address, Pravasee Banga Sahitya Sammelan, Banaras, 3 March 1923, reprinted in *Rabindra Rachanavalee*, vol. XII.

———. 'Bharatvarsher itihaser dhara' (The course of Indian history), *Pravasee* (1319 BS, 1912 CE); reprinted in *Rabindra Rachanavalee*, vol. IX.

———. 'Satyer ahvan', *Prabasee* (Kartik, 1328 BS, 1921 CE); reprinted in *Rabindra Rachanavalee*, vol. XII, and in *Kalantar* (Calcutta, 1969), translated into English as 'Call of Truth' in S. Bhattacharya (ed.), *The Mahatma and the Poet* (1997), pp. 68–87.

Tagore, Soumendranath. *Biplabi russia* (Revolutionary Russia). Calcutta, 1930.

Wadud, Kazi Abdul. *Hindu musalman virodh* (The Hindu–Muslim conflict). Calcutta, 1935.

INDEX

ABOUT THE AUTHOR

Sabyasachi Bhattacharya is Tagore National Fellow, Ministry of Culture, Government of India. He was earlier Vice Chancellor of Visva-Bharati, Santiniketan, and Professor at the Centre for Historical Studies, Jawaharlal Nehru University, New Delhi. He has also held teaching and research appointments at the University of Chicago; St Antony's College, University of Oxford; and El Colegio de México. His recent publications include *Talking Back: The Idea of Civilization in the Indian Nationalist Discourse* (2011), *Rabindranath Tagore: An Interpretation* (2011); *Vande Mataram: The Biography of a Song* (2004), and *Mahatma and the Poet: Letters and Debates between Gandhi and Tagore, 1915–1941* (ed., 2002).